TOURISM MANAGEMENT

D0927737

One of the leading texts in the field, *Tourism Management* is the ideal introduction to the fundamentals of tourism as you study for a degree, diploma or single module in the subject.

It is written in an engaging style that assumes no prior knowledge of tourism and builds up your understanding as you progress through this wide ranging global review of the principles of managing tourism. It traces the evolution and future development of tourism and the challenges facing tourism managers in this fast growing sector of the world economy. This book is highly illustrated with diagrams and colour images, and contains short case studies of contemporary themes of interest, as well as new data and statistics.

This 5th edition has been revised and updated to include:

- new content on: sports, festivals and event tourism, social media impacts on tourism and the effects of the global economic downturn on tourism, as well as emerging themes in tourism such as slow travel, dark tourism, volunteer tourism and medical tourism
- updated case studies on BRIC markets and new case studies from the Middle East and Asia
- enhanced tourism and sustainable development coverage, which runs throughout the book as a major theme, highlighting the challenge of climate change and future tourism growth
- a transport section with more international perspectives from China and South America
- an updated companion website with: additional case studies, quizzes, PPTs, further reading, web reading and video links.

Stephen J. Page is Professor at the School of Tourism, Bournemouth University, holds an Honorary Doctorate from the University of West London, is an Honorary Professor at the University of Wales and works as a Tourism Consultant with different organizations including the United Nations World Tourism Organization, VisitScotland, Scottish Enterprise, Highlands and Islands Enterprise, Harrah's Casinos and Sky Tower, Auckland, New Zealand among many other clients. He is the author and editor of 39 books on Tourism, Leisure and Events and has been the Associate and Reviews Editor of the leading tourism journal – *Tourism Management* – since 1996.

'Anyone interested in tourism management will value this book because of its breadth and scope. If you are concerned with the heated issues of managing visitors and their impact as well as the future range of management problems that the tourism industry need to address, this is the book you cannot afford to miss.'

Barry Mak, PhD, Associate Professor, School of Hotel and
Tourism Management, The Hong Kong
Polytechnic University, Hong Kong

'The newly revised 5th edition of *Tourism Management* is an excellent textbook, comprehensive and easy to read, that covers the fundamentals of tourism management issues with appropriate resources; much more than a general academic treatment of the topic of tourism management. It is a multi-purpose book, serving as classroom textbook, reference book and business guidebook for practitioners and professionals in the field of tourism.'

Muzaffer Uysal, Professor of Tourism and Hospitality
Management, Virginia Tech, USA

'*Tourism Management* is an ideal text for students who are either embarking on tourism studies as a field of study or for students taking a one-off "expedition" into tourism studies. Extensively updated with a more focused emphasis on sustainability, many additional case studies and an expanded global coverage this text certainly meets the needs of the contemporary student.'

Bruce Prideaux, Professor, Marketing & Tourism,
College of Business, Law & Governance,
James Cook University, Australia

5th Edition

TOURISM MANAGEMENT

STEPHEN J.PAGE

Routledge
Taylor & Francis Group

LONDON AND NEW YORK

First published 2015
by Routledge
2 Park Square, Milton Park, Abingdon, Oxon OX14 4RN

and by Routledge
711 Third Avenue, New York, NY 10017

Routledge is an imprint of the Taylor & Francis Group, an informa business

British Library Cataloguing in Publication Data
A catalogue record for this book is available from the British Library

Library of Congress Cataloging in Publication Data
Page, Stephen
Tourism management/Stephen J. Page. – Fifth edition.
    pages cm
    Includes bibliographical references and index.
    1. Tourism–Textbooks. 2. Tourism–Management–Textbooks.
    I. Title.
    G155.A1T59237 2014
    910.68–dc23   2014017096

ISBN: 978–1–138–78457–4 (hbk)
ISBN: 978–1–138–78456–7(pbk)
ISBN: 978–1–315–76826–7 (ebk)

Typeset in Stone Serif, Avenir and Rockwell
by Florence Production Ltd, Stoodleigh, Devon, UK
Printed and bound by Ashford Colour Press Ltd, Gosport, Hampshire

Contents

4 Transporting the tourist I: Surface transport   105

7 Tour operating and travel retailing

225

8 Visitor attractions and events 271

9 The management of tourism　　　　305

10 The public sector and tourism　　　　341

11 Managing the visitor and their impacts — 375

CASE STUDIES

INNOVATIONS IN SUSTAINABILITY

Preface

This book is written as a simple, plain language introduction to tourism and assumes no prior knowledge of what tourism is and how it affects our everyday lives. To read it you need to ask one question: Why is there so much interest in tourism? If you are inquisitive about tourism and how it has developed as a business then read on. This is a book which looks at what the tourism industry is and does, and why it is such an important global business. In simple terms it shows how tourism is organized, run and managed – and how our desire to take holidays and use our leisure time creates an industry which is expanding and is sometimes seen as out of control. This book does not pull any punches: it is not full of jargon, buzzwords and academic gobbledegook – there are far too many books like that which fail to convey the excitement that tourism engenders. It tells a story chapter by chapter about how tourism has developed, what tourism is and how specialist businesses meet the insatiable demand for holidays and travel. Where technical terminology is used, it is explained in lay terms for the general reader. The book offers many insights into a fascinating business which is changing so fast that even commentators find it hard to keep abreast of it.

The book takes a global look at what tourism is with examples from various countries and places, and asks: *If tourism is so important to our economies and society, what can we do to manage it? Whose responsibility is it? Is it too late to control it?* Such questions can only be answered after explaining how the tourism industry exists as a large unwieldy set of interests that are united by one key principle: making money from the visitor and their pursuit of pleasure or travel. The book is comprehensive in the way it treats the different elements of the tourism sector and questions what the challenges of managing tourism are.

Tourism Management will be essential reading for anyone interested in tourism – including tourists – and who want to understand how the business works, how it makes profits and what are the effects of its activities on destinations. The book examines all the key trends now affecting the tourism industry from the impact of technology to the way low-cost airlines have transformed the market for leisure travel.

We are all living in an age of major social and economic transformation, and tourism is part of that transformation. Reading this book will at least help you understand what is driving these changes in tourism and what is likely to stimulate future changes. For the tourism manager, the book will undoubtedly spell out a few home truths. For the general reader, it will show how difficult being a manager in tourism actually is – and the problems that we, the travelling public – *the tourists* – actually pose for businesses – as well as the opportunities and the challenges.

I hope you enjoy reading this book. It is certainly not the largest book ever written on tourism, but it is a clear, lucid and frank assessment which is easy to follow and above all shows how everything fits together – since tourism is not a simple business, all about holidays – or is it? Why not read on and find out! Happy reading.

New to the fifth edition

This edition has been completely rewritten, updated and revised to refocus the book's key messages on the management of tourism with a stronger focus on sustainability. As a result, the following new features have been developed:

- new short and concise innovation in sustainability features to showcase best practice or very innovative actions by businesses or the public sector to help manage the effects and impacts of tourism
- new case studies throughout, with other case studies updated
- a greater focus on concepts and ideas being represented in a visual or graphical format
- a greater global focus throughout the book both at the general level through trends and developments and with a greater geographical spread of case studies derived from developed, developing and emerging countries as tourism destinations
- new PowerPoint slides that make the book's visual and graphical material more accessible, with a new website with online questions and links
- an expanded format and extended discussion of key themes of current interest in global tourism, including the growing importance of social media and how both tourists and the tourism sector are harnessing its power.

Companion website information

A companion website accompanies this book at www.routledge.com/cw/page/ and includes additional resources for both students and lecturers.

Student resources

- Suggested further reading for each chapter.

- Supplementary readings and indicative questions that extend and develop key themes in each chapter.

- A case study archive.

- Further web reading.

- Links to a selection of multi-media resources.

- A test bank of multiple choice questions for each chapter for students to test their understanding.

Instructor resources

- PowerPoint slides with line figures, illustrations and photographs from the book.

1 Tourism today

Why is it a global phenomenon embracing all our lives?

Learning outcomes

This chapter provides an overview of tourism as a subject of study and after reading the chapter you should be able to understand:

- why tourism has emerged as a major leisure activity
- how tourism can be defined as an human activity
- how to distinguish between domestic and international tourism
- why tourism has to be measured and the importance of tourism statistics
- the scale and importance of tourism at a global scale and some of the reasons for its growth
- why tourism is a difficult activity to manage.

Introduction

The new millennium has witnessed the continued growth of interest in how people spend their spare time, especially their leisure time and non-work time. Some commentators have gone as far as to suggest that it is leisure time – how we use it and its meaning to individuals and families – that defines our lives, as a focus for non-work activity. This reflects a growing interest in what people consume in these non-work periods, particularly those times that are dedicated to travel and holidays which are more concentrated periods of leisure time. This interest is becoming an international phenomenon known as 'tourism': the use of this leisure time to visit different places, destinations and localities which often (but not exclusively) feature in the holidays and trips people take part in. The World Travel and Tourism Council (WTTC) estimates that travel and tourism as economic activities generate around US$6 billion, which is expected to grow to US$10 billion by 2015. At a global scale, travel and tourism supports around 260 million jobs: this is equivalent to 8 per cent of world employment and 9 per cent of world GDP.

Therefore, the growing international significance of tourism can be explained in many ways. In an introductory text such as this, it is important to stress at the outset the following types of factors and processes in order to illustrate the reasons why tourism assumes an important role not only in our lives but also globally:

- *tourism is a discretionary activity* (people are not required to undertake it as a basic need to survive, unlike consuming food and water)
- *tourism is of growing economic significance* at a global scale, with growth rates in excess of the rate of economic growth for many countries
- *many governments see tourism as offering new employment opportunities* in a growing sector that is focused on service industries and may assist in developing and modernizing the economy
- *tourism is increasingly becoming associated with quality of life issues* as it offers people the opportunity to take a break away from the complexities and stresses of everyday life and work – it provides the context for rest, relaxation and an opportunity to do something different. This is increasingly being associated with notions of well-being and how holidays assist with relaxation, recuperation and personal goals outside of work
- *tourism is becoming seen as a basic right in the developed, Westernized industrialized countries* and it is enshrined in legislation regarding holiday entitlement – the result is that many people associate holiday entitlement with the right to travel on holiday
- *in some less developed countries, tourism is being advocated as a possible solution to poverty* (described as 'pro-poor' tourism)
- *holidays are a defining feature of non-work* for many workers
- *global travel is becoming more accessible* in the developed world for all classes of people with the rise of low-cost airlines and cut-price travel fuelling a new wave of demand for tourism in the new millennium. This is potentially replicating the demand in the 1960s and 1970s for new popular forms of mass tourism. Much of that earlier growth was fuelled by access to cheap transport (i.e. the car and air

travel) and this provided new leisure opportunities in the Western world and more recently in the developing world and newly industrializing countries

- *consumer spending on discretionary items such as travel and tourism is being perceived as a less costly item in household budgets.* It is also much easier to finance tourism with the rapid rise in credit card spending in developed countries, increasing access to travel opportunities and participation in tourism
- *technology such as the internet and the growing importance of social media has made booking travel-related products easy* and placed travel within the reach of a new generation of computer-literate consumers who are willing to get rid of much of the traditional ritual of going to a travel agent to book the annual holiday. Such technology now opens many possibilities for national and international travel at the click of a computer mouse and to check-in for a flight via a mobile phone.

It is evident that tourism is also becoming a powerful process affecting all parts of the globe. It is not only embraced by various people as a new trend, a characteristic or defining feature of people's lives, but is also an activity in which the masses can now partake (subject to their access to discretionary forms of spending). This discretionary activity is part of wider post-war changes in Western society with the rise in disposable income and spending on consumer goods and services. Yet tourism is not just a post-war phenomenon as it can be traced back through time as shown in Further Web Reading 1. This highlights how important tourism was in past societies as well as the historical processes of continuity and change which help us to understand tourism development throughout the book. The first major wave of growth in consumer spending was in home ownership, then in car ownership and then in accessing tourism and international travel. In fact international travel (and domestic travel, i.e. within a country) is a defining feature of the consumer society. Whilst the car has given more people access to tourism and leisure opportunities within their own country, reductions in the price of aeroplane tickets has made international travel and tourism products and services more widely available. For example, the number of air travellers in the UK is expected to rise to 475 million by 2030. This is not without its environmental cost.

Travel and sustainability

There is a growing global concern about the ability of the earth's environment and resources to sustain the continued expansion of economic activity, including tourism. Whilst scientists have pointed to these concerns since the 1960s, these environmental issues have only really begun to permeate government and people's thinking since the rise of global concerns over climate change, the international Kyoto Treaty seeking to address greenhouse gas emissions and the Stockholm Conference in 2013. Tourism is centre stage in these concerns because travel for leisure purposes is not a fundamental necessity, and it contributes to CO_2 emissions through the consumption of fossil fuels used to transport people on holiday, at the destination and in the accommodation they use. Transportation causes around 75 per cent of the CO_2 emissions generated by tourism, with aviation responsible for around 40 per cent of these emissions. Improving energy efficiency in transportation may be expected to generate a reduction of 32 per cent in the emissions per passenger kilometre between 2005 and 2035. However, the quantity of emissions varies depending on the mode of transport used, with long-haul travel the greatest contributor to highly emission-intense trips.

The issue of tourist travel and its global environmental effect through pollution is a thorny one since tourism is internationally significant and has an important role in society, as we have already seen. There is an almost unanimous reluctance among government policy-makers to directly limit or restrict tourist travel due to its economic effects on destination areas. Consequently, many prefer to adopt the politically acceptable and palatable adaptation strategies – seeking to adapt human behaviour and destinations to the effects of climate change (see Case Study 1.1). Many people openly admit to being supportive of 'green' and 'sustainable' principles but are unwilling to sacrifice their annual or additional holiday to reduce carbon emissions: likewise, few are willing to sacrifice an overseas destination for a less carbon-consumptive and polluting domestic holiday. This assumes a more interesting dimension when one sees some sections of the tourism industry responding to consumer interest in green issues, by offering more 'green' and 'sustainable' holidays, recognizing a business opportunity. Critics have labelled this harnessing of green issues as one way of gaining a competitive edge without a

CASE STUDY 1.1
THE MALDIVES, TOURISM AND SEA LEVEL CHANGE

Climate change has become a dominant theme in the analysis of the future for small island nations which are little more than a metre above sea level. This has become a major problem for governments when the scale of sea level change is set against natural changes in the land level which is sinking at a rate of around less than a centimetre per year. However, this means that in less than 100 years some island states such as the Maldives may be flooded and therefore uninhabitable. The Maldives is a collection of 1200 small islands (198 of which are inhabited) and it is dependent upon tourism as its main source of external earnings, accounting for over 28 per cent of GDP and almost 60 per cent of foreign earnings receipts. The dependence upon tourism has meant that the country's 600 000 international visitors each year are a key source of revenue for the country's economy and, should climate change combine with sea level rises to accelerate the pace of change, the country's tourism industry could be completely eradicated. Therefore in spite of the country's natural beauty, and 80 tourist resorts located across 80 different atolls (i.e. small islands that are just above sea level), its competitiveness as a destination may well be threatened by natural environmental changes. To address these threats, the capital Male has built a 3m sea wall for just one island, while other islands in the Maldives suffer periodic flooding. Despite these major challenges the country's government is seeking to try and mitigate the worst impacts of climate change. However, its resources are very limited and the scale of the problem huge. It is a story that can be repeated across many similar island archipelagos across the South Pacific where climate change may accelerate the pace of sea level rises, putting the livelihoods and entire destination in peril for the future.

Table 1.1 Key studies on tourism and sustainability

Tourism and its ability to be sustainable as an activity have been major growth areas of research since the 1990s. The guiding principles of sustainable tourism are based on the management of resources, the environment, the economy and society/its culture for the long term so that they are not compromised or damaged by tourism development. A number of key studies exist which provide a very wide ranging overview of the subject's development:

- Krippendorf, J. (1987) *The Holiday-Makers*. Oxford: Butterworth-Heinemann.

  This landmark study questioned the necessity of long-haul travel and the impact of tourism, including the damage it caused to the environment.

- Connell, J. and Page, S. J. (eds) (2008) *Critical Concepts in Sustainable Tourism*, Vols 1–4. London: Routledge.

  This extensive review of the landmark studies published on sustainable tourism charts the development of research in the area and navigates the reader through the 40 years of research in the area.

- Mowforth, M. and Munt, I. (2008) *Tourism and Sustainability: Development, Globalization and New Tourism in the Third World*. London: Routledge.

  This is a complex but critical review of the sustainability debate which challenges current thinking and many of the conventional ideas that tourism can easily be translated into a sustainable activity, particularly in less developed countries.

- UNWTO/UNEP (2005) *Making Tourism More Sustainable, A Guide for Policy-Makers*. Madrid: UNWTO.

  This report outlines many of the principles which can be harnessed to try and make tourism sustainable.

complete commitment to implementing sustainability principles in their business practices as 'greenwash' (see Table 1.1).

This reflects the fact that tourism in this respect is a phenomenon that is constantly evolving, developing and reformulating itself as a consumer activity. Tourism, as a consumer activity, is constantly being developed by the tourism industry and individual businesses, as marketing is used to develop new ideas, products and services, and destinations. The challenge for the tourism industry is in adopting new ideas developed in research, such as service-dominant logic (i.e. where the prevailing focus is on the exchange of service from the provider to the consumer rather than a passive provision of service – see the discussion in Chapter 9), which may also assist, with the use of social marketing techniques, in adapting human behaviour so that people extend the daily activities which embrace sustainability ideals (e.g. recycling, reuse and minimizing the use of natural resources) to their holidaytaking behaviour. Of course, the cynic may argue that the most sustainable form of tourism is none at all if you are serious about your own footprint on the planet.

The tourism sector has embraced new ideas (including in some cases sustainability) and pursued strategies focused on developing niche products reflecting the way that tourism has developed a more specialist focus (see Table 1.2). Tourism appeals to the

Table 1.2 Niche forms of tourism

Tourism is a dynamic phenomenon and a highly trend-driven activity in a post-modern society where travellers constantly seek new and diverse experiences. This has led the tourism sector to harness marketing techniques to create different products and experiences for very specific market segments based on consumers' interests and values. A range of some of the key trends and developments in recent years are listed below with a brief explanation of their underlying philosophy and examples.

Trend	Explanation
Slow travel	Travel to a destination and savouring the journey by not flying, such as taking the train or bicycle so that the rush and stress is taken out of the travel experience and it is slowed down
Low-cost travel	Travel by budget carriers which provide very cheap tickets for those who can book a long way in advance
Volunteer tourism	Travel to destinations to volunteer one's services to help with community or environmental projects (e.g. rebuilding a community after a natural disaster)
Sport tourism	Travel to watch or participate in sport such as to visit the Olympic Games
Health and well-being tourism	Travel to improve one's quality of life and health with treatments at spas or health resorts
Medical tourism	Travel overseas to get low-cost medical treatment in countries such as India
Film tourism	Travel to a location or fictitious area popularized in a movie or television programme (e.g. New Zealand and the Lord of the Rings trilogy)
Dark tourism	Travel to a location or locations that have been associated with death, disaster or macabre events, such as prisons or sites of torture (e.g. Auschwitz concentration camp)

Further reading: Novelli, M. (ed.) (2004) *Niche Tourism*. Oxford: Elsevier.

human imagination. As an activity it knows no bounds: it is global and it affects the environment it occurs in, the people who host it, the economies it seeks to benefit and the tourists who consume it as an experience, product and an element of their lives. With tourism having this all-embracing role, it is no surprise that many commentators, researchers and governments have agreed on the need to manage it as a process and activity, especially since it has the potential to snowball and grow out of proportion if it is not managed. Therein lies the basic proposition of this book – tourism needs managing if it is to be successful and beneficial rather than a modern-day scourge. For this reason, sustainability has a key role to play in helping to transform the very damaging and resource-consumptive nature of tourism activity.

Yet one of the fundamental problems in seeking to manage tourism is in trying to understand *what it is*: how it occurs, why it occurs where it does, the people and environments that are affected by it and why it is a volatile activity that can cease as quickly as it can start. These types of questions are what this book seeks to address. It will also look at why tourism as a consumer activity is built on dreams, images and

INNOVATION IN SUSTAINABILITY 1.1
SUSTAINABILITY AS A PHILOSOPHY TO TRANSFORM THE IMPACT OF TRAVEL AND TOURISM

Sustainability as a concept is becoming more embedded into mainstream tourism thinking as it moves from a niche concept to a way of thinking or philosophy that should underpin all areas of tourism activity and behaviour. Despite the many barriers which exist in promoting sustainability to make holidays and tourist behaviour less environmentally damaging, at an operational level the tourism sector is increasingly showing signs of embracing and implementing sustainability ideals. In recognition of this, and to demonstrate how organizations and businesses are innovating in the field of sustainability, this new edition will illustrate how innovations have been developed and implemented to showcase examples of best practice, new policies or approaches that have been developed and challenges which sustainability faces.

The sustainability concept

As Page and Connell (2010) argue, *sustainability* is now a commonly used term in everyday use which arose from a growing consensus during the 1980s over concern with environmental issues and the impact of different forms of economic development, particularly its link to climate change and global warming. This international growth in environmentalism has meant that there is a greater emphasis on the protection, conservation and management of the environment as a natural and finite resource (although some elements are renewable such as water, with the ability to replenish itself).

This concept of sustainability has been refined within the public sector, particularly in the planning profession, to *sustainable development* which highlights the vulnerability of the environment to human impacts and the need to consider its long-term maintenance. As Page and Connell (2014) illustrate, much of the initial stimulus to a global awareness of sustainable development can be traced to the influential 1987 World Commission on Environment and Development (WCED) report, Our Common Future (WCED 1987), which asserts that 'we have not inherited the earth from our parents but borrowed it from our children'. In other words, sustainable development is based on the principle of 'meeting the needs of the present without compromising the ability of future generations to meet their own needs' (WCED 1987). Translating these principles into practice has been a major challenge for policy-makers and governments as it requires changing existing ways of doing things and people's attitudes, and a new way of thinking about how human activity impacts both the resources of the planet that are finite (i.e. cannot be replenished such as oil or coal) and those which are infinite (those which can be replenished such as water), which can be adversely affected by pollution from human activity related to tourism or directly compromised by the pressures from tourism (see Case Study 1.2). For this reason, where sustainability is championed by the public sector it will often require a range of tools that can transform our thinking and behaviour in the form of specific interventions as illustrated in Figure 1.1, where excessive levels of conspicuous consumption associated with tourism may need to be curtailed or modified (i.e. controlled or adapted). This underlines what many commentators argue, that sustainability really needs to be at the heart of all tourism activity to reduce the consumption of carbon and associated pollution arising from tourism.

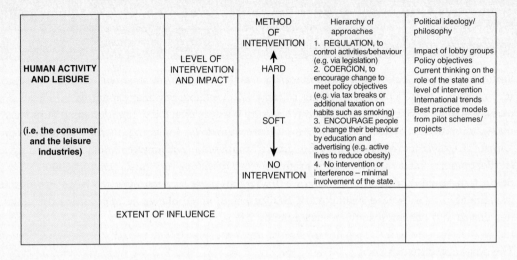

Figure 1.1

Levels of public sector intervention to regulate individual/group behaviour in society: Implications for leisure planning and sustainability

Source: Page, S.J. and Connell, J. (2010) *Leisure: An Introduction.* Harlow: Pearson

CASE STUDY 1.2
WATER EQUITY ISSUES AND SUSTAINABILITY IN THE DEVELOPING WORLD

Water is a fundamental human need for both drinking and sanitation and, as Tourism Concern argues, water equity is concerned with ensuring that development does not infringe on the needs of local people in destination areas to gain rights to water for personal needs so that they can live in dignity. In the developed world, water is taken for granted but, in many developing countries, particularly in fragile environments where tourism has developed (e.g. in coastal communities where resort development has occurred), access to water is far from equitable. Some researchers have highlighted the conflict which exists between tourists and residents over access to water. This was embodied in a campaign by Tourism Concern in 2012: in Goa, a local resident uses 14 litres of water a day; a hotel guest uses 1785 litres of water; in Zanzibar research has highlighted that residents consume on average 93.2 litres of water a day and tourists' use ranges from 686 to 3195 litres a day depending upon the accommodation type they stay in. In the Dominican Republic, estimates of tourist use of water range from 259 to 1483 litres a day, while only 48 per cent of the population have access to potable water (which is water that is safe enough to drink or with low risk of harm). In the case of the Dominican Republic, the UN has estimated that only 10 per cent of the population has continuous access to uninterrupted water supplies. This pattern is replicated in other developing countries where mass resort-based tourism has led to overconsumption of water supplies for tourism purposes in environments that are arid, subject to seasonal droughts and water-intensive in the products and experiences offered to overseas tourists. The unsustainability of these mass resort models has been characterized by indirect water-consumptive activities such as golf and swimming in hotel pools and by heavy consumption for direct use (e. g. toilet flushing, washing and bathing, and washing of hotel towels daily), whilst residents are often forced to travel long distances to seek water (where piped supplies do not exist or access to fresh supplies of water are limited).

Therefore issues of water scarcity in some developing countries with expanding tourism industries (see the discussion later in this chapter), and the prioritization of supplies for tourism and agricultural use, make both the issue of the development of tourism and identifying the unsustainable nature of its growth contentious. Whilst some tour operators have sought to address the issue by raising awareness of water use amongst tourists as consumers, this has been shown to have very little impact on consumer behaviour. This again reinforces the problem of being 'green at home' and seemingly responsible towards the environment but wishing to 'treat themselves' on holiday, which is compounded by a degree of ignorance about the scale and significance of the water equity issues in specific destinations.

what people like to do; this is notoriously difficult to understand as it involves entering the realms of psychology and the mind of the individual tourist. Furthermore, these psychological elements are bound up in notions of enjoyment, feelings, emotions and seemingly intangible and unseen characteristics. The issue is further complicated by the way in which an individual's tastes and interests change throughout their life. In other words, being a tourist is based on the principle of non-work and enjoyment of one's free time in a different locality, and results in an experience, a treasured memory and something personal which develops through our life course.

Why study tourism? Is it just about enjoyment and holidays?

Tourism and its analysis have become a relatively recent field of study among academics, researchers and commentators. Some of the very early student textbooks on tourism (see Table 1.3) can be dated to the early 1970s (although there are examples of other reviews of tourism dating to the 1930s, 1940s and 1950s), with a second wave being produced in the 1980s and then a massive explosion in the late 1980s and 1990s as tourism education and training expanded worldwide. Since the 1990s, a wide range of more specialist and niche books have been published on particular aspects of tourism research.

Table 1.3 The evolution of the study of tourism: Key studies during the period 1930–1970s

Lennard, R. (1931) *Englishmen at Rest and Play*. Oxford: Clarendon Press.

Ogilvie, I. (1933) *The Tourist Movement*. London: Staples Press.

Pimlott, J. (1947) *The Englishman's Holiday*. London: Faber and Faber.

Lickorish, L. and Kershaw, A. (1958) *The Travel Trade*. London: Practical Press Ltd.

Burkart, A. and Medlik, S. (1974) *Tourism, Past Present and Future*. London: Heinemann.

Goeldner, C. (1974) *Tourism, Principles and Practice*. New York: Wiley.

Page, S. J. and Connell, J. (eds) (2008) *Tourism, Volumes 1–6: Sage Library of Tourism and Hospitality Management*. London: Sage. (This collection of seminal articles shaping the development of tourism research documents the period since the 1920s and is an important starting point to trace the development of the subject.)

There are a range of commonly recognized problems in studying tourism, a number of which are important to the way in which we understand whether it is just about enjoyment and holidaytaking:

- tourism is a multidisciplinary subject which means that a wide range of other subjects, such as psychology, geography, economics, to name but a few, examine it and bring to it a range of ideas and methods of studying it. This means that there is no overarching academic agreement on how to approach the study of tourism – it really depends on how you are looking at tourism, and the perspective you adopt which determines the issues you are interested in studying
- this has led to a lack of clarity and definition in how to study tourism, something that other researchers have defined as *reductionism*. What this means is that tourism is normally defined by reducing it (hence 'reductionism') to a simple range of activities or transactions (i.e. *What types of holidays do people choose?* or *How do people purchase those holidays?*) rather than by focusing on the framework needed to give a wider perspective or overview of tourism.

These problems often compound the way people view tourism as a subject, emphasizing the holiday or enjoyment aspects of travelling (in one's spare time or on business) as the defining features or reference point of tourism. To the general public tourism is something everyone knows about – it is something many have engaged in and so have an opinion on what it is, its effects and widespread development.

Admittedly, tourism is about pleasure and enjoyment, but its global growth and expansion are now creating serious societal problems and issues; a fundamental understanding of tourism is required if we are to manage and control the impacts and problems it can cause. Some critics argue that tourism epitomizes the extreme of post-modern consumption in a society that spends on travel and tourism because it can and not for an intrinsic need for holidays as access to travel is, in relative terms, very cheap and affordable for many. One way of beginning to understand that tourism is more than holidays and enjoyment is to think about why tourism is so important in modern society (i.e. its social, cultural and economic significance) by looking at an important process which has led to the demand for it – the rise of the leisure society.

The leisure society

Tourism is now widely acknowledged as a social phenomenon, as the nature of society in most advanced developed countries has now changed from one which has traditionally had an economy based on manufacturing and production, to one where the dominant form of employment is services and consumer industries (i.e. those based on producing consumer goods and services). At the same time, many countries have seen the amount of leisure time and paid holiday entitlement for their workers increase in the post-war period so that workers now have the opportunity to engage in the new forms of consumption such as tourism. These changes have been described as being part of what has been termed the *leisure society*, a term coined in the 1970s by sociologists. They were examining the future of work and the way in which society was changing, as traditional forms of employment were disappearing and new service-related employment, increased leisure time and new working habits emerged (e.g. flexi-time and part-time work). Some commentators described this as a 'leisure shock' in the 1980s since many workers were still not prepared for the rise in leisure time and how to use it.

As society has passed from the stage of industrialization to one now described as post-industrial, where new technologies and ways of communicating and working have evolved, sociologists such as Baudrillard (1998) in *The Consumer Society: Myths and Structures*, have argued that we have moved from a society of work and production to one in which leisure and consumption now dominate. This has been reflected in social changes, such as the rise of new middle classes in many developed and developing countries, and these middle classes have a defining feature, which is the concern with leisure lifestyles and consumption. The new-found wealth among the growing middle class has been increasingly spent on leisure items, and tourism is an element of this (e.g. in 1911, 1 per cent of the population had 70 per cent of the wealth; this dropped to 40 per cent in 1960 and 23 per cent in 2002 in the UK). The international growth in holidaytaking is directly related to this new middle class. The increasing mobility of this group has been reflected in a massive growth globally in their propensity to travel and the growth of a society focused on leisure, of which tourism is prioritized as a key element of their household budgets and as a form of conspicuous consumption, as the following statistics suggest:

- factors promoting these changes include cheaper air fares and changing patterns of personal expenditure. For example, *The Family Spending Survey 2008* (published in

2009) by the Office for National Statistics found that household spending in the UK included £60.10 a week on recreation and culture, ranked second to transport at £63.40. This recreational spending included £13.60 a week spent on overseas package holidays and 1.10p on UK-based package holidays: this is over four times the amount spent in real terms in 1968

- the amount spent on overseas holidays has increased more than sevenfold since 1971, when 6.7 million trips were taken, rising to 68.2 million overseas trips in 2008, although dropping to 58.5 million trips in 2013, with those in managerial and professional employment (the new middle classes) spending double that of other employed classes

- in 2012, the UK received 31 million inbound tourists from overseas (overseas tourists); for UK residents, 57 million holiday trips of one night or more were taken in the UK (domestic holidays); 18.9 million domestic business trips of one night or more were taken; and 45.1 million trips of one night or more were taken to visit friends and relatives

- the economic significance of holidays in the UK for the period 2008–2012 illustrates the economic effects of tourism. For example, as Figure 1.2 shows, expenditure by overseas tourists to the UK and UK residents rose from £116 billion to £129 billion despite the effects of the economic slowdown that emerged in 2008–2009 as a result of the global financial crisis. Figure 1.2 shows that, whilst overseas tourists spending in the UK grew from £19 to £21 billion, the economic downturn saw a change in consumer behaviour as outbound trips overseas saw the first major consistent decline since the 1970s as the concept of the 'staycation' developed. Staycation is described as spending one's leisure time in the UK rather than taking overseas holidays, with economic austerity and low consumer confidence in the economy (and poor exchange rates making overseas holidays much more expensive) contributing towards more day trips and domestic holidays. This illustrates the impact of economic factors (e.g. the economic slowdown)

- not surprisingly, the rise in such travel has seen air travel grow exponentially. In the period 1980–2008, there was a 204 per cent increase in the number of air passengers at UK airports, with the number of domestic passengers rising from 7.5 to 22.8 million. Similarly, the number of overseas passengers increased by 342 per cent from 42.9 to 189.8 million, despite recording a slight decrease on 2007 figures.

This snapshot of the UK shows that tourism is a major element of the leisure spending of households, and tourist travel to the UK is a major driver of the economy. The growing significance of travel and tourism in household spending reflects what researchers have described as 'leisure lifestyles'. A study for the United Nations World Tourism Organization in 2013 illustrated how interconnected tourism is within the global economy, identifying the impact of the drop in overseas holiday spending by developed countries like the UK and USA. It found that:

- low-income countries (less developed countries) depended upon tourism for 45 per cent of their exports in 2009

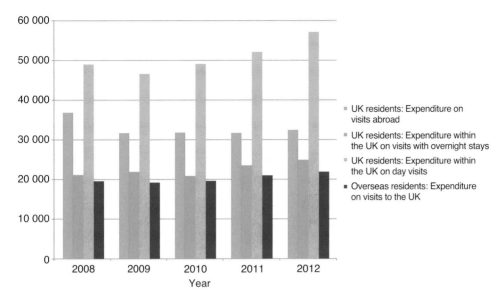

Figure 1.2
Tourism expenditure in the UK, 2008–2012

Source: UK-TSA 2008–2011 (ONS)

- international tourism accounted for US$306 billion in tourism receipts and 36 per cent of the volume of international tourism, with a wide geographical distribution, as illustrated in Figure 1.3
- the economic crisis affected countries with a high level of dependence upon tourism with between a 4 per cent drop (e.g. in the Maldives) to a 9 per cent drop (e.g. in Costa Rica), although these percentage drops were much greater for high spending markets such as the UK and US
- the tourism sector in these countries responded by downsizing their operations, with lay-offs and by reducing their outgoings, which hit the lower paid and female employees to a greater degree
- in the Maldives, 1477 low paid workers, mainly immigrant workers, lost their jobs and a 2030 per cent cut in the Maldivian tourism workforce occurred.

Source: UNWTO (2013) *Economic Crisis, International Tourism Decline and its Impact on the Poor*

Interest in tourism in Europe, North America and other parts of the world has been given an added boost by the impact of new technology such as the internet and the worldwide web, which has rendered knowledge and awareness of tourism and the opportunities to travel worldwide more accessible. The worldwide web has been used as a medium to portray travel options and the product offerings of destinations, so that people can search and explore travel options at a global scale from the ease of a computer terminal. In Europe, the impact of this new technology in the early years of the twenty-first century has generated a new tourism boom akin to the rise in international tourism in the 1970s, with new forms of technology and the supply of cheaper forms

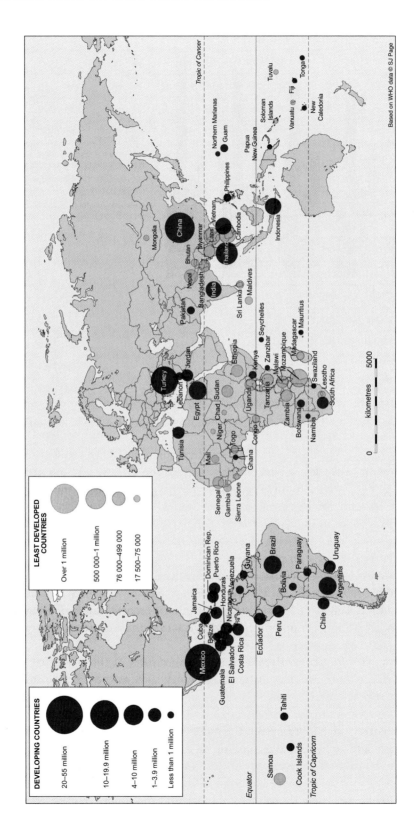

Figure 1.3
The geographical distribution of tourism in the less and least developed world

Source: developed from UNWTO data

of travel (i.e. the low-cost airlines) fostering this demand. Over 90 per cent of some low-cost airline bookings are now made online, which illustrates the power of the internet and its role in reaching a new customer base in the tourism sector. This has given rise to *e-tourism*, which is the digitization of all elements in the tourism supply chain,[1] whereby the supply and demand for tourism can be met through new virtual forms of distribution such as the worldwide web, as opposed to conventional methods such as travel agents and paper brochures. This has certainly revolutionized tourism and the access to travel knowledge and information, hitherto largely within the confines of travel agents and travel organizers: now everyone can be their own travel agent if they have access to the technology.

Other commentators have also pointed to the changing sophistication of tourists as consumers, especially the middle classes with their pursuit of authentic and unique experiences in the developed world and the expanding, fast growing middle classes in the BRIC economies (Brazil, Russia, India and China). This is part of what Pine and Gilmore (1999) identified as the *experience economy*, which is the next stage in the evolution of society from a service economy. They argue that businesses need to create experiences which create a sensation and can personalize the experience to build a relationship with the consumer, and they suggest four areas of experience that we need to focus on:

- entertainment
- education
- aesthetics (i.e. an ability to immerse oneself in something) and;
- escapism in what is consumed.

This has major implications for the types of tourism experience we develop now and in the future and it has gained momentum with the growth of the internet, which now allows consumers to seek out these experiences globally.

The internet and social media

e-tourism is only the first stage of the internet's impact upon tourism. The first wave of internet technology created an online travel community where tourism businesses were able to market to and communicate with consumers through electronic media. This has been followed by a new wave of web-based communities known as Web 2.0 (also described as *computer-generated media* or *social media*) where the online content is created by online users and made available to other users via the Web 2.0 interactive technology. The importance of this technology is that it allows consumers to communicate about social themes such as holidays and travel. So the increasing use of the internet to make bookings and reservations for travel online has been combined with consumer ratings and reviews online through travel sites such as TripAdvisor.com. Therefore, many of the previous principles of travel planning, where the advice and knowledge of travel agents was seen as a key determinant of holiday decision-making have now been replaced by the technological power of the internet, social media and consumer ratings which offer greater insights into the very intangible nature of tourism experiences from those who have already consumed the product or service.

Access to and use of internet technology is increasing and one important feature which many studies confirm is that this technology is increasingly used to search out and peruse travel options, as well as for making bookings. With these issues in mind, attention now turns to what is meant by the terms 'tourism', 'tourist' and 'travel'.

Concepts: Tourism, the tourist and travel

Attempts to define tourism are numerous and very often the terms 'travel' and 'tourism' are used interchangeably. According to the international organization responsible for tourism, the World Tourism Organization (UNWTO):

> Tourism is defined as the activities of persons travelling to and staying in places outside their usual environment for not more than one consecutive year for leisure, business and other purposes not related to the exercise of an activity remunerated from within the place visited. The use of this broad concept makes it possible to identify tourism between countries as well as tourism within a country. 'Tourism' refers to all activities of visitors, including both 'tourists (overnight visitors)' and 'same-day visitors'.
>
> (www.world-tourism.org)

This seemingly straightforward definition has created a great deal of debate. In fact, controversy has surrounded the development of acceptable definitions since the League of Nations' attempt to define a tourist in 1937 and subsequent attempts by the United Nations conference in 1963 which considered definitions proposed by the then IUOTO (now UNWTO). There have also been attempts to clarify what is meant by the term 'visitor' as opposed to 'tourist' and the distinction between tourists who travel within their own country (domestic tourists) and those who travel to other countries (international tourists). What the debates on defining tourism at a technical level show is that it is far from an easy task in agreeing what constitutes a 'tourist'. For example, should we include someone who is a visitor staying in a second home?: they are technically away from their homes, but are staying in another form of property that they own. Similarly, how far away from your home area must you travel before your activity is deemed tourism? A further problem is associated with the category of cruise ship passengers who dock at a port and visit briefly, not staying overnight, or cross-Channel trippers who may cross an international boundary but then return within a day and do not stay overnight.

To try and encompass many of these anomalies and problems, the UNWTO produced guidelines and a useful categorization for defining a tourist, which is shown in Figure 1.4. What is increasingly obvious is that new forms of research on tourism are needed to understand how the phenomenon loosely defined as tourism is evolving, as it is far from static. For example, research on tourism and migration has identified the short-term migration of the elderly who winter in warmer climates – such as the UK pensioners

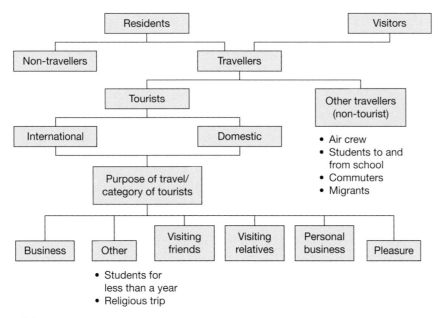

Figure 1.4
The classification of tourists

Source: developed and modified from Chadwick (1994)

who overwinter in the Mediterranean – as a new type of tourist. These patterns of tourism migration incorporate owners of second homes, tourists and seasonal visitors who spend two to six months overseas in locations such as Tuscany, Malta and Spain. For example, over 300 000 people own a second home in the UK and over 170 000 have purchased overseas properties. In the USA estimates of domestic second-home ownership range between 3.6 million and 9.2 million properties, the majority of which are located in coastal or rural areas. This pattern of seasonal tourism and migration also generates flows of people known as 'visiting friends and relatives', and these are somewhat different to the conventional images of package holidaymakers destined for these locations in Europe. In the USA, a long-established trend of a family vacation is the holiday home. Some commentators also suggest that existing definitions of tourism are dated and are being challenged by new forms of tourism such as students engaging in a Year Abroad or volunteering.

Therefore, the following definition of tourism might be useful where tourism is

the field of research on human and business activities associated with one or more aspects of the temporary movement of persons away from their immediate home communities and daily work environments for business, pleasure and personal reasons.

(Chadwick 1994: 65)

In the USA, there is a tendency still to use the term 'travel' when in fact 'tourism' is meant. What is clear is that tourism is associated with three specific issues:

- 'the movement of people;
- a sector of the economy or an industry;
- a broad system of interacting relationships of people, their needs [sic] to travel outside their communities and services that attempt to respond to these needs by supplying products'.

Source: After Chadwick (1994: 65)

From this initial starting point, one can begin to explore some of the complex issues in arriving at a working definition of the terms 'tourism' and 'tourist'.

Probably the most useful work to provide an introduction to tourism as a concept and the relationship with travel is Burkart and Medlik's (1981) seminal study *Tourism: Past Present and Future*. This identified the following characteristics associated with tourism:

- tourism arises from the movement of people to and their stay in various destinations
- there are two elements in all tourism: the journey to the destination and the stay including activities at the destination
- the journey and the stay take place outside the normal place of residence and work, so that tourism gives rise to activities that are distinct from those of the resident and working populations of the places through which tourists travel and in which they stay
- the movement to destinations is of a temporary, short-term character, with intention to return within a few days, weeks or months
- destinations are visited for purposes other than the taking up of permanent residence or of employment remunerated from within the places visited.

Source: Burkart and Medlik (1981: 42)

All tourism includes some travel but not all travel is tourism, while the temporary and short-term nature of most tourist trips distinguishes it from migration. But how does tourism fit together – in other words how can we understand the disparate elements? One approach is to look at tourism as an integrated system, which means that one has to ask how tourism is organized and what the defining features are.

An organizing framework for the analysis of tourism

The most widely used framework is that developed by Leiper (1990 – see Hall and Page 2010 for a posthumous review of his work) who identified a tourism system as comprising a tourist, a traveller-generating region, tourism destination regions, transit routes for tourists travelling between generating and destination areas, and the travel and tourism industry (e.g. accommodation, transport, the firms and organizations supplying services and products to tourists). This is illustrated in Figure 1.5 and shows that transport forms an integral part of the tourism system, connecting the tourist-generating and destination region together. Thus, a 'tourism system' is a framework which enables one to understand the overall process of tourist travel from both the supplier and purchaser's perspective

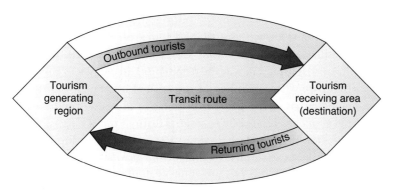

Figure 1.5
Leiper's tourism system
Source: redrawn from Page (1995); based on and modified from Leiper (1990)

(known respectively as 'supply' and 'demand') while identifying the organizations which influence and regulate tourism. It also allows one to understand where the links exist between different elements of tourism, from where the tourist interacts with the travel organizer (travel agent or retailer), the travel provider (airline, or mode of transport), the destination area and tourism sector within the destination. This approach is also helpful for understanding how many elements are assembled by the tourism sector to create an experience of tourism. One major element in this experience of tourism is the tour, which is a feature of holidays and the use of leisure time.

The tour, holidays, leisure time and the destination

What is evident from Leiper's model of the tourism system is that the tour – which is a trip, travel anywhere for pleasure, leisure or business – is a vital element. The tour is an underpinning feature of tourism, a prerequisite for tourism to occur – the consumer has to be brought to the product or experience, and has to travel, and it is a reciprocal event – the traveller travels out and back. Transport and single or multiple locations are involved. The conventional definition of touring inevitably implies travel to one or more places, called 'destinations'. A destination typically comprises attractions (e.g. natural and man-made), and needs to be accessible, have available packages to attract visitors and provide ancillary services (such as tour guides) and amenities (such as accommodation and retailing). This notion of a destination is increasingly being used as a framework for tourism management by public sector organizations to understand how the visitor experience of a place can be developed and enhanced as well as how the synergies between businesses can be developed and the competitiveness of the destination can be improved. In other words, the destination concept acts as a holistic framework in which tourism activity can be understood as a system, where the inter-connections and relationships between tourists, the tourism system and containing context (the destination) are understood so that impacts upon the environment and residents or on the local and national economy can be more precisely assessed.

For the tourist, there are various forms of touring: the excursion by road or rail which may have a scenic element known as a touring route; or some cruises, where the ship tours a range of destinations or ports of call. Conversely, the excursion element may be something that the tourist undertakes at the destination on a day-trip basis or in the form of a more sustained trip, with a planned or unplanned itinerary. Whilst the holiday is something which encompasses the entire experience or use of leisure time for a holiday, the tour is a distinct element of the holiday and has distinct travel patterns. These patterns contribute to the development of places as destinations which develop and grow through time. Some researchers have attempted to explain the growth, stagnation and decline of tourist resorts such as spas in terms of a resort life cycle. The work of Butler, published in 1980, suggested that resorts follow a specific cycle of growth. The initial exploration by tourists is followed by a period of involvement, often with patronage by a royal figure who started a trend towards visitation (e.g. King George III visiting Weymouth in England) or by its wider popularization as a resort for the elite to visit. This set the stage and created tourism tastes and fashions emulated by the visitors. The next stage of Butler's model is development, followed by consolidation and then stagnation. At this point, the resort may decline or action may be taken by agents of development (i.e. an entrepreneur, the public sector or a combination of both) to rejuvenate the resort, and this rejuvenation is the last stage of the model. Figure 1.6 illustrates this pattern through time and shows the creation (i.e. birth) and decline (i.e. death) of resorts. Although such models are highly generalized and simplify the reality of resort development, they are a starting point for the analyses of resorts such as spas through history. The model has also been used in recent years as a basis to try and understand what point specific destinations are at in their life cycle, since the model follows the marketing concept of the product life cycle, where products may have definite or indefinite life courses. The same applies to tourist

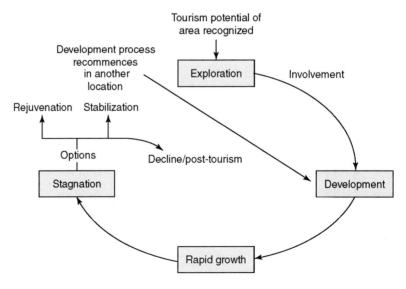

Figure 1.6
The resort life cycle

Source: developed and modified from Butler (1980)

destinations which can decline when tourist tastes and patterns change and so fall out of favour and require a new focus or attraction to bring the visitors back.

In view of these issues, which help to understand the nature of tourism as an entity, attention now turns to the scale, significance and importance of tourism as an international activity.

Measuring tourism

Once we agree a general definition of what tourism is, we can look for methods that add precision to the scale, volume and significance of tourism as a global activity. Measuring tourism also helps to understand some of the problems which planners and decision-makers need to address in planning for tourism and future growth scenarios. There are three basic considerations in trying to define tourism as an activity, which are:

1   What is the purpose of travel (e.g. business travel, holidaymaking, visits to friends and relatives)?
2   What time dimension is involved in the tourism visit, which requires a minimum and a maximum period of time spent away from the home area and the time spent at the destination? In most cases, this would involve a minimum stay of more than 24 hours away from home and less than a year as a maximum.
3   What situations exist where some countries may or may not choose to include travellers, such as cruise passengers, travellers in transit at a particular point of embarkation/departure and excursionists who stay less than 24 hours at a destination, as tourists?

There are four main reasons why measuring tourism is important (Figure 1.7).

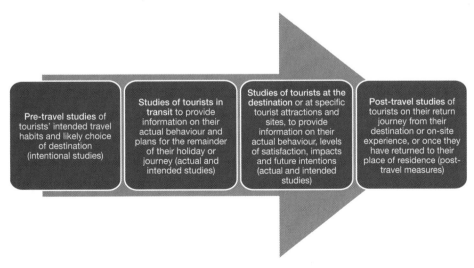

Figure 1.7
Ways of measuring tourism

Source: author

The growth of global tourism and volatility in demand

At a general level, measuring tourism through the collection, analysis and interpretation of statistics is essential to the measurement of the volume, scale, impact and value of tourism at different geographical scales from the global to the country level down to the individual destination. At the simplest level, this is shown in Figure 1.8, which demonstrates the trends in global tourism since 1950 and forecasts to 2030.

Figure 1.8 uses the UNWTO arrival statistics for each year and their forecasts and shows that international tourist arrivals have not simply grown year on year. A number of downturns have occurred in tourist arrivals, more recently caused by the impact of foot and mouth cattle disease in the UK, 9/11 and Bali (September 2002) terrorist events and other factors (e.g. the economic crisis in Argentina, the strength of the US dollar, conflict in the Middle East and the SARS (Severe Acute Respiratory Syndrome) outbreak). One could term the period since 2000 as one in which international tourism has operated in 'turbulent times'. Part of this turbulence, as Glaeßer (2006) notes, is the impact of natural catastrophes on tourism. For example, in the twentieth century there have been 50 000 natural disasters but between 1990 and 2005 there have been 500–700 such catastrophes each year. These events have periodically interrupted or at worst devastated the tourism industry (e.g. the earthquake that devastated Haiti in 2009), contributing to the notion of turbulence in tourism activity. In other words, a range of factors impact upon visitor arrivals at an international level, because tourism

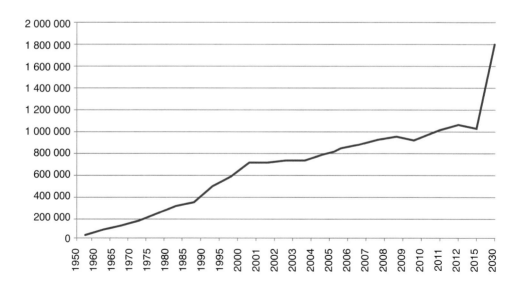

Figure 1.8
The growth of international tourism since 1950 and forecasts to 2030

Source: UNWTO data

is a very fickle activity (i.e. it is very vulnerable to the external factors mentioned above which act as deterrents to travel) and adverse events can act as shock waves which send ripples across the world and impact upon people's willingness to travel for pleasure reasons. This is because tourism needs relative stability for such activity to occur and the vulnerability to shock effects has been described as volatility in tourism demand which reacts very quickly to these crises or shock events such as wars, currency fluctuations and political instability. Tourism also responds to very positive factors such as hosting the Olympic Games, which may lead to a sudden change in the volume of visitors. One of the most recent shock events that have impacted on global tourism is the global credit crunch. Whilst this has had different types of impacts on various tourism markets (the most substantial being on business travel), its continued existence has led to a global decline in visitor arrivals internationally. In addition, in 2008 the effect of the credit crunch was compounded by the outbreak of a global pandemic associated with swine flu which initially developed in Mexico and spread by travellers returning to their home areas or by visiting new areas so that a number of fatalities occurred in the affected countries as shown in Figure 1.9.

At the same time, major religious events can be a major stimulus to tourist travel, for example pilgrimages to locations such as Lourdes in France, where its waters are seen as having healing properties. Other religious events such as the Pope's Christmas message attract large audiences in Rome, while other religious faiths have similar examples. At a global scale, recent trends in international tourism can be summarized as follows:

* international tourism is dominated by Western European destinations and, in 2012, international arrivals globally had exceeded 1 billion for the first time
* new areas for tourism activity, such as Asia and the Pacific (including the growing economies of Singapore, Thailand, South Korea, Taiwan and China) are beginning to develop their volume of visitor arrivals at the global scale and are experiencing the highest rates of tourism growth, as illustrated in Figure 1.10
* the top destinations worldwide in terms of arrivals in 2013 were: France, the USA, Spain, China and Italy
* more established destinations in N. W. Europe and the USA have seen slower growth compared to emerging regions such as Africa, N. E. Asia, Eastern Europe, S. E. Asia and the Middle East. What these rates of growth mean for individual destinations can be seen in Case Study 11.1, which examines Vietnam.

But one of the enduring problems of tourism statistics is that they are an incomplete source of information because they are often only an estimate of the total pattern of tourism. In addition, such statistics are often dated when they are published because there is a significant time lag in their generation, analysis, presentation and dissemination. This is because many published tourism statistics are derived from sample surveys, with the results being weighted or statistically manipulated to derive a measure which is supposedly representative of the real-world situation. Hence, many tourism statistics at

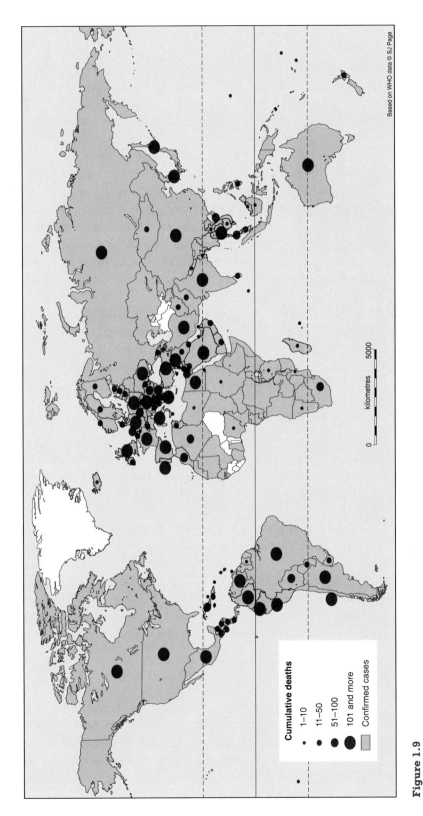

Figure 1.9

The global distribution of deaths from swine flu in 2008–2009

Source: based on UN World Health Organization data

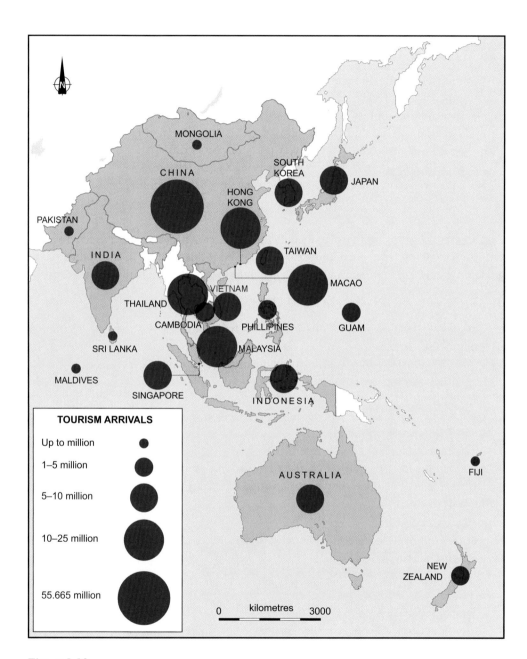

Figure 1.10
The geographical distribution of tourism in Asia Pacific

Source: developed from UNWTO data

a country or regional level often state that they are estimates of tourism for this reason. In reality, this often means that tourism statistics may be subject to significant errors depending on the size of the sample.

The typical problems associated with measuring tourism are as follows:

- tourists are a transient and highly mobile population making statistical sampling procedures difficult when trying to ensure statistical accuracy and rigour in methodological terms
- interviewing mobile populations such as tourists is often undertaken in a strange environment, typically at ports or points of departure or arrival where there is background noise which may influence responses
- other variables such as the weather may affect the responses.

Source: Latham (1989)

Even where sampling and survey-related problems can be minimized, such tourism statistics have to be treated carefully as they may be influenced by how the tourist was measured and the type of approach used. The main ways of measuring tourists through surveys are as follows:

- pre-travel studies of tourists' intended travel habits and likely choice of destination (intentional studies)
- studies of tourists in transit to provide information on their actual behaviour and plans for the remainder of their holiday or journey (actual and intended studies)
- studies of tourists at the destination or at specific tourist attractions and sites, to provide information on their actual behaviour, levels of satisfaction, impacts and future intentions (actual and intended studies)
- post-travel studies of tourists on their return journey from their destination or on-site experience, or once they have returned to their place of residence (post-travel measures).

Such studies can also be used to examine different facets of the tourist as the following three approaches suggest:

- measurement of tourist volume, enumerating arrivals, departures and the number of visits and stays
- expenditure-based surveys which quantify the value of tourist spending at the destination and during the journey
- measurement of the characteristics and features of tourists to construct a profile of the different markets and segments visiting a destination.

In the commercial world, tourism data are also collated by organizations that specialize in their collection and analysis including market research companies. Tourism consultants may also be commissioned specifically to collect data for feasibility studies of tourism developments or new business opportunities, and much of the information remains confidential to the client due to its commercial sensitivity. But, in most cases, national governments collate tourism statistics through studies of domestic and international tourism which are then assembled by the UNWTO.

Once we have an understanding of how tourism is measured and collated, then we can begin to think about what the patterns and trends in tourism mean at a global level and what the implications are, particularly in terms of the more critical issues of what forces are affecting tourism as a global activity.

New forces affecting tourism: Globalization, inequality and the developed and developing world

When one looks at the patterns of tourism, and those areas which are growing in terms of international tourism, it is evident that the majority of outbound travellers are from the developed countries of Europe and North America, Australasia and the new middle class in many developing countries. In some cases, the tourists are travelling to developing countries where the standard of living often means the majority of the population lives at subsistence level or at a much lower standard than the visitor. The contrast in wealth between visitor and host is often very large and it highlights a clear inequality between those who have the disposable income to enjoy the luxury of international and domestic travel and the tourism employees who are working at low wage rates and in low-paid, unskilled jobs. This situation is made worse by the growing impact of globalization.

Globalization is a process associated with the growth of large international companies and corporations, which control various forms of economic development and production internationally from their host country, making goods and delivering services at a lower cost using low overheads and cheap labour in developing countries. Tourism is no exception to this: large multinational hotel chains and tour operators use developing countries and destinations as the basis for their tourist product. In these situations, the economic linkages with the local community are limited, so that low-skill jobs and low economic benefits are traded off against the profits and economic benefits of tourism development being expropriated (i.e. returned) to the country of origin of the multi-national firm. In many cases, the weakly developed nature of local economic linkages in developing countries' tourism economies mean they are often trapped into such exploitative relationships because they do not have the indigenous capital or entrepreneurs to set up tourism businesses. A lack of education, know-how and power to negotiate with multinationals to maximize the benefits for local people means that tourism can develop as a form of exploitation for such communities. This may mean that, rather than importing foodstuffs, such as internationally recognizable brands, to meet the tastes of tourists, local products should be developed to nurture the linkages with the local economy, so local people may benefit.

Tourists bring their leisure lifestyles with them on holiday and these are increasingly consumptive and conspicuous. Their spending power could be harnessed for the benefit of the local economy. A growing problem in many tourism destinations worldwide is that the growth of tourism and expropriation of its profits means that the environmental resource base which is used to attract tourists (e.g. attractive beaches, wildlife and the cultural and built environment) is not invested in and may be spoilt. More and more, attention is turning to the extent to which tourism is a sustainable economic, social and environmentally based activity. That we should use the environment without conserving it for future generations is one of the central arguments in the sustainable tourism debate. This also raises the issue of inequalities related to tourism; for example, tourist use of local resources required by residents can destroy those resources and environmental quality. This means that local people, governments and international agencies have a responsibility to lobby and take action to ensure that tourism development which occurs in different countries and locations is not only sustainable but seeks to minimize negative impacts as far as possible. It should not marginalize vulnerable groups such as children and the local workforce: the International Labour Organization (ILO) has estimated that 10–15 per cent of the tourism workforce worldwide is comprised of children who do not enjoy appropriate standards of labour and employment conditions (see the work of Tourism Concern at tourismconern.org.uk). Among the common human rights abuses which Tourism Concern have highlighted are: the forced eviction of people to make way for tourism development; environmental damage resulting from tourism which impacts upon the resources people depend upon for their livelihoods; exploitation of tribal people as tourist attractions; and poor levels of pay and poor working conditions for employees in the tourism sectors.

Tourism needs to be developed in an ethical manner so that exploitation is not its hallmark. This is a theme which will be returned to later in the book; at this point it is enough to emphasize that tourism development and activity not only needs to be socially and environmentally responsible, it must be sustainable and long term rather than short term and exploitative (so that the goose that lays the golden egg is not killed off). The tourism industry needs to work with communities, local bodies and people to ensure that tourism is a win–win activity for everyone and is integrated into the local community rather than just exploiting its local assets. This may require a significant change in emphasis in the way tourism is developed and managed but it is an enduring theme, which is worth highlighting at different points in the book (see Case Study 1.3 for more detail).

Tourists and tourism businesses have a greater responsibility to ensure that tourism is promoted as an activity which will not only enhance global understanding and interaction between people of different cultures and societies, but will also promote dialogue, benefits and opportunities for the tourist, the host and the environment. So, in some situations, tourism may be a way of providing the stimulus and means for preserving and conserving endangered species and environments as well as providing benefits beyond those which normally accrue to the tourism industry. Tourism has to operate as a profitable activity but, for its long-term future, mutually beneficial relationships and links between the industry, people and the environment must exist

CASE STUDY 1.3
TOURISM AND POVERTY ALLEVIATION

Extreme poverty is a major problem for many developing countries which have a large proportion of their population living a subsistence lifestyle, often existing on less than $1 a day. At the same time, many of these countries have seen their tourism economies expand as tourists seek new destinations and governments embrace the expansion of this activity to generate foreign revenue. A considerable body of research from consultants and academics has arisen on how this expansion of tourism may be harnessed to address the development problems associated with poverty (see Scheyvens 2007, 2011; Mitchell and Ashley 2009). This new thinking has been described as pro-poor tourism which is designed to develop ways to maximize the benefits from tourism to raise local people out of poverty. This involves measures that will: encourage the employment of local people (as opposed to expatriate labour); provide opportunities for local people to supply goods to tourists and tourism businesses; and help the creation of micro-enterprises so that people can develop their own businesses. However, many obstacles have been identified in implementing pro-poor tourism strategies in less developed countries which include: a lack of awareness and understanding in poorer communities which limits their understanding of the opportunities available; a lack of skills and entrepreneurial talent to capitalize on the opportunities; a lack of access to finance to create new businesses focused on tourism; and cultural concerns over how tourism may affect their way of life. Where success stories of pro-poor tourism exist, these examples of best practice need to be shared so that tourism can be harnessed to address abject poverty through case studies of best practice which outline the principles and success factors associated with implementing such an approach. This is vital if the benefits of tourism development are to be harnessed in the future to address poverty.

Further reading

Mitchell, J. and Ashley, C. (2009) *Tourism and Poverty Reduction: Pathways to Prosperity*. London: Earthscan.

to bring financial and sustainable benefits for all and enhance the reputation and image of tourism as a global phenomenon. This is the underlying basis of the pro-poor tourism lobby. In this way the welfare and benefits of tourism to tourists can also be extended to the host population and help to address many of the inequalities which exist in the growing globalization of tourism activity as multinational enterprises seek to exercise greater control of the choice and nature of tourism being offered to consumers. Although this book will not be able to address all of these issues, it is hoped that they will be at the forefront of the reader's mind so that they are aware of the implications of the tourism industry and its activities at a global, national and local level throughout the book.

A framework for the book

The title of this book is *Tourism Management* and therefore it is useful to present an organizing framework for the book and what is meant by the term 'tourism management'. What is often seen and used as an ambiguous term is the word 'management'. Therefore, in this section, the relationship of tourism with management and its meaning in the context of this book is examined.

Tourism and management as a focus for the book

At a very general level, the word 'management' as applied to tourism refers to how tourism needs to be managed as a growing activity at a global, national and local level in order that its often contradictory forces (i.e. the pursuit of profit as a private sector activity and impact on the resource base it uses such as a beautiful coastline on a Pacific island) are reconciled and balanced so that tourism develops and is pursued in a sustainable manner. This means that there is a need to examine the basic principles associated with the term 'management' and how they can be integrated with tourism as an activity. The basic functions associated with management which focus on planning, organizing, leading and controlling are illustrated in Figure 1.11.

Each of these functions involves decision-making by managers, businesses, tourist destinations or organizations so that they can be harnessed to achieve the objectives and tasks associated with managing tourism. The word 'organization' is often used as an all-embracing term to refer to the type of tourism entity which is involved with tourism as a business or at another level. These businesses are motivated by their involvement in tourism to make a profit and, therefore, the efficient organization and management of their activities is essential to ensure that company or organizational

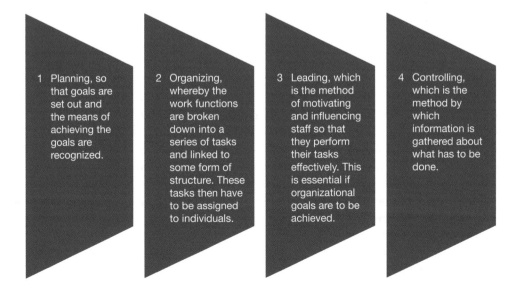

1 Planning, so that goals are set out and the means of achieving the goals are recognized.

2 Organizing, whereby the work functions are broken down into a series of tasks and linked to some form of structure. These tasks then have to be assigned to individuals.

3 Leading, which is the method of motivating and influencing staff so that they perform their tasks effectively. This is essential if organizational goals are to be achieved.

4 Controlling, which is the method by which information is gathered about what has to be done.

Figure 1.11
The functions of management

Source: author

objectives are met. There is a school of management thought which argues that management only occurs when chaos occurs and that the function of management is to impose order and structure on that chaos. Within organizations dealing with the tourism sector (e.g. travel agents, airlines, tour operators and associated businesses), resources are harnessed (e.g. employees, finance, capital, technology, equipment and knowledge) to provide an output, which in the case of tourism is normally a product or experience consumed by the tourist or service. This output is achieved through the management of the resources. One critical element of that management process is related to the way in which businesses have to address the following issues:

- *What should we produce as a business to meet a certain form of tourism demand?* (i.e. should we produce an upmarket high-cost holiday package for ecotourists using tailor-made packages or aim for mass market, low-cost package holidays?)
- *How should it be produced?* (i.e. should we contract in supplies to provide each element of the package product to reduce costs or should we produce each element to ensure quality control and consistency in product delivery?)
- *When, where and how should we produce the tourism product?* (i.e. do we produce an all-year-round or seasonal tourism product?)
- *What destinations/places should be featured in the tourism experience?*
- *What form of business or businesses do we need to produce the tourism services and products so that we meet demand?*

Tourism businesses need to address these issues for their long-term viability, and success or failure will depend upon the management of their organizations' resources to meet demand by consumers in an efficient and profitable manner. It is the concept of supply (i.e. what a business produces) which helps us to understand how the wide range of tourism businesses and organizations (and quite often businesses which do not see themselves as servicing tourists' needs such as taxi companies) combine to link the tourist with the services, experiences and products they seek in a destination.

Managing tourism demand and supply: The perennial management challenge for tourism organizations

Sessa (1983) categorized the supply of tourism services by businesses as follows:

- *tourism resources*, comprising both the natural and human resources of an area
- *general and tourism infrastructure*, which includes the transport and telecommunications infrastructure
- *receptive facilities*, which receive visitors, including accommodation, food and beverage establishments and apartments/condominiums
- *entertainment and sports facilities*, which provide a focus for tourists' activities
- *tourism reception services*, including travel agencies, tourist offices, car hire companies, guides, interpreters and visitor managers.

These 'elements of tourism' which combine at a destination highlight the scope of tourism supply, but a number of less tangible elements of supply (i.e. the destination image) also need to be considered. The business environment in which businesses operate can also have a major bearing on tourism supply. For example, in most countries tourism operates within a free market economy, and individual businesses operate in open competition. However, in some countries certain sectors of the tourism industry receive assistance from government through infrastructure provision, marketing and promotional support from tourist boards and other agencies. It is also apparent that, when governments decide to promote inbound tourism to destinations (also see Further Web Reading 1), they cannot easily control the consequences of marketing, promotion and demand. The competition for overseas visitors to stimulate economic development and GDP growth often means that the associated impacts and implications of growth in inbound markets have to be managed once a boom in arrivals has occurred. The premise of much tourism promotional activity supported by governments and the private sector is achieving growth in inbound arrivals from international visitors as they are generally higher-spending visitors than domestic visitors. This has translated into competition for visitors globally, as more countries target tourism as a key economic sector to grow, and so we need to understand the issues of competition for visitors between countries and between businesses within countries.

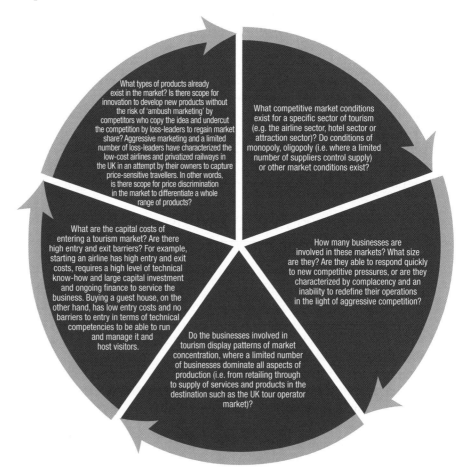

Figure 1.12
Factors affecting the competitive environment for tourism businesses and organizations

Source: author

The competitive environment which affects tourism businesses and their operation needs to be considered in relation to a number of underlying economic issues which are summarized in Figure 1.12.

What Figure 1.12 illustrates is that the market conditions and business environment in which tourism operates is far from static. They are constantly changing, requiring businesses to adapt and to develop strategies to retain their market presence.

For tourism businesses, recognizing these evolving patterns, new trends and the need for innovation (i.e. new ideas and products) to address market conditions re-emphasizes the importance of managerial skills in the supply of tourism products and services. This also highlights what Mintzberg (1973) identified as the nature of managerial work in organizations – short-term coping, disparate activities and more concern with brevity, variety and increasing fragmentation. Tourism managers and businesses are no exception to this and Mintzberg's research has an important bearing on how managers performed certain roles (see Table 1.4) labelled as interpersonal, informational and decisional roles. The ten managerial work roles which Mintzberg identified illustrate the scope of activities which operating and managing a tourism business requires, as well as some of the complexities of how the individual business interacts with the wider body of interests conveniently labelled the 'tourism industry'. It also suggests how important prevailing market conditions are when they impact upon how a business operates, manages and

Table 1.4 Mintzberg's ten managerial roles

Interpersonal roles

Figurehead	Symbolic head: obliged to perform a number of routine duties of legal and social nature
Leader	Responsible for the motivation of subordinates; responsible for staffing and training
Liaison	Maintaining self-developed network of outside contacts/informers who provide information and favours

Information roles

Monitor	Through seeking and receiving a variety of special information, develops thorough understanding of organization and environment
Disseminator	Transmits information received from outsiders and subordinates to members of the organization
Spokesperson	Transmits information to outsiders on organization's plans, serves as expert on organization's industry

Decisional roles

Entrepreneur	Searches organization and its environment for opportunities to bring about change
Disturbance handler	Responsible for corrective action when organization faces important, unexpected disturbances
Resource allocator	Responsible for the allocation of organizational resources of all kinds
Negotiator	Responsible for representing the organization at major negotiations

Source: reproduced from S. Chareanpunsirikul and R. Wood, Mintzberg, managers and methodology. *Tourism Management*, 25: 551–556, © 2002, with permission from Elsevier

responds to opportunities, threats and shortcomings in its own organization. Yet, to do this, a business needs also to understand its relationship to other tourism businesses. A convenient way to explain this is by using the tourism supply chain concept.

The tourism supply chain

As tourism is an amalgam of different interests, activities, stakeholders and businesses, the supply chain concept helps us to understand how different interests are functionally linked together to form a distinct method of service delivery. The supply chain concept originates in economics and has been used to explain how different businesses enter into contractual relationships to supply services, products and goods, and how these goods are assembled into products at different points in the supply chain. Tourism is well suited to the concept of the supply chain because the product, service or experience that is consumed is assembled, and comprises a wide range of suppliers. All too often our knowledge of the supply chain is quite restrictive, since a wide range of components are consumed in tourism including the use of bars, restaurants, handicrafts, food, infrastructure and related services. A schematic diagram of a typical tourism supply chain is shown in Figure 1.13. This shows that, once the consumer has chosen a destination and product, the decision to purchase involves contacting a tourism retailer (e.g. a retail agent, a direct-selling company or an internet-based seller such as www. expedia.co.uk). Having chosen a booking medium and selected a package from a tour operator, the package is then assembled. The tour operator enters into contractual relationships with tourism suppliers such as airlines (although larger tour operators may also own their own charter or scheduled airline), hotel operators and suppliers of associated services such as airport transfers. These suppliers, in turn, contract suppliers

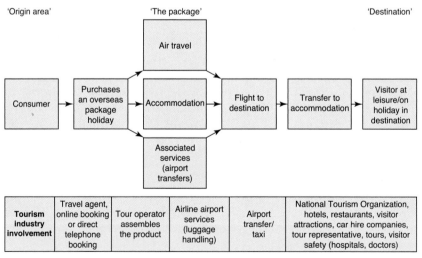

Figure 1.13
A typical supply chain

Source: author

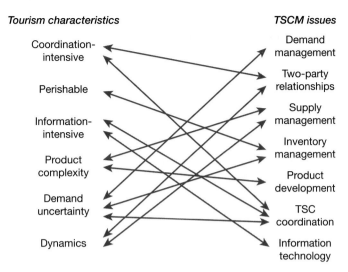

Figure 1.14
Tourism characteristics and related TSCM issues

Source: redrawn from Song (2011) *Tourism Supply Chain Management*. Oxford: Routledge, with permission from Taylor & Francis

who service their business needs: in-flight caterers, airline leasing companies, airport terminal services (i.e. check-in services, baggage-handling, flight controllers, customer service agents for visitors and those with special needs, such as the disabled).

With so many organizations involved in the supply chain in relation to tourist spending and activity, it is clear that these are critical break or pressure points where the service provision could potentially fall down. In fact Zhang *et al.* (2009) found that we need to recognize a number of underlying characteristics of tourism as a business which makes tourism supply chain management (TSCM) essential to the efficiency and profitability of tourism enterprises, as shown in Figure 1.14.

The business strategies that travel companies can pursue to develop their supply of tourism services and products include:

* focusing on core business (i.e. a holiday company focusing on selling holidays rather than being vertically integrated and operating its own airline and hotels)
* seeking to diversify its products. The leading French holiday company Club Méditerranée (Club Med), which traditionally sold packages to its 120 holiday resorts, has used this strategy. Since 1999 and its acquisition of Jet Tours (France's fourth-ranked tour operator, which operated to 113 summer and 81 winter locations) it has diversified its operations to sell non-Club Med packages. Rewe in Germany has pursued a similar diversification strategy with its acquisition of a wider range of tour operating businesses in the long- and short-haul market
* choosing to operate in all segments of the tourism market. TUI has adopted this tactic, and others such as Kuoni are moving towards that goal
* non-holiday companies may choose to enter the market: easyJet entered the cruise holiday business in 2005.

To implement these business strategies, companies in the tourism industry have adopted marketing-related concepts such as branding to differentiate their products in an increasingly competitive marketplace. For example, Club Med relaunched its worldwide image to re-emphasize its famous name and association with consumers, and particularly its dominant position in the French market. Thomas Cook, now owned by the German company C&N Touriste, has used its global image and historic association with pioneering tourism to continue its expansion throughout Europe (see Plates 1.1, 1.2 and 1.3).

Managing the tourism sector

There is also a debate among tourism researchers who argue that tourism is a unique sector in that it displays characteristics of partial industrialization, which are explained more fully by Leiper (1990: 25), where

> only certain organisations providing goods and services directly to tourists are in the tourism industry. The proportion of (a) goods and services stemming from that industry to (b) total goods and services used by tourists can be termed the index of industrialisation, theoretically ranging from 100 per cent (wholly industrialised) to zero (tourists present and spending money, but no tourism industry).

What Leiper's approach to the tourism sector shows is that managing the broad phenomenon called 'tourism' is complex for a number of reasons:

- the tourism industry is not a homogenous sector or segment of the economy: it is made up of various organizations directly involved in tourism (i.e. those which directly service tourist needs) and those indirectly involved, which may be described as allied industries (i.e. food suppliers, retailers and other service providers)
- some of the organizations directly involved in tourism are responsible for encouraging and promoting tourism development and marketing
- the allied industries do not always see themselves as tourism-related enterprises
- the destination or area which the tourists visit is not the sole responsibility of one business or group of businesses; usually the public sector intervenes to ensure that business objectives (i.e. profit and increasing tourism numbers and revenue) are balanced with local needs and business interests (known as 'stakeholder interests') in relation to the resource base which tourism utilizes (i.e. beaches, attractions, the infrastructure and overall environment)
- the public sector is responsible for trying to liaise with, plan and manage this diverse group of interests that are associated with tourism as a phenomenon, as well as having an underlying responsibility in many cases for the marketing and promotion of the destination.

Therefore, one can see how complex the management of tourism is when the interests and variety of organizations involved in tourism are considered and then the concept of partial industrialization is introduced.

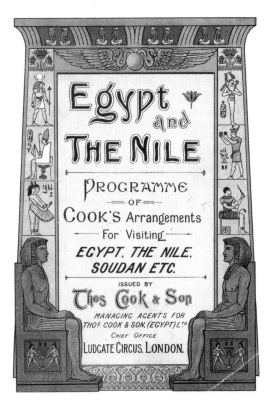

Plate 1.1 (top left)
Thomas Cook brochure advertising Egypt and Nile trips 1900

Source: Thomas Cook

Plate 1.2 (top right)
Thomas Cook brochure advertising Egypt and Nile trips 1904

Source: Thomas Cook

Plate 1.3 (left)
Thomas Cook relaunch of its Egyptian tourism heritage with the 1981/1982 brochure advertising holidays to Egypt and Nile cruises

Source: Thomas Cook

From this discussion, who is responsible for tourism management can be examined at a number of levels, although this is not an exclusive list but a range of illustrations:

- at the individual business level the manager(s) is (are) involved with the functioning and running of the enterprise
- at the destination level, responsibility often lies with a public sector-led agency such as a tourism department (either as a stand-alone body or as part of a local authority department). In extreme situations where a destination is deluged with tourists due to its popularity, the public sector may lead with a public–private sector partnership involving business interests to manage the visitors on the ground
- at the country level, it is the National Tourism Organizations, funded by the public sector through taxes and sometimes with private sector members, who promote and market the country as a place to visit and attempt to manage the diverse interests involved in tourism
- at each level, be it the individual business, destination or country, a complex web of interactions and interrelationships exist which need to be taken into account in the decisions, interests and actions taken to manage tourism.

In each of these illustrations, the functions of management are harnessed. Tourism management as a pursuit, however, is further complicated in that there is a great debate as to what tourism is, what needs to be managed and who should be responsible. The fact that tourism can be seen as an experience based on the pursuit of pleasure and profit raises many complex issues such as whether the tourist is consuming a product, experience or service, and it leads to many debates on what to manage and how far management controls should be exercised by the tourism industry and public sector.

So how does this book address these questions?

One way is to view the managerial process of tourism as a multilayered process, in which the various organizations and stakeholders involved in tourism engage at different levels through time. Figure 1.15 demonstrates this. The focus begins with the individual business, and the management processes (controlling, planning, leading and organizing) are continuous through the interconnected stakeholder groups, from the individual business through to the various interests known as the tourism industry. These interests and the connections between management at different levels and between groups means that, in reality, these groups also have to be aware of external factors that will impact upon management such as the visitor, the business environment, consumer trends, the growth of the leisure society and political processes affecting tourism at government level. The book is organized in such a way that these issues are explained in a manner where the links between different elements of the tourism sector are addressed through examples and case studies. Each chapter builds upon the one preceding to develop the knowledge and understanding of what the tourism industry is, the management challenges facing each sector and how tourism affects changes in different contexts. Accommodating, anticipating and responding to that level of change is one of the major challenges for tourism management in the new millennium.

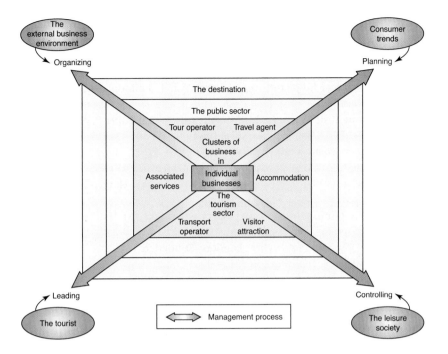

Figure 1.15
A framework for tourism management

Source: author

CHAPTER REVIEW

Note

1   The supply chain comprises all the elements of a tourism experience which the tourism sector combines and links together to produce a holiday, such as transport, accommodation and attractions.

 ## References

Baudrillard, J. (1998) *The Consumer Society: Myths and Structures*. London: Sage.

Burkart, A. and Medlik, S. (1981) *Tourism, Past Present and Future*, 2nd edn. London: Heinemann.

Butler, R. (1980) The concept of the tourist area cycle of evolution: Implications for the evolution of resources. *Canadian Geographer*, 24(1): 5–12.

Chadwick, R. (1994) Concepts, definitions and measures used in travel and tourism research. In J. R. Brent Ritchie and C. Goeldner (eds) *Travel, Tourism and Hospitality Research: A Handbook for Managers and Researchers*, 2nd edn. New York: Wiley.

Glaeßer, D. (2006) *Crisis Management in the Tourism Industry*. Oxford: Butterworth-Heinemann.

Hall, C. M. and Page, S. J. (2010) The contribution of Neil Leiper to Tourism Studies. *Current Issues in Tourism*, 13(4): 299–309.

Latham, J. (1989) The statistical measurement of tourism. In C. P. Cooper (ed.) *Progress in Tourism, Recreation and Hospitality Management*, Vol. 1. London: Belhaven.

Leiper, N. (1990) *Tourism Systems: An Interdisciplinary Perspective*. Palmerston North, New Zealand: Department of Management Systems Occasional Paper 2, Massey University.

Mintzberg, H. (1973) *The Nature of Managerial Work*. New York: Harper Row.

Page, S. J. (1995) *Urban Tourism*. London: Routledge.

Page, S. J. and Connell, J. (2014) *Tourism: A Modern Synthesis*, 3rd edn. Andover: Cengage.

Pine, B. and Gilmore, J. (1999) *The Experience Economy*. Boston: Harvard University Business School Press.

Scheyvens, R. (2007) Exploring the tourism–poverty nexus. In C. M. Hall (ed.) *Pro-Poor Tourism: Who Benefits? Perspectives on Tourism and Poverty Reduction*. Bristol: Channel View.

Scheyvens, R. (2011) *Tourism and Poverty*. London: Routledge.

Sessa, A. (1983) *Elements of Tourism*. Rome: Catal.

UNWTO (2013) *Economic Crisis, International Tourism Decline and its Impact on the Poor*. Madrid: UNWTO.

World Commission on Environment and Development (1987) *Our Common Future*. Oxford: Oxford University Press.

Zhang, Xinyan, Song, Haiyan and Huang, George Q. (2009) Tourism supply chain management: A new research agenda. *Tourism Management*, 30(3): 345–358.

 Further reading

The best international overview of tourism can be found in:

Page, S. J. and Connell, J. (2009) *Tourism: A Modern Synthesis*, 3rd edn. London: Cengage.

For an overview of how tourism and leisure fit together, the best review to date can be found in:

Page, S. J. and Connell, J. (2010) *Leisure: An Introduction*. Harlow: Pearson.

 Questions

1   Why is tourism such an important activity in the twenty-first century?
2   How would you classify tourists?
3   Why is tourism management important for a business operating in the tourism sector?
4   How stable is tourism as an economic activity?

 Access additional resources

- For students: Multiple choice questions for each chapter, video links and further reading.
- For instructors: PowerPoint slides with tables and diagrams, additional case studies, video links and further reading.

2 Tourism

Its origins, growth and future

Learning outcomes

This chapter provides an historical perspective of the evolution of tourism as a business activity through the ages and some of the management challenges it has faced. After reading the chapter you should be able to understand:

- the underlying processes affecting tourism: continuity and change
- the importance of the resort life cycle
- the role of coastal resorts in leisure and tourism during the nineteenth and twentieth centuries
- the role of historical sources such as diaries in reconstructing past patterns of tourism activity
- the evolution of tourism in the inter-war and post-war period
- the factors associated with future trends in tourism development such as space tourism.

Introduction

Tourism is not a recent phenomenon. Whilst it was argued in the last chapter that tourism has become a widely accessible product in the consumer-led leisure society, the historical roots of tourism can be traced back almost to the origins of civilization. What the historical study of tourism indicates is that the nature of what tourists do in their leisure time may have changed, as technology has expanded the opportunities for travel. At the same time, tourism has evolved from being an activity which was the preserve of the 'leisured classes' (i.e. the aristocracy) who had both the leisure time and means to engage in travel, to a mass phenomenon. Throughout history, and even to a degree today, what distinguishes the higher social classes' experience of tourism from a mass product, is its highly individualized consumption when compared to the communal consumption of accommodation and transport, in particular, of the mass market experience. This chapter will show that tourism has varied in terms of its accessibility to different groups in society throughout history, and that the development of a leisure ethic and increased prosperity have created new tourism opportunities.

In any historical overview of tourism, two underlying themes are important: *continuity* and *change*. Continuity means that tourism has continued to be an important process, which remained influential in the leisure lifestyles of certain social classes. Change on the other hand characterizes the evolution of tourism through the ages, since tourism is a dynamic, ever-changing phenomenon. Much of the change is based upon the interaction between the demand for and supply of tourism opportunities through time. In terms of supply, key factors promoting the development of tourism can be explained by the role of innovations (i.e. new ideas) that have generated new products, experiences and destinations and released a latent or pent-up demand for tourism. Part of this change in tourism resulted from the innovations of individual entrepreneurs such as Thomas Cook in the nineteenth century, the introduction of new technology (e.g. the railway, the car and jet aircraft) in expanding the endless possibilities for tourist travel. In simple terms, destinations were developed for tourists and tourists visited them, creating an interaction which is implicit in all forms of tourism: a movement from origin area to destination and vice versa. The discovery and development of these destinations also exhibits elements of continuity and change through time as tourism is a dynamic activity which rarely remains static.

There are comparatively few studies documenting the long-term history of tourism, with many studies focused on specific eras or epochs in time. Much of historians' attention has focused on the evolution of mass tourism in both a domestic setting (i.e. the rise and demise of the English seaside resort) and international setting (i.e. the post-war growth and development of the package holiday). But equally important is the historical evolution of tourism from classical times since it established many of the principles of today's use of leisure time for holidays and travel.

Tourism in classical times

The ancient civilization of Greece was not so much important for any major development of tourism, but more for the Greek philosophers' recognition, endorsement and promotion of the concept of leisure, upon which tourism is based. Aristotle considered leisure to be a key element of the Greek lifestyle, where slaves and other people should do the work required and the Greek freemen should put their leisure time to good use.

This positive leisure doctrine may well have been the original 'leisure lifestyle', which encouraged the pursuit of music, philosophy, non-work and measures of self-development as elements of Greek society. The development of the Olympic Games after 776 BC did provide a vital stimulus for tourism based upon a major sporting event. Greeks travelled to the site of the Olympic Games and were housed in tented encampments, creating a sport tourism event. International travel in Greek times was limited due to the Greek wars.

In contrast, the rise of Rome and the Roman Empire was based upon the twin elements of military conquest and administration. The state and private individuals created leisure facilities (i.e. spas, baths and resorts) and enjoyed similar leisure lifestyles to the Greeks. The construction of colosseums for events and spectator sports, as epitomized in the recent film *Gladiator*, created the supply of tourism-related facilities. Therefore, two elements of tourism can be discerned in Roman society: first, domestic tourism focused on urban places where the resorts and facilities/events existed, so that the middle classes in Roman society had somewhere to spend their 200 holidays a year. Second, the conquest of overseas territories and their administration created a demand for business-related travel related to the territorial management and control of these peoples. The middle classes also had expanded opportunities to travel afforded by new territories, trade and the provision of roads linking the Roman origin area to seaside resorts, summer villas and historical sites, which might be visited for health, pleasure and spiritual reasons.

Rome also emerged as an important urban tourism destination because of its capital city function. To service tourist needs, inns, bars and tour guides as well as souvenir sellers developed. In this respect, many elements of modern tourism were established in Roman times, which were mainly made possible by the political stability and provision of infrastructure and facilities, and were stimulated by a prosperity among the middle classes who enjoyed travel for leisure and business.

The Middle Ages

In the years following the demise of the Roman Empire, historians have described the years from 500 AD through to the accession of Henry VII in 1485 as the Middle Ages. The early part of this period has also been described as the Dark Ages, a time when the civilization and progress of the Roman era declined. In place of the pleasure-seeking society of the Roman era, the rise of Christianity and the development of monastic orders saw a society evolve which was based on landed estates, a feudal system of peasants and nobility. Yet even in these seemingly dark times, tourism can be discerned with the emergence of festival and event-based tourism stimulated by the activities of the nobility and knights. Jousting tournaments and spectatorship from peasants and other nobility saw a demand emerge for temporary accommodation and travel to these events.

Pilgrimages were invariably viewed by researchers as the oldest form of non-economic travel, motivated by religious fervour. Pilgrimage can be dated to the Ancient Greeks and travel to the Olympic city, Olympia. Many researchers, however, trace Christianity and pilgrimages to around the fourth century, with trips made on a voluntary basis or as a penitence, initially very localized in scale and growing during the first crusade with pilgrimages to Jerusalem. The period from the eleventh to the thirteenth century saw pilgrimages encouraged in Christian countries, with trips by nuns and priests permitted by their superiors and popularized in Geoffrey Chaucer's *The Canterbury Tales*, with visits to the shrine of Thomas Becket who had been murdered in Canterbury Cathedral. Other notable locations in Europe, such as Santiago de Compostela in Spain, were among a number of popular destinations for Italian pilgrims. By the fourteenth century, changing attitudes towards pilgrimages began to develop and by the fifteenth century, the spread of the Black Death and labour shortages saw a slowing down of pilgrim traffic in Europe. By the sixteenth century, pilgrimages were being challenged by thinking associated with the Protestant reformers of the Reformation that opposed the cult of saints, driving much of the activity underground. The difficulties of early pilgrim travellers should not be underestimated as diary accounts outline the problems of travel on unmade roads, the threat to life posed by bandits, the limited availability of accommodation, disease and the time involved to make such perilous journeys, as outlined by Theilmann (1987). Travel was difficult in the Middle Ages due to the poor quality of access, although this poor access created a demand for accommodation and hospitality services (e.g. food, drink and entertainment) en route. The amount of business travel to centres of commerce across Europe and farther afield was modest in comparison with the present. A neglected feature of the history of tourism is the contribution of exploration and subsequent colonization of native people as a precursor to the development of business tourism based upon trade and increased flows of international trade. Shackley (2006) examined this theme and, in the case of South America and the Caribbean, focused on the voyages of discovery by Christopher Columbus (Figure 2.1) and later explorers that paved the way for subsequent colonizers. For example the Conquistadores, who subjugated the ancient Aztec Empire of Mexico, led by Cortes in the 1520s, and later the Incas in Peru, led by Pizarro, changed the nature of travel and tourism to the region. As Shackley suggests, these incursions not only transformed South America but also saw the introduction of the horse which revolutionized transport in the region. Spanish colonization of Mexico and Peru was accompanied by religious colonization of the interior by the Jesuits, as embodied in the film, *The Mission*.

However, it should be recognized that the feudal society which existed across Europe in the Middle Ages did not really begin to see any significant change until the Renaissance, with a quest for knowledge and discovery.

The Renaissance and Reformation

The Renaissance originated in Italy after 1350 and reached its zenith in England during Elizabethan times. The earlier trends in festivals and fairs continued, again forming a nucleus of domestic tourism activity. The rise of travelling theatres and the patronage of the arts created opportunities for travel. The Reformation, in contrast, emerged after 1500 with the ideas of Luther and Calvin with their religious zeal that created what has been termed the Protestant work ethic. This is a notable turning point in the history of leisure and thereby tourism, as these Lutheran and Calvinistic ideas questioned the

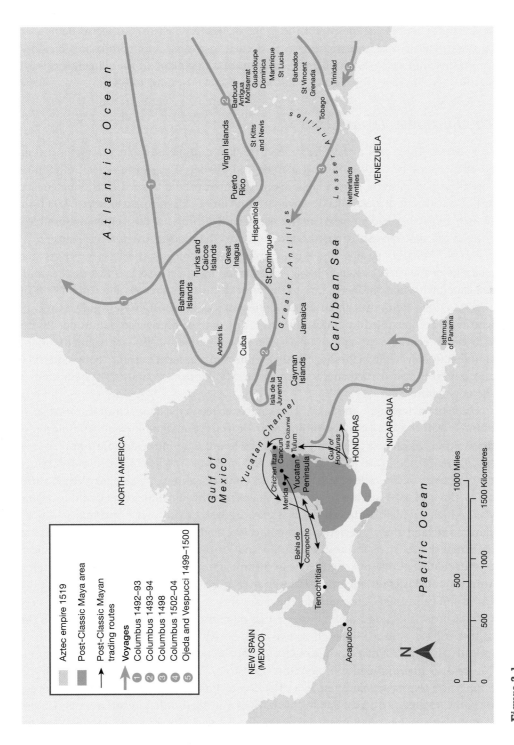

Figure 2.1

Pre-colonial Central America and the Caribbean

Source: redrawn from Shackley (2006)

value of leisure, portraying it as idleness, when individuals should devote themselves to a life of good work rather than leisure and enjoyment of pleasure. These ideas can be seen more clearly in the rise of the industrial society, where leisure was denigrated by the capitalists and entrepreneurs who needed to create a more profitable economy.

Another important development in tourism that originated in the sixteenth century was the Grand Tour, which emerged as an aristocratic form of tourism.

The European Grand Tour

The 'Grand Tour' was a traveller's circuit of key destinations and places to visit in Europe, mainly by the wealthy, aristocratic and privileged classes in pursuit of culture, education and pleasure. The origins of such tours can be discerned in those elements of Roman society that travelled to Greece in pursuit of culture and education. As a form of tourism, it reached its peak in the eighteenth century. Some commentators have gone as far as to suggest it was the forerunner of the modern overseas holiday.

Within Western Europe, the Grand Tour is recounted in the diaries, letters and memoirs of travellers as well as being documented in guidebooks and historical records associated with tourism. According to the most detailed research on the Grand Tour by Towner (1985, 1996) the typical tourists in the sixteenth century were young aristocrats who were accompanied by tutors, although this may be an oversimplification. By the eighteenth century, the emerging middle classes formed a growing element of the Grand Tour. Towner (1985) estimated that in the mid-eighteenth century between 15 000 and 20 000 British participants toured continental Europe, around 0.2–0.7 per cent of the population.

Much of the interest in the Grand Tour can be related to the Renaissance and emergence of interest in classical antiques, promoted by learning and developments in philosophy that encouraged travel to expand the human mind. One interesting historical source, J. Hall's 1617 book *Quo Vadis? A Just Censure of Travell as it is commonly undertaken by the Gentleman of Our Nation*, epitomized this educational trend, where gentlemen spent up to three years travelling to gain an education. This emerging travel culture which was centred on mainland Europe saw a growing link to knowledge and interest in the classics, art and the appreciation of architecture and an intellectual thought prior to the expansion of mass forms of education and learning. The Grand Tour was far from a static entity as ideas from Europe were imparted back to England and changing fashions and tastes in the interests of Grand Tourists can also be discerned between 1550s and early 1800s. For example, the emergence of interest in landscape and scenery viewing from the 1760s and a wider range of pursuits characterized such tours. The coming of the railways in each area combined with the expansion of the tourism industry. Figures 2.2 and 2.3 illustrate some of the typical Grand Tour routes taken in Europe and the dominance of certain centres (i.e. Paris, Turin, Florence, Naples and Rome). The rise in popularity of Switzerland as a consequence of the pursuit of scenery was also notable, with new modes of transport on land, inland waterways and rivers (e.g. the appearance of steamers on Swiss lakes in the 1820s) creating opportunities for scenic tourism. In the UK, travellers such as Celia Fiennes during the 1680s and Daniel Defoe in the 1720s reflected the traits of the European Grand Tour in their changing

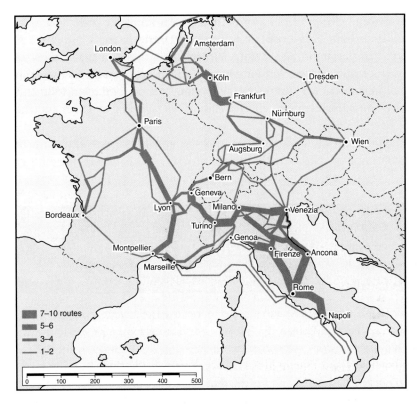

Figure 2.2

Grand Tour routes in Europe, 1661–1700

Source: © Elsevier; reprinted from *Annals of Tourism Research, Vol. 12,* J. Towner, The Grand Tour: A Key Phase in the History of Tourism: 297–333, © 1985, with permission from Elsevier

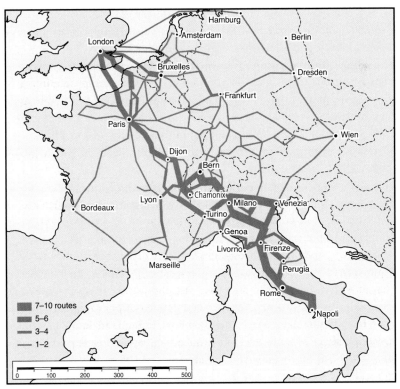

Figure 2.3

Grand Tour routes in Europe, 1884–1820

Source: © Elsevier; reprinted from *Annals of Tourism Research, Vol. 12,* J. Towner, The Grand Tour: A Key Phase in the History of Tourism: 297–333, © 1985, with permission from Elsevier

attitudes to landscapes and scenery as elements of tourism. The Romantic poets, including Wordsworth, spearheaded the discovery of England's Lake District in the 1790s onwards while Walter Scott's novels glamorized Scotland. Writers and artists were drawn to these landscapes with their scenic qualities. A similar interest in landscape and wilderness can be observed in the new world (i.e. the USA) in the same period, and after 1830 this was popularized by American literature (e.g. *The Last of the Mohicans* in 1826) and the concept of the Western frontier.

An enduring theme from Elizabethan times was the growth of spas as a form of tourism development and it reflects both the continuity and change in the history

CASE STUDY 2.1
CHANGING PATTERNS OF SPA DEVELOPMENT AS A FORM OF TOURISM

There is a long historical tradition of taking mineral waters during tourist trips for health and pleasure in Western society that can be dated back to Roman times with over a thousand baths existing in ancient Rome. These *aquae*, as they were known, were distributed throughout the Roman territories. What is notable, in terms of the continuity and change in the history of tourism, is that they declined after Roman times (i.e. changed) but formed the basis for the future growth of spa resorts in later times (i.e. continued). Examples are Bath in the UK, Aquae Calidae in Vichy, Aquae Mattiacae in Germany and hot springs in the Bay of Naples. Whilst Roman spas were less exclusive than those designed for the later users, in some countries (Hungary), spas continued in use from Roman times to the Middle Ages. But why did spas develop as sites for tourist consumption?

At a general level, certain factors were a prerequisite for development: the existence of a spring to provide the waters, individuals or agents to promote development and favourable conditions relating to accessibility and trends which promoted spa visiting. In addition the associated development of accommodation, hospitality and ancillary services, often coalesced to comprise a distinct spa resort. In fact, in colonial America, Philidelphia had spas at Abington, Bristol and Yellow Springs; these urban centres supported nearby springs, and access to the outlying springs led to the development of resorts and facilities in the urban centres.

In many spas that developed in England between 1660 and 1815, patronage by royalty, the nobility and the growing affluent classes stimulated the demand. Entrepreneurs, public authorities or a partnership of both led to the growth of spas (e.g. Bath), with individual landowners amongst the gentry or aristocracy providing the land and thus the basis for tourism based speculative development. In Harrogate in Yorkshire, public-sector promotion by the Corporation in the 1720s provided the basis for development as did the Federal Parks Department in Canada at Radium Hot Springs in the 1920s. In some cases such as Rotorua in New Zealand, the advances in spa-based health treatments (e.g. hydropathy) saw the New Zealand Tourism and Publicity Department manage and promote the major facilities as a basis to stimulate tourism development. In Scotland, late Victorian and Edwardian entrepreneurs created a range of successful and unsuccessful hydro hotels providing the focal point of a spa and health tourism at locations such as Dunblane and Crieff.

of tourism. In mainland Europe, Lennard (1931) observed that only 12 spas existed in Europe in the late sixteenth century. However, by the mid-seventeenth century, the pursuit of health remedies for the sick gradually saw the growth of pleasure travel to such spas (see Case Study 2.1).

In England, 173 rural spas were created between 1558 and 1815, many of which had a short existence compared to their urban counterparts. Whilst certain spas had an enduring history (i.e. Buxton and Bath), others such as Wellingborough were in existence in the late 1600s but had disappeared by 1711. Probably the most well-known example of spa development is Bath in England. It emerged from its Roman origins with an enduring pattern of visitation during the Middle Ages due to the medicinal value of its waters. One illustration of its rapid expansion was its rise in population from under 2000 in the 1660s to 13 000 in the 1760s and 33 000 in 1801 mainly as the spa-based growth of the town continued. Patronage of Bath initially, in the sixteenth century, was by visitors from London and southern England, then gradually expanded to a national market that included courtiers, the aristocracy, gentry, clergy and professional classes (both the infirm and those of good health seeking cures and preventative medicine). Some estimates of visitor numbers suggest that 8000 tourists visited annually in the early 1700s, rising to 12 000 by the 1750s and 40 000 by 1800. The visiting season was expanded (initially July to mid-August), providing the basis for further investment and development in the town. Much of the public and private sector development was speculative in nature and the market fuelled this in turn for visitors. Expansion continued as improvements in transportation linked the resort to a wider range of visitor markets with better roads and expanded coach services reducing travel times. Interestingly, the advent of the railways had a limited effect on Bath because it was evolving from a spa function to a residential and retirement centre. What did develop was a specialized leisure resort with a highly developed tourist infrastructure and associated facilities akin to a modern resort. What was notable in many countries was that spa resorts emerged as inland tourism destinations and their importance began to wane by the nineteenth century as a new genre of tourism emerged – the seaside resort.

Tourism and the coast: Transition from spas to the seaside resort

Coastal areas emerged in the late eighteenth century in many European and North American countries as the new form of tourism destination for the leisured classes. This was at a time when spas and other inland resorts were still expanding,

The coast up to the eighteenth century had not been a revered landscape, where religious ideals, cultural attitudes and tastes had not encouraged coastal visiting: on the contrary, the coast was considered an environment to avoid due to the forces of nature and evil. During the eighteenth century, the impact of poets, artists (such as Constable) and romanticists led to the beach and coastline being discovered as a site for pleasure, a place for spiritual fulfilment and for tourism as bathing slowly developed as a social and leisure activity between 1750 and 1840.

CASE STUDY 2.2
THE EVOLUTION OF TOURISM IN THE USA, 1750s TO 1850s – FROM SPAS AND MINERAL SPRINGS TO THE COAST

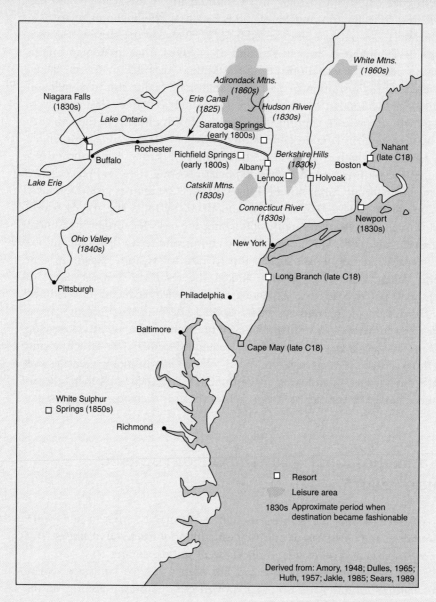

Figure 2.4
The development of selected leisure destinations in the eastern USA by the mid-nineteenth century

Source: *An Historical Geography of Recreation and Tourism*, J. Towner (1996) © John Wiley and Sons Ltd, reproduced with permission

According to Weiss (2004) the slow speed of travel and Puritan work ethic negated against the growth of tourism alongside the pressures of establishing new settlements and the risks involved with early travel. The growth of tourism is attributed to the middle of the eighteenth century where travel was localized to travel to spas and mineral springs akin to similar trends in Europe. Weiss traces this trend in the USA to the 1660s when Bostonians went to Red Springs. By the 1800s there were 22 spas distributed across the settled areas of the USA. Weiss estimates that between 11 000 to 44 000 visits were made to spas around 1800, equivalent to 1 per cent of the nation's population. Associated with early spa development was hotel development for overnight stays and improvements to transportation such as the railroads and steamboats, which expanded the scope of such trips to a wider range of people from a different strata of society. From the early 1800s other trends in tourism emerged such as the fashionable Tour, an American variant of the Grand Tour, popularized in the 1830s and 1860s by a guide book of the same name first published in 1822. As the main form of information for tourist promotion, the guide book popularized travel to emerging destinations such as Niagara Falls and other scenic wonders for visitors from the north-east seaboard with attractions along the Hudson River and other river valleys. Seaside resorts also developed in this period as illustrated in Figure 2.4. Weiss points to the emergence of Newport, Rhode Island as a seaside destination with accommodation for 85 guests in 1831 and around 1000 visitors in the locality. Similar growth occurred at Nahant as well as Cape May and Long Branch. By the 1850s Cape May had accommodation capacity for 2400 guests. The fashionable Tour described 106 tourists attractions to visit in 1826 and by the 1832 edition, this had grown to 368 attractions in 16 states as Weiss traces the number of spas alone as totalling 94 by 1855. By the outbreak of the Civil War, Weiss estimated that the number of tourists travelling to Cape May alone could have totalled 17 000. At Niagara, Weiss trace the growth in tourism from 20 000 in 1838 to 45 000 in 1847 up to 80 000 in 1850 based on historical studies of the destination. Consequently, Weiss summarizes the volume of tourism in the 1850s as 100 000 visits annually to spas, 100 000 to coastal destinations and 80 000 to Niagara yielding an estimate of 250 000 to 300 000 domestic trips a year equivalent to around 1 per cent of the population.

Further reading

Weiss, T. (2004) Tourism in America before World War II. *The Journal of Economic History*, 64(2): 289–327.

A number of key landmarks in the early history of coastal tourism can be recognized, including:

- Dr Russell's (1752) treatise on the use of seawater for health reasons as well as bathing
- the popularization of sea-bathing by royal patronage (e.g. George III bathing at Weymouth in the late eighteenth century)
- royal patronage of resorts (e.g. Brighton by the Prince Regent)
- the combining of health reasons to visit with pleasure and fashion

- the search by Europe's social elite, from the late eighteenth century onwards, for more exclusive and undiscovered destinations
- the rise of resorts with a wide range of social and ancillary services to meet the needs of visitors (i.e. reading rooms, accommodation, assembly rooms, promenades, excursions and entertainment).

Table 2.1 Visitors to Margate 1812/1813 to 1835/1836 based on the records of the Margate Pier and Harbour Company

Year	Visitor numbers
1812–13	17 000
1815–16	21 931
1820–21	43 947
1830–31	98 128
1835–36	105 625

Source: extracted from J. Pimlott (1947) *The Englishman's Holiday: A Social Holiday.* London: Faber and Faber

The early patronage by the upper classes soon gave way to a growing access to coastal recreation and tourism as transport technology made resorts accessible. The provision of paddle steamers in the 1820s between London and the Kent coast resorts is one example of this. For example, Margate on the north Kent coast received 18 000 visitors, mainly from London, who could afford to travel by hoy or sailing boat. The rise of the paddle steamer led to a rapid growth in visitors as Table 2.1 shows. Data in Table 2.1 from the Margate Pier and Harbour Company shows how over a 20-year period, travel to Margate and north-east Kent became fashionable for the affluent London population as the annual visitation in the pre-railway era rose above 100 000 visitors a year. The paddle steamer was an important innovation for the seaside resort, starting a process of growth and development fuelled by visitor demand and culminating in the railway era.

The railway era did not necessarily lead to a rapid development in coastal tourism *per se*, but when combined with other factors discussed later (i.e. the availability of leisure time and statutory holidays) railways did facilitate the growth of tourism. Even so the railway era, from the 1840s onwards, also connected many coastal resorts to the main sources of demand – the urban industrial heartland of the UK. The major cities provided the principal sources of demand. But while much attention has focused on the growth in coastal tourism, in the UK the 1851 Great Exhibition heralded the early establishment of the package holiday. Some 6 million people visited the Great Exhibition in 1851 in London, many purchasing organized accommodation and travel from travel clubs (by saving up through weekly payments) or from agents such as Thomas Cook, who arranged travel for 165 000 excursionists. Some travellers arrived by rail while others from Scotland journeyed by steamer, spending up to two nights in London.

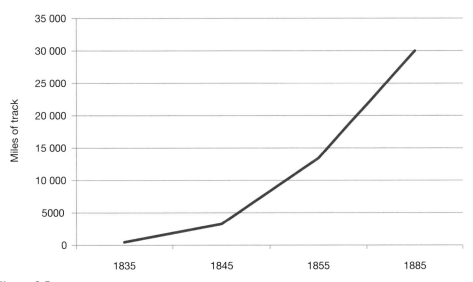

Figure 2.5
The growth of the UK railway network 1835–1885

Source: data from UNWTO

The first provision of a package by Thomas Cook can be dated to 1841 and the famous Leicester to Loughborough hiring of a train to travel to a temperance meeting. What marks this auspicious point in history is the pre-purchasing of tickets for re-sale by an agent including the travel arrangements made by the organizer, Thomas Cook, for his 570 passengers on this excursion. Yet it would be misleading to attribute the growth in domestic tourism in the UK during the railway age solely to the efforts of Thomas Cook.

The first railway was opened in 1830: the Liverpool to Manchester line. By 1842 there were over 23 million passenger journeys a year by rail. Much of this traffic can be attributed to the early promotional activities of the railway companies. For example, the Great Western Railway carried 1000 passengers on its first excursion train in 1844 while, in the same year, 360 000 passengers travelled from London to the coastal resort of Brighton. This reflects the rapid expansion of the railway network as illustrated in Figure 2.5.

The UK was not alone in this railway fever. For example, Europe's rail network grew from 673 miles in 1835 to 195 833 miles in 1885 as similar patterns of growth occurred in tourist and leisure travel. One sign of the scale of growth in domestic tourism in Great Britain by 1854 was recorded in the *Royal Hotel Guide* which listed over 8000 hotels, many developed in the expanding coastal resorts and cities. Whilst a good number of the establishments in cities and towns would have been based on the old coaching inns, new investment and development contributed to the continued growth of coastal areas. In 1851 Thomas Cook launched its advertising brochure the *Excursionist*. This brochure promoted company products and services including excursions and special events, to encourage travel and included advertisements from hotels and transport

Plate 2.1
Thomas Cook's *Excursionist* publication

Source: Thomas Cook

companies. The *Excursionist* highlighted the power of advertising (see Plate 2.1) to generate travel business, selling 100 000 copies a month in the 1880s in English and foreign editions.

However, the real sustained changes to tourism and leisure patterns in Victorian England (in parallel with many other countries worldwide) was the introduction of holiday time. The 1871 and 1875 Bank Holiday Acts in the UK provided four statutory days' holiday, giving workers the opportunity to engage in coastal tourism more fully. These Acts made the coastal resorts in the UK more accessible to the working classes; the middle-class workers had already begun to take more extensive holidays from the 1850s.

A social differentiation in coastal resorts also existed, where developers, municipal authorities and businesses positively attracted certain types of visitor. In north-west England, Blackpool developed as a working-class resort, meeting the needs of the Lancashire textile towns, where cheap rail travel and savings schemes promoted holidaytaking. The different timings of industrial holidays in various towns in north-west England also enabled resorts to extend the traditional summer season, so that accommodation and hospitality services had a wider range of business opportunities and resorts such as Blackpool developed a highly specialized tourism industry.

In terms of the supply of coastal resorts in England and Wales, no major population centre was more than 70–80 miles from a coastal area. In the eighteenth century, a number of early resorts such as Scarborough combined a spa and coastal tourism trade; the majority of resorts were in southern England due to their proximity to London and its large population. During the industrialization and urbanization of England in the late eighteenth and early nineteenth century, a number of other regional markets developed in south-west England and in a limited number of northern and Welsh locations. By 1851, a continuous growth of resorts from Devon to Kent emerged in southern England, complemented by the rising popularity of the Isle of Wight, Wales, north-west and eastern England. By 1881 growing access to the coast led to more specialized resorts, with specific markets emerging, and the growing social divide of visitors to certain resorts (i.e. the middle classes went to Bournemouth and the working classes to Southend, Margate and Blackpool). By 1911, the current-day pattern of resorts was well established, although oversupply and seasonality were common problems for the holiday trade in these resorts. In Scotland, resort development in western districts dependent upon the urban population of Glasgow provided a wide range of opportunities, where the integration of rail and steamers provided a complex system of destinations by the 1880s.

Running parallel to the mass tourism phenomenon of the coastal resorts were the origins of the modern tourism industry, with the emergence of commercially organized tourism by Thomas Cook. As discussed above, Cook organized the first package tours, initially utilizing the Victorian railway system (Leicester to Loughborough in 1841), with railway tours to Scotland in 1848 and overseas tours in the 1850s. In 1866, Cook organized his first tours to America and passenger cruises on the River Nile in the 1880s. Other entrepreneurs, including Henry Lunn, also organized overseas packages for skiing in Switzerland in the 1880s and the upper and middle classes engaged in new overseas tours as well as domestic tourism to coastal resorts.

Tourism in the Edwardian and inter-war years

By the 1900s, coastal tourism, overseas travel by passenger liner and the rise of socially segregated travel offered a wider range of international holiday options to the elite in Western society. The imperial trade of many European powers also created a demand for business travel and limited volumes of recreational travel. For example, by 1914 up to 150 000 American visitors entered the UK each year. The Edwardian years saw the continued expenditure of the middle classes on overseas travel and a growing fascination with rural and scenic areas, popularized by the pursuit of outdoor activities such as shooting and hunting in the Highlands of Scotland and cycling. Almost 10 per cent of *Black's Shilling Guide to Scotland* (1906) was devoted to cycling, using hotels and other accommodation establishments. The railway extended access to mountain climbing activities in the Highlands (e.g. the Ladies Scottish Climbing Club was founded in 1908), reflecting the growing emancipation of women and their role as travellers in Edwardian society. Hiking also emerged as a popular activity, with the rise of the Scottish Youth Hostels Association in 1931. The emergence of sleeper services on long-distance rail routes encouraged the middle classes to travel further afield.

One of the historical sources that enables us to understand how and where the Edwardians travelled is the guide book. An interesting example is the *Queens Newspaper Book of Travel* (1910), which had been published annually since 1903 and was compiled by a travel editor who was a geographer. This provided descriptions of places visitors from the UK might visit domestically and overseas, or where they might be stationed in the British Empire. It had candid insights as this extract on visiting Rangoon, in Imperial Burma, shows:

> A damp place; and the first feeling on arrival is generally one of prostration, followed by slight ague and fever; but this in robust people soon passes away, and although Rangoon is not regarded as a healthy station, yet of late years sanitary improvements have somewhat bettered its climate ... All clothing should be packed in airtight cases. One requires an abundant supply of Indian gauze underclothing (not less than three changes a day, even to corsets).

Guide books like this also highlight a neglected feature of tourism history: the development of business travel to manage colonies. They also reveal the travel activities of the colonists, such as the seasonal migration of the British in India to hill settlements in the summer to avoid the high temperatures of the lowland cities. Similarly, the rise of tourism between the colonial mother country and the colonies has not been accorded much attention, although it tends to follow the resort life cycle: following the exploration and colonization, tourism developed initially through business travel, then visits to family and relatives and then trips to different destinations. These patterns would appear to have developed across the colonial continents of Africa, Asia and the Pacific islands in parallel with the overt exploitation of the indigenous labour and resource base. However, the First World War was a significant interruption to the continued growth of leisure travel, as Case Study 2.3 shows.

CASE STUDY 2.3
TOURISM AND THE FIRST WORLD WAR

The First World War (1914–1918) slowed the growth of international tourism, although domestic tourism continued in a number of countries, as its R&R (rest and recuperation) function after the ravages of war provided a renewed boost for many resorts. There is a widespread debate on the impact of the war on global travel as most studies of tourism assume it curtailed travel other than troop movements, since this is how researchers depict the impact of war on tourist travel. Yet what is interesting is that *The Times* carried daily advertisements for travel between the UK and many of the colonies and dominions on cruise liners owned by White Star, Cunard Line, Union Line, Nippon Yasen Kaisha, the Orient Line, P&O and City and Hall Lines, for example, as well as Royal Mail steamers, to New Zealand, Australia, South Africa, Hong Kong, Singapore, the USA, Canada and the Mediterranean. These advertisements were not related to troop movements, but to travel for business and pleasure. Therefore, tourism did not cease. Recent research by Page and Durie (2009) has shown that domestic travel did not cease in the First World War despite the efforts of the government to limit the use of railways to the war effort. Even the increase in rail fares and propaganda by the wartime government did not deter domestic travel, as a famous series of posters by London Transport even encouraged it after a series of fatal zeppelin bombing raids on London. Whilst many of the east coast resorts suffered German shelling, which led to their loss of tourists in the 1914–1918 period, this demand was simply displaced to other locations. In fact, new forms of demand for domestic holidays and leisure were generated in the UK during 1914–1918 by the emancipation of women and their employment in high-paid, high-risk munitions work.

This demand saw the patronage of many working-class resorts such as Blackpool by the female munitions workers – *the munitionettes*.

In the initial aftermath of the First World War, demand for coastal holidays surged in 1919 as resorts such as Blackpool were claiming they were 'full up' and bulging at the seams whilst new forms of travel emerged. For example, between 1904 and 1914, the number of cars in Britain rose from 8465 to 132 015 and by 1926 this had risen to 683 913. This, combined with the growth of coach travel, as surplus military vehicles were converted to charabancs after 1918, generated more road-based and flexible travel than was offered by the more rigid timetables of railways. Even so, research by the National Railway Museum in York, UK has found that, in 1934 alone, 700 boat trains operated between London and Tilbury docks – one example of a passenger terminal for sea passengers on scheduled services, indicating the scale of rail travel to connect with international sea transport.

Air travel also saw its embryonic growth after the First World War, with Thomas Cook offering scenic flights over battlefields in Europe. The first passenger flights from London to Paris also commenced, marketed by Thomas Cook and others. The growth in air travel globally increased from 1 million miles flown in 1919 to 70 million miles in 1930 and 234 million miles in 1938 on the eve of the Second World War.

Likewise, the route network expanded from 3200 miles in 1919 to 156 800 in 1930 to 349 100 in 1938. This is reflected in the example of Britain's Imperial Airways which commenced with a daily London-to-Paris service in 1922 as well as to other European destinations and the Middle East and India. Its route network saw passenger numbers grow from 11 000 in 1924 to 24 000 in 1930 and 222 000 in 1938.

Plate 2.2
A 1933 Thomas Cook brochure for air services

Source: Thomas Cook

CASE STUDY 2.4
TOURISM IN THE INTER-WAR YEARS

An interesting study published in 1933 by Ogilvie, *The Tourist Movement: An Economic Study*, is one of the first systematic studies of the statistical analysis of tourism in the UK, tracing tourist movements back to the Edwardian period. It also contains a wealth of data on tourism in other European countries and much of the detail which historians of tourism require to trace the development of tourism as an economic activity. For example, it analyses the problem of measuring tourist numbers and much of the discussion pre-dates the later discussion of tourist bodies like the World Tourism Organization (UNWTO). Using Board of Trade figures, Table 2.2 indentifies the flow of British subjects living in the UK who travelled to Europe between 1913 and 1931 and the problems of measurement. It also shows that the flow of travel between the UK and Europe (excluding the First World War) was roughly equal in each direction and grew from around 760 000 to just over 1 million trips by 1931. Estimates of overseas British (typically from colonial countries) and overseas visitors from other countries who

Table 2.2 British subjects, residents in the United Kingdom or overseas travelling between the United Kingdom and Europe 1913 and 1921–1931

Year	Inward from Europe	Outward to Europe	Balance inward
1913	763 420	761 019	2401
1921	561 903	553 099	8804
1922	640 392	639 050	1342
1923a	783 644	777 191	6453
1924	826 684	811 880	14 804
1925	927 618	924 083	3535
1926	969 712	959 559	10 153
1927	1 002 350	976 494	25 856
1928	1 113 831	1 093 715	20 116
1929	1 115 100	1 093 798	21 302
1930b	1 151 688	1 125 125	26 563
1931	1 077 477	1 029 991	47 486

a   From 1 April 1923, the figures exclude traffic with the Irish Free State.

b   Tables I, V and VI of the annual *Statistics in regard to alien passengers*. In the *Board of Trade Journal* of 3 March, 1932, p. 306, the number of British passengers inward in 1930 is given as 1 138 881, the result of subtracting 411 110 aliens from a total of 1 549 991 passengers. This figure for aliens, however, is 12 807 too high, the compiler having apparently added together aliens from Europe (373 757) and all transmigrants inward (37 353), instead of only transmigrants *from Europe* (24 546), as had been correctly done for 1929 and previous years. The same *Journal* gives the number of British passengers outward in 1930 as 1 100 377, based upon an aliens total of 404 480, which I do not understand; the correct total of aliens, including transmigrants *to Europe*, being 379 732 (which is adapted for the calculation in the text) and the incorrect total resulting from the inclusion of *all* outward transmigrants being 404 350.

Source: Ogilvie (1933)

travelled to the UK are shown in Table 2.6. Again, the estimates show that around 500 000–600 000 trips were made to the UK in the 1920s and early 1930s.

In terms of outbound travel from the UK, Table 2.7 shows that British residents' and overseas residents' trips overseas are not dramatically dissimilar to many patterns we observe today. Around 80 per cent of trips were to Europe and the Mediterranean and around 20 per cent of trips were further afield, with much of this travel being dependent upon shipping routes and cruise lines. Ogilvie (1933) also indicated that these patterns of travel were made and grew to 11 295 in 1925, to 22 388 in 1928 and 24 294 in 1931. Similarly, the growth of the use of the car as a form of travel to Europe by British residents is apparent from records of the Royal Automobile Club (RAC) and Automobile Association (AA) with around 15 000 overseas travellers crossing to and from Europe and 50 000–60 000 British residents making the same crossing. Ogilvie also documented the rise of sea traffic between mainland UK and the Irish Free State (Eire, which was formed in 1923) which grew from around 250 000 trips a year in 1923 to 370 000 by 1931.

Figure 2.6
Visitors to the United Kingdom, 1921–1931

Source: Ogilvie (1933)

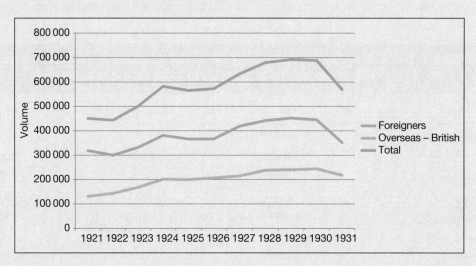

Figure 2.7
United Kingdom residents abroad, 1921–1931

Source: Ogilvie (1933)

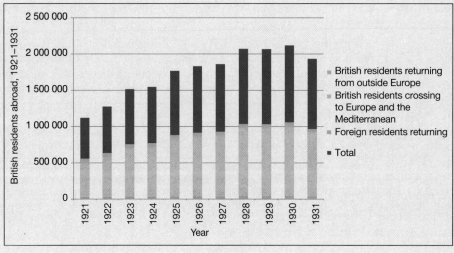

The depression in industrial economies during the 1920s and 1930s suppressed the demand for international and domestic tourism from all those but the wealthiest (illustrated by the international growth in air travel), although recreational pursuits replaced some of the demand for travel and new forms of low-cost tourism such as working holidays emerged among poorer working-class families (e.g. Londoners from the East End picking hops in Kent in the autumn). Mechanization in the post-war period gradually removed some of these tourism opportunities, but also created new ones. The construction of second homes on plots of land in the green belt or coastal areas by the working classes in the 1930s was a new, chaotic and unplanned form of domestic tourism. Many such dwellings were subsequently removed by planning acts in the 1930s and 1940s. Many of these trends were part of a transition from the Edwardian period through to the 1930s. Lickorish and Kershaw (1958: 42) argue that:

> The First World War brought about many changes which were to influence the volume of tourism. It had wrought great social changes: people returning from the war expected new opportunities, better living standards, more breadth to their lives; the war had broken down international barriers, and it had resulted in the fostering of an ideal, an optimistic, peaceful internationalism – just the climate in which tourism was most likely to flourish . . . The post-war era saw a rise in the standard of living of the working and middle classes in America and certain European countries.

Indeed, Lickorish and Kershaw (1958) noted that the 1930s were important because countries began to recognize the economic importance of tourism. This was accompanied by the League of Nations encouraging the simplification of frontier formalities, removing visa fees and provision of customs passes for tourists' cars and international driving licences. It also led to many destinations increasing the role of government to nurture this growing tourism economy (see Web Case 2.2). Statistical accounts of tourism from the Edwardian and inter-war period give a number of insights about those who were able to travel abroad as Case Study 2.4 shows.

A number of interesting insights into the tourism activities of the population in the 1930s are provided by Rowntree's (1941) *Poverty and Progress: A Second Social Survey of York* based on research from 1935. Rowntree found, among a largely working-class population in the town of York, that there was a growth in interest in the Youth Hostel Association among those under 25 years of age, with 4753 guest nights spent in York's youth hostel each year. The research also showed the importance of worker organizations, such as the Cooperative Holiday Association and its later offshoot, the Cooperative Holiday Fellowship, in promoting holidays in the outdoors as part of the health and fitness movement. Some of this was attributed by Rowntree to the reduction in working hours since 1900 from a typical 54-hour week in a factory to a 44- to 48-hour week. A similarly rich source of historical evidence on the holiday habits, activities and behaviour of the British population in the late 1930s is the Mass-Observation project. The Mass-Observation social research organization was set up in 1937 to collate an anthropology of the British population using a wide range of survey methods, including participant observation. The records along with other sources such as diaries are kept at the University of Sussex, UK. One interesting feature of this project was that it confirms what many historians suggest, that holidays

CASE STUDY 2.5
THE GROWTH OF THE BRITISH HOLIDAY CAMP

Probably the most influential development in the 1930s was the rise of the holiday camp, epitomized by the entrepreneur Billy Butlin. In 1936 Butlin bought a plot of 40 acres of land in Skegness and built the first holiday camp, with holidays at between 35 shillings and £3 a week advertised in the *Daily Express* newspaper. In the 1920s only 17 per cent of the population had paid holidays and during the 1930s only 3 million of the population had holiday with pay. This had changed by 1939 when 11 million people in the UK received holidays with pay and Butlins attracted almost 100 000 visitors to Skegness and to a second camp at Clacton in Essex. It is estimated that by 1948 one in twenty holidaymakers stayed at Butlins camps. The origins of the holiday camp concept can be traced to the organized workers associations' cycling and tent camps earlier in the twentieth century. By 1939, a wide range of such camps emerged as planned commercialized resorts which provided a fantasy world and offered relatively cheap domestic holidays. At the same time, second homes developed as a more widespread phenomenon in many countries. Greater advertising, promotion and marketing by tour operators, resorts, transport providers (e.g. the railways and shipping companies), combined with the popularization of travel in guide books, saw inter-war tourism begin to acquire many of the hallmarks of commercialized travel that continued into the post-war period.

Further reading

Ward, C. and Hardy, D. (1986) *Goodnight Campers: The History of the British Holiday Camp.* London: Mansell.

were firmly embedded in working-class culture. For example, when a sample of the population were asked what they would economize on, holidays (irrespective of social class) were deemed to be important elements not to be sacrificed.

One of the major innovations was the holiday camp (see Case Study 2.5). The unrivalled success of the holiday camp idea as a mass holiday product in the inter-war and post-war years also led Thomas Cook to enter the market in the 1950s by building a more exclusive development at Prestatyn in Wales modelled on a nautical theme, as illustrated in the promotional materials of the time (see Plates 2.3–2.5).

The Second World War impeded the growth of international tourism. Yet even on the eve of the Second World War in 1939, fewer than 50 per cent of the British population spent more than one night away from home. However, the number of car owners had risen from 200 000 in 1920 to 2 million in 1939. Other notable developments were the emergence of embryonic passenger airline services challenging the dominant passenger liners, and providing the seeds of the post-war transformation of many societies to adopt the overseas travel bug. In other parts of the world, such as communist Russia, the state used tourism as an organized form of R&R for workers, with sanatoria and resorts developed along the Black Sea and in other locations. For the elite, holiday homes (dachas) near the urban centres were also developed.

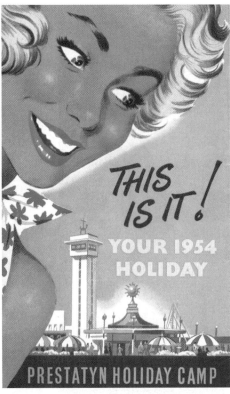

Plate 2.3 (above)
Thomas Cook brochure advertising Prestatyn:
It's Perfect – at Prestatyn Holiday Camp

Source: Thomas Cook

Plate 2.4 (top right)
Thomas Cook brochure advertising Prestatyn
Holiday Camp: This Is It! Your 1954 Holiday

Source: Thomas Cook

Plate 2.5 (right)
Thomas Cook brochure advertising Prestatyn
Holiday Camp: Look! Here's Your 1955 Holiday

Source: Thomas Cook

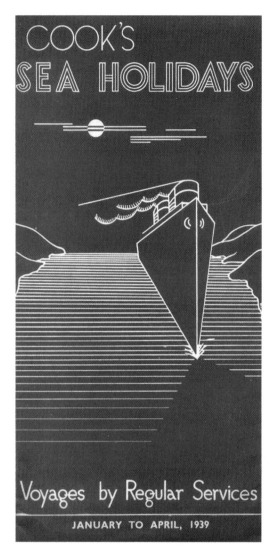

Plate 2.6
The 1930s were the heyday of cruising
epitomized in the Thomas Cook brochure from
1939

Source: Thomas Cook

Plate 2.7
The immediate post-war years saw cruise and passenger
liner travel challenged by the expansion of air travel

Source: Thomas Cook

The Soviet Union has been described as a country that pursued 'proletarian tourism', where the state, via state tourism organizations, determined the collective good by providing holidays that benefited the productive capacity of the state. This was accomplished through workers being given holidays designed to enhance their intellectual and physical well-being as a means of self-improvement. This trend developed in the 1920s and persisted through to the end of the Stalinist era, when diplomatic relations and outside travel was gradually permitted by Kruschev. Similar patterns of state-led tourism were also apparent in the Soviet-controlled East Germany, where countryside recreation became a popular focus for state-organized, worker-based tourism. In post-war Romania, state-organized tourism was directed towards three specific forms of tourism: mountain tourism, spas and the coastal areas around the Black Sea.

Access to new forms of transport (notably road-based) in the inter-war period, opened up the countryside and a wider range of domestic tourism destinations to the population in many countries. The emergence of new forms of domestic tourism (i.e. the holiday camp), cruise liners and air travel led to changing tastes and trends in holidaytaking. Whilst many resorts and transport providers responded to a widening range of opportunities for travel and holidaying, with the use of marketing and promotion (see Web Case 2.2), the real rise of mass tourism was a post-war phenomenon.

Post-war tourism: Towards international mass tourism

In Chapter 1 the trend in international tourism, dating back to the 1950s, illustrated the phenomenal growth in international travel, which was punctuated by peaks and troughs in demand. Many of the current trends in tourism can be dated to the post-war period, particularly the rise in demand for holidays. This period saw a growth in income, leisure time and opportunities for international travel. In the immediate post-war period, surplus military aircraft were converted to passenger services and the 1950s saw the introduction of jet airliners.

In the UK, the tourism industry employed about 5 per cent of the population (Lickorish and Kershaw 1958) and it generated £750 million a year in expenditure, of which £111 million was spent by overseas visitors. Travel remained one of the largest elements of household expenditure. In contrast, the USA domestic market in 1956 was worth US$17.5 billion, with an annual growth rate of 5–10 per cent and visitor volumes equivalent to half of the national population. Almost 85 per cent of vacation travel was by car, and accounting for 15 billion miles travelled, a growth from 11.5 billion miles in 1955. The car was opening up other areas, particularly more remote rural areas and the scale of this impact saw the State of Texas' tourism industry valued at US$26 million (Lickorish and Kershaw 1958).

Lickorish and Kershaw (1958) provide an interesting snapshot and cross-section of tourism in the UK in the 1950s. For example, tourism in Scotland was estimated to be worth £50 million in 1956, comprising £20 million spent by Scottish holidaymakers, £19 million by visitors from other parts of the UK and £11.5 million by overseas visitors. Yet Britain received only 610 000 overseas visitors a year from Western Europe, with

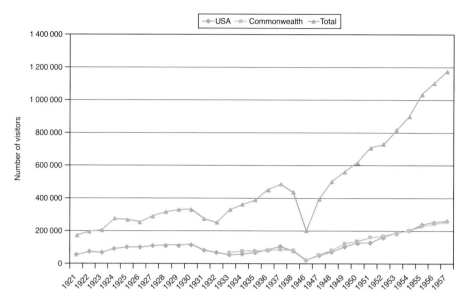

Figure 2.8
Number of visitors to Britain, 1921–1957 (no data available for 1939–1945)

Source: based on tabulated data in Lickorish and Kershaw (1958: 339)

much of the market attributed to the USA and Commonwealth tourism, as Figure 2.8 shows for the period 1921 to 1957. In 1957, Britain received 262 730 visitors from the USA, 254 590 from Commonwealth countries and the balance from Europe. This reflects the close historic ties the UK had with the USA and Commonwealth. The latter's ties were reinforced and strengthened during the First World War but subsequently weakened in the Second World War and in the 1950s as former British colonies sought independence. What Figure 2.8 also shows is the devastating impact of the Second World War on international travel, but in the immediate aftermath of 1945, visitor arrivals did quickly return to pre-war levels (i.e. by 1948) illustrating the resilience of tourism to crisis such as war. Figure 2.8 also shows that after 1945 inbound tourism to the UK grew exponentially into the 1950s, outstripping the growth recorded in the 1920s and 1930s illustrating a continued upward trend, which then continues to grow significantly in the 1950s and 1960s through to the more recent period.

As airlines bought new jets, older aircraft became available to charter holiday companies to operate services to holiday destinations. In the UK Vladimir Raitz is credited with offering the first air-related package holiday and Horizon Holidays (purchased later by Thomson Holidays) was soon followed by a number of other tour operators. By 1959, 2.25 million Britons took foreign trips, 76 769 of which were to Spain. In 1966, 94 per cent of these overseas trips were to Europe; this number dropped to 86 per cent in 1974 as other destinations were developed.

Figure 2.9 shows the impact of the rise of the package holiday in Spain, which led to the growth of Mediterranean resorts. By 1965, Spain had become Europe's leading tourism destination with 14 million visitors a year (which had grown to nearly 48 million in 2001). Spain saw its share of the UK holiday market rise from 6 per cent in

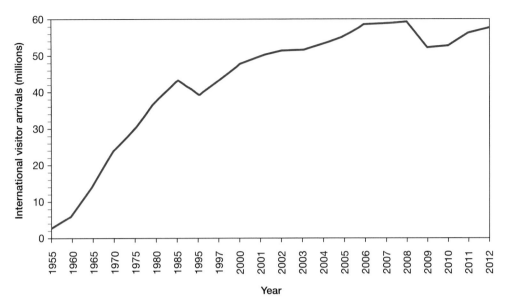

Figure 2.9
The growth of tourism in Spain since 1955

Source: author

1951 to 30 per cent in 1968. In the late 1960s package holidays to Mallorca cost £30, which was equivalent to a week's salary. The ill-fated Clarkson's tour operator saw the number of its clients grow from 16 000 in 1966 to 90 000 in 1967, a sign of the massive growth in package holidays. Consumer spending on domestic holidays rose by 80 per cent between 1951 and 1968, and on overseas holidays by 400 per cent. In 1951 a UK holiday cost on average £11, a foreign holiday £41. By 1968 the prices were £20 and £62 respectively and the numbers of Clarkson's clients had risen to 175 000. However, the oil crisis in the 1970s, the Arab–Israeli war and the oil embargo of 1973 saw fuel price increases which led to a massive drop in tourist travel. In 1974, Clarkson's collapsed with tourists stranded in 75 resorts in 26 coastal areas. This resulted, in part, from a sustained price war among tour operators in the UK.

During the 1960s the numbers taking foreign holidays was set to rise by 230 per cent and by 1967 there were 5 million British holidaymakers going abroad. This rose to 7.25 million in 1971 and 8.5 million in 1972 but dropped to 6.75 million in 1974 due to the oil crisis. Yet throughout this period, the proportion of the population *not* taking a holiday remained almost constant at around 40 per cent and this is similar to the proportion recorded in the 1990s.

In the 1970s, 1980s and 1990s there was an increasing proliferation of tourism products and experiences, and a growing global reach for travel. The growth in leisure time, however, did not lead to a major change in the proportion of people taking holidays. In the period 1950–1988 UK spending on holidays increased sixfold in real terms. Therefore, changes in supply (i.e. by the tourism industry) and demand have seized upon the rise in consumer spending and associated factors such as:

- changes in demand for domestic and international travel, particularly business travel, new markets in visiting friends and relatives (VFR) (e.g. reunions among migrant groups) and the pursuit of new travel experiences
- transportation improvements, especially the introduction of jet aircraft, the wide-bodied jet (i.e. the DC10 and Boeing 747 jumbo jet), and the proliferation of high-speed trains and larger aircraft such as the Airbus A380
- the development of new forms of holiday accommodation (i.e. the change from the holiday camp to timeshare, self-catering and second homes)
- innovations by tour operators, including the rise of the holiday brochure, new forms of retailing such as direct selling, buying via the internet, more competitive pricing and the evolution of one-stop shop retailing (i.e. the package, insurance, holiday currency, airport transfers and pre-flight accommodation and car parking)
- greater availability of information on destinations to visit from the media, brochures, guide books, the internet and travel programmes
- increased promotion of destinations by governments, growing consumer protection to ensure greater regulation and resort promotion in the media and via the internet.

These factors certainly promoted the development of mass tourism in the Western industrialized nations in the post-war period, especially in the 1960s and 1970s. Many of the trends identified in the UK are part of a wider change in Western society towards consumption of tourism products. Looking at the past is interesting because many of the issues we face in modern tourism may already have existed in the past, and so are not necessarily new. Even so, the past may not always be a guide to the future, especially given the speed of change in society, the rapid pace of technological innovations and the effect of wider societal trends. For this reason, no discussion of the origins and growth of tourism is complete without some consideration of the future.

The future of tourism

Anticipating changes in tourism has attracted a great deal of interest from economists who seek to model the changes in demand based on past and future growth assumptions. But this approach alone ignores some of the underlying changes in the nature of society that shape the tourist of the future. An interesting example is Brazil, where the emerging middle class is over 30 million people, who are among the top spenders in the USA according to the Brazilian Central Bank. For this reason, some consideration of the following key trends over the next decade will help to understand how tourism consumption and development may be affected:

- the ageing of society in the Western industrialized nations, with the over-50 age group – the 'new old' who are active and far from elderly and uninterested in tourism – which is a growing market sector
- a growth in single households, with later marriage and child-bearing as well as increased rates of divorce and single parenthood

- information technology becoming an all-embracing element of our lives, increasingly used by consumers and part of the globalized society
- consumers becoming more environmentally conscious; this will be balanced by increased searches for hedonistic experiences (i.e. those based on pleasure) and more flexible leisure time
- tourism consumers looking for greater convenience and ease of access, with the media playing a much greater role in shaping our tastes and preferences

CASE STUDY 2.6
EMERGING OUTBOUND MARKETS: THE BRIC AND MINT ECONOMIES

Some of the more established tourism markets in Europe and North America have begun to see their tourism economies grow at relatively modest rates. Conversely, there are a range of fast growing emerging economies which are developing significant rates of GDP, creating enhanced affluence for some of their population, who are emulating the consumer behaviour of the developed world. One facet of that new consumerism is growth in domestic and international tourism. Currently, interest is focused on the booming BRIC economies (Brazil, Russia, India and China) which have seen major growth among their rapidly expanding middle classes. UNWTO and the European Tourism Commission examined the characteristics of the growing markets of Russia, China and India, identifying their potential as major drivers of sustained future international tourism growth, as these are people with limited experience of international travel. Existing studies by UNWTO (2011) suggest that the BRIC countries are experiencing and will achieve growth of over 10 per cent in outbound travel, which is more than double that of mature Western economies with rates of less than 5 per cent per annum. Interest is also developing in the next group of countries which will be the successors of the BRIC countries, and analysts suggest that the next group of fast growing economies which will emerge are the MINT countries (Malaysia, Indonesia, Nigeria and Turkey), with their fast growing population, a youthful population structure, access to expanding economies and, for three of the MINT countries, being commodity producers associated with the growing global demand for raw materials. Both the BRIC and MINT countries are indicative of a gradual shift of economic power from the developed former colonial powers to developing economies. One of the defining features of these MINT economies is that existing notions of the distribution of wealth, patterns of urbanization and industrial development reveal a mix of developed nation attributes of conspicuous consumption abutting abject poverty, deprivation and slums in less developed world environments.

Further reading

UNWTO (2011) *Policy and Practice for Global Tourism*. Madrid: UNWTO.

UNWTO and European Tourism Commission (2009) *The Russian Outbound Travel Market with Special Insight into the Image of Europe as a Destination*. Madrid: UNWTO.

UNWTO and European Travel Commission (2009) *The Indian Outbound Travel Market with Special Insight into the Image of Europe as a Destination*. Madrid: UNWTO.

- technology providing consumers with new opportunities to access tourism opportunities
- some regions of the world growing, and others expected to grow, their economies and GDP at a much faster rate, creating a demand for both domestic and outbound travel as illustrated in Case Study 2.6.

One potential approach used by some futurologists to understand future changes in tourism has been the use of scenario planning (see Chapter 12): stories or possible views on what might happen at a future point in time. This approach seeks to use creative thinking to understand how future changes and events may shape the unknown, building a picture of what the tourism consumer of 2015 might look like. In essence, looking at the future is about grappling with uncertainty, beyond the planning horizon of most individuals and businesses. In contrast the approach used by economists, namely econometrics – using past trends and future growth assumptions to forecast changes – is seen as more scientific and precise. The problem in many cases, is that forecasts are rarely achieved. To illustrate how the scenario and forecasting approach have been used, the example of New Zealand's international tourism prospects is reviewed in Web Case 2.4 because it is an example of where many growth forecasts were achieved.

Whilst the forecasts of future tourism illustrate the importance of looking ahead in trying to anticipate changes, one new trend which is emerging as a potential growth area is space tourism.

Space tourism

Since a member of the public joined a Russian space flight in 2001, there has been a growing interest in the future growth of space tourism. However, interest in space tourism is not new, with NASA publishing various reports on space tourism in the 1990s, particularly its 1998 report, *General Public Space Travel and Tourism*. In the USA, 12 million people per year visit NASA's Air and Space Museum in Washington, the Kennedy Space Center in Florida and the Johnson Space Center in Texas, while 2 million a year visit Space World in Japan.

In market research studies, the market for space travel in the USA alone is estimated to be US$40 billion a year. Much of the future potential market is dependent upon reusable launch vehicles that can carry commercial passengers. Research indicates that once ticket prices can be generated at US$10 000, the market will be expanded. However, this is some way off, with the Russian launch vehicle costing US$10 million. Some commentators consider that it will be possible to achieve space tourism in the next 50 years based on short sub-orbital flights. In the longer term, other possibilities may include:

- short earth orbital flights using reusable spacecraft
- orbital tourism in space hotels located around the earth's orbit
- moon and Mars tourism.

For the tourist, seeing the earth from 100 km above its surface will provide a lifetime memory. There will also be a leisure space for activities such as weddings, sports and games. Yet engineers recognize that for technology to advance, major developments in propulsion systems are required. For the tourist, certain medical and physical preparations will be necessary, including familiarization with short sub-orbital flights, an ability to perform emergency procedures and learning coping strategies to deal with claustrophobia, isolation and personal hygiene. Policy changes may also be necessary to modify the Liability Convention (1971) of the UN that makes the launching country liable for compensation for losses or damage. However, the existing investment by governments in the USA, Europe and Japan of US$20 billion in space agencies indicates that state funding has already underwritten an element of the investment costs in space tourism, and it has a potential to generate an economic return.

In 2005, space tourism moved a step nearer to reality when British entrepreneur Richard Branson signed a £14 million agreement to build five spaceliners in the USA with Mojave Aerospace Ventures to utilize the technology devised for SpaceShipOne. This space craft reached an altitude of 112 km (368 000 ft) equivalent to 69.6 miles above the earth's surface in 2005. Virgin are planning flights in the near future at a cost of £100 000 each and they estimate that 3000 people are prepared to pay this price. In 2008, over 200 people had pre-booked space flights and over 80 000 had expressed an interest in these flights. The Virgin Spaceship will have five passengers, involve a week of pre-flight training, and will last three hours after travelling at 21 500 miles per hour (three times the speed of light) following the launch from the mother ship at 50 000 feet. The highlight will be three minutes of weightlessness before returning to earth. The development of Virgin's first spaceport to launch its space tourism flights in the Mojave desert, New Mexico, is expected to cost US$225 million to build but may create 500 jobs and over U$1 billion in tourism revenue over a ten-year period.

The future demand for space tourism as a luxury travel experience could grow from a conservative estimate of 150 000 trips a year on 1500 flights (generating revenue of US$10.8 billion with a ticket price of US$72 000) to 950 000 trips on 9500 flights (with a ticket price of US$12 000). The flights would rendezvous with a space hotel, unload incoming passengers and transport returning passengers to earth. What is evident is that in the early years of space tourism the demand will be low and price will be high. This will change as the activity becomes more acceptable – similar to any product life cycle.

Conclusion

The history of tourism can be characterized by continuity and change in the form, nature and extent of tourism activity. The growing globalization and global extent of tourism activity can be explained by wider social access to travel, enabled by a range of factors promoting travel (e.g. income and leisure time). The impact of innovations and entrepreneurs has significantly changed the course of the history of tourism, and the example of Richard Branson's Virgin Galactic is likely to change it again.

The emergence of mass tourism in the period since the 1960s is a dominant feature of the international expansion of world travel. With the prospect of space travel now a reality, along with more exploratory forms of marine tourism to the ocean's depths, tourism continues to push the bounds of humanity's endurance and quest for discovery and something new. Underwater hotels already exist: futurist notions of underwater tourism are now a reality. What is clear is that tourism has continued to develop and evolve through time, and many current trends will wane as new ones emerge, although these may use existing resources, places and experiences. In some cases new environments, places and experiences will continue to be developed. Tourism is always changing, and the challenge for the tourism manager and entrepreneur is to anticipate new trends and tastes and to meet them.

CHAPTER REVIEW

 ## References

Lennard, R. (1931) *Englishmen at Rest and Play*. Oxford: Clarendon Press.

Lickorish, L. and Kershaw, A. (1958) *The Travel Trade*. London: Practical Press Ltd.

Ogilvie, I. (1933) *The Tourist Movement*. London: Staples Press.

Page, S. J. and Durie, A. (2009) Tourism in war time Britain 1914–1918: Adaptation, innovation and the role of Thomas Cook & Sons. In J. Ateljevic and S. J. Page (eds) *Tourism and Entrepreneurship*. Oxford: Butterworth-Heinemann.

Pimlott, J. (1947) *The Englishman's Holiday*. London: Faber and Faber.

Shackley, M. (2006) *Atlas of Travel and Tourism Development*. Oxford: Butterworth-Heinemann.

Theilmann, J. (1987) Medieval pilgrims and the origins of tourism. *Journal of Popular Culture*, 20(4): 93–102.

Towner, J. (1985) The grand tour: A key phase in the history of tourism. *Annals of Tourism Research*, 12(3): 297–333.

Towner, J. (1996) *An Historical Geography of Recreation and Tourism in the Western World 1540–1940*. Chichester: Wiley.

Weiss, T. (2004) Tourism in America before World War II. *The Journal of Economic History*, 64(2): 289–327.

 ## Further reading

There are a number of excellent sources available on the historical development of tourism including:

Walton, J. (1983) *The English Seaside Resort: A Social History 1750–1914*. Leicester: Leicester University Press.

Walton, J. (2000) *The British Seaside: Holidays and Resorts in the Twentieth Century*. Manchester: Manchester University Press.

Walton, J. (2000) The hospitality trades: A social history. In C. Lashley and A. Morrison (eds) *In Search of Hospitality: Theoretical Perspectives and Debates*. Oxford: Butterworth-Heinemann.

Walton, J. and Smith J. (1996) The first century of beach tourism in Spain: San Sebastian and the Playas del Norte from the 1830s to the 1930s. In M. Barke, J. Towner and M. Newton (eds) *Tourism in Spain: Critical Issues*. Wallingford: CAB International.

There are also recent articles in the *Journal of Tourism History*.

Questions

1   Why is the historical study of tourism useful in understanding the management problems many destinations face in the new millennium?

2   How can you explain the continuity and change in the historical development of tourism?

3   What is the value of the resort life cycle model in explaining tourism growth and development?

4   What are the future prospects for space tourism?

Access additional resources

- For students: Multiple choice questions for each chapter, video links and further reading.
- For instructors: PowerPoint slides with tables and diagrams, additional case studies, video links and further reading.

Demand

Why do people engage in tourism?

Learning outcomes

This chapter examines the reasons why people go on holiday and the explanations developed to understand the motivating factors associated with leisure travel. After reading this chapter, you should be able to understand:

- the concept of tourism demand and the ways it may be defined
- the role of motivation studies in explaining why people go on holiday
- the different motives used to develop classifications of tourism
- the role of consumer behaviour in explaining why people select certain holiday products.

Introduction

Understanding why people choose to travel and to become tourists seems at first sight a very simple issue. In fact it is a very complex area and, whilst we can all think of simple reasons why people choose to go on holiday, the area has also been extensively studied by psychologists (who study how humans behave, interact and react to external and internal stimuli) trying to derive explanations that apply to groups and individuals to the perennial question: *why do people go on holiday?* Theoretical research has sought to classify travellers into groups in order to generalize the reasons for being involved in tourism. However, there needs to be a recognition that not all tourists are the same. They are diverse and have a wide range of motivations to travel which vary by wealth, age, stage in the life cycle, lifestyle and personal and group preferences. As the tourism industry relies upon travellers choosing to go on holiday, understanding what motivates them to visit specific places and resorts has major economic consequences.

The explanation of why people travel for pleasure, business and other reasons has become further clouded by a fundamental problem: psychologists attempt to develop theories about why people choose to travel but these theories are detached from the way the tourism industry uses very practical marketing-based approaches to understand the same question. One of the distinguishing features of tourists is that they are outsiders in the places they visit. Tourism is different to other forms of consumption but there is a tendency to treat tourists in the same vein as we would other consumers, and to apply the same methods of study from consumer behaviour and the field of marketing. However, as Pearce (2005: 9) argues, 'There are several critical dimensions that create differences between tourist behaviour and consumer behaviour. One such major difference lies in the extended phases that surround tourist activities'. These include:

- an anticipation or pre-purchase stage
- an on-site experience
- a return travel component
- the extended recall and recollection stage.

In this respect, the essential feature of the tourist experience, even in the pre-purchase and recall stage, is about being somewhere (notably somewhere else than at home). Unlike many other consumer purchases, a tourism experience may be enduring, having a long-lasting impact in terms of reflection and psychological enrichment of one's life (see Table 3.1). In contrast to other tangible goods such as a car, a holiday is more about our dreams, expectations of enjoyment and satisfaction. The nature of the experience in terms of meaning, value and people-to-people contact distinguishes the consumption of tourism from the way many other products are purchased.

This chapter explores the way in which the academic study and practical application of principles associated with tourism demand have been applied to understanding what motivates tourists as consumers. Motivation is important in terms of the personal satisfaction which the tourist derives from consuming the experience; it is also a component of visitors' perceptions of destinations and should affect how those marketing and promoting a destination present it.

Table 3.1 Characteristics of the positive psychologists' study of tourism

There has been a growing recognition by psychologists that tourism research on tourists' experience of holidays can be better understood by embracing a number of new approaches associated with the following concepts:

- positive psychology, which is focused on how individuals and groups can make their normal life more fulfilling through experiences such as holidays

- fulfilment, which Filep and Pearce (2014:2) define as 'achievement of something desired, promised or predicted' based on the Oxford English Dictionary definition. Fulfilment embraces notions of well-being

- happiness, which is largely a conscious state of mind although psychologists have developed various theories to explain this state of mind

- tourist behaviour, which is the setting in which individuals/groups have encounters and experiences that will impact upon their happiness and fulfilment derived from holidays.

Further reading: Filep, S. and Pearce, P. (eds) (2014) *The Tourist Experience and Fulfilment.* London: Routledge.

Source: developed from S. Filep and P. Pearce (eds) (2014) *The Tourist Experience and Fulfilment*

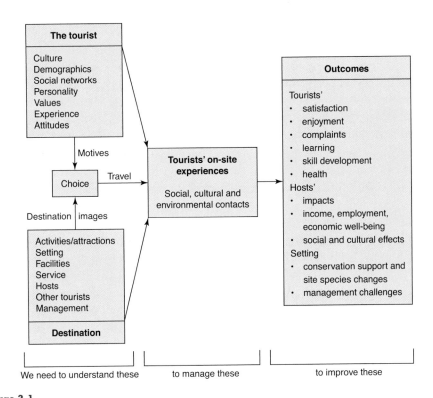

Figure 3.1
Concept map for understanding tourist behaviour

Source: *Tourist Behaviour*, P. Pearce (2005) © Channel View Publishers, reproduced with permission

Attempts to classify and group tourists into categories or to develop a model of tourist motivators are fraught with problems, as motivation is a highly individualized element of human behaviour. It affects and conditions how people react and behave as well as their attitudes to tourism as something they consume. In other words, while a range of motivating factors can be considered in promoting travel, a range of highly personal and individualized elements still exist beyond these. There is no universal agreement on how to approach the tourist demand for travel products and services, although this chapter will explore a number of approaches and possible reasons why human beings engage in tourism as a recreational activity. If we understand what prompts people to leave their home area and to travel to other places, then we may be able to develop approaches that help us to manage these visitors and their impacts. It may be possible to help plan for a more enjoyable experience at the place(s) they visit. Motivation may help to explain why certain places developed as successful tourism destinations and then continued to grow, stagnated or declined as tastes, fashions and perceptions of tourism changed. One interesting way to view the wider significance of tourist behaviour, as mapped out by Pearce (2005) is to consider the tourist, their motives in choosing a destination and a mode of transport, and their interaction with the destination (Figure 3.1).

What is tourism demand?

Tourism demand has been defined in numerous ways, including 'the total number of persons who travel, or wish to travel, to use tourist facilities and services at places away from their places of work and residence' (Mathieson and Wall 1982: 1) and 'the relationship between individuals' motivation [to travel] and their ability to do so' (Pearce 1995: 18). In contrast, more economic-focused definitions of demand are more concerned with 'the schedule of the amount of any product or service which people are willing and able to buy at each specific price in a set of possible prices during a specified period of time' (Cooper *et al.* 1993: 15).

There are three principal elements to tourism demand:

1   *effective* or *actual demand*, which is the number of people participating in tourism, commonly expressed as the number of travellers. It is normally measured by tourism statistics – typically, departures from countries and arrivals at destinations

2   *suppressed demand*, which consists of the proportion of the population who are unable to travel because of circumstances (e.g. lack of purchasing power or limited holiday entitlement). It is sometimes referred to as 'potential demand'. Potential demand can be converted to effective demand if the circumstances change. There is also 'deferred demand' where constraints (e.g. lack of tourism supply such as a shortage of bed-spaces) can also be converted to effective demand if a destination or locality can accommodate the demand

3   *no demand*, is a distinct category for those members of the population who have no desire to travel and those who are unable to travel due to family commitments or illness.

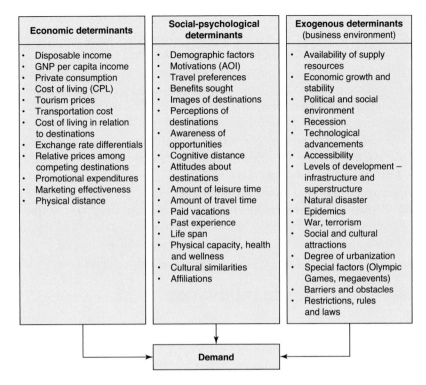

Economic determinants	Social-psychological determinants	Exogenous determinants (business environment)
• Disposable income • GNP per capita income • Private consumption • Cost of living (CPL) • Tourism prices • Transportation cost • Cost of living in relation to destinations • Exchange rate differentials • Relative prices among competing destinations • Promotional expenditures • Marketing effectiveness • Physical distance	• Demographic factors • Motivations (AOI) • Travel preferences • Benefits sought • Images of destinations • Perceptions of destinations • Awareness of opportunities • Cognitive distance • Attitudes about destinations • Amount of leisure time • Amount of travel time • Paid vacations • Past experience • Life span • Physical capacity, health and wellness • Cultural similarities • Affiliations	• Availability of supply resources • Economic growth and stability • Political and social environment • Recession • Technological advancements • Accessibility • Levels of development – infrastructure and superstructure • Natural disaster • Epidemics • War, terrorism • Social and cultural attractions • Degree of urbanization • Special factors (Olympic Games, megaevents) • Barriers and obstacles • Restrictions, rules and laws

Demand

Figure 3.2
Determinants of tourism demand

Source: Uysal (1998) © Routledge, reproduced from D. Ioannides and K. Debbage (eds), *The Economic Geography of the Tourist Industry*, p. 87, Fig. 5.2, Routledge

An interesting study by Uysal (1998) summarized the main determinants of demand (see Figure 3.2): economic, social-psychological and exogenous factors (i.e. the business environment). This useful overview provides a general context for tourism demand and many of the factors help to illustrate the complexity of demand, but it does not adequately explain how and why people decide to select and participate in specific forms of tourism, which is associated with the area of motivation.

The motivation dichotomy: Why do people go on holiday?

In a very comprehensive assessment of tourist motivation, Mountinho (1987: 16) defined motivation as a 'state of need, a condition that exerts a push on the individual towards certain types of action that are seen as likely to bring satisfaction'. This means that demand is about using tourism as a form of consumption to achieve a level of satisfaction for an individual, and involves understanding their behaviour and actions and what shape these human characteristics. This seeks to combine what the tourist desires, needs and seeks from the process of consuming a tourism experience that involves an investment of time and money. The expectations a tourist has as a consumer in purchasing and consuming a tourism product or experience is ultimately shaped by a wide range of social and economic factors which Uysal (1998) listed in Figure 3.2 and which are shaped by an individual's attitudes and perception of tourism.

Yet tourist motivation is a complex area dominated by the social psychologists with their concern for the behaviour, attitudes and thoughts of people as consumers of tourism. A very influential study published in 1993 by Phillip Pearce suggested that in any attempt to understand tourist motivation we must consider how to develop a concept of motivation in tourism, how to communicate this to students and researchers who do not understand social psychology and what practical measures need to be developed to measure people's motivation for travel, particularly the existence of multi-motivation situations (i.e. more than one factor influencing the desire to engage in tourism). Pearce (1993) also discussed the need to distinguish between intrinsic and extrinsic forces shaping the motivation to become a tourist; he explored these issues further in *Tourist Behaviour* (2005).

Intrinsic and extrinsic motivation

There is no all-embracing theory of tourist motivation due to the problem of simplifying complex psychological factors and behaviour into a universally acceptable theory that can be tested and proved in various tourism contexts. This is illustrated in Table 3.2 which summarizes some of the main theoretical approaches developed in motivation research. The different approaches illustrate that there is no general congruity between the approaches (i.e. there is no common agreement or approach) which explains the complexity of trying to derive general explanations of motivation among tourists. This resulted in a large number of individual studies of tourist motivation dating back to the 1970s (Table 3.3) which adopt different theoretical and conceptual standpoints. One immediate complication is the problem of understanding what drives an individual to travel. For example, while a business traveller is obviously travelling primarily for a work-related reason, there are also covert (or less overt) reasons which are related to that individual's needs and wants. The individual is a central component of tourism demand, as

> no two individuals are alike, and differences in attitudes, perceptions and motivation have an important influence on travel decisions [where] attitudes depend on an individual's perception of the world. Perceptions are mental impressions of ... a place or travel company and are determined by many factors, which include childhood, family and work experiences. However, attitudes and perceptions in themselves do not explain why people want to travel. The inner urges which initiate travel demand are called travel motivators.
>
> (Cooper *et al.* 1993: 20)

What this illustrates is that the individual and the forces affecting their need to be a tourist are important. These forces can be broken down into *intrinsic* and *extrinsic* approaches to motivation. The intrinsic motivation approach recognizes that individuals have unique

Table 3.2 Theoretical approaches to tourist motivation

Needs-based approaches

- Assumes that tourists select destinations to satisfy their needs
- Sees pleasure-related travel as being designed to meet tourist needs
- Epitomized by need-based motivation research such as Maslow (1943, 1954)
- Argues that human needs motivate human behaviour based on a very generic hierarchy of human needs.

Values-based approaches

- Highlights the importance of human values on tourist motivation and why tourists seek to consume certain experiences
- Used widely in consumer behaviour research and embodied in the VALS study by Mitchell (1983) on values and lifestyles
- Used to segment tourists into groups to help understanding.

Benefits sought or realized approaches

- Focuses on causal factors in terms of what benefit a tourist expects to gain from travel and holidays
- Typical approaches have looked at: the attributes of a destination and the benefits it may offer; the psychological benefits which a tourist may gain from a service or holiday.

Expectancy-based approaches

- Uses developments in employment motivation research based upon job preferences and satisfaction
- Is based upon the assumption that the concept of attractiveness of achieving an outcome is the prime motivator
- Is characterized by Witt and Wright's (1992) study.

Other approaches

- Push/pull factors.

personal needs that stimulate or arouse them to pursue tourism. Some of these needs are associated with the desire to satisfy individual or internal needs – for example, becoming a tourist for self-improvement or what is termed 'self-realization', so as to achieve a state of happiness. It may also help boost one's ego (a feature termed ego enhancement) because of the personal confidence building that travel can encourage. In contrast, the extrinsic motivational approach examines the broader conditioning factors that shape individuals' attitudes, preferences and perceptions but are more externally determined – for example, the society and culture one lives in will affect how tourism is viewed. In the former Soviet Union tourism was a functional relationship that was conditioned by the state that sent workers for rest and recreation so they could return refreshed to improve output and productivity. In contrast, in a free market economy the individual is much freer to choose how and where they wish to travel, within certain constraints (e.g. time, income and awareness of opportunities).

At a general level, tourism may allow the individual to escape the mundane, thereby achieving their goals of physical recreation and spiritual refreshment as well as enjoying social goals such as being with family or friends. In this respect, extrinsic influences on the tourist may be family, society with its standards and norms of behaviour, peer pressure from social groups, and the dominant culture. For example, one of the cultural motivators of outbound travel from New Zealand among youth travellers (those aged under 30 years of age) is the desire to do the 'Overseas Experience' (the 'big OE'). This

Table 3.3 Key publications on tourist motivation

Study	Contribution
Lundberg, D. (1971) Why tourists travel. *The Cornell Hotel and Restaurant Administrative Quarterly*, 26(February): 75–81.	Used 18 motivation statements to assess key travel motives
Cohen, E. (1974) Who is a tourist? A conceptual clarification. *Sociological Review*, 22(4): 527–555.	Discussion of what a tourist is and creation of typologies using different tourist roles
Crompton, J. (1979) Motivations for pleasure vacation. *Annals of Tourism Research*, 6(4): 408–424.	Devised a classification of tourist motives for pleasure travel
Dann, G. (1981) Tourist motivation: An appraisal. *Annals of Tourism Research*, 8(2): 187–219.	Review of the tourism studies published to the late 1970s and the role of push and pull factors
Pearce, P. (1982) *The Social Psychology of Tourist Behaviour*. Oxford: Pergamon.	First major review of the field to examine the different motivational research up to the early 1980s and importance of social psychology
Iso-Ahola, S. (1982) Towards a social psychology theory of tourism motivation: A rejoinder. *Annals of Tourism Research*, 9(2): 256–262.	A response to Dann's (1981) study; presents a social psychological model of tourist motivation
Witt, C. and Wright, P. (1992) Tourist motivation after Maslow. In P. Johnson and B. Thomas (eds) *Choice and Demand in Tourism*. London: Mansell.	Review of the literature and contribution which expectancy theories can make to motivation research
Harrill, R. and Potts, T. (2002) Social psychological theories of tourist motivation: Exploration, debate and transition. *Tourism Analysis*, 7(2): 105–114.	A review of the main social psychological models of tourist motivation
Prentice, R. (2005) Tourism motivations and typologies. In A. Lew, A. Williams and C. M. Hall (eds) *A Companion to Tourism*. Oxford: Blackwell. 261–279.	A useful synthesis of the field challenging some of the main assumptions on tourist motivation
Pearce, P. (2005) *Tourist Behaviour*. Clevedon: Channel View.	An update of his 1992 book and a new synthesis of the tourist behaviour field, with a focus on motivation
Pearce, P. and Lee, U. (2005) Developing the travel career approach to tourist motivation. *Journal of Travel Research*, 43(3): 226–237.	A study in which Pearce readjusts his concept of the travel career ladder to the travel career pattern which concludes that 'a core of travel motivation factors including escape, relaxation, relationship enhancement, and self-development seem to comprise the central backbone of motivation for all travelers' (p. 226)
Clarke, J. and Bowen, D. (eds) (2009) *Contemporary Tourist Behaviour*. Wallingford: CABI.	A collection of articles that reviews current research and thinking on tourist motivation.

Plate 3.1
Motivation for travel for a dream holiday is epitomized by this Pacific Island destination with the sun, sea and sand (3s) elements

Source: author

often gives travellers a chance to engage in a cultural form of tourism by visiting Europe, seeing relatives and friends and achieves a number of social goals. The big OE also has an intrinsic function as a long-haul trip and a sustained time away from the home environment encourages independence, self-reliance and greater confidence in one's own ability and judgement, and will contribute to ego enhancement. In the UK there has also been a trend towards a similar experience before commencing study at university; it is known as the 'gap year' and a similar style of travel, working holiday, voluntary activity or round-the-world trip takes place which is explored in more detail in Web Case 3.1 and Case Study 3.1.

While analysis of tourist motivation is about the underlying psychological value and features of being a tourist, actual tourism demand at a practical level is derived through a consumer decision-making process. From this process, it is possible to describe three elements, which condition demand:

1   *energizers of demand*, which are factors that promote an individual to decide on a holiday
2   *filterers of demand*, which are constraints on demand that can exist in economic, sociological or psychological terms despite the desire to go on holiday or travel
3   *affecters*, which are a range of factors that may heighten or suppress the energizers that promote consumer interest or choice in tourism.

CASE STUDY 3.1
VOLUNTEER TOURISM

One of the principal challenges for researchers examining tourist motivation is to try to understand what factors promote a specific tourist experience such as volunteering. Volunteer travel has seen a major growth and volunteer organizations have developed to provide opportunities for volunteers, often on projects located in the less developed world. As a market segment, volunteer tourists spend in excess of US$3000 a trip and TRAM (2008) estimated the size of the global market as 1.6 million volunteers per year. This was valued at between £832 000 and £1.3 million. The number of volunteer tourism organizations is estimated to be 300 globally, and the physical profile of travellers tends to be those aged 20 to 30 years of age. Among the market for volunteer tourists, TRAM (2008) identifies two specific segments:

- those who are unskilled but educated
- a smaller, more highly skilled and older experienced group.

Research conducted in Australia and other countries points to the altruistic motivation (i.e. a willingness to give something back without any expectation of personal reward) alongside specific factors that influence the level of satisfaction derived from the experience including:

- an opportunity to develop a skill or additional knowledge
- the chance to contribute to a worthwhile project
- to have fun and enjoy oneself
- to experience a new environment or setting.

Overseas tourists volunteering in Australia's Northern Territory participated in projects based in schools, care centres and marine wildlife conservation schemes. According to TRAM (2008) 90 per cent of overseas volunteer placements were located in Latin America, Asia and Africa. This reflects the flow of volunteering from developed to developing countries. A study by Campbell and Smith (2006) of sea turtle conservation in Tortuguero, Costa Rica highlighted the environmental values of volunteers. This is aligned with the growing awareness of sustainability issues among specific tourist markets. TRAM (2008), however, points to concerns over the value of volunteer tourism when the projects are poorly managed, so that the traveller receives personal gratification but the project receives little benefit from the volunteer.

Further reading

Campbell, L. and Smith, C. (2006) What makes them pay? Values of volunteer tourists working for sea turtle conservation. *Environmental Management*, 38(1): 84–98.

Holmes, K. and Smith, K. (eds) (2009) *Managing Volunteers in Tourism*. Oxford: Butterworth-Heinemann.

TRAM (2008) *Volunteer Tourism: A Global Analysis*. Arnhem: ATLAS.

Wearing, S. and McGee, N. (2013) Volunteer tourism: A review. *Tourism Management*, 38: 120–130.

These factors directly condition and affect the tourist's process of travel decision-making although they do not explain why people choose to travel. For this reason, it is useful to understand how individuals' desires and need for tourism fit into their wider life.

This partly reflects upon the intrinsic motivations, and one useful framework devised to understand this is Maslow's hierarchy of human needs.

Maslow's hierarchy model and tourist motivation

Maslow's (1954) hierarchy of needs remains one of the most widely discussed ideas on motivation. It is based on the principle of a ranking or hierarchy of individual needs (Figure 3.3), based on the premise that self-actualization is a level to which people should aspire. Maslow argued that if the lower needs in the hierarchy were not fulfilled then these would dominate human behaviour. Once these were satisfied, the individual would be motivated by the needs of the next level of the hierarchy. In the motivation sequence, Maslow identified 'deficiency or tension-reducing motives' and 'inductive or arousal-seeking motives' (Cooper *et al.* 1993: 21), arguing that the model could be applied to work and non-work contexts, such as tourism and leisure. Yet how and why Maslow selected five basic needs remains unclear, although it appears to have a relevance in understanding how human action is related to understandable and predictable aspects of action compared to research that argues that human behaviour is essentially irrational and unpredictable. Maslow's model is not necessarily ideal, since needs are not hierarchical in reality because some needs may occur simultaneously. But such a model does emphasize

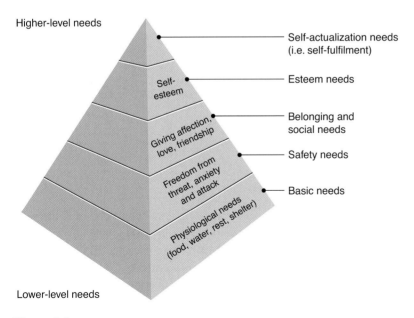

Figure 3.3
Maslow's hierarchy of individual need

Source: author

Table 3.4 Push and pull factors used to explain holidaytaking	
Push factors	Pull factors
Escape	Ease of access
Socializing	Cost of travel
Fun/excitement	Promotional images of destination
Relaxation	Tourist attractions/events
Prestige	Sun, sea, sand
Educational motives	

the development needs of humans, with individuals striving towards personal growth, and these can be understood in a tourism context.

Maslow's work has also been developed since the 1950s when work began on specific motivations beyond the concept of needing 'to get away from it all'. For example, 'push' factors that motivate individuals to seek a holiday have been researched and compared with 'pull' factors (e.g. promotion by tourist resorts), which act as attractors (see Table 3.4).

Ryan's (1991: 25–9) analysis of tourist travel motivators (excluding business travel) identified a range of reasons commonly cited to explain why people travel to tourist destinations for holidays:

- a desire to escape from a mundane environment
- the pursuit of relaxation and recuperation functions
- an opportunity for play
- the strengthening of family bonds
- prestige, since different destinations can enable one to gain social enhancement among peers
- social interaction
- educational opportunities
- wish fulfilment
- shopping.

From this list, it is evident that tourism is unique in that it involves real physical escape reflected in travelling to one or more destination regions where the leisure experience transpires ... [thus] a holiday trip allows changes that are multi-dimensional: place, pace, faces, lifestyle, behaviour, attitude. It allows a person temporary withdrawal from many of the environments affecting day to day existence.

(Leiper 1984, cited in Pearce 1995: 19)

It is also evident that fashion and taste have a major bearing on the destinations people choose to go to for holidays.

Even so, the ranking of UK package destinations has remained fairly consistent in terms of the locations chosen, with Spain maintaining its prominent position as the most popular country (see Chapter 2). Spain also maintained its position as the overall top choice of destination for UK holidaymakers followed by France.

The tourism tradition of motivation studies: Classifying and understanding tourist motives

A large number of studies of tourist motivation (see Tables 3.2 and 3.3), dating back to the 1970s, took many of Maslow's ideas forward and then applied more socio-psychological ideas in a tourism context. In most of the studies of tourist motivation, a common range of factors tend to emerge. For example, Crompton (1979) emphasized that socio-psychological motives can be located along a continuum which explains why certain tourists undertake certain types of travel. In contrast, Dann's (1981) conceptualization is one of the most useful attempts to simplify the principal elements of tourist motivation into a series of propositions (i.e. general statements which characterize tourists) including:

- travel as a response to what is lacking yet desired
- destination pull is in response to motivational push
- motivation may have a classified purpose (this was the focus of many of the earlier studies of motivation)
- motivation typologies
- motivation and tourist experiences.

This was simplified a stage further by McIntosh and Goeldner (1990) into:

- physical motivators
- cultural motivators
- interpersonal motivators
- status and prestige motivators.

On the basis of motivation and using the type of experiences tourists seek, Cohen (1974) distinguished between four types of travellers:

1   *the organized mass tourist*, on a package holiday, who is highly organized and whose contact with the host community in a destination is minimal
2   *the individual mass tourist*, who uses similar facilities to the organized mass tourist but also desires to visit other sights not covered on organized tours in the destination
3   *the explorers*, who arrange their travel independently and who wish to experience the social and cultural lifestyle of the destination
4   *the drifters*, who do not seek any contact with other tourists or their accommodation, wishing to live with the host community.

**Figure 3.4
Plog's
psychographic
types**

Source: Plog, S.
(2001) Why
destination areas
rise and fall in
popularity: an
update of a Cornell
Quarterly classic.
*The Cornell Hotel
and Restaurant
Administration
Quarterly*, 42(3):
13–24

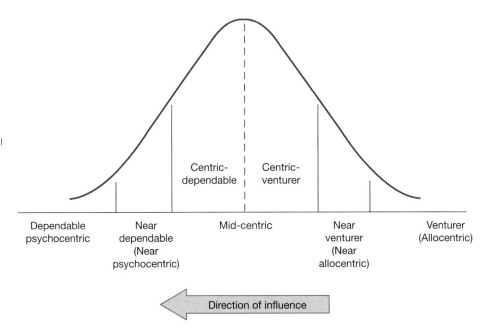

Clearly, such a classification is fraught with problems, since it does not take into account the increasing diversity of holidays undertaken nor the inconsistencies in tourist behaviour. Other researchers suggest that one way of overcoming this difficulty is to consider the different destinations tourists choose to visit and then establish a sliding scale that is similar to Cohen's (1972) typology, but without such an absolute classification.

One such attempt was by Plog (1974), who devised a classification of the US population into psychographic types, with travellers distributed along a continuum from psycho-centrism to allocentrism (see Figure 3.4). The psychocentrics are the anxious, inhibited and less adventurous travellers while at the other extreme the allocentrics are adventurous, outgoing, seeking out new experiences due to their inquisitive personalities and interest in travel and adventure. This means that, through time, some tourists may seek out new destinations, while others will follow the more **adventurous as** the destinations develop and appear safe and secure. But some of the **criticisms of Plog's** model are that it is difficult to use because it fails to distinguish **between extrinsic** and intrinsic motivations. It also fails to include a dynamic **element to encompass** the changing nature of individual tourists. Pearce (1993) suggested that **individuals have a** 'career' in their travel behaviour where people

> start at different levels, they are likely to change levels during their life-cycle and they can be prevented from moving by money, health and other people. They may also retire from their travel career or not take holidays at all and therefore not be part of the system.
>
> (Pearce 1993: 125)

Pearce (2005) has argued that a travel career is a dynamic element in a tourist's holidaytaking habits, influenced by travel experience, stage in the life cycle and age.

Initially he developed the idea of a travel career ladder (Pearce 1993), which was built on Maslow's hierarchial system and had five motivational levels:

1   biological needs
2   safety and security needs
3   relationship development and extension needs
4   special interest and self-development needs
5   fulfilment or self-actualization needs.

Later Pearce (2005) de-emphasized the hierarchical elements of a ladder in favour of a reformulated travel career pattern (TCP) approach arguing that 'the pattern of motivations and their structure rather than the steps on a ladder' (Pearce and Lee 2005: 228) were more important. The TCP placed a greater emphasis on how motivations form patterns which may link to the notion of travel careers. The notion of the TCP is that tourists will have different motivating patterns over their life cycle which will be impacted upon by their experience of travelling. This reflects better the complexity of understanding tourist motivation, although studies of this have suggested a tourist's experience of domestic and international travel and age were important factors in identifying influences on TCPs. What Pearce (2005) concludes is that we may discern three layers of travel motivation:

•   *layer 1*, the common motives at the core of the TCP: novelty, escape, relaxation, enhancing and maintaining human relationships
•   *layer 2*, a series of moderately important motivators related to self-actualization (i.e. focused on the inner self) that surround this core set of motivations and a number of externally focused motives such as interaction with the host society and environment
•   *layer 3*, an outer layer with lesser importance including motives such as nostalgia and social status.

These factors may also vary in importance according to the culture of the travellers, and the relative significance of these motives may also change during the TCP of individuals.

From the discussion of motivation so far, it is apparent that the key principles are as summarized in Table 3.5.

The important point here is that motivation is about how a general need/want (in this case the desire to travel) is translated in a context where it can be fulfilled. This is often simplified to push and pull factors but it does raise issues about the ways in which tourists as consumers respond to specific stimuli that encourage them to engage in tourism. Goodall (1991) identified the relationship between needs, wants and preferences and goals amongst travellers, where push and pull factors existed. Much of the discussion is focused on consumer behaviour and the role of marketing in providing the stimuli that lead people to choose specific motivations for going on holiday. For this reason, the role of consumer behaviour in tourism is important in understanding the practical ways consumers choose to become tourists.

> **Table 3.5 Summary of tourist motivation: Key principles**
>
> - Tourism is a combination of products and experiences which meet a diverse range of needs
> - Tourists are not always conscious of their deep psychological needs and ideas. Even when they do know what they are, they may not reveal them to researchers, family and friends
> - Tourism motives may be multiple and contradictory, with some working in harmony and others working in direct opposition (i.e. push and pull factors)
> - Motives may change over time and be inextricably linked together (e.g. perception, learning, personality and culture are often separated out but they are all bound up together)
> - Dynamic models of tourist motivation such as Pearce's (2005) TCP are crucial to understanding not only the role of motivation but also the way that such motives will evolve, change and be conditioned by changes in lifestyle, life cycle and personal growth and development.

Consumer behaviour and tourism

Consumer behaviour concerns the way tourists as purchasers of products and services behave in terms of spending and their attitudes and values towards what they buy. Their age, sex, marital status, educational background, amount of disposable income, where they live and other factors such as their interest in travel directly affect this. For marketers who sell and promote tourism products and services, these factors are crucial to the way they divide tourists into groups as consumers so that they can provide specific products that appeal to each group. One frequent approach used by tourism marketers to achieve this goal is 'market segmentation' (i.e. how all the above factors can be used to describe different groups of consumers).

There are a range of approaches one can use in market segmentation though the most commonly used is *demographic or socio-economic segmentation*, which occurs where statistical data such as the census are used together with other statistical information to identify the scale and volume of potential tourists likely to visit a destination. Key factors such as age and income are important determinants of the demand. For example, the amount of paid holidays and an individual or family's income both have an important bearing on demand. One powerful factor shaping demand in a demographic context is social class, which is related to income, social standing and the way status evolves from these factors. Social class is widely used by marketers as a way of identifying the spending potential of tourists. In the UK, the Institute of Practitioners in Advertising uses the following socio-economic grouping of the population with six groups:

A   Higher managerial, administrative or professional
B   Middle managerial, administrative or professional
C1 Supervisory, clerical or managerial
C2 Skilled manual workers
D   Semi- and unskilled manual workers
E   Pensioners, the unemployed, casual or lowest grade workers.

This is after Holloway and Plant (1988), although other classifications have been devised with various emphases in different countries. The key point to stress from any classification is how social class, employment or economic status impact upon participation in tourism. In most cases, professionals enjoy higher incomes and this affects their consumption of tourism in general terms. However, other factors may come into play: the stage in the family life cycle may inhibit a young professional with children while a working couple in another occupational group may have fewer constraints and therefore more money to spend on holidays. Many studies of income and social class indicate that those in groups AB have a greater propensity to take overseas holidays than those in groups DE as illustrated by the consumption of ecotourism (see Case Study 3.2). This also raises wider social debates about how income and class can contribute to social exclusion of those groups unable to participate in tourism. Two other notable factors which impact upon tourism in terms of consumer behaviour are gender and ethnicity.

Gender and ethnicity

Gender has a powerful impact on participation in tourism, since many studies indicate that women in households are the holiday decision-makers. Yet with changes in the existing composition of two-parent households and the growth in single-parent households, the notion of the nuclear family is changing in many Western societies. The consequences are that many tourism providers are having to rethink the nature of the traditional family holiday. Similarly, new trends in holiday consumption can be discerned with children exerting greater pressure on parents in the selection of holiday destinations (e.g. pester power), demanding visits to child-oriented destinations (e.g. Disneyland) and locations associated with children's television series (e.g. the Isle of Mull in Scotland where the fictitious *Balamory* BBC Television series was filmed has been receiving up to 250 000 visitors a year, a significant proportion generated by pester power).

Gender has also become a defining feature in the identification of the gay and lesbian market. In the USA this comprises 10 per cent of the tourism market and they are now wooed as a high-spending group (this has led to the use of terms such as the 'Pink Pound' in the UK). In the USA, such households have income above the national average. The Tourism Industry Association (TIA) in the USA estimate this market is worth US$54.1 billion a year. However, the gay and lesbian market is also very discerning and seeks destinations with a gay or lesbian involvement that is integrated in the community. Among the top reasons to visit a destination are: holidaying with a boyfriend/girlfriend; attending Gay Pride festivals; holidaying with a group of friends; purchasing a holiday package and taking advantage of internet travel specials.

In the USA, the top destinations for gay men in order of preference are New York, San Francisco, Hawaii, Palm Springs, Fort Lauderdale, West Hollywood, Miami/South Beach and Key West. Lesbians travelled to San Francisco, Provincetown, New York, Hawaii, Key West, West Hollywood, Miami/South Beach, Fort Lauderdale and Palm Springs.

Ethnicity has also been identified as an important factor shaping tourist travel behaviour and consumption patterns. Many Western societies now have multicultural

CASE STUDY 3.2
THE EMERGENCE OF ECOTOURISM MARKETS IN BRAZIL

The sustainability debates highlighted in Chapter 1 have slowly filtered into tourist consumer behaviour, reflected in high value spending among ecotourists. However, the practicalities of embracing the principles of sustainability means many people are very aspirational about practising sustainability. This means, as a DEFRA study (Dresner *et al.* 2007) found, that people have very good intentions about wanting to be more environmentally sustainable. In their daily lives, people may want to be environmentally responsible and do the right thing (e.g. recycling) but they do not follow it through with action, as discussed in Chapter 1. This is especially the case with holidaytaking. For example, tourists are reluctant to forego long haul travel as a form of consumption. Consequently, the development of sustainable forms of travel, particularly niche products such as the ecotourism, remains a relatively small segment of the overall market. Ecotourism pursuits as an environmental form of tourism are supposed to have a minimal impact on the environment, so it is one form of sustainable tourism particularly as it has environmental goals at its heart, such as wildlife conservation. Ecotourism is a relatively recent phenomenon, especially in many developing countries, and Brazil is no exception. As a destination Brazil has seen its international visitor numbers rise from 5 million in 2002 to nearly 7 million in 2008. As an ecotourism destination its attraction can be related to its:

*   environmental diversity including a wide range of ecosystems and landscape
*   large areas of wilderness such as the Amazon Basin and a network of National Parks
*   wildlife diversity.

Whilst there has been a long history of explorers and scientists who have visited Brazil as nature-oriented travellers (e.g. Charles Darwin), the development of ecotourism can be dated to around 1985 and the decision by the state tourism organization – Embratur to develop new products and the establishment of tour operators focused on ecotourism and the domestic market. The focus on the domestic market reflects the rapid growth of domestic tourism in Brazil and the growth of the middle class with increasing affluence, some of which has been spent on tourism. Around 6 per cent of domestic visitors cite ecotourism as a major motivation to travel, although this rises to 10 per cent amongst the most affluent social groups. Embratur has estimated the potential market for domestic ecotourists to be around 4 million and international research shows that these visitors are amongst the higher spending consumers. Even so, the market for ecotourists needs further investment in the infrastructure to support the development of these markets, although one project in Brazil has won the coveted Condé Nast ecotourism award.

Further reading

Dresner *et al.* (2007) *Public Understanding of Sustainable Leisure*. London: DEFRA.

Sarigöllü, E. and Huang, R. (2005) Benefits segmentation of visitors to Latin America. *Journal of Travel Research*, 43(3): 277–293.

Tangeland, T. and Aas, O. (2011) Household composition and the importance of experience attributes of nature-based tourism activity products – A Norwegian case study of outdoor recreationalists. *Tourism Management*, 32(4): 822–832.

populations, with race and ethnicity assuming a more prominent role in travel markets. According to the TIA in the USA, the emerging Hispanic travel market now accounts for 13.7 per cent of the national population, which is set to grow to 162.6 million (around 25 per cent) of the US population by 2050. This is a substantial market despite their low average household incomes. The Hispanic groups in the USA have made growing use of the internet, although there are differences in consumer behaviour between native-born and recent Hispanic migrants. In terms of tourism, the US Hispanic market purchasing is concentrated in California and Texas. The majority of their travel is for leisure, especially to see family, friends and relatives. Popular domestic destinations in the USA are California, Texas, Florida, Nevada, Arizona and New Mexico. Therefore the examples of gender and ethnicity show that it is important for the tourism sector to understand how consumers can be broken down into discrete groups or segments.

Psychographic segmentation

A more sophisticated approach to segmentation (which was discussed above in the motivation study by Plog, 1974) is *psychographic segmentation* which is often introduced to complement more simplistic approaches based on socio-economic or geographic data. It involves using socio-economic and life-cycle data to predict a range of consumer behaviours or purchasing patterns associated with each stage. Examining the psychological profile of consumers to establish their traits or characteristics in relation to different market segments further develops this. By combining the behaviour of tourists and their value system comprising their beliefs and how these affect their decision to purchase, the marketers can communicate more effectively with potential consumers by under-standing what motivates their decision to purchase certain types of products and services. One example of psychographic segmentation is a specialized product such as ecotourism (travelling to engage in wildlife viewing, visiting natural areas and having a concern with the natural environment); here, segmentation is possible using a range of variables such as the age profile of the ecotourists, how they choose to travel, how they book their holidays, what type of budget they have and their motivation for being an ecotourist. This is illustrated in Case Study 3.2. This is one component of the growth of alternative forms of tourism (see Table 3.6) of which ecotourism is one element.

Once the supplier of the services or products has considered these issues, the next stage to examine is how tourists decide to purchase certain products – particularly the most frequent purchase, which is the holiday.

Purchasing a holiday

A study undertaken in Canada in March 2002 by TripAdvisor found that consumers often take as long as a month to purchase quite complex holiday products online and that illustrates how important it is for businesses to understand how consumers select products both online and from more traditional distribution channels such as travel agents. It also highlights the importance of marketing efforts by tourism businesses to tempt the consumer to book a product. Consumers have a range of holiday options

Table 3.6 Alternative forms of tourism: Terminology

- **Alternative tourism** has emerged as an all-embracing concept in the broader literature on sustainable tourism within which a number of distinct strands of thought have developed that are characterized by a greater concern for ethical tourism behaviour

- **Ecotourism** is responsible travel to natural areas to conserve the environment and benefit local people

- **Community-based tourism** is designed to involve local people and stakeholders to ensure that the benefits of tourism development are retained within the community

- **Pro-poor tourism** is intended to ensure that the poor over-proportionally benefit from tourism development

- **Fair trade and tourism** is an alternative mechanism to help alleviate poverty among the producers and suppliers of tourism goods and services in the supply chain

- **Justice tourism** is an approach founded upon ethical and equitable principles as well as respect, sharing and equality for all ideology

- **Ethical tourism** is based upon the assumption that the fundamental principles of tourism as both a business activity and transaction between the industry and consumer are inherently 'unethical', being exploitative, damaging to the environment and local people, because tourism is a conspicuous form of consumption. The term is often used interchangeably with 'responsible' and other similar terms

- **Responsible tourism** is primarily characterized by the tourism industries and tourists acting in a responsible manner in terms of their actions, activities and behaviour.

Source: adapted from C. Weedon (2014) *Responsible Tourism Behaviour*. London: Routledge

available at specific points in time and their choice is based on the preferences of the individual, family and other groups. One other notable group that has seen a growth in volume and significance in the UK is the stag and hen party market, as discussed in Web Case 3.2.

The following factors exert a powerful influence on the decision to purchase tourism products and services:

- the personality of the purchaser
- the point of purchase
- the role of the sales person
- whether the individual is a frequent or infrequent purchaser of holiday products
- prior experience.

Any explanation of consumer behaviour in tourism also needs to be aware of the motivations, desires, needs, expectations, and personal and social factors affecting travel behaviour. These are in turn affected by stimuli which promote travel (i.e. marketing and promotion), images of the places being visited, previous travel experiences, and time and cost constraints. What this type of debate on tourists as consumers shows is that marketing and promotion are fundamental in a business which seeks to create a four-step process which takes the consumer from a stage of unawareness of a product or service through to a point where they want to consume it. Within marketing, much of the attention focuses on using well-known brands and household names in travel (i.e. Thomson Holidays in the UK and other World of TUI brands in Germany and other European countries) to promote awareness. Marketers describe this process as the AIDA model: Awareness, Interest, Desire, Action.

The AIDA process has been used by the mayor in the Maipo River region, an area just outside the Chilean capital Santiago, to create a unique tourism destination – a UFO tourism zone. The Awareness has been created by UFO sightings over two decades, while the Interest has resulted from increased publicity. To stimulate and satisfy the Desire to visit, the Action is based on plans to erect two observation centres, signposts of sightings and the provision of workshops.

Much of the efforts in marketing are focused on consumer behaviour, seeking to understand how individuals perceive things and digest the information and messages that advertising and promotion use to develop a tourism image. These images impact not only upon the holiday selection process and decision to go on holiday but also, and more importantly, upon destinations – the specific places tourists will visit.

The tourist image of products and places

It is generally acknowledged that many consumers will select a range of destinations (often three to five) when considering where to go on holiday. A major element in the decision to select a specific destination is the image of the place. The tourist(s) select the destination through a process of elimination but this is not a straight linear process from A to B to C. Often, people will look at options, re-evaluate them and reconsider specific places based on their knowledge, the images portrayed in the media and the opinions of individual(s) and group members. This can make travel decisions a lengthy and complex process based on compromise. For example, the 9/11 attack on the USA and other terrorist threats created widespread negative images of international travel and one immediate beneficiary of this was the growth of domestic tourism in many countries. This required government and tourism agencies to promote not only 'business as usual' in New York to encourage people to travel again, but to restore negative images portrayed by the media. This is because cities have large volumes of overseas tourists as the statistics for 2009 suggest for the following cities: Paris (14.8 million); London (14.1 million); Singapore (9.7 million); New York (8.7 million); Istanbul (7.51 million); Hong Kong (7 million).

Image can be a powerful process where destinations (such as London and Paris) have memorable elements in the landscape which feature as icons to promote aware-ness and travel to the destination (e.g. the Eiffel Tower in Paris), leading to tourists associating positive reasons to travel to well-known icons that are safe and popular such as Amersterdam's canals (Plate 3.2). In some cases, over-popular images of destina-tions or specific attractions may mean that a degree of caution has to be used to downplay the destination in peak season; this is sometimes called 'de-marketing'. In addition, destinations have to create images of their tourism offerings and locality that help to differentiate them from the competition. In Australia, there has been a rise

Plate 3.2
Visitors to Amsterdam pursue a wide range of activities during their visit

Source: Istock

in wine and food tourism based on local products, and specialist producers in areas such as Margaret River in Western Australia have helped regions to emerge as newly created and re-imaged, with emphasis being placed on the uniqueness of the place. One additional way in which destinations have re-imaged themselves is through the development of a comprehensive programme of redevelopment that has allowed them to reposition themselves as in the case of Calvià (see Innovation in Sustainability 3.1).

Another example is a desolate area in northern China on the Tibet–Qinghai plateau, where attempts by local government in 2002 have begun to turn a former nuclear weapons research centre (No. 221 Plant, owned by the China Nuclear Industry Corporation) into a tourist attraction. Established in 1958, the site was used to test nuclear bombs and nuclear waste is buried there. Some 16 nuclear tests were carried out over a 30-year period. Negative images and publicity present a major challenge to those creating positive images of the region for visitors, which the Qinghai Provincial Tourism Association are basing on the region's cultural heritage (Tibetan culture and architecture) and the natural environment (varying from snow-capped mountains to desert-style dunes). To attract visitors, a number of festivals have been staged based on horse racing and Buddhist rituals.

Yet much of the image of a destination is not concerned with the tangible elements, since tourism is a combination of tangible perceptions of place and emotional feelings about locations (Plate 3.3).

Plate 3.3
Visitors to urban areas wishing to absorb the culture and ambience often find a hop-on-hop-off bus a convenient means of sightseeing

Source: author

INNOVATION IN SUSTAINABILITY 3.1
REPOSITIONING A RESORT TO ADDRESS MASS TOURISM DEMAND – CALVIÀ, MALLORCA

Dr Joanne Connell, Exeter University Business School

The Municipality of Calvià is one of the largest destinations on the island of Mallorca, accounting for about one-third of the tourists to the Balearic Islands. It is a municipality of 143km^2 with a 60-km coastline, 50 000 inhabitants and around 1.6 million visitors a year. Tourism development in Calvià boomed in the 1960s based on short-term economic gain, but it was one of the first areas to experience the negative effects of mass tourism. Lack of planning regulations resulted in urban sprawl and a significant range of environmental impacts, epitomized by poor water quality, deforestation, unsympathetic building styles and dense development. Figure 3.5 outlines the consequences of unsustainable tourism growth. By the 1980s, Calvià had become a stagnating destination where lower-spending tourists were attracted to the poor-quality hotels and bars and a pattern of inappropriate behaviour based on the European 'lager lout' image set in. Calvià City Council, concerned at the problems of managing an 'ageing' tourist destination, proposed a series of policies and actions to assist the sustainable development of tourism in the resort. The strategy, published in 1995, was based on the global framework of Local Agenda 21 (LA21), the Action Plan arising from the United Nations Conference on Environment and Development (Rio de Janerio, 1992) to stimulate sustainable actions at a local level (i.e. the destination level). The mission statement for the Calvià plan was 'To develop a philosophy, strategy and programme of actions for the tourism sector based on sustainable development' and the objectives of the LA21 are set out in Figure 3.6.

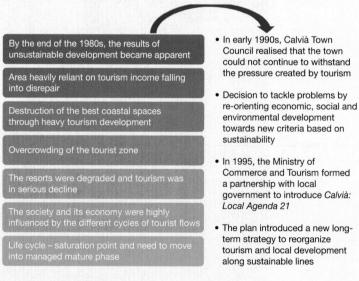

Figure 3.5
Consequences of unsustainable tourism growth

Source: J. Connell

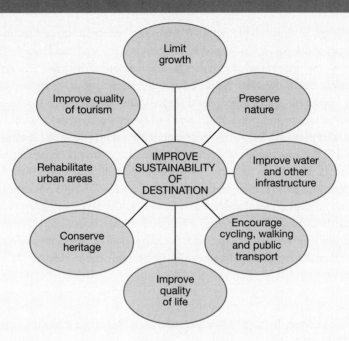

Figure 3.6
Objectives of LA21 in Calvià

Source: J. Connell

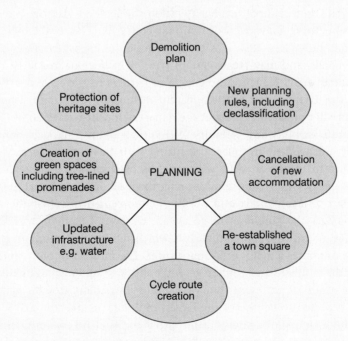

Figure 3.7
Major outcomes of the Calvià LA21 process: Planning aspects

Source: J. Connell

The long-term aim of the project was to achieve a modern coastal tourism destination offering high-quality and more appropriate bed-space capacity, and this was incorporated into the Local Development Planning Regulations, the outcomes of which are summarized in Figure 3.7. Sea water quality is monitored on a weekly basis, obsolete hotels have been demolished, reducing bed-space capacity and removing ugly buildings, while a proposed large-scale development has been halted. Environmental management in hotels and other buildings has been encouraged – such as waste recycling, reduced electricity, and purchase of more environmentally sound products. A wide acceptance of the principles of Agenda 21 has been established through broad community consultation and participation. A significant spin-off to the Calvià initiative is the transferability of the concept of environmental management and improvement to similar resorts. Indeed, Aguiló *et al.* (2005) found that prices of holidays were now higher than in other areas of the Balearic Islands as Calvià enters a restructuring phase using the principles of sustainability, whilst meeting the needs of visitors and repositioning the destination. Sharing good practice and integrating the principles of Agenda 21 in plans for sustainable development are seen as the way forward for the local authorities in Mediterranean resorts.

Further reading

www.calvia.com

Aguiló, E., Alegre, J. and Sard, M. (2005) The persistence of the sun and sand tourism model. *Tourism Management*, 26(2): 219–231.

Even when rational feelings question the logic of visiting somewhere, the desire to see something may override rational concerns. This is related to risk behaviour in holiday purchases. Risk is a complex topic, not least because it is very personal to individuals, and may create certain types of behaviour in tourists. The low-risk tourist will book early, reducing the perceived barriers to travel, and may return to the same resort or country due to the apparent feelings of safety and security. In contrast, risk takers will be less worried about the impact of tourist-related crime, will be less concerned about the stability and certainty offered by booking a package holiday and may choose to be independent travellers organizing their travel and itinerary themselves. Tourists seeking to minimize risks will seek out well-known brands that guarantee quality experiences. Often, these groups prefer the reassurance of booking at travel agents where the face-to-face contact and positive reinforcement of what the experience will offer encourages the purchaser to go ahead. Outbound Chinese travellers comprise one of the fastest growing tourism markets which reflects the country's rapid industrialization and position as a major economic power. The number of outbound trips has risen from 620 000 in 1990 to 47 million in 2009 and 57.7 million in 2012 (see Web Case 3.3 for more detail). It represents one of the most important growth markets for the future as it is expected to be one of the largest outbound markets in 2015.

This example of China illustrates that the demand for tourism is variable. Although demand may perform in a constant manner, the overall effect of demand factors is that they are constantly under review by consumers and some fluctuations will inevitably occur when adverse events such as 9/11 occur.

The future of tourism demand

The growth of domestic and international tourism demand depends on a wide range of factors, some of which have been discussed in this chapter. The example of the Chinese outbound market vividly illustrates the scale of tourism growth that has occurred in a relatively short time frame (i.e. since 1983) and the prospects of it becoming a major outbound market by 2015.

Irrespective of these trends are more profound changes which are occurring among tourism consumers. Whilst the Chinese are a young and buoyant outbound and domestic market, many other industrialized countries have recognized that their tourists now have much higher expectations of what they purchase and consume as tourists and are somewhat 'mature' markets. For this reason it is interesting to reflect upon some of the consumer trends now affecting tourist consumption which may shape the quality as well as the nature of tourism demand in the next decade:

- consumers are more discerning of tourism purchases, irrespective of what they pay, and have high expectations of quality
- in a post-modern society, some researchers argue that the consumer gains as much satisfaction from the process of purchasing as they do from consumption, implying that the purchase process needs to meet these raised expectations
- many consumers across the globe are now more e-savvy and able to use technology to establish the range and extent of travel and holiday options, leading to a greater demand for value-adding in the purchase and consumption process
- more experienced travellers are seeking more innovative, unusual and targetted products which fit with their lifestyles, perception of their lifestyle and needs. The traditional annual holiday of one to two weeks, purchased through a travel agent from a mass produced brochure, will no longer be the norm
- the tourism industry will be faced with more discerning clients, a proportion of whom will be willing to purchase a portfolio of products that appeal to their time-poor, cash-rich lifestyles. Ease of consumption will be the new buzzword: the holiday or trip will be an opportunity to de-stress and will not commence with stress, disorganization and lack of attention to detail
- marketing techniques which allow targeting, segmentation and client identification to capture the individual needs of the traveller, will provide premium profits for the tourism provider
- low-cost, high-volume mass products such as low-cost airline travel will continue to fill a niche for independent price-sensitive travellers without any restrictions from government
- consumers are continuing to be heavily influenced by branding, brands and advertising which create an image of the market position, consumer benefits and promise made by tourism products. This trend is likely to continue, with destinations and operators using the brand image to create a unique appeal to certain markets and groups
- new product development to appeal to individualized aspects of demand (e.g. health and wellness tourism) will see further growth, as niche products aimed at specific

groups with these interests are developed (see Case Study 3.3). Penn (2007) has described the growing importance of microtrends (i.e. trends affecting at least 1 per cent of the population) as keydrivers of niche leisure interests which can be combined into tourism products.

CASE STUDY 3.3
EMERGENT FORMS OF TOURISM DEMAND – DEMENTIA AND TOURISM

There is developing awareness amongst tourism researchers that tourism per se is outside the reach of many, and thus is a privilege or a consumer good for those able to 'access' tourism and experiences associated with holidays. At the same time, the population of tourism consumers in the developed world is ageing as the UNWTO (2010) report outlines. Travel and tourism growth is largely predicated upon access to holidays based on the able-bodied and those who enjoy good health. Yet there have been major changes in the developed world, with legislation to make tourism more accessible to all, via disability legislation. But such legislation does not recognize global trends in ageing, with the number of people aged 60 and over likely to triple from 894 million in 2010 to 2.43 billion in 2050. Within this expanding demographic group are predictions of major growth in those suffering from dementia, estimated at 35 million globally. These numbers are expected to increase from 65.7 million in 2030 to 115 million in 2050. Dementia as a disease leads to a decline in memory and cognitive functions, impacting upon one's independence and ability to undertake fulfilling activities alone.

Researchers in leisure studies consider the 'constraints' which such people face as the disease progresses, as structural constraints develop linked to the absence of environments, activities and experiences which those with dementia and caregivers can participate in. Recent research by Page *et al.* (in press) argues that this actually provides a market opportunity for destinations or providers able to develop Dementia-Friendly Tourism experiences that embrace the notion of tourism for all and inclusivity. This study was part of a growing recognition globally of the effect of dementia on society. The UK Prime Ministerial Group on dementia identified this as a priority area for action, seeking to create 20 towns and cities which will become dementia-friendly by 2015. In the UK alone, dementia care costs £23 billion a year and enhanced tourism experiences are viewed as one way of enhancing the well-being of those living with dementia. Whilst research and action on these issues is at an early stage, it illustrates where a latent form of tourism demand exists for a population that has enjoyed great personal mobility and freedom in the developed world that then finds its lives constrained by a progressive medical condition.

Further reading

Page, S. J., Innes, A. and Cutler, C. (in press) Developing dementia-friendly tourism destinations: An exploratory analysis. *Journal of Travel Research*.

Conclusion

The reasons why people choose to engage in tourism are diverse and multifaceted. No one simple explanation can be advanced to explain motivation for tourism. Instead it is a process of understanding the psychology of tourist decision-making based upon the reasons why they wish to travel and take holidays. To simplify some of the reasons, researchers have developed lists of factors and typologies of tourists to try to suggest how humans can be grouped into common types of consumers of tourism. Understanding the individual is a time-consuming process that is not easily reduced to questionnaire surveys or face-to-face interviews on the beach asking tourists why they are there. The tourist has to be understood like an onion: they comprise a number of layers which need to be peeled away to uncover the extrinsic and intrinsic motivational forces. To continue the analogy, over-analysing the tourist may mean that removing all the layers leaves nothing to be eaten and digested; and while slicing the onion in half may reveal the complex thinking and factors shaping human behaviour associated with tourism, predictable and rational behaviour is not necessarily revealed. Consequently, a range of motivational approaches may provide conflicting information. However, what is certain is that taking a holiday and travelling are firmly embedded in modern society and although fashions, tastes and changes in travel habits may alter outward motivation, deep down the intrinsic motivation is a highly personal process for each and every tourist.

CHAPTER REVIEW

 References

Cohen, E. (1972) Towards a sociology of international tourism. *Social Research*, 39: 164–182.

Cohen, E. (1974) Who is a tourist? A conceptual clarification. *Sociological Review*, 22: 527–555.

Cooper, C. P., Fletcher, J., Gilbert, D. G. and Wanhill, S. (1993) *Tourism: Principles and Practice*. London: Pitman.

Crompton, J. (1979) An assessment of the image of Mexico as a vacation destination. *Journal of Travel Research*, 17(Fall): 18–23.

Dann, G. (1981) Tourist motivation: An appraisal. *Annals of Tourism Research*, 8(2): 187–219.

Goodall, B. (1991) Understanding holiday choice. In C. Cooper (ed.) *Progress in Tourism, Recreation and Hospitality Management*, Vol. 3. London: Belhaven.

Holloway, J. C. and Plant, R. V. (1988) *Marketing for Tourism*. London: Pitman.

Maslow, A. (1943) A theory of human motivation. *Psychological Review*, 50: 370–396.

Maslow, A. (1954) *Motivation and Personality*. New York: Harper and Row.

Mathieson, A. and Wall, G. (1982) *Tourism: Economic, Physical and Social Impacts*. Harlow: Longman.

McIntosh, R. W. and Goeldner, C. (1990) *Tourism: Principles, Practices and Philosophies*. New York: Wiley.

Mitchell, A. (1983) *The Nine American Lifestyles*. New York: Warner.

Mountinho, L. (1987) Consumer behaviour in tourism. *European Journal of Marketing*, 21(10): 3–44.

Pearce, D. G. (1995) *Tourism Today: A Geographical Analysis*, 2nd edn. Harlow: Longman.

Pearce, P. (1993) The fundamentals of tourist motivation. In D. Pearce and R. Butler (eds) *Tourism Research: Critique and Challenges*. London: Routledge.

Pearce, P. (2005) *Tourist Behaviour*. Clevedon: Channel View.

Pearce, P and Lee, U (2005) Developing the travel career approach to tourist motivation. *Journal of Travel Research*, 43: 226–237.

Penn, M. (2007) *Microtrends: The Small Forces Behind Big Changes*. London: Allen Lane.

Plog, S. (1974) Why destination areas rise and fall in popularity. *The Cornell Hotel and Restaurant Administration Quarterly*, 15(November): 13–16.

Ryan, C. (1991) *Recreational Tourism: A Social Science Perspective*. London: Routledge.

UNWTO (2010) *Demographic Changes and Tourism*. Madrid: UNWTO.

Uysal, M. (1998) The determinants of tourism demand: A theoretical perspective. In D. Ioannides and K. Debbage (eds) *The Economic Geography of the Tourist Industry: A Supply-side Analysis*. London: Routledge.

Witt, C. and Wright, P. (1992) Tourist motivation after Maslow. In P. Johnson and B. Thomas (eds) *Choice and Demand in Tourism*. London: Mansell.

 # Further reading

The best studies to explore in this complex area are:

Argyle, M. (1996) *The Social Psychology of Leisure*. Harmondsworth: Penguin.

Clarke, J. and Bowen, D. (eds) (2009) *Contemporary Tourist Behaviour*. Wallingford: CABI.

Maslow, A. (1943) A theory of human motivation. *Psychological Review*, 50: 370–396.

Mitchell, A. (1983) *The Nine American Lifestyles*. New York: Warner.

Pearce, P. (1982) *The Social Psychology of Tourist Behaviour*. Oxford: Pergamon.

Pearce, P. (1993) The fundamentals of tourist motivation. In D. Pearce and R. Butler (eds) *Tourism Research: Critique and Challenges*. London: Routledge.

UNWTO and European Travel Commission (2008) *The Chinese Outbound Travel Market*. Madrid: UNWTO.

 # Questions

1   Why is tourist motivation important for tourism managers to understand?

2   What is the role of consumer behaviour in understanding what tourists want to purchase? Do consumers always follow rational decision-making approaches when purchasing products such as holidays?

3   Should the consumer be the starting point for the analysis of tourism demand?

4   How useful is Maslow's model in understanding tourist motivation? Has it been made redundant and superseded by specific social psychology studies of tourism, or is it still the basis for all analyses of tourist motivation?

 # Access additional resources

- For students: Multiple choice questions for each chapter, video links and further reading.
- For instructors: PowerPoint slides with tables and diagrams, additional case studies, video links and further reading.

4 Transporting the tourist I

Surface transport

Learning outcomes

Transport forms the vital link between tourists and destinations. It also provides the focus for many tourist activities such as sightseeing and cruising. After reading this chapter, you should be able to understand:

- the relationship between transport and tourism
- the significance of different modes of surface transport and their contribution to tourism
- the role of operational issues in developing competitive modes of tourist transport.

Introduction

The pursuit of tourism through the ages has stimulated a steady growth in the range of destinations visited. This is directly related to changes in transport technology and its affordability, or diffusion of tourism from a travelling elite initially to a wider mass market. As Page and Connell (2014) argue,

> Fundamentally, human mobility is structured around distinct methods of transport: self-propelled modes (e.g. walking); augmented modes (using technology or tools to amplify our bodily effort such as skiing) and fuelled modes (especially motorized transport) . . . [and] these modes also require the infrastructure . . . to accommodate each form of transport and tourism.
>
> (p.155)

The two principal drivers from a supply perspective have been the aircraft for international travel and the car for domestic travel. As Stradling and Anabele (2008) argue, the three notions of propulsion, combustion and consumption are what characterize modern-day travel, and these can be directly related to tourism as a form of conspicuous consumption as well as to the growth in greenhouse gases from the consumption of oil-based fuels. In the nineteenth century the building of railways and cheap fares (combined with increases in leisure time) permitted a mass market development of seaside trips in many

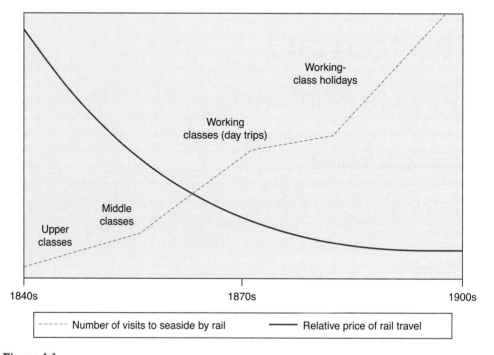

Figure 4.1
Hypothetical example of the impact of railway technology on the growth of coastal tourism in Victorian and Edwardian England

Source: author

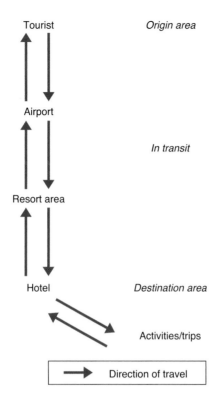

Figure 4.2
Tourist travel from origin to destination area and return
Source: author

European countries, initially as day trips and later as holidays, as this form of tourism became more widely available. This is illustrated in Figure 4.1, which shows how the innovation of rail travel and its decreasing costs led to growing numbers of people travelling as tourists as previous modes of transport (e.g. the paddle steamer) were replaced by mass forms of transport. What this example also shows is that transport is a vital facilitator of tourism: it enables the tourist to travel from their home area (origin) to their destination and to return. This tourist trip has a reciprocal or two-way element: the tourist travels out on a mode of transport and then returns at a set period of time later. These simple principles of tourist travel which were introduced in Chapter 1 are reiterated here so that they can be used as a basis to differentiate different forms of tourist travel.

In the example shown in Figure 4.2, the tourist travels on a number of different forms of transport from the origin to destination area. Conventionally, each element of travel has been viewed as a passive element, as a means to an end (reaching the destination area). However, this is now very outdated. Travellers often have unrealistic expectations of transport providers, especially budget travellers who expect the standards of provision and customer care offered by full-price well-known airline brands when delays or operational problems occur. This is emphasized in the following extract:

> the purchaser of the tourism product (*the tourist*) must experience the trip to access the product, the quality of the transportation experience becomes an important

aspect of the tourist experience and, therefore a key criterion that enters into destination choice. Poor service, scheduling problems, and/or long delays associated with a transportation service, for example, can seriously affect a traveller's perceptions and levels of enjoyment with respect to a trip. Tourists require safe, comfortable, affordable, and efficient intermodal transportation networks that enable precious vacation periods to be enjoyed to their maximum potential.

(Lamb and Davidson 1996: 264–265)

It also illustrates the interrelationships between transport and tourism where four main elements exist:

1 the tourist
2 the relationship between transport and the tourist experience
3 the effect of transport problems on the tourist's perception
4 the tourist's requirement for safe, reliable and efficient modes of transport.

Transport, tourism and the tour

The mode of transport by which tourists seek to travel may be the main motivation for a holiday or the containing context of a holiday, and this is the case with a cruise or coach tour. In these examples, the basic element of tourism, the tour (which takes in a number of destinations on an itinerary) is followed. The basic principle of a tour is shown in Figure 4.3: the tourist travels to the point of departure, then boards the

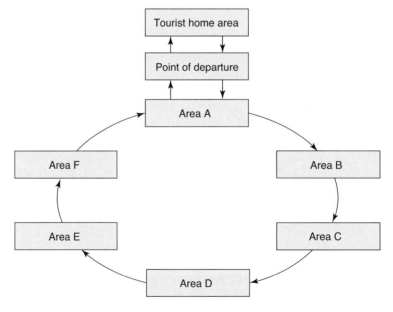

Figure 4.3
A tour with an itinerary, visiting different areas

Source: author

mode of transport (a coach or cruise ship) and engages in the tour, which follows a set route over a period of time. At each point of call (Areas A to F), the mode of transport may require an overnight stay on the mode of transport (the cruise ship) or in serviced accommodation, and time is made available for visiting attractions and for sightseeing. The coach or cruise then travels to the next area. Eventually the tour returns back to the point of departure and the tour is completed. In recent years, cruise companies have introduced the concept of fly-cruises to offer more compact, time-efficient cruises. Passengers fly to a point of departure where they undertake a cruise or part of a cruise before returning by ship or aircraft. At a less organized level, the principles of touring are inherent in the activities of holidaymakers who undertake domestic driving holidays or tours in their destination area. Within destinations, the distances tourists travel from their accommodation vary from very restricted to unrestricted patterns of movement, influenced by the availability of accommodation, the ease of access, their attitudes to travel and length of stay. In Figure 4.4, based on the movement patterns of visitors within Hong Kong, a variety of movement styles from the hotel exist, including cross-border trips into mainland China. The availability of attractions and tours clearly shapes the nature of the movement patterns, but what is clear is the diversity of movement styles, making generalizations difficult. Other research on tourist behaviour also suggests that, the longer visitors spend in a destination, the greater familiarity they develop and this encourages greater exploration, particularly away from the known tourist hot spots. The recent development of global positioning technology associated with mobile phones has also generated new opportunities to track tourists within destinations to better understand their behaviour, activities and time budgets so as to assess how much time they devote to specific activities such as shopping, sightseeing and visiting attractions, which has great value for tourism managers.

Therefore, transporting the tourist, the tour and travel in general are fundamental elements of the dynamic phenomenon known as tourism.

The movement of people, often in large volumes, requires specific managerial skills and an understanding of logistics – particularly of how the transport system and its different elements are managed. For the transport sector, managing the supply of transport so it meets demand and operates in an efficient, timely and convenient manner is an underlying feature for transporting tourists. For this reason, this chapter and Chapter 5 examine the transport sector and the principal modes of transport by land, water and air. In each case the management issues involving tourists will be highlighted and key concepts associated with each mode of transport. However, prior to discussing land-based transport it is useful to examine a number of concepts that are used in understanding how tourist transport is shaped by government.

Policy issues in tourist transport

Much of the provision of transport which tourists use is a direct response of private sector firms' desire to provide a service which is a profitable enterprise in its own right. Yet the provision of transport does not occur in an unconstrained market with no

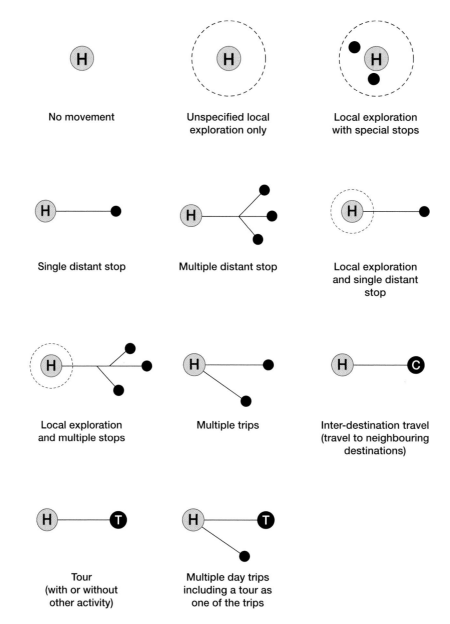

Figure 4.4
Movement styles

Source: McKercher, B. and Lau, G. (2008) Movement patterns of tourists within a destination. *Tourism Geographies*, 10(3): 355–374

controls or regulation. Whilst tourists may wish to travel and transport operators want to provide a service, governments develop policies and regulatory frameworks to facilitate, sometimes constrain, and manage transport provision. Governments may pursue policies that promote a high level of regulation or policies that promote total deregulation. For example, in a highly regulated environment, the government may operate its own airline (a 'flag carrier'), to promote tourism development in a country. In contrast, in a highly deregulated environment, the government may adopt a 'hands-off' approach, wanting competition and the market to determine what services are provided. Whilst policy objectives may set the direction the government wants to pursue, governments also have responsibility for the provision of infrastructure given the high capital costs of airports, ports and railways, roads, bridges and waterways. One example of this involvement is shown in Table 4.1 for Scotland, which has a devolved government for some transport issues. However, in recent years, governments have tried to defray these high capital costs by encouraging private sector investment and leasing the asset to the developer for 20–25 years so they recoup the cost plus a profit, then the asset returns to the state. These changing approaches to transport policy have followed distinct phases in countries such as the UK, where Button and Gillingwater (1983) identified four eras, each of which had a clear impact on tourism development and provision. A fifth era that has developed since the 1990s can also be discerned:

1   *the Railway Age*, from the 1840s onwards, during which private sector investment was employed to develop land-based transport (except during the First World War when state control was exercised)
2   *the Age of Protection*, which dominated the 1920s and 1930s when road transport emerged and unplanned car and coach travel developed. Governments intervened to prevent excessive competition, which in the USA led to the 1935 Motor Carriage Act that protected the Greyhound Bus Operators by giving this one operator a monopoly on inter-urban bus travel
3   *the Age of Administrative Planning* followed the Second World War, with the weaknesses exposed in railway companies leading to nationalization and a national passenger network to ensure national efficiency. The financial costs of large-scale nationalization led to major subsidies, which were restructured in the 1960s after the Beeching Report (the network was cut back considerably). In 1968, the Transport Act in the UK led to further reorganization of public transport with the creation of the National Bus Company (NBC)
4   *the Age of Contestability* characterized the USA in the 1970s and the UK in the 1980s. It was based on the principles of deregulation to achieve greater efficiency and to reduce public subsidies. In the UK, it led to the sale of state-owned assets (e.g. the sale of the NBC) and the establishment of private transport providers such as British Airways, Sealink Ferries and Stena, and, in the early 1990s, to the privatization of British Rail and UK airports (see Web Case 4.2).
5   *the Age of Public–Private Partnerships* has emerged in the UK since the Labour government entered power in the late 1990s. It has seen continuity with previous policies of privatization and a greater emphasis on private sector expertise to manage transport infrastructure. Concerns for efficiency and renewed investment in infrastructure have led to complex solutions to harness public–private partnerships in redeveloping aged infrastructure like the London Underground. Where the private sector assesses the risk of investment as not justified in terms of likely returns, the state has had to reinvest using taxpayers' funds. Where competition is seen as

beneficial, it is promoted, particularly in air travel. Even so, for the tourism sector there is a recognition that policy issues may be a key element of the drivers of change for transport and tourist travel. Scenario planning looking at transport and tourism in 2025 identified a range of policy issues for the national tourism organization (Visit Scotland). The relationship between transport and tourism, especially the potential for innovation in sustainability (see Page *et al.* 2010 for more detail), can be enhanced through the use of scenario planning to understand how changes in technology and new consumer preferences may encourage greener travel options in the future. This is a theme we return to later in the chapter in terms of new trends such as slow travel (see Innovation in Sustainability 4.1: Slow travel).

One additional level of policy measure that is important in Europe is the role of the European Union and its attempt to develop pan-European policies towards transport provision. EU states have been slow to engage in rail competition following EU Directive 91/440 in 1991 that sought to separate infrastructure from operations. Sweden initially separated its operations from infrastructure, followed by the UK and Germany in 1994. France established the RRF infrastructure authority in 1997 (although most of its

Table 4.1 The scope and extent of the Scottish Executive's* involvement in national transport planning and management in Scotland

- Aviation is a reserved issue for the UK government (though rail links serving airports are in the Scottish Executive's remit)
- ScotRail franchise, costing £250 million a year
- Network Rail in Scotland, £300 million a year
- Direct funding to vital air services (Barra, Campbeltown and Tiree to Glasgow) and operation of ten airports in the Highlands and Islands
- Ferry subsidies to the Northern Isles, Clyde and Hebrides services
- Provision of the Bus Operator Grant
- Encouraging 'Smarter Choices in Travel'
- International connectivity by air and the Air Route Development Fund, administered by Scottish Enterprise
- International connectivity by sea is a matter for the private sector
- Cross-border connectivity
  - advice to UK government on rail franchises
  - 148 short-haul flights per weekday Scotland to London, of which 98 are London–Edinburgh/Glasgow
  - promotion of rail as a more sustainable option and use of Air Route Development Fund to reduce reliance upon London-based connecting flights.

* In 2007 the Scottish Executive was renamed the Scottish Government

Source: adapted from Scottish Executive (2006) *Scotland's National Transport Strategy: A Consultative Summary*

responsibilities are delegated to SNCF) while the Netherlands implemented similar changes in July 2001, but poor management led to virtual re-nationalization.

To compete with air-based traffic and to address European air congestion, the EU proposed plans for a trans-European network (TENS) of high-speed road and rail links in Europe. The EU pointed to success in new high-speed operations (e.g. Spain's AVE route from Madrid to Seville saw the share of air traffic drop from 40 per cent to 13 per cent and the Paris–Brussels THALY service led to a 15 per cent drop in car usage), but these are the exception rather than the norm. These flagship projects are frequently used to justify additional investment, given that road and air congestion add 6 per cent to EU fuel consumption.

This discussion of policy issues illustrates that government policy can directly affect the supply of transport services in its use of regulation–deregulation measures. Notable entrepreneurs in the transport sector have responded to the opportunities afforded by transport policy changes (e.g. the deregulation of the bus industry and railway system after 1985) as the rise of Stagecoach as a global transport operator in the UK has shown (also see Case Study 4.1 on Megabus.com). The rise of Virgin and easyJet as transport brands has also followed a similar pattern. Policy changes such as deregulation have also altered the shape and nature of transport provision for tourists (as the discussion

Plate 4.1
Car parking at this beach resort illustrates the management issues associated with accommodating the impact of the car and domestic tourism

Source: author

CASE STUDY 4.1
INNOVATION IN COACH TRAVEL – STAGECOACH'S MEGABUS.COM

In August 2003, the UK's Stagecoach bus company launched a low-cost internet-booking coach service based on trips between the UK's main cities. Its dark blue vehicles proudly boasted single fares for £1.00 plus a booking fee (see Plate 4.2). By 2005, the Megabus network had developed a network of services covering 40 UK cities, with around 1.5 million passengers a year, and two-hourly services on major trunk routes (e.g. London–Birmingham) and lesser frequencies on longer distance routes (e.g. London–Aberdeen). By 2010, the network was carrying 2 million passengers a year and this had grown to 5 million passengers a year in 2013. This was the first major competition of any significance for the UK's National Express inter-city coach service which operates to 1200 possible pick-up/drop-off locations in the UK. The service is modelled on the low-cost airline model of ticketless travel, with seats being yield managed and cheaper fares for travellers the longer in advance they book. Fares are from £1 for a single ticket plus a 50 pence booking fee. They also offer integrated coach and rail services from the East Midlands on Megabus Plus routes where you catch a coach to East Midlands Parkway and a train to London (see Table 4.2 for a summary of the UK operations).

Interestingly, post-nationalization, around 80 per cent of National Express services are operated by contracted-out services and this is effectively a monopoly on long-distance coach travel (with a few notable exceptions). It was over 20 years ago that the National Express monopoly over long-distance coach travel was challenged by the ill-fated British Coachways Consortium of private operators. This group ran competing services on trunk routes between major cities, but lost considerable sums of money when National Express reduced its prices to undercut them (it was effectively being subsidized by the National Bus Company parent organization at the time). Since that time, there has been little national competition on the National Express network, with the exception of the impact of the low-cost airline market in seeking to attract price-sensitive travellers.

In contrast to British Coachways, Megabus.com has introduced sophisticated yield management systems like those used by airlines and railway companies with a strong brand and web presence (Plates 4.3 and 4.4). This allows the operator to price each seat according to demand and supply,

Table 4.2 Summary of megabus.com UK operations: Key highlights

- In 2003–2013, 30 million passengers carried on operations in UK and Europe, with 54 million miles travelled
- Megabus vehicles are 14 times more fuel efficient than an equivalent trip by car
- In 2013, 100 coaches were serving 60 towns and cities in the UK, with 5 million passengers carried annually
- New product innovations include:
   o megabusplus.com, a coach-rail integrated service linking London with the north of England
   o megagold, a new luxury brand daytime service linking Scotland and England with overnight services using convertible flatbeds, based on convertible leather seats (i.e. 55 daytime seats convert to 42 beds). The service is time competitive with sleeper train services between London and Scotland.

Source: Megabus

Plate 4.2
Advertisement for Megabus: Launch of Megabusplus.com

Source: Stagecoach

Plate 4.3 A Megabus vehicle

Source: Stagecoach

Plate 4.4 Booking online for Megabus

Source: Stagecoach

increasing the prices where demand is highest. Some of the lead-in fares of £1 have closely mirrored the promotional tools used by the low-cost airlines (Chapter 5). Online sales have also been complemented by a call centre for telephone bookings. The company initially invested £6.6 million in a fleet of luxury double-deckers to increase the comfort level on longer-distance routes with coaches serving other routes (Figure 4.5). In 2006, the company invested £11 million in 45 new 63-seater vehicles with air conditioning and other passenger comfort features. Business was helped in September 2005, following the London terrorist attack, by the provision of 100 000 free seats (booking fee only) to and from London, which was intended to boost leisure travel and to stimulate demand which was affected adversely by the terrorist event. Megabus has won innovation awards such as Transport Innovation of the Year at the UK's National Transport Awards and Scottish Transport Awards.

The Stagecoach parent company has acquired a 35 per cent share in its main Scottish rival – Citylink (the National Express equivalent), which carries around 3 million passengers a year to 200 destinations. This joint venture is expected to generate annual revenue of £18 million in the Scottish coach market. (However, in October 2006, the Competition Commission ruled that the Citylink and Megabus operations must be separated and operated as different companies.) The existing 65 per cent share of Scottish Citylink was retained by the parent company Comfort Delgro, which operates the Metroline bus services for Transport for London; Dublin's rail services (Aerdart); Comcab (a computerized taxi service in London with 3700 vehicles); SBS Transit in Singapore (a rail–bus operator); and Citylink coach services in Eire. The impact of Megabus.com has led other long-distance coach operators such as National Express to offer a similar priced product for travellers who book in advance – its Fun Fares – as a response to the competition. Fares are £1 to £10, with no booking fee on many routes. By 2008, easyBus has also begun to operate a limited number of services from north London (Hendon) to Milton Keynes for £1 to £5 fares. By 2010 the company was operating 15 full size easyBus coaches from Luton Airport to London for fares from £2 single if pre-booked in advance and 19 seater coaches from London to Heathrow and Gatwick Airport with £2 fares.

These developments in the coach market illustrate the importance of large transport integrated operators and new entrants with the investment power to add value to travel products through innovation and high specification vehicles globally. This is reflected in Stagecoach's announcement in October 2005 that it was to replicate the low-cost coach product with a trial of the low-cost train product – Megatrain.com. This, however, was equally problematic for the company as there were numerous regulatory obstacles which the company had to overcome. The company introduced the lead-in £1 fares on its South West Trains franchise between London, Portsmouth and Southampton. It offered 3000 off-peak seats a week (40 per departure) on the services provided on the new state-of-the-art Desiro trains. The scheme overcame government regulations (in the Ticketing and Settlement Agreement), after the 34-week trial period, to stimulate a low-cost revolution on the rail franchises it holds, thereby filling off-peak capacity and improving revenue generation. By 2010, Megatrain.com was offering £1 fares to 30 locations in the UK on the three rail franchises it was involved with. In April 2006, Megabus also commenced operation in the USA, initially between Chicago and Midwest states with advance booking from US$1 a seat. Between April 2006 and August 2007, Megabus in the USA carried 500 000 passengers between 20 cities (Plate 4.7). By 2010, the company was operating services to 32 locations in the USA and had carried 5 million passengers since the service's inception. These new initiatives not only mirror some of the

Plate 4.5 Megabus gold service in the UK

Source: Stagecoach

Plate 4.6 Megabus sleeper interior

Source: Stagecoach

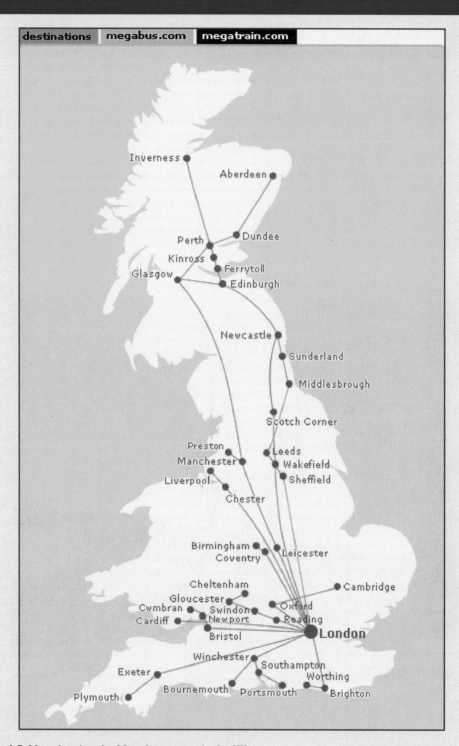

Figure 4.5 Map showing the Megabus routes in the UK

Source: Megabus

Table 4.3 Summary of Megabus North American operations: Key highlights

- Since 2006, 25 million passengers carried
- The services operate in 30 US states and 2 provinces of Canada
- Some 120 destinations served and 200 000 trips per annum made
- The company has created 1000 jobs since it was established
- It operates a fleet of 81 double-decker coaches
- In terms of carbon savings, two double-decker coaches can carry as many passengers as three conventional coaches
- The company is credited with reviving the declining long-distance coach market in the USA, with rates of growth of 5 to 7 per cent per annum, described as 'the megabus effect'.

Source: Megabus

Plate 4.7 Megabus USA in Dallas   Source: Stagecoach

trends in the low-cost airlines market, they also mark a major step forward in terms of innovation in generating demand for land-based travel at a time when concerns about the environmental costs of low-cost air travel are growing. In 2006, Stagecoach (the Megabus parent company) reported the findings of its evaluation of the environmental effects of low-cost easyJet flights compared to Megabus departures. It found that Megabus coaches were, on average, six times more fuel efficient than easyJet flights, with seven times less CO_2 emissions per passenger. The company has won many environmental awards and it demonstrates how the coaches it uses emit 60 per cent less CO_2 than a car. The company has also launched services in Canada with an initial $16 million investment in 15 top of the range environmentally friendly double-decker coaches built in Belgium by Van Hool. The coaches contain free WiFi, reclining seats, safety belts, reading lights, DVD and eight channel CD capabilities.

Stagecoach has been heralded as a major operator seeking to also move passengers from car-based travel to public transport modes, with improved marketing, information and initiatives encouraging a reduction in car use and also winning many public transport awards for its innovative approach to road travel.

of air transport in Chapter 5 shows). In some cases deregulation has increased choice; in other instances an initial increase in choice has been followed by consolidation that has actually reduced choice. Recognizing the linkages between transport and tourism can also yield invaluable business opportunities.

Land-based transport

Land-based transport is often neglected in discussions of transport and tourism, and yet it forms the dominant mode of travel for many domestic tourist trips. Air travel normally attracts more attention due to the scale and pace of development in this market since the early 1970s. However, land-based transport has a long history and covers a number of distinct motorized forms: the car, bus and coach travel and rail travel as well non-motorized forms (e.g. walking and cycling). Regions and countries should consider the concept of seamless transport systems for tourists. This means that the individual transport networks that exist for each mode of tourist transport need to be planned and integrated into a holistic framework. This will ensure that the tourist's experience of transport is a continuous one which is not characterized by major gaps in provision and a lack of integration (e.g. airports need to be linked to tourist districts so that visitors transfer from one mode of transport to another with relative ease). In countries which have a large land mass, such as Australia (see Figure 4.6) land-based transport offers a complementary mode of transport to the comprehensive network of internal air services. Land-based travel by car offers the opportunity to explore the iconic attractions in the outback such as Uluru (Ayers Rock).

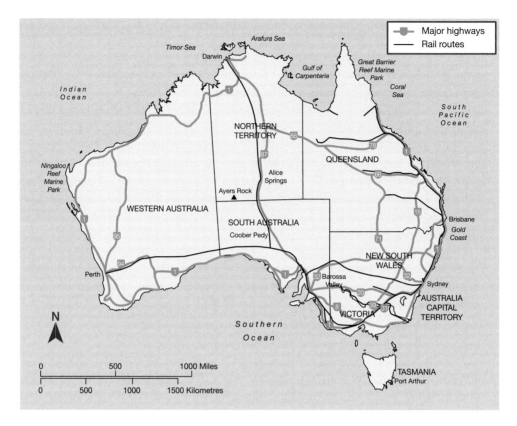

Figure 4.6
Land-based transport infrastructure in Australia

Source: Shackley (2006)

The car and tourist travel

In the post-war period, the growth of car ownership has made tourist travel more flexible but it has also induced overuse at accessible sites. Ease of access, fuelled by a growth in road building and the upgrading of minor roads in many developed countries, has been a self-reinforcing process, leading to overuse and a greater dominance of passive recreational activities. Car ownership expanded rapidly in most countries in the 1970s and 1980s, adding pressure to the road network especially at holiday times (e.g. the August holiday exodus from Paris to holiday destinations). Among the key factors which affect the use of roads by tourists are access, the quality of the infrastructure, grades of road and signage to steer tourists to tour areas, which may be off the beaten track. Intermodal connections (i.e. connections between different modes of transport) between airports, ports and rail termini and tourist areas are also important. There is also recognition that tourist areas need to develop new linear land and water corridors that integrate various forms of transport to explore scenic regions.

Probably the most influential study of car usage among recreationalists was Wall's (1971) study of Kingston-upon-Hull in the UK (also see Table 4.4 for other key studies).

Table 4.4 Key studies in car-based tourism

The main text by Page (2009) provides a synthesis of the literature on car-based tourism, which is an underdeveloped area of research, and some of the major research studies to consult are:

Study	Contribution
Cullinane, S. and Cullinane, K. (1999) Attitudes towards traffic problems and public transport in the Dartmoor and Lake District National Parks. *Journal of Transport Geography*, 7(1): 79–87.	Car drivers' attitudes towards congestion and problems in National Parks
Beunen, B., Jaarsma, C. and Regnerus, H. (2006) Evaluating the effects of parking policy measures in nature areas. *Journal of Transport Geography*, 14(3): 376–383.	Use of policy measures to address issues of car-based congestion in natural areas
Beunen, R., Regnerus H. and Jaarsma, C. (2007) Gateways as a means of visitor management in national parks and protected areas. *Tourism Management*, 29(1): 138–145.	Use of gateways as a method of reducing congestion at other areas in National Parks
Connell, J. and Page, S. J. (2008) Exploring the spatial patterns of car-based tourist travel in Loch Lomond and Trossachs National Park, Scotland. *Tourism Management*, 29(3): 561–580.	A unique study using Geographical Information System technology to map tourist car-based itineraries to develop a plan for car-based tourists in a National Park
Dickinson, J. and Robbins, D. (2008) Representations of tourism transport problems in a rural destination. *Tourism Management*, 29(6): 1110–1121.	Analysis of tourist transport issues in a rural environment
Prideaux, B. and Carson, D. (eds) (2011) *Drive Tourism: Trends and Emerging Markets*. London: Routledge.	Overview and set of chapters on the global growth of car-based tourism

It highlighted the importance of seasonality and the timing of pleasure trips by car and the dominance of the car as a mode of transport for urban dwellers. It also considered the role of the journey by car as a form of recreation in itself; the car is more than just a means of transport. Wall also found that the majority of pleasure trips were day trips less than 100 km away from Hull, being concentrated in a limited number of resorts along the Yorkshire coast and southerly part of the region. This is broadly similar to many leisure trips by car today. In the EU, over 4.4 billion passenger kilometres a year were travelled by car. The numbers were led by Germany which had a 19 per cent share of all such journeys followed by France, Italy and the UK. This reflects the dominant position of these car-owning countries and the general increase in the EU's road network from 3.9 million km in 1990 to 4.82 million km.

Eaton and Holding (1996) identified the growing scale of such visits to the countryside by visitors in cars. In 1991, 103 million visits were made to National Parks in the UK (Countryside Commission 1992), the most popular being the Lake District and Peak District Parks. It was estimated in 1992 that car traffic would grow by 267 per cent by the year 2025. Rising car usage has coincided with the decline in public transport usage for tourist and recreational trips. Yet many National Parks seem unlikely to be able to cope with the levels of usage predicted by 2025, given their urban catchments and the relative accessibility by motorway and A roads in the UK. Eaton and Holding (1996) reviewed the absence of effective policies to meet the practical problems of congestion facing many sites in the countryside in Britain. This situation is little different over two decades later, with many National Parks besieged by cars in the peak season – which seems to be at odds with the conservation goals intended when National Parks were initially conceived. This problem is worse when looking at visitors and their cars concentrated at 'honey pots' (locations which attract large numbers in a confined area) in National Parks. Research by Connell and Page (2008) reaffirmed many of these issues in Scotland's first National Park, created in 2001, the Loch Lomond and Trossachs National Park. By understanding the types of itinerary the visitors undertook by car within the National Park, it was possible to identify where the key 'honey pots' were and the implications for managing these sites and car use.

The UK Tourism Society's response to the Government Taskforce on Tourism and the Environment (English Tourist Board/Employment Department 1991) highlighted the impact of the car by commenting that

> no analysis of the relationship between tourism and the environment can ignore transportation. Tourism is inconceivable without it. Throughout Europe some 40 per cent of leisure time away from home is spent travelling, and the vast majority of this is by car . . . Approaching 30 per cent of the UK's energy requirements go on transportation . . . [and] . . . the impact of traffic congestion, noise and air pollution . . . [will] . . . diminish the quality of the experience for visitors.

A number of sensitive areas, including Yosemite National Park in the USA, have had to develop management plans to control the impact of the car. Yosemite had allowed access by car since 1917, but by the 1920s it was handling 1 million vehicle movements a year and over 3 million by the 1950s. The 1980 and 2000 Final Yosemite Valley Plan introduced out-of-park car parks and a shuttle bus for peak periods as management tools.

One additional area that is worthy of discussion in terms of road transport is the car hire industry. This is neglected in many studies of tourism and transport, and yet it is a major driver of car-based activity. The car hire business can be divided into three distinct segments:

1   airport rentals, which often command a 15 per cent premium charge over and above other rentals due to the charges imposed by airport authorities. These are based on the principle that this is a captive market which is able to pay the price demanded. This may be the case for corporate travel, where such prices have been discounted on the basis of volume of business, but leisure travellers pay premium prices
2   downtown rental locations
3   replacement vehicles for corporates and individuals whose cars are off the road being repaired or serviced.

In Europe the car hire business is dominated by the main brands, which also dominate the US market: Avis, Budget, National (formed from Eurodollar and Alamo) and Hertz.

The scale of the industry is illustrated by two of the market leaders: Avis, which has a fleet of over 80 000 vehicles in Europe, and Hertz, with 7000 rental locations worldwide. The traditional ownership patterns in which car manufacturers were key stakeholders have changed as manufacturers have reduced their involvement. Many car hire companies have looked at leasing vehicles rather than purchasing now that second-hand car values have dropped in Europe due to oversupply of new vehicles. The cost of car hire for tourists varies considerably by country, reflecting tax regimes and other local factors. In Europe, Finland is the most expensive, being 48 per cent dearer than the cheapest rental costs in Belgium and Luxembourg. In the USA, the car rental market is worth in excess of US$16.5 billion. The market sustains varying pricing strategies, a feature observed by the American Automobile Association in 2002 when they noted that hire car rates in the same city could vary between 18 and 190 per cent for the same product. Typically, rates varied around 77 per cent, with the greatest variations in key tourist destinations in states such as California and Nevada. Unsurprisingly a common complaint amongst car hirers is that hidden charges and a lack of transparency dominate the retailing of this product. Overall the most lucrative markets for car rental are France, Germany, Italy, Spain and the UK, which reflects the domestic and international tourism markets in each country, which dominate patterns of tourism in Europe.

Cycling

Bicycles are used by tourists either occasionally by those visiting a destination, who may hire a cycle for a day, or for long-distance cycling holidays undertaken by the more determined. In the USA, bicycle tourism can be dated to the 1890s when this mode of recreational transport became extremely popular, given the freedom it provided on the evolving road network. In Europe, cycling is the main mode of daily transport for 31 per cent of people in the Netherlands compared to 7 per cent of the population in the EU and 2 per cent in the UK. Lumsdon (1996: 5) defines cycle tourism as cycling that is 'part of or the primary activity of, a holiday trip . . . it falls within a categorization of activity holidays'. The UK Department of Transport statistics suggest that up to 40 per cent of cycle journeys are for leisure purposes:

> Leisure cycling has great potential for growth, it can be a stimulus to tourism, it is a high-quality way to enjoy the countryside and a good way to introduce people to cycling for their everyday transport needs. To encourage leisure cycling there needs to be small scale improvements, especially near where people live, followed by better signposting, marketing and information. Flagship leisure routes, using quiet roads or disused railway paths, can increase the profile and boost leisure cycling in town and countryside.
>
> (Department of Transport 1996: 13, cited in Lumsdon 1997: 115)

But who are the typical cycle tourists and what motivates them to use this form of transport? The Scottish Tourist Board's (1991) innovative study on the *Tourism Potential of Cycling and Cycle Routes in Scotland* indicated that cycling had grown in popularity as a recreational activity in the 1970s and 1980s, with the Cyclists Tourist Club having

40 000 members in the UK. A later study by the Countryside Commission (1995), *The Market for Recreational Cycling in the Countryside*, identified some of the main motivations for cycling, including:

- keeping fit
- having fun
- getting some fresh air
- accessing the countryside.

In a tourism context, Lumsdon's (1996) study simplifies the market segments involved in cycle tourism to include:

- *holiday cyclists*, comprising couples, families or friends who seek a holiday where they can enjoy opportunities to cycle but not necessarily every day. They seek traffic-free routes and are independent travellers who are not interested in a package holiday. While they are likely to take their own bikes on holiday, a proportion of them will hire bikes. They are likely to cycle 25–40 km each day that they travel by bike
- *short-break cyclists*, who seek to escape and select packages that will provide local knowledge (with or without cycle hire) and comfortable accommodation. They are likely to travel in groups and to cycle 25–40 km a day
- *day excursionists*, who are casual cyclists who undertake leisurely circular rides of 15–25 km. They are not prepared to travel long distances to visit attractions or facilities but prefer to seek quiet country lanes, which are signposted. They tend to comprise 25–30 per cent of the market for cycling and are increasingly using their own bikes rather than hiring them.

The Royal Commission on Environmental Pollution (HMSO 1994) identified the role of cycling as a mode of personal transport that is sustainable and has minimal pollution and effects on others. It recommended that cycle trips should be quadrupled to 10 per cent of all journeys in the UK by 2005, highlighting the need for further infrastructure to achieve such growth targets. By 2004 SUSTRANS, the National Cycle Network (NCN) that has promoted cycle routes, found that 201 million trips a year were being made on the NCN and that 60 million of these were on traffic-free components of the NCN. The impact of new trends such as slow travel (see Chapter 1) illustrate the significance of cycling as a means of developing tourism at a slower pace for visitors (see Dickinson and Lumsdon 2010).

The UK's national cycle network

SUSTRANS is a national sustainable transport and construction company operating as a charity that designs and builds routes. One of its early aims was to develop a 2000-mile national cycle network to link all the main urban centres in the UK, using a combination of traffic-calmed roads, cycle paths, disused railway lines and river/canal paths. This aim was realized in 1996 via a grant of £43.5 million from the Millennium

Commission (comprising 20 per cent of the total cost) to form a 10 400-km route on the basis of its original vision. This was the UK's National Cycle Network. By 2005 it had achieved its ambitious target to expand to 16 000 km and it now stretches to 22 500 km. In 2000, over 23.5 million cycling trips were made on the network rising to 77 million in 2004 and the rise in cycling saw 386 million cycle and walking trips made in 2008. By 2013 this had reached 486 million trips. Estimates seem to indicate that the network has the potential to generate 750 million cycling and walking trips per annum by 2015. SUSTRANS (2002) argues that the network generates £635 million from cycle tourism, with the following economic impacts:

- £146 per domestic trip (based on expenditure of £30–£35 a night)
- £300 per overseas cycling holiday trip
- £9 per trip for each cycling day trip
- £4 per local leisure cycling trip.

A SUSTRANS report (Transform Scotland 2013) on the value of cycle tourism in Scotland found that cycle tourism contributed between £106 to £228 million for the economy, which rises if the economic value of mountain biking is added.

Indeed the UK Leisure Day Visits Survey in the UK recognized that the average cycle day trip comprises 62.9 km in length, 3.6 hours in duration and with a party size of 4.6.

The market segments for cycle tourism trips identified by SUSTRANS (2002) comprised:

- infrequent leisure cyclists
- occasional leisure cyclists
- frequent leisure cyclists
- cycling enthusiasts.

Each of these has specific product requirements as Table 4.5 shows.

The C2C cycle route is indicative of the generative effect it may have. The C2C route is a 270-km coast-to-coast route in northern England which attracts over 10 000 cycle tourists to an economically marginal area (West Cumbria and the North Pennines). This has generated an annual expenditure of £100 per person and £1.1 million for the local tourism economy. A subsequent study in 2006 of the four long-distance cycle routes in north-east England found that they directly contributed £9.6 million to the local economy and up to £13.4 million to the wider economy. This reflects the importance of public–private partnerships brokered by SUSTRANS such as the £20 million investment in the Valleys Cycle Network in South Wales to connect towns, employment, visitor attractions and green spaces.

There is also a European Cycle Route Network and some of the principal routes are:

- the 5000-km Atlantis route (Isle of Skye, Scotland, to Cadiz, Spain)
- the 470-km Noordzee route (Den Helder in the Netherlands to Boulogne-sur-Mer in France).

Table 4.5 Cycle tourism market segments and product requirements

Market segment	Types of activity required	Product requirements
Infrequent leisure cyclists	• Traffic-free cycling • Packaged cycle touring holidays	• Traffic-free cycle paths • Cycle hire • Packaged cycling holidays
Occasional leisure cyclists	• Day cycle rides (20–25 miles on quiet country roads and traffic-free paths) • Centre-based cycling short breaks • Access to countryside from town and home	• Circular day cycle routes with maps and information • Safe places to leave the car while cycling • Ideas for cycling short breaks • Cycle parking and storage • Cycle repair/rescue
Frequent leisure cyclists	• Day cycle rides (30–35 miles on quiet country roads and traffic-free paths) • Centre-based cycling short breaks • Access to countryside from town and home	• Circular day cycle routes with maps • Safe places to leave the car while cycling • Cycle access by train (for some) • Ideas for cycling short breaks and cycle touring holidays • Cycle friendly accommodation • Cycle parking and storage • Cycle repair/rescue
Cycling enthusiasts	• Day cycle rides (up to 40–50 miles primarily on quiet country roads) • Independent cycle touring holidays and short breaks • Access to countryside from town and home	• Ideas for day cycle rides – cycling enthusiasts tend to plan their own rides, using cycle route leaflets for ideas and information • Cycle access by train (generally more important for cycling enthusiasts than for other market segments) • Cycle friendly accommodation • Cycle parking and storage • Cycle repair

Source: Lumsdon (1996)

In addition, Eurovelo (a project of the European Cyclists Federation) developed 14 long-distance cycle routes in Europe which are 45 000 km currently and expected to grow to 70 000 km by 2020.

According to Lumsdon (1996: 10–12), there are three ways that the National Cycle Network may contribute to sustainable tourism (i.e. tourism which does not further damage or harm the resource base upon which it depends):

1 by encouraging tourists to switch from cars to cycles at their destination. This could reduce recreational car journeys at the destination by 20–30 per cent

2 by reducing car-based day excursions, particularly at 'honey pot' attractions or sites near to resorts and urban areas. The National Cycle Network may offer 'escape routes' to allow tourists to get off the beaten track

3   by encouraging growth in cycle-based holidays, in both the short-break and longer
     duration categories.

Cycle tourism is certainly beginning to assume a much higher profile in the UK and their
use for leisure encourages people to become more avid cyclists and to reduce car usage.
Therefore, cycling can potentially make a major contribution to switching to more
sustainable tourist and commuter use of transport.

Cycling offers an opportunity to savour one's environment and surroundings and
this is part of a new philosophy – slow travel (see Innovation in Sustainability 4.1).

INNOVATION IN SUSTAINABILITY 4.1
SLOW TRAVEL

The development of mass tourism has largely been based on a high carbon-use culture where
consumptive behaviour linked to flying and car patronage has been the norm. A philosophical shift
in consumer thinking is required to encourage behaviour change away from high carbon travel; this
has been marked by the rise of the term 'slow travel'. As Dickinson and Lumsdon (2010) illustrate,
slow travel is a throwback to travel in past times when travel was slow and people engaged with the
communities and environments they visited. The notion of slow travel has seen its growth in parallel
with other similar trends in food consumption, with slow food a reaction to the fast food culture of
the late twentieth century. The notion was also popularized at a city-destination level by the Cittaslow
(Slow City) movement based on three underpinning concepts:

•   do things at the right speed
•   adapt one's attitude towards time and one's use of it
•   the pursuit of quality over quantity.

The slow travel concept has become associated with lower carbon use (i.e. avoiding flights and car
use) and a shift towards overnight train travel and cycle trips, as well as home stays. Although various
definitions and approaches to characterize slow travel have emerged, the optimum mode of travel
is non-motorized, being 'slow' in duration and far less intensive and environmentally damaging. As
a result, this renders the economic principles of transport being related to time savings to get from
A to B in the fastest manner redundant. In conventional models of economic development, travel
cost/time were fundamental to destination development and linked to market size, accessibility and
cost; with slow tourism, these issues are not important, as the time-travel cost becomes less significant.

A wide range of slow travel websites have developed where more carbon-neutral options (i.e.
walking and cycling) challenge the carbon-intensive paradigms of mass tourist travel that have
dominated since the mid-nineteenth century (see Chapter 2). As existing studies argue, slow travel
needs to be framed, as Figure 4.7 suggests, in a holistic framework whereby three key elements
exist: the content, the ingredients and the outcome. What is evident from existing studies is that slow
travellers can be understood on a continuum ranging from hard slow travellers (i.e. the environmental
motivations and lifestyle factors shape their choice of slow travel) to 'soft slow travellers' who are

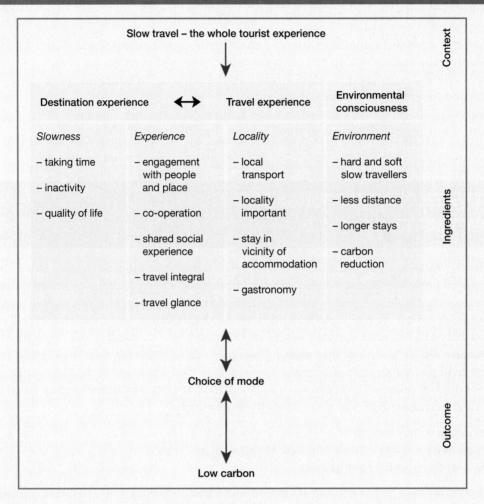

Figure 4.7
Slow travel – the whole tourist experience

Source: Dickinson, J., Lumsdon, L. and Robbins, D. (2011) Slow travel: Issues for tourism and climate change. *Journal of Sustainable Tourism*, 19(3): 294, reprinted by permission of Taylor & Francis

environmentally aware, but continue to fly to the destination to engage in a slow travel holiday. It is clear that the greater engagement in slow travel needs policies and infrastructure to break the inertia of modern-day carbon-intensive travel, thereby popularizing the notion of slowness as a key to relaxing, having fun, achieving one's holiday objectives and enjoying oneself in a responsible and sustainable manner.

Further reading

Dickinson, J. and Lumsdon, L. (2012) *Slow Travel*. London: Earthscan.

Kieran, D. (2012) *The Idle Traveller: The Art of Slow Travel*. London: Automobile Association.

Coach and bus travel

Bus and coach travel assumed a growing significance in the 1930s in most countries (see Chapter 2). There is a tendency to interchange the terms 'bus' and 'coach' which may create confusion and complexity. Bus travel usually refers to a specific form of urban and rural passenger transport which tourists may use at the destination they are staying at. In the UK, a bus trip is defined as a 24-km or less trip, with coach travel replacing that travel over 24 km. In other European countries, specific terms (such as the Autocar in France) distinguish coach travel from bus travel. However, such a definition does not distinguish between the market for international and domestic coach services. The European Conference of Ministers of Transport (1987) classifies the international coach travel market in terms of three categories of service (scheduled, shuttle and occasional services):

- *scheduled services* (lines). These services transport passengers at specified times, often based on a timetable, over specified routes. They involve the picking up and setting down of passengers at established stops. Such services are provided under a licence for a prescribed period for which the service is offered. Timetables, tariffs and the vehicles to be used are also specified and particular conditions are attached to the service provided, such as the pan-European Eurolines service. These services are sometimes called 'express coach services' and are operated by consortia of companies or individual operators
- *shuttle services*. These consist of trips transporting groups of tourists or individuals from the same point of departure to the same destination. Later the traveller will be transported back to the original departure point and the service usually involves accommodation for the group at the destination. The service must comply with the conditions of an itinerary and length of stay, and no passengers are carried on the last outward or first inward journey. These services are often referred to 'holiday shuttles'
- *occasional services*. These include a range of different services such as:
  o closed-door tours (one vehicle is used throughout the journey for the same group and the tour returns to the original point of departure), often referred to as 'continental coach holidays' or 'continental coach tours'
  o services with the return trip unladen
  o all other services (e.g. day excursions, private hire, tours, airport shuttles, urban excursions such as hop-on-hop-off all-day ticketed tours).

In the UK, the coach tourism holiday market is estimated to be worth £2–4 billion a year, with 11 million holidays sold. Shearings (prior to the Wallace Arnold merger) had a 14 per cent share of the market and in 2007 it dropped the Wallace Arnold brand and operated 44 hotels under its own name. The majority of these holidays are still sold through travel agents.

The market segments to which coach travel appeals is far from homogenous, and ranges from the 'youth travel market' for express domestic and continental services to the elderly markets which dominate coach tours. In 2005, Shearings' in-house research found that 89 per cent of its clients booked six or more holidays a year, which illustrates the significance of the elderly market. Coach travel has an image that appeals to low-income groups and of being a slow mode of surface transport. Even so, the scale of coach travel on express services was such that London's Victoria coach station handles over 9 million passengers a year. In recent years, a number of new trends have come to dominate coach travel including the rise of the multimodal operator such as Stagecoach, which has global coach and bus operations and operates over 28 000 vehicles.

There is a tendency to underplay the role of local bus services and urban services in the tourism industry; tourists may use these when staying in a destination (see Lumsdon 2006). Lumsdon's study highlights the neglect by tourists of use of the bus and the dominance of the car. For example, in the UK access to a car increased from 14 per cent of householders in 1951 to 75 per cent in 2012. To redress the shift to the car, Lumsdon developed a model (Figure 4.8) which outlines the key stages that tourism and transport planners need to follow to design bus services for greater tourist use. As Figure 4.8 shows, the existing network and goals of a network for tourist use need to be identified.

This may require augmenting the existing network (i.e. redesigning it) to create an experience to engage tourists, including integration with other transport modes. The designed network needs to be expressed as a service which is then marketed/branded, and the service then needs to be delivered. The resulting service and its success/failure need to be measured against the initial goals to understand how to refine the service further to meet users' expectations (also see Innovation in Sustainability 11.1 on the exemplar of tourist bus service development in the New Forest National Park).

In the UK, the bus industry is largely controlled (post-deregulation in 1985, when the National Bus Company was sold off as 70 units for £1 billion), by five major organizations that have a turnover of £3.3 billion. In 1990, these groups had 5 per cent of the market and this grew to 66.5 per cent in 2002 as a process of consolidation occurred. The ownership pattern is dominated by First Group; Stagecoach; Arriva; Go-ahead; National Express; the rest of the market was accounted for by small operators and the public sector.

In Europe, patterns of bus and coach travel based on express services tend to be point to point (i.e. city to city) or city to city via non-urban areas terminating at a major coach terminus, many of which date to the 1930s when the market first developed. They tend to use major transport corridors (i.e. motorways) wherever possible to gain economies in travel time so that they are price and time competitive with rail travel. In contrast, coach tours, particularly packaged tours, have a tendency to follow what are called 'milk runs': they follow a set itinerary to showcase the main attractions. In the UK, milk runs with a strong heritage appeal might typically depart from London, visit Oxford, Stratford-upon-Avon, Bath, Chester, the Lake District and Scotland, and return on the east coast via York and Cambridge to London, depending on the length of the tour.

Coach tourism in the UK generated £153 million for the UK economy (an average of £219 per trip and £57 per night). Of this, £28 million was contributed by overseas coach trips to the UK.

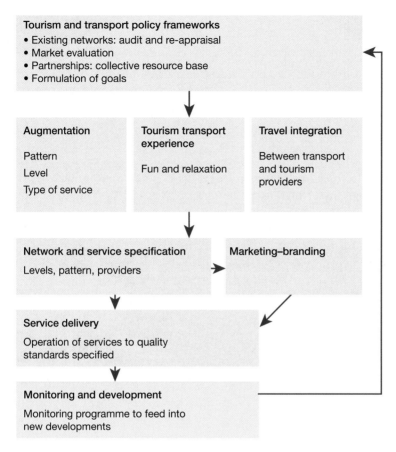

Figure 4.8
Bus services

Source: Lumsdon (2006: 762)

According to the North West Regional Development Agency (NWRDA) study in 2008 on coach tourism in England's north-west, the coach market was predominantly based upon 60- to 70-year-old travellers who:

- took 2 million trips a year to the region
- spent £120 million a year as a result of coach tourism in the region
- accounted for around 1:20 of all domestic staying trips in north-west England
- visited two dominant locations: Blackpool (50 per cent) and the Lake District (30 per cent).

The market has seen increased pressure from low-cost airlines although the luxury end of the market still has considerable potential for growth along with special interest tours (e.g. seeing behind the film set of a popular drama series). Combined with forecasts of an ageing population, the NWRDA report suggests this may be an opportunity for the coach market along with the increasing investment in higher-specification vehicles.

Plate 4.8
Eden Project, Cornwall
Source: author

The structure, organization and management of coach and bus operations in each country is specifically shaped by the history, regulations and policies towards transport, and by a strong tradition of visiting established destinations – except where a major draw such as the Eden Project in Cornwall (see Plate 4.8) or new attractions in cities act as a hub for day excursions or visits.

Rail travel

Globally, railways are a major mode of moving tourists and leisure trippers around countries and between countries. In the USA, rail travel has the smallest proportion of passengers carried on any mode of transport (0.3 per cent), since the car dominates (with 85 per cent of passenger kilometres) followed by air travel (10 per cent) and coach (3.1 per cent). In Europe, rail travel has a 6.5 per cent share of passenger trips, higher than air travel, although passenger cars account for nearly 85 per cent of trips followed by bus and coach travel (8.6 per cent). In Europe, railways are a major business with a 75 billion euro turnover per annum, employing 1 million people. The role of rail in European passenger traffic has slipped from its 10 per cent share of traffic in 1970 to around 6 per cent in 2002 and remained static thereafter. At the same time, state subsidies for rail have grown, with the EU railway system costing taxpayers over 35 billion euros annually in grants for infrastructure projects and support.

With increasing congestion on many of the developed countries' road and air networks, rail travel has a number of natural advantages over competing modes of transport. The convenience of rail travel for short- to long-distance trips from one city centre to another remains. In a European context, rail travel fulfils a wide range of functions for travellers as it is convenient for daily commuting needs, business trips and recreational travel. Three specific types of recreational rail user can be discerned within Europe: day-trippers, domestic tourists and international tourists who use rail travel as part of their itinerary to visit visitor destinations.

Much of the growth in European rail travel has been in the high-speed rail services but they only carry 13 per cent of all European rail passengers. The use of rail in relation to tourism and leisure travel occurs under a number of journey types, with a combination of types in the typical tourism and leisure journey:

• the use of dedicated rail corridors which connect major gateways (airports and ports) of a country to the final destination, or as a mode of transit to the tourist accommodation in the nearby city

Plate 4.9
Railways which offer a scenic journey, such as the St Ives Bay Line in Cornwall, can also be a tool for destination marketing and branding, as illustrated by the train advertising

Source: author

- the use of rapid transit systems and metros to travel within urban areas
- the use of high-speed and non-high-speed intercity rail corridors to facilitate movement as part of an itinerary or city-to-city journey, typically for business and leisure travel. These journeys may cross country borders, forming international networks
- the use of local rail services outside urban areas, often used in peak hours by commuters to journey to/from mainline/intercity rail terminals en route to other destinations
- the use of rail services in peripheral tourist destinations (e.g. the Caledonian Sleeper operated by the ScotRail franchise which serves the London to the Highlands of Scotland market) which sometimes have a scenic value as tourist journeys in their own right (e.g. the Central Otago, New Zealand, Taireri Gorge half-day rail tour or St Ives line (Plate 4.9))
- purpose-built rail excursions/holidays on historic services such as the Orient Express in Europe, the 1851-mile Ghan from Adelaide to Darwin in Australia that takes two days (see Figure 4.6). The most famous journey is probably the Trans-Siberian railway (Case Study 4.2).

CASE STUDY 4.2
TOURIST TRAVEL BY RAIL – THE TRANS-SIBERIAN RAILWAY

The Trans-Siberian railway (TSR) is by far the longest single rail route, covering a 9000-km route starting in European Russia and travelling eastwards, ending on the eastern coast of Vladivostok (Figure 4.9). The tourist rail journey travels through a series of time zones, crossing the mountain range – the Urals – to the Siberian 'taiga' landscape and steppes. The route has a long history, being constructed between 1891 and 1916 as the main method to transport troops to protect Russia's eastern territories at a time of territorial ambitions from other colonial powers. The tourist journey takes around six days, with various alternative routes now available after the route passes Siberia, with a route to Beijing via Mongolia (the Trans-Manchuria service); the Trans-Mongolian service from Moscow to Beijing travels through Ulaanbaatar and Mongolia and the Tran-Siberian proper follows the original Moscow to Vladivostok route. Many of the stations en route offer opportunities for sightseeing as well as periodic stops where local people and bazaars offer food and drink, complementing the on-board dining. Key destinations to visit en route include: Moscow, Lake Baikal, Ulaanbaatar, Terelj National Park, Beijing and Yekaterinburg. The main tourist season for travel is May to September, peaking around July, with many companies marketing a trip on the route as a trip of a lifetime. From a tourism development perspective the TSR offers important economic development opportunities for many of the remoter communities along the rail route in a post-communist era. Following the collapse of communism, many of the communities along the railway line have had to forge new economic development pathways now that they have the power to be self-determined regions and areas after the passing of centralized state control under the command economy model.

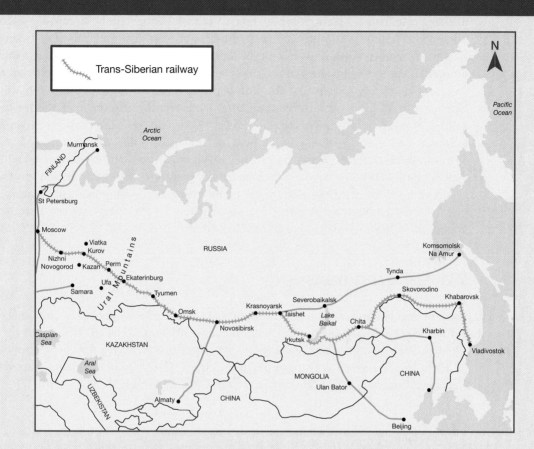

Figure 4.9 Trans-Siberian railway   Source: Shackley (2006)

Further reading

Shackley, M. (2006) *Atlas of Travel and Tourism Development*. Oxford: Butterworth-Heinemann.

It is clear that rail travel, aside from commuting, offers a wide range of options for tourist and leisure travel. In Europe rail continues to have a slow rate of overall growth compared to other modes of transport: at a pan-European level, rail travel is constantly outperformed by the increase in air and car-related travel of around 2–4 per cent per annum in the volume of passenger kilometres travelled.

Despite the declining importance of rail (excluding high-speed services), a wide range of issues have been suggested as important in trying to attract more tourists to use rail as a mode of travel. These include improved marketing to raise awareness of new services, better ticketing options such as through tickets and more seamless travel across rail networks, e-commerce, frequent traveller schemes and greater attention to service quality issues as well as addressing safety issues for passengers travelling alone. In addition, a wide range of business issues was highlighted for railway companies including broadening their distribution channels (e.g. in 2002, the Caledonian Sleeper adopted e-ticketing and paperless check-ins in line with innovations from the airline sector). Attempts to improve customer usability of rail services (e.g. simplification of ticketing systems to remove confusion over tickets and prices) have been proven to generate a substantial volume of business in their first year of operation. It is also notable that rail operators are slowly recognizing the link between transport and tourism, with value-for-money fares for leisure travel stimulated in Europe by the onset of the low-cost airlines. Physical improvements to the travel environment have also illustrated the need to invest in a better travelling environment for tourists with new rolling stock and state-of-the-art travel facilities. Virgin Trains' new service enhancements on trunk routes which include music channels, laptop sockets and the segregation of mobile phone users have now been mirrored in innovations by other rail companies. Developments in e-commerce such as the Trainline.com (in which Stagecoach has a controlling interest) have been important in making rail a more accessible option for travellers.

Water-based transport

The potential of water- or sea-based transport has been greatly overlooked in most analyses of tourism, largely because much attention has been given to the growth in tourism by air since 1945. Yet, prior to the development of rail and air travel, sea-based travel was of major importance in crossing water (e.g. ferries), for pleasure on inland waterways (e.g. canal boats) or as a mode of tourist travel (e.g. cruising) (see Plate 4.10).

Cruises

Many modern-day shipping companies such as P&O developed water-based transport as a means of travelling between continents, linking the UK with its empire in India and the Far East during the nineteenth century. In 1842, the P&O passenger ship *Hindustan* undertook its inaugural trip, stimulated by the company's contract to carry mail from Southampton to Calcutta. By 1844, P&O had also begun deep-sea cruises in the Mediterranean and in the late 1880s other companies (it was later to acquire) began cruises. For example, in 1886 the North of Scotland and Orkney and Shetland Company began cruises to the Norwegian fjords at a cost of £10, while in 1889 the Orient Line began cruises to Norway and the Mediterranean. By 1890, the P&O line had developed a global network of direct and connecting passenger services which remained largely unaltered (with the exception of the withdrawal of Indian services after that country's independence) up until the 1960s when air services began to challenge passenger liners. The 1920s and 1930s were the heydays of luxury cruise liners competing to be the fastest crossing across the Atlantic Ocean between Europe and North America. The era was characterized by the Art Deco movement, with luxurious fittings and glamour associated with cruise liners (see Plate 4.10). What is apparent from Figure 4.10 is the demand for business travel between the UK and its imperial territories. P&O became a global brand in the nineteenth century, much earlier than many of the marketing debates on the internationalization of the tourism industry

Plate 4.10 1920s cruise of the tropics organized by Thomas Cook

Source: Thomas Cook

in the 1960s, although monopoly contracts on mail services did help to support its expansion of the passenger routes. The company reconfigured its business activities after the development of passenger airliners. For example, in the 1970s P&O invested in its North American market and the growing demand for cruises as passenger liner business declined. In fact the company has a history of adapting to new business environments. For example, it adapted a ship no longer needed for mail services in 1904 for the cruise line Vectis: this was the first time it had developed a dedicated cruise liner that carried 160 first-class passengers in absolute luxury. Cruising is not a new concept, although it has certainly seen a revival at a global scale since the 1990s and has become a more popular activity, no longer just the pursuit of elderly customers or the rich which characterized its growth from the late nineteenth century. Globally, Peisley (2006) suggests the market has grown from 6 million passengers in 1995 to 16 million in 2007 and may rise to 34 million by 2015.

The industry organization in the USA, the Cruise Lines International Association (CLIA), represents members who offer around 95 per cent of the cruise capacity in North America. It has seen passenger sales rise from 3.6 million in 1990, to 5 million in 1997, 8.8 million in 2004 and 21 million in 2013. This, in part, reflects the growth in cruise ship capacity added by CLIA members who plan to introduce 24 ships in 2014–2015, a US$8 billion investment. The USA dominates world cruise line passenger volumes, followed by Europe.

At a global scale, three companies dominate the cruise market:

- Carnival (incorporating the Carnival Corporation and the former P&O Cruises)
- Royal Caribbean Cruises
- Star Cruises.

With many cruise ships now costing in excess of US$300 million and able to accommodate 2000–3000 passengers, capital costs for this area of tourist transport are massive. In fact the worldwide cruise ship business is worth over US$16 billion. Whilst much of the cruise business is focused on the Caribbean followed by Europe, the Far East has entered the market together with Australasian/Pacific island cruises, where Star Cruises has a market presence, challenging traditional patterns of cruises. The cruise line industry has been dominated by product innovations to attract a growing variety of passengers and the rise of luxury brands again in the market, akin to superyachts, are signalling a revival in cruising for the rich which characterized the heydays of the 1920s and 1930s.

Ferries

Ferries are more functional modes of tourist transport than cruise ships and are used to cross stretches of water. In the lead-up to the opening of the Channel Tunnel, many ferry operators attempted to market the UK's short-sea ferry crossing as cruises. In Europe, Dover and Calais are the two most important international passenger ports with 13.5 and 13 million passengers travelling through each. This is followed by travel over the Öresund between Sweden and Denmark. Much of the international maritime travel

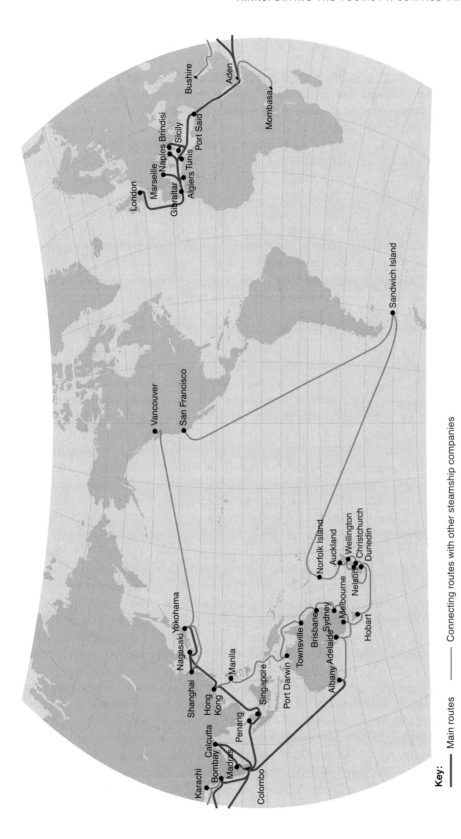

Key:

—— Main routes   —— Connecting routes with other steamship companies

Figure 4.10

Schematic diagram of the steamer routes operated by the Peninsular and Orient Steam Navigation Company in 1890

Source: redrawn and redesigned from Horwath and Horwath (1986) *The Story of P&O: The Peninsular and Oriental Steam Navigation Company.* London: Weidenfeld and Nicolson

in Europe is based on travel within the EU member countries. In reality, ferries offer travellers a different element in their holiday, trip or excursion and a time for rest, relaxation and a break from their main form of transport. One of the most frequently crossed waterways is the English Channel. The construction of the Channel Tunnel offered an all-weather mode of crossing this stretch of water yet, despite the concerns over the Channel Tunnel's impact on UK ferry services, passenger volumes through the Port of Dover have risen from 11 million in 1994 to 16.2 million in 2002. But since 2002, they have dropped to 13.5 million in 2009 and 12 million in 2013. At the same time, passenger volumes in the Channel Tunnel reached 18 million by 2013 as the volume of coaches dropped. These dropped from a peak of 165 000 a year in 1997 to 106 000 in 2006 and 81 000 in 2009. One consequence of the increased competition from the Channel Tunnel and low-cost airlines was the merger of the two Dover–France ferry companies, Stena Line and P&O Ferries. The major blow for the ferry companies was the loss of duty-free sales on board ferries in 1999, which had accounted for 65 per cent of profits from short-sea ferry routes. This gave an estimated loss of revenue of £350 million for UK–European services and led to price rises on fares of up to 40 per cent, which, together with rises in fuel costs, resulted in a drop in passenger volumes of between 16 and 20 per cent.

The majority of travellers travelling by ferry from the UK used short-sea routes across the English Channel (66 per cent), the Western Channel in southern/south western England/Irish Sea (25.8 per cent) and the North Sea (7.6 per cent) (see Figure 4.11).

A recent expansion of seasonal sea catamaran services has also provided more route options for passengers. In the short-sea sector, a number of smaller, peripheral ferry services from Sheerness, Folkestone and Ramsgate have been cut as the industry has focused operations in Dover. In addition, the company Hoverspeed withdrew its hovercraft services in September 2000 after 32 years of operation and then its catamaran service in 2005. The rapidly changing competitive environment has meant that tourism managers have had to carefully set out future strategies to ensure the viability of their business, and in some cases, operations were closed, rationalized, merged or sold. In 2004, P&O Stena Line further rationalized its UK fleet, operating 25 vessels to counter the drop in patronage due to low-cost airlines, and then closing 4 of its 13 routes after full-year losses of £40 million. Businesses have had to keep sight of their existing and future passengers via more active marketing campaigns to extol the virtues of cross-channel ferry travel now Eurotunnel and low-cost airlines have become well established in this market. A comparison of the route network of ferry operations in 2000 and 2014 indicates that the ferry companies have relocated surplus capacity away from the competitive short-sea crossing of Dover–France to other short-sea crossings which have more revenue generation potential. The port in Dover has diversified and expanded the cruise business.

A rapid period of change in the holiday market and turmoil in the operating environment highlights the importance of being proactive in managing the tourism business. In each case, operators have sought to add value to the services they provide by upgrading onboard facilities, particularly food and beverages, children's lounges and business lounges, and increasing the size of ferries so they can carry over 2000 passengers in some cases. For some locations, such as the Highlands and Islands of Scotland and the Greek islands (with up to 60 000 ferry departures in the peak months), ferries provide the vital link between the mainland tourism market and the destination.

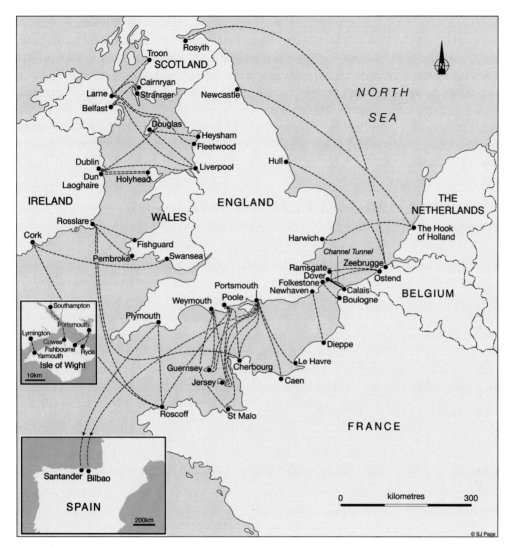

Figure 4.11
Travel by ferry from the UK to Europe

Source: author

Inland waterways

Inland waterways are another relatively neglected area of study in tourism research. They are seen as the product of a bygone era, linked to industrialization from the late eighteenth century onwards when canals and waterways were developed in many European countries to transport products from source areas to market. Yet many towns and cities with waterways and river networks have seen a renaissance in their regeneration for tourism purposes in the late twentieth century, with Birmingham, UK, a case in point. It is the junction of many of the UK's canals and waterways, with a well-developed riverboat and canal-based holiday market. Much of this regeneration activity has been a successful partnership of waterway agencies such as the former British Waterways Board (BWB) and local authorities, often supported in the UK by grants from the Lottery and Millennium funds. BWB managed 3220 km of canals and rivers in the UK with a budget of almost £200 million, part of which has been spent on re-opening old canals for leisure and in creating a new focus for tourism such as the Millennium Wheel in Falkirk, Scotland. In 2012, BWB ceased to exist and the Canal and River Trust was established to care for the infrastructure. In other contexts, such as the Norfolk Broads, a major holiday and boating industry exists which is based on inland waterways (see Web Case 4.1).

Managing land- and surface-based tourist transport

The various modes of transport examined in this chapter have highlighted the diversity and wide range of uses which tourists, make of transport, from linking the home to the nearest departure point through to using transport as a holiday context (e.g. a cruise). Integrating the transport modes to ensure a seamless travel experience without major service interruptions is a major challenge for the tourism industry, since transport functions are often contracted out to suppliers who may not have a tourism ethos (e.g. coach operators or taxis). In each case, transport providers interface with tourists, and so ensuring they are good ambassadors for tourism has become a priority for many destination areas as has ensuring those people who interface with tourists recognize the service standards which travellers now experience in other areas of the service economy. Yet the consumption of tourism has not only been associated with pleasure and enjoyment, as new trends related to the impact of transport and travel have focused attention on the resource use (i.e. carbon consumption) of such trips. For this reason, Innovation in Sustainability 4.2 outlines some of the debates over and measures taken to reduce carbon consumption.

The transport sector has been very slow to embrace these ideas on sustainability since it has been operationally led and focused on operating vehicles, plant and capital investment rather than looking at the tourist as a customer and the need to adopt a 'greener' approach to travel. This issue permeates most forms of surface-based transport, as tourism and service provision in the air transport sector have been more innovative.

Much of the planning and integration of surface transport has been achieved in many European capitals by innovative and forward-looking planning in the post-war period and purpose-building new infrastructure; in some older European capitals existing infrastructure still has gaps in the provision of terminals, with visitors often having to travel from central areas to airports on systems that are not integrated and are complicated to use. Transport provision needs champions within each destination area so that the tourist can be easily connected with terminals, attractions, accommodation and gateways, such as ports and airports – a theme which will be returned to in Chapter 5. Airports are the most obvious example of where the private sector takes the lead in integrating transport and tourism. The work of BAA in the UK illustrates this, with each airport having a surface transport strategy, working within the UK government's encouragement

INNOVATION IN SUSTAINABILITY 4.2
MONITORING AND REDUCING CARBON CONSUMPTION
IN TOURISM

With growing concerns over climate change and the contribution of tourist travel to this issue, researchers have examined the carbon footprint of tourists and tourism activities, and the wider use of carbon by the tourism industries. Carbon is produced when fossil fuels such as coal or oil combust and produce carbon dioxide (CO_2) which then enters the atmosphere. The period since the industrial revolution, where economic growth was largely dependent upon fossil fuels for energy, has seen growth in CO_2 emissions concentrating in the atmosphere, which causes a retention of heat within the atmosphere. The combination of other gaseous emissions such as nitrogen oxide, CFCs and methane means that the process of 'radiative forcing' is what causes CO_2 and other gases to contribute to global warming.

In the UK, greenhouse gas emissions from transport in 2011 comprised: the car (40 per cent); buses/coaches (3 per cent); light and heavy lorries (23 per cent); non-road transport (6 per cent) and international shipping and aviation (27 per cent). More concerning was the fact that UK greenhouse gas emissions from aviation rose from 11 per cent of transport emissions in 1990 to 21 per cent by 2011.

The scientific analysis of carbon consumption is crucial to understanding the impacts of different emissions from fossil fuels, particularly as air travel (see Chapter 5) produces proportionally more greenhouse gases than land-based transport. In this respect, aviation makes a greater contribution to global warming via the radiative forcing process as it generates both CO_2 and other gaseous emissions. One particularly innovative study that sets out to measure the carbon footprint of Dutch holiday makers is by de Bruin *et al.* (2013) *Travelling Large in 2012: The Carbon Footprint of Dutch Holidaymakers* (www.cstt.nl). This study is influential as it shows that:

- the average CO_2 emission per person per day in the Netherlands is 27.2 kg

whereas

- the average CO_2 emission per average Dutch holiday per day is 48.9 kg.

In total, almost 8 per cent of the Dutch carbon footprint for all forms of holiday is attributable to tourism. The study also highlights the eco efficiency of specific holiday types (i.e. domestic and overseas travel) and modes of travel. Previous reviews of the period 2002–2009 have shown that, whilst Dutch CO_2 emissions dropped 3.1 per cent, holiday emissions increased by 16.5 per cent. Therefore, tourism remains a problematic sector for policy-makers as it is running contrary to domestic day-to-day behaviour on sustainability. This illustrates the importance of innovations by transport providers to substitute air travel with less carbon-consuming modes such as rail travel, illustrated by Eurostar.

The Eurostar operation provides cross-channel rail services between London and Paris and London and Brussels via the Channel Tunnel. In April 2007 the company launched its Tread Lightly campaign to reduce CO_2 emissions, seeking to cut these by 35 per cent per passenger per journey. One strand of its strategy was to offset its carbon use by investing in projects that reduce the use of CO_2 by the same amount. The company was the first train operator to make all passenger journeys carbon neutral in 2007, reducing emissions by an estimated 40 000 tonnes of CO_2 compared to flying over comparable distances. Other sustainability measures achieved through the Tread Lightly Plan include:

- waste recycling at Eurostar's London depot
- a reduction of 70 per cent of waste being sent to landfill
- on-board catering services using biodegradable and recyclable paper and plastic crockery
- recycling of old uniforms into new clothing and accessory products.

Other targets include improved on-board waste handling and investment in a new generation of more environmentally friendly trains by 2015.

Further reading

De Bruijn, K., Dirven, R., Eijgelaar, E. and Peeters, P. (2013) *Travelling Large in 2012: The Carbon Footprint of Dutch Holidaymakers in 2012*. Breda: The Centre for Sustainable Tourism and Transport, NHTV. www.cstt.nl

Eurostar (2009) *Tread Lightly Report*. London: Eurostar. www.eurostar.com

of the use of public transport for more journeys. A third of passengers travel to BAA's three London airports by public transport and it is seeking to expand that to 50 per cent. Specific initiatives include the development of the Heathrow Express, the St Pancras Express, the M4 spur road bus lane, discounted London Underground travelcards being issued to airline staff, public–private sector partnerships to improve railway stations, enhancements to bus services (including a subsidy to the Glasgow Airport link) and environmental levies on car parking to support public transport initiatives. Given the significance of these, it is useful to turn in the next chapter to the important role of airports as transport terminals as receiving and sending areas for air travellers.

CHAPTER REVIEW

 References

Button, K. J. and Gillingwater, K. (eds) (1983) *Future Transport Policy*. London: Routledge.

Connell, J. and Page, S. J. (2008) Exploring the spatial patterns of car-based tourist travel in Loch Lomond and Trossachs National Park. *Tourism Management*, 29(3): 561–580.

Countryside Commission (1992) *Trends in Transport and the Countryside*. Cheltenham: Countryside Commission.

Countryside Commission (1995) *The Market for Recreational Cycling in the Countryside.* Cheltenham: Countryside Commission.

Dickinson, J. and Lumsdon, L. (2010) *Slow Travel and Tourism.* London: Earthscan.

Eaton, B. and Holding, D. (1996) The evaluation of public transport alternatives to the car in British National Parks. *Journal of Transport Geography*, 4(1): 55–65.

English Tourist Board/Employment Department (1991) *Tourism and the Environment: Maintaining the Balance.* London: English Tourist Board.

European Conference of Ministers of Transport (1987) cited in S. Page (1994) The European coach travel market. *Travel and Tourism Analyst*, 1: 19–39.

HMSO (1994) *Royal Commission on Environmental Pollution*, Eighteenth Report, Transport and the Environment, Cmmd. 2674. London: HMSO.

Lamb, B. and Davidson, S. (1996) Tourism and transportation in Ontario, Canada. In L. Harrison and W. Husbands (eds) *Practising Responsible Tourism: International Case Studies in Tourism Planning, Policy and Development.* Chichester: Wiley.

Lumsdon, L. (1996) Future for cycle tourism in Britain. *INSIGHTS*, A27–A32.

Lumsdon, L. (1997) Recreational cycling: Is this the way to stimulate interest in everyday urban cycling? In R. Tolley (ed.) *The Greening of Urban Transport Planning for Walking and Cycling in Western Cities*, 2nd edn. Chichester: Wiley.

Page, S. J (2009) *Tourism Management*, 3rd edn. Oxford: Routledge.

Page, S. J. and Connell, J. (2014) *Transport and Tourism.* In A. Lew, C. M. Hall and A. Williams (eds) *Companion of Tourism.* Oxford: Blackwell.

Page, S. J., Yeoman, I., Connell J. and Greenwood, C. (2010). Scenario planning as a tool to understand uncertainty in tourism: The example of transport and tourism in Scotland in 2025. *Current Issues in Tourism*, 13(2): 99–137.

Peisley, T. (2006) *A Worldwide Analysis to 2015: Boom or Bust.* Colchester: Seatrade.

Scottish Tourist Board (1991) *Tourism Potential of Cycling and Cycle Routes in Scotland.* Edinburgh: Scottish Tourist Board.

Shackley, M. (2000) *Atlas of Travel and Tourism Development.* Oxford: Butterworth-Heinemann.

Stradling, S. and Anabele, J. (2008) Individual transport patterns. In R. Knowles, J. Shaw and I. Docherty (eds) *Transport Geographies: Mobilities, Flows and Spaces.* Blackwell: Oxford, 179–195.

SUSTRANS (2002) *Cycle Tourism: Information Pack TT21.* SUSTRANS online. www.sustrans. org.uk, accessed 11 October 2002.

Transform Scotland (2013) *The Value of Cycle Tourism.* Edinburgh: SUSTRANS.

Wall, G. (1971) Car owners and holiday activities. In P. Lavery (ed.) *Recreational Geography.* Newton Abbot: David and Charles.

Further reading

Competition Commission (2009) *Investigation of the Supply of Airport Services in the UK by BAA.* London: Competition Commission. www.berr.gov.uk

Gibson, P. (2006) *Cruise Operations Management.* Oxford: Butterworth-Heinemann.

Hickman, R. and Bannister, D. (2007) Looking over the horizon: Transport and reduced CO_2 emissions in the UK by 2030. *Transport Policy*, 14(5): 377–387.

Knowles, R., Shaw, J. and Docherty, I. (eds) (2008) *Transport Geographies: Mobilities, Flows and Spaces.* Oxford: Blackwell.

Lumsdon, L. (2006) Factors affecting the design of tourism bus services. *Annals of Tourism Research*, 33(3): 748–766.

Lumsdon, L. and Page, S. J. (eds) (2004) *Tourism and Transport: Issues and Agenda in the New Millennium.* Oxford: Elsevier.

Page, M. (2005) Non-motorised transportation policy. In K. Button and D. Hensher (eds) *Handbook of Transport Strategy, Policy and Institutions*. Oxford: Elsevier, 581–596.

Peeters, P., Szimba, E. and Duinjnisveld, M. (2007) Major environmental impacts of European tourist transport. *Journal of Transport Geography*, 15(2): 83–93.

Prideaux, B. and Carson, D. (eds) (2011) *Drive Tourism: Trends and Emerging Markets*. London: Routledge.

Român, C., Espino, R. and Martin, J. (2007) Competition of high-speed train with air transport: The case of Madrid–Barcelona. *Journal of Air Transport Management*, 13(5): 277–284.

Tol, R. (2007) The impact of a carbon tax on international tourism. *Transportation Research D*, 12(2): 129–142.

The most comprehensive book on transport and tourism is:

Page, S. J. (2009) *Transport and Tourism: Global Perspectives*, 3rd edn. Harlow: Prentice Hall.

 # Questions

1   How would you develop a model of tourist transport and its relationship to tourist activity?
2   Why is the car so important to tourist activity patterns? What advantages and disadvantages does it have compared with other modes of surface travel?
3   What role does transport play as a focus for tourist activities?
4   How important is the integration of different forms of transport to achieve a seamless tourism experience?

 # Access additional resources

- For students: Multiple choice questions for each chapter, video links and further reading.
- For instructors: PowerPoint slides with tables and diagrams, additional case studies, video links and further reading.

Transporting the tourist II

The aviation sector

Learning outcomes

This chapter examines the role of the aviation industry in tourism as a global phenomenon which is responsible for enabling people to travel to destinations worldwide. On completion of the chapter, you should be able to understand:

- the structure and organization of the aviation sector and the role of airports in the handling of tourists as travellers

- key trends in the airline sector and the importance of the low-cost airlines as a new business sector

- the way in which airlines market their businesses to travellers.

Introduction

In Chapter 4, the role of surface transport highlighted the fundamental link between tourism and transport in a number of different contexts. One of the underlying themes was how transport (the industry) is linked to the tourist (the consumer), which in simple terms raises a fundamental question: how are these two elements managed so that consumer needs are met? This returns to many of the issues initially developed in Chapter 1 on the role of tourism management and who should manage such issues. This chapter addresses these issues by focusing on the aviation sector, since it has seen the greatest volume growth in passengers of all forms of transport (excluding car usage and ownership). It is focused on a complex transport system upon which the tourist experiences directly impact. This is shaped from the point they enter an airport through to the point they get off their aircraft at the destination, a process that is repeated on the return journey. In other words, the management of the tourist by the airline industry reveals an integrated transport system, which can largely be defined as:

> the process whereby individual (and groups of) airlines seek to organize, direct and harness their resources, personnel and their business activities to meet the needs of their organization and customers in an effective and efficient manner.
>
> (Page 2002: 209)

This also involves the close working relationship of the airlines with airports to ensure the smooth, safe and reliable processing and transfer of tourists through the system with the minimum of disruption and inconvenience. As the airline industry carries a large volume of passengers and the airport system has to be able to process the volume of travellers in an efficient manner, its effective management is crucial so that the system continues to have the capacity to allow the flow of travellers through the system. Therefore, this chapter commences with a discussion of the role of the airport as a terminal facility that links the tourist with the supply of transport – air transport. It offers a seamless travel process from departure to arrival in principle, although sometimes service interruptions and unavoidable delays may cause problems in the air transport system. This is followed with a discussion of air travel, emphasizing its growth and significance as a mode of tourist transport, how it is regulated, the role of airlines' operations and the significance of recent developments in the airline market, including the rise of low-cost airlines and future prospects for global air travel.

The role of the airport as a tourist terminal facility

Airports are one of the most highly developed and complex environments that tourists will experience as over 40 per cent of tourist trips are by air. Airports operate as well-developed systems, where a wide range of tourist interactions occur. At a simple level the airport is the point of processing for travel to a destination through to a highly developed shopping and retail environment. Other analogies of airports as post-modern citadels of tourism and consumption have led commentators to examine the architecture, subtle design features and careful management measures devised to encourage consumers to spend their money, with layouts designed to nurture a captive audience. Airports are more than

Table 5.1 World's top 30 airports by total passengers in 2009

Rank	City	Code	Total passengers	% CHG 2008–2009
1	ATLANTA, GA	ATL	88 032 086	−2.2
2	LONDON	LHR	66 037 578	−1.5
3	BEIJING	PEK	65 372 012	16.9
4	CHICAGO, IL	ORD	64 158 343	−6.1
5	TOKYO	HND	61 903 656	−7.2
6	PARIS	CDG	57 906 866	−4.9
7	LOS ANGELES, CA	LAX	56 520 843	−5.5
8	DALLAS/FORT WORTH, TX	DFW	56 030 457	−1.9
9	FRANKFURT	FRA	50 932 840	−4.7
10	DENVER, CO	DEN	50 167 485	−2.1
11	MADRID	MAD	48 250 784	−5.1
12	NEW YORK, NY	JFK	45 915 069	−4.0
13	HONG KONG	HKG	45 558 807	−4.8
14	AMSTERDAM	AMS	43 570 370	−8.1
15	DUBAI	DXB	40 901 752	9.2
16	BANGKOK	BKK	40 500 224	4.9
17	LAS VEGAS, NV	LAS	40 469 012	−6.3
18	HOUSTON, TX	IAH	40 007 354	−4.1
19	PHOENIX, AZ	PHX	37 824 982	−5.2
20	SAN FRANCISCO, CA	SFO	37 338 942	0.3
21	SINGAPORE	SIN	37 203 978	−1.3
22	JAKARTA	CGK	37 143 719	15.2
23	GUANGZHOU	CAN	37 048 712	10.8
24	CHARLOTTE, NC	CLT	34 536 666	−0.6
25	MIAMI, FL	MIA	33 886 025	−0.5
26	ROME	FCO	33 723 213	−4.0
27	ORLANDO, FL	MCO	33 693 649	−5.5
28	SYDNEY	SYD	33 451 383	0.4
29	NEWARK, NJ	EWR	33 399 207	−5.6
30	MUNICH	MUC	32 681 067	−5.4

Total passengers: arriving and departing passengers, direct passengers counted once.

Source: ACI, reproduced by permission of ACI

just transport termini where tourists transfer from a ground-based form of transport to air-based forms of transport. In larger capital cities, airports are major integrated transport hubs, with a wide range of feeder routes by public transport and road (including other air travellers in transit) who are sorted, sifted, channelled and directed towards departing flights as part of their tourism experience. Airports have changed out of all recognition from their early 1930s origins when they were simple buildings that provided a waiting area for flights. Today they are multi-million-pound businesses, with vast capital investment in transport infrastructure to facilitate the air travel function, as well as a large number of other functions – including retailing, support services, car hire, onward travel by other modes of transport and large car parking facilities, as well as a cargo function.

As Table 5.1 shows, despite the effects of a global economic slowdown, the demand for air travel in many markets in 2011–2012 saw continued growth in mainland China, with rates of growth of over 10 per cent for a number of airports in Asia and the Middle East and slower growth in the USA and Europe. The scale of the numbers using these terminal areas reinforces the size of the management challenge for airport operators in ensuring that business activities run smoothly. The Airport Council International (www.aci.org), which represents 575 airport operators worldwide with 1663 airports in 179 countries carrying 4.8 billion passengers, identified the following key issues as challenges for airports in ensuring the visitor experience is maintained:

- the need to cope with larger aircraft size, as 600-seat aircraft are likely to be introduced on long-haul routes
- the need to embrace technological change such as new navigation systems so that the capacity at individual airports can be increased to cope with demand. This is important given the Boeing Commercial Airplane Group (2010) *Current Market Outlook 2010* indication that future demand will lead to a greater use of medium-haul aircraft (e.g. Boeing 777s and the new 787 dreamliner), increasing the number and frequency of aircraft wishing to take off and land at airports worldwide. This prediction runs counter to the forecasts of Airbus, which has replaced the jumbo jet with the new A380, able to carry in excess of 550 passengers on trunk routes
- the recognition that air travel has now begun to reach a mass market rather than the elite group it served in the 1950s and early 1960s

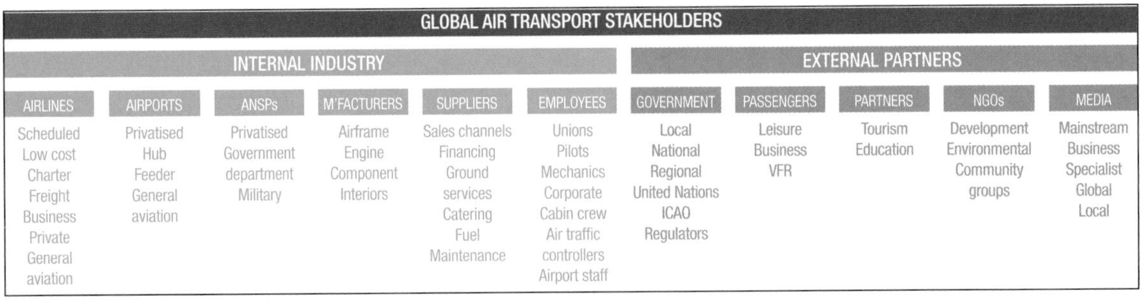

GLOBAL AIR TRANSPORT STAKEHOLDERS										
INTERNAL INDUSTRY						EXTERNAL PARTNERS				
AIRLINES	AIRPORTS	ANSPs	M'FACTURERS	SUPPLIERS	EMPLOYEES	GOVERNMENT	PASSENGERS	PARTNERS	NGOs	MEDIA
Scheduled	Privatised	Privatised	Airframe	Sales channels	Unions	Local	Leisure	Tourism	Development	Mainstream
Low cost	Hub	Government	Engine	Financing	Pilots	National	Business	Education	Environmental	Business
Charter	Feeder	department	Component	Ground	Mechanics	Regional	VFR		Community	Specialist
Freight	General	Military	Interiors	services	Corporate	United Nations			groups	Global
Business	aviation			Catering	Cabin crew	ICAO				Local
Private				Fuel	Air traffic	Regulators				
General				Maintenance	controllers					
aviation					Airport staff					

Figure 5.1
Global air transport stakeholders

Source: ATAG

- a need to speed up the passenger flows at airports, including the removal of bottlenecks and delays with baggage handling, by introducing new technology and smart technology to track travellers and their personal belongings
- addressing security issues at airports, which are seen as one of the weakest links, as well as enhancing safety matters for travellers.

In each case, the ACI recognize the importance of investing in the airport system and its constituent parts so that the interface with the traveller is enhanced. Perhaps one of the greatest challenges for the airport sector is in recognizing and acknowledging the fact that:

> The airport cavalcade can baffle or startle the inexperienced passenger ... Laden with suitcases and packages, calm and rational people grow uptight, defensive with aggression, fail to allow themselves time to familiarise themselves with the layout or study the free guides to terminals.
>
> (Barlay 1995: 48)

This quotation illustrates the importance of designing passenger-friendly environments that are welcoming, have a relaxed feel (such as London Stansted's terminal building designed by Sir Norman Foster) and provide opportunities for travellers to reduce the stress, anxiety and uncertainty associated with air travel.

For the airport sector, various issues affect how the traveller perceives the terminal including:

- speed of check-in
- efficiency of passport control and customs clearance
- luggage retrieval
- availability of shops, duty-free and associated services
- a spacious and relaxed environment to wait prior to boarding the aircraft.

Source: developed from Barlay (1995: 49) cited in Page (2009)

This identifies the themes that airport managers need to address as they become more customer-oriented, and investment in new terminals and redevelopments integrate the latest thinking on passenger-friendly environments. This is somewhat of a culture change for airports as traditionally they were largely operationally focused and only paid lip service to the needs of travellers. The airport manager's focus has changed out of all recognition since the impact of privatization and the need for a greater consumer orientation in order to generate profits for shareholders and other investors.

The greater commercialization in airport operations has been coupled with the development of global airport companies (such as BAA plc and Amsterdam Schipol) and non-airport transport companies that have entered airport management. As a result, airports have become part of the wider globalization of transport and tourism activities. Such companies recognize that managing airports is not just about providing some of the services and facilities which travellers need; it is also about coordinating, planning, leading and communicating between the airport and the diverse range of ancillary services such as handling agents, concessionaires (i.e. businesses which operate under licence or franchise on airport premises, such as retailers), government bodies (e.g. the Federal Aviation

Authority in the USA) and industry bodies (e.g. ACI) as well as the airlines. Airport operations have certainly seen a greater emphasis on business skills and communication such as marketing than on their traditional, operationally led focus since a wave of commercialization has swept through the airport sector. This is also reflected in the evolution of airports as business entities that recognize their different revenue streams.

What is an airport and how is it operated?

In physical terms, Doganis (1992) defines an airport as:

> Essentially one or more runways for aircraft together with associated buildings or terminals where passengers . . . are processed . . . the majority of airport authorities own and operate their runways, terminals and associated facilities, such as taxiways or aprons.
>
> (Doganis 1992: 7)

The evolution of airports in many countries has followed a complex pattern based on historical, legal and other factors (i.e. changing government policy and the different roles of public and private sector involvement). Explaining airport development in many instances has been associated with opportunities for the expansion of gateway airport terminals and the post-war reuse of former military bases and available sites, as well as new-build projects. Airport development in part mirrors the expansion of tourism in the post-war period, but the lead times for airport development due to the capital intensive nature of their sunk costs means that development horizons are at least ten years for new runways and terminals and associated infrastructure (i.e. expanding new road infrastructure to cope with demand). A well developed literature on airports now exists including a number of academic journals that examine air transport issues such as the *Journal of Air Transport Management* (also see Table 5.2).

However, Doganis (1992: 7) distinguishes between the three principal activities of airports:

- essential operational services and facilities
- traffic-handling services
- commercial activities.

Whilst the dominant activity to be considered for the safe and efficient management of the airport as a terminal area are its passenger flows, it is clear that the airport houses a complex system in which a wide range of interrelated activities take place.

The scope of activities broadly encompasses the following:

- ground handling
- baggage handling
- passenger terminal operations
- airport security
- cargo operations
- airport technical services
- air traffic control

Table 5.2 Key studies on air transport and tourist travel
Graham, A., Papatheodorou, A. and Forsyth, P. (eds) (2008) *Aviation and Tourism: Implications for Leisure Travel*. Aldershot: Ashgate.
Gross, S. and Luck, M. (eds) (2013) *The Low Cost Carrier Worldwide*. Farnham: Ashgate.
Iatrou, K. and Oretti, M. (2007) *Airline Choices for the Future: From Alliances to Mergers*. Aldershot: Ashgate.
Janic, M. (2007) *The Sustainability of Air Transportation*. Aldershot: Ashgate.
Page, S. J. (2009) *Transport and Tourism: Global Perspectives*, 3rd edn. Harlow: Pearson Education.
Shaw, S. (2007) *Airline Marketing and Management*, 6th edn. Aldershot: Ashgate.
Taneja, N. (2005) *Fasten Your Seatbelt: The Passenger is Flying the Plane*. Aldershot: Ashgate.
Vasign, B., Fleming, K. and Tacker, T. (2008) *Introduction to Air Transport Economics*. Aldershot: Ashgate.
Wensveen, J. (2007) *Air Transportation: A Management Perspective*, 6th edn. Aldershot: Ashgate.

- aircraft scheduling (take-off/landing slot allocation)
- airport and aircraft emergency services
- airport access.

Source: after Page (2009)

The way in which airports are managed is also partly determined by their pattern of ownership. New forms of ownership have emerged as the demand for air travel has grown and state involvement in airport provision has been reduced, allowing owners to pursue commercial strategies so they can invest and grow their capacity and ability to respond more quickly to the market. There are four main types of ownership:

1 *state ownership with direct government control*, characterized by a single government department (e.g. a Civil Aviation Department) which operates the country's airports. The alternative to a centralized government pattern of control and management is localized ownership, such as municipal ownership
2 *public ownership through an airport authority*, usually as a limited liability or private company
3 *mixed public and private ownership* is an organizational model that has been adopted at larger Italian airports, where a company manages the airport, with public and private shareholders
4 *private ownership* was a model of limited appeal prior to the wave of privatization in the 1980s; an example is the UK government's privatization of BAA in 1987.

Privatization is seen as a politically sensitive issue, since it involves the transfer of state assets accumulated from taxpayers' revenue in major capital assets that may give the private sector significant commercial opportunities.

However, the most fundamental issues that are involved in any airport development are:

- costs
- the economic features of airports

- sources of revenue
- methods of charging and pricing airport aeronautical services
- the type of commercial strategy to adopt
- potential sources of commercial revenue
- the most appropriate management structure for an airport as a commercial/non-commercial organization
- financial performance indicators.

Source: based on Doganis (1992) and Ashford *et al.* (1991)

Aside from revenue issues, managers of airport facilities need to understand the costs and economic characteristics of airports so as to recognize both the commercial potential and where fixed costs exist. By far the largest cost, as one would expect since tourism is a people industry, is staffing costs. These are often in excess of 40 per cent of the operational costs, though these are closely followed by ongoing capital charges (i.e. interest payments on loans and the cost of depreciation on the capital assets) and security costs are a growing concern for airport operators. Other operational costs (e.g. electricity, water and supplies) typically comprise 11 per cent of costs while maintenance and administrative costs can account for the remaining costs. In contrast to costs, revenue can be divided into two categories:

1   operating revenues, which are generated by directly running and operating the airport (e.g. the terminal area, leased areas and grounds)
2   non-operating revenues, which include income from activities not associated with the airport core business which airport analysts divide into aeronautical or traffic revenues and non-aeronautical or commercial revenues.

For the airport there is a range of possible revenue sources (though not all airports necessarily collect or use the revenue in a set way):

- landing fees (which the ACI have suggested do not exceed 4 per cent of airlines' operating costs)
- airport air traffic control charges
- aircraft parking
- passenger charges
- freight charges
- aircraft handling services.

In terms of non-aeronautical revenue, Doganis (1992) outlines the following sources:

- rents or lease income from airport tenants
- recharges to tenants for utilities and services provided
- concession income (e.g. from duty-free and tax-free shops)
- direct sales in shops operated by the airport authority
- revenue from car parking where it is airport operated

- miscellaneous items
- non-airport related income (e.g. through land development or hotel development).

Within a European context, Doganis noted that aeronautical revenue accounted for 56 per cent of revenue and non-aeronautical revenue for 44 per cent of income. In the USA, airports generated more revenue from commercial sources (e.g. concessions, 33 per cent; rents, 23 per cent; car parking, 4 per cent; other non-aeronautical sources, 17 per cent and aeronautical fees, 23 per cent). In terms of non-airport revenue, airports need to understand the scope of airport users, who comprise:

- passengers (departing, arriving and transferring between flights)
- the airlines, which are major consumers of space for storage, maintenance, staff and catering
- airport employees
- airline crews
- meeters and greeters (i.e. those who are accompanying or meeting friends and relatives departing or arriving by air)
- visitors to airports, particularly where airports market their shopping facilities and opportunities to observe aircraft activity in purpose-built viewing areas
- local residents
- the local business community.

Source: based on Doganis (1992: 115)

Airports also operate in a globally competitive environment, and so continued investment is vital for them to remain attractive to airlines and passengers. The lobby group, the Air Transport Action Group (ATAG), has highlighted the €120 billion that European airports have committed to infrastructure investment between 2009 and 2015, although this is dwarfed by the major investment being made in Middle Eastern hubs such as Abu Dhabi and Qatar.

Among some of the more contentious issues which airport management has to deal with are passenger safety and security, and environmental issues as shown in Web Case 5.1.

The international airline industry

The airline industry developed as a commercial enterprise during the 1930s as technological advances in aviation enabled companies to develop regular passenger services, cross-subsidized by the provision of freight and air postal services. In the post-war period, modern-day air transport emerged as an international business, providing services and products for a diverse group of users including scheduled and non-scheduled (charter) transportation for air travellers and cargo transportation for businesses.

(Page 2002: 209)

Table 5.3 The global aviation industry: Key facts

- It contributes to 8 per cent of world GDP
- Aircraft have the greatest load factors of any form of scheduled transport mode, typically over 70 per cent
- The airline industry carried 3 billion passengers worldwide in 2012
- There are 3750 airports globally
- Air transport supports 56 000 000 jobs internationally, of which 8.36 million are direct employment in aviation
- There are 1715 airlines globally with a fleet of 23 000 aircraft
- In Africa, airports employ 430 000 people, 21 000 of whom work in airports, which contributes US$9.2 billion to GDP
- Air transport is a highly competitive and capital intensive industry
- For the period 2010 to 2029 Boeing forecast that the demand for new aircraft will rise to 36 300, which is almost a doubling of capacity
- The volcanic ash cloud in Iceland in April 2010 led to passengers being stranded and losses for the global aviation industry of US$1.8 billion
- Passenger demand for air travel in Asia-Pacific is set to grow at over 7 per cent per annum as the proportion of GDP derived from aviation in Asia Pacific rises, as passenger demand is forecast to increase 234 per cent in the period 2010 to 2029.

Sources: Boeing, IATA and ATAG

The airline industry is truly a global business, and the effects of 9/11 and the ensuing financial problems experienced by many airlines only led to a slight drop in international tourist arrivals to 689 million in 2001, from 697 million in 2000. The international aviation industry is clearly very resilient as illustrated in Table 5.3. It is clear that the pace of change in the aviation sector is rapid and understanding the nature of underlying and current trends is important from a tourism management perspective so managers and the industry can understand how to respond to such issues. Table 5.2 illustrates some of the key studies that have examined the international airline industry in the specialist area of study aviation management.

Trends in the airline industry in the new millennium

The airline industry in its broadest form, as shown in Figure 5.1, is a complex amalgam of transport-related sectors and interest groups which operate, regulate and interact with the aviation sector. The previous section reviewed one of these sectors – the airport – and in this section the focus is on the trends and patterns of development of the airline sector: passenger airlines. These can be divided into two distinct groups:

1   *scheduled services*, which operate between destinations to a predetermined timetable and take the form of two types of services, one operated by domestic airlines and

one by international airlines. There are over 650 airlines which provide scheduled services internationally. Quite often, a country may run a state-owned airline (known as a flag carrier such as Lan in Chile) that safeguards the tourism market for the destination and air access. Other airlines can be part publicly and part privately owned or wholly privately owned. Where airlines operate on high-volume routes between major destinations, these are termed 'trunk routes', which are fed by feeder or regional airlines. This, the hub and spoke operation, is illustrated in Figure 5.2. Yet one innovation noted by Boeing Commercial Airplane Group (2002, 2004) is the rise in point-to-point, or city pair flights, using medium-sized aircraft that remove the hub-and-spoke pattern of development; this may be observed in Figure 5.2. These point-to-point flights are also illustrated later with reference to the low-cost carriers that have pioneered this concept, often using secondary, lesser-known airports at a distance from the major tourist destination, with lower landing costs

2   *charter airlines*, which do not operate to published timetables, being chartered to tour operators (travel intermediaries) who then sell the seats. In recent years, charter aircraft have also pioneered the sale of seat-only sales, which account for up to 20 per cent of their sales, particularly on Mediterranean holidays. Charters have, therefore, been associated with leisure travel and one example of their large-scale use is for the Hajj pilgrimage to Mecca, during which up to a million visitors travel for a religious event each year. Many scheduled carriers or tour operators also have their own charter airlines as part of an integrated tourism business.

The scale of growth in air travel has been phenomenal since the 1960s, and ATAG, a lobby group for the aviation sector, has used a list of factors that have been used to explain this growth. These include:

- falling real cost of air travel
- increased international trade and economic activity, which necessitates travel
- rising disposable incomes
- political stability
- a gradual relaxation of travel restrictions in many countries e.g. South Korea and China allowed greater outbound travel in the 1990s; China allowed greater inbound travel in the 1990s)
- greater leisure time and tourism promotion
- rising air transport liberalization
- new countries with low levels of air transport activity expanding their traffic volumes (e.g. East Asia-Pacific).

These factors are reflected in a series of trends in air travel since the 1970s, which Doganis (2001) explains in terms of the following:

- the effects of increasing liberalization (at the same time as airports were being privatized to accommodate changes in demand), which have removed many of the

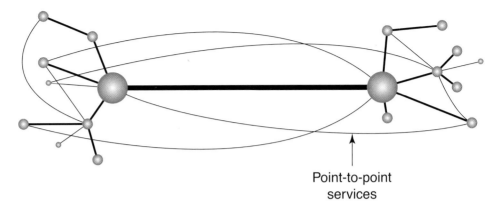

Point-to-point
services

Figure 5.2
Hub and spoke service with point-to-point services

Source: © Boeing Commercial Airplane Group (2001: 41) *2001 Current Market Outlook*. Seattle: Boeing
Commercial Airplane Group

existing controls on air route capacity and frequency of services, where monopoly,
duopoly or collusion prevented fair and open competition. This can lead to an
initial growth of 30 per cent in demand following liberalization

- the relatively low price of aviation fuel since the mid-1980s, which typically accounts
for 30–33 per cent of airline operating costs (but rose sharply in the new millennium)

- actual declines in the growth rate of air travel from growth rates of up to 12 per cent
in the 1960s and 7.8 per cent growth per annum prior to 1987, to 4.8 per cent per
annum between 1987 and 1997

- major restructuring in the nature of supply and market demand for air travel
since the 1970s. Doganis (2001) found that in 1972 the USA and Europe were
dominant, with 66 per cent of all international air travel. In the 1990s, this had
dropped to 50 per cent as Asian airlines with lower cost bases (i.e. greater flexibility
in staff utilization and lower salary and operating costs) reconfigured the nature
of air transport supply as demand from Asia-Pacific also expanded. One consequence
in the USA was the merger of United and Continental in 2010 as shown in Case
Study 5.1

CASE STUDY 5.1
CREATING THE WORLD'S LARGEST AIRLINE: THE
UNITED–CONTINENTAL MERGER IN 2010

The airline industry and its management faces many challenges – from a demand perspective, it
needs to attract customers and to retain them and from an operational perspective, the issue of cost
needs to be addressed in terms of people, the fleet it operates and its finances. In the USA, the
deregulation and the rise of the low-cost model of operation have impacted substantially on the full

service airlines that have not adopted a low-cost model of operation, with the US airline industry suffering losses of US$5.1 billion in 2008 (in part due to fuel costs) and US$1 billion in 2009. This has led to full service airlines seeking out partners to merge with to ensure their long-term survival. These corporate responses have assumed a significant role when some airlines have filed for bankruptcy protection and in May 2010, two of the US's larger full service airlines – United and Continental – announced plans to merge with a view to being operational by late 2010. United is the third largest airline in the USA and Continental the fourth largest. Each airline had made a loss in the first three months of 2010 (US$146 million by Continental and US$82 million by United) and the merger is expected to generate over US$1 billion in synergies by 2013 for new revenue such as new route options as well as between US$200 and US$300 million in cost savings. The decision to merge will create the world's largest airline with over 1200 aircraft trading as United with aircraft liveries painted in the Continental colours and the strap line – *Let's Fly Together*.

This will create an airline combining United's network serving 230 overseas and domestic destinations with 3400 flights a day and 46 000 employees. United's network is 60 per cent domestic and 40 per cent international. In contrast, Continental had 2700 daily flights to the Americas, Asia and Europe and employed almost 41 000 staff with a network equally split between domestic and international traffic. The combined airline had little route overlap and the new airline will have combined passengers of 144 million a year with 370 destinations in 59 countries thereby achieving greater economies of scale through merger.

- The yields (the actual profitability of an airline seat or flight) have dropped since the 1990s, reflected in lower revenue per passenger kilometre, due to increased capacity on many flights/routes and lower prices. Doganis (2001) found that the percentage of passengers travelling on promotional fares (i.e. discounted rates) rose from 51 per cent to 71 per cent in the early to late 1990s and this has continued. To address the falling yields, airlines have had to reduce the unit costs of operation (i.e. the cost of each individual input which goes into a flight including in-flight service, staffing and associated costs). Where airlines have failed to reduce costs quicker than drops in yields, they have been forced to raise the number of passengers they carry (loadings) or face financial problems
- The growth in globalization and international ownership of airlines. The most notable privatization in the 1980s was British Airways. Accompanying these changes are greater involvement in collaboration and partnerships (e.g. airline alliances), greater concentration of airlines in a large number of global carriers and increased numbers of mergers and agreements for working together
- A constant decline in fare levels has forced a response by the airline industry: to bypass travel agents and their commissions, which have been as high as 12 per cent of operating costs. This is known as 'disintermediation', and involves selling direct to the customer and using paperless tickets, both of which remove the role of a travel agent
- Infrastructure constraints, induced by liberalization and more airlines seeking take-off and landing slots at congested gateway or hub airports, as well as pressure on airlines to be more environmentally responsible and reduce noise emissions.

Managing the airline industry

From the previous discussion, it is evident that the aviation sector has experienced and continues to undergo rapid change. Adapting to such change is a key challenge for management so that it can ensure profitability. Many airlines began life as state-owned enterprises, and this indicates the need for massive investment since the airline industry is very capital intensive, requiring a steady and predictable long-term stream of revenue to absorb the high capital and operating costs. For example, a Boeing 737 can cost US$30 million new and that excludes some of the fit-out costs: deploying such resources to their optimum use is critical. The airlines of many smaller countries are still subsidized and maintained for political reasons especially in Asia-Pacific and South America.

One of the most volatile issues for individual airlines is the cost of aviation fuel that can be up to 14 per cent of operating costs. For example, in 2008, the price of oil rose to almost US$150 a barrel, then dropped to US$70 a barrel in 2010. For BA, this meant its annual fuel bill dropped £600 million in 2009/10 compared to 2008/09 when its annual fuel bill rose to over £3 billion. This was also a factor causing six US airlines to seek bankruptcy protection in 2008 due to soaring oil prices that impacted on their operating costs when their revenue was relatively static. For example, American Airlines saw its annual fuel bill rise by US$6 billion in 2008. One way airlines try to stabilize these huge swings in oil prices is to engage in the process of hedging (i.e. paying a predetermined price for fuel to offset potential higher costs) although if oil prices drop then the airline will pay an above market price.

Airline management requires airlines to balance those issues they have to deal with on a day-to-day basis (operational issues) and longer-term basis (strategic issues) together with their marketing. In reality, the management process for airline companies is an ongoing activity that requires a predetermined structure within the organization to ensure that all the business activities are adequately integrated to meet the needs of its internal customers (those within the organization) and the external business needs (the customer or purchaser of services and products). This involves overseeing the activities of airline operations (domestic and international airline business) and diverse activities that affect the organization's main business (e.g. ground handling, planning, human resource management and reservations). To streamline and ensure different parts of an airline work efficiently, many larger companies have been organized into functional business units and in some cases have outsourced, franchised or disposed of elements of the business that are not profitable or central to core activity. This is most noticeable in low-cost airlines, which have stripped out all but the basic elements needed for the business to function. Yet

> airline managers are not free agents. Their actions are circumscribed by a host of national and international regulations. These are both economic and non-economic in character and may well place severe limitations on airlines' freedom of action.
>
> (Doganis 1991: 24)

One of the ways in which the management of airlines have been evaluated is through their performance. Case Study 5.2 illustrates the performance of airlines in the second largest market for air travel – China.

As a result, regulation is a major factor affecting the business environment for aviation and this is a very complex area involving politics, decision-making, governments, airlines and changing international pressure for greater liberalization.

CASE STUDY 5.2
THE PERFORMANCE AND COMPETITIVENESS OF CHINESE AIRLINES

A study by Wang *et al.* (in press) highlighted that China's airlines are among some of the most profitable globally, with their profits in 2010 four times higher than US airlines' and twice as profitable as European airlines'. This has been related not only to a booming Chinese economy, but the deregulation of the domestic aviation market and the rise in foreign involvement, with many airports also partially privatized. Much of the profitability in the Chinese aviation sector arises from the domestic market and that market is characterized by the domination of the three largest airlines (Air China, China South and China Eastern) which have a 70 per cent share of the market, based on their subsidiary airlines which serve the main hubs, thereby reducing competition on the routes. The result, as Wang *et al.* (in press) show, is increased market concentration.

Wang *et al.* evaluated the productivity of Chinese airlines by looking at key inputs to airline operation (labour, fuel, materials, flight equipment, ground property and equipment) and the outputs (passenger services, freight services and incidental services) to construct measures of productivity. Comparing US and Chinese airlines, Wang *et al.* found that the Chinese airlines had lower levels of productivity, suggesting inefficiencies in the aviation system. The result is that the Chinese aviation sector has scope for greater efficiency gains. At the same time, Chinese airline yields calculated by dividing total passenger revenue by total revenue passenger kilometres were comparable to the USA, although the Chinese aviation market lacks major competition domestically. As a result, Wang *et al.* explain the highly profitable nature of the Chinese aviation sector as a function of:

- lower input prices than international rivals including relatively low levels of staff remuneration. This leads to lower input costs
- Chinese airlines were able to charge similar or greater prices than comparable US airlines due to market control and an absence of deregulation measures.

Further reading

Wang, K., Fan, X., Fu, X. and Zhou, Y. (in press) Benchmarking the performance of Chinese airlines: An investigation of productivity, yield and cost competitiveness. *Journal of Air Transport Management*.

Regulating international air transport

Within many sectors of the tourism industry, there is a great debate on why certain activities need to be regulated. In the case of air travel, regulation is needed for a number of reasons. Appropriate international regulation and supervision of the industry ensures airlines do not operate in an unsafe manner. Regulations set minimum standards for operating aircraft, and non-economic regulations are designed to cover the safety and operational guidelines for airline services. There are regulations concerning, for example,

- the airworthiness of aircraft, their maintenance and overhaul and the training of engineers who undertake this work
- the numbers and type of flight crew and cabin staff required on specific types of flight together with their qualifications and training
- the aviation infrastructure such as airports, meteorological services, en route navigational facilities and safety standards.

Technical and safety standards are developed and policed by civil aviation bodies in each country (for example, the Civil Aviation Authority in the UK). Technical standards and safety procedures are incumbent upon airline managers, and adhering to high standards of technical expertise and safety is now seen as essential to maintaining a competitive advantage. Other forms of regulation include environmental regulations associated with the noise and emissions that airlines create and the effects in and around airports and their local population. As mentioned above, many airports have begun to develop stringent environmental conditions that airlines must meet if they operate from their airports – otherwise they may be fined or banned.

The economic regulation of airlines can be traced back to the Paris Convention (1919) which established the principle that states have sovereign rights over their territory (i.e. their airspace). This led to the eventual development of bilateral agreements between countries to allow airlines rights to overfly their airspace and the right to operate into and out of other countries. In 1944, the Chicago Convention led to multilateral agreement on the:

- exchange of air traffic rights, or 'freedom of the air' (see Table 5.4)
- control of fares and freight tariffs
- control of frequencies and capacity.

As a result the operating environment for air travel was rigidly regulated, although agreement on the first two freedoms was not completed until the International Air Services Transit Agreement (1944). The outcome of the Chicago Convention was the establishment of the International Civil Aviation Organization (ICAO), an inter-governmental agency to act as a forum to discuss major aviation issues. In addition, the International Air Transport Association (IATA) was established as a rival to ICAO in 1945, to represent the interests of airline companies. IATA's primary purpose remains coordination and standardization of airline operations, representing airlines in a diverse range of negotiations with airport authorities, ICAO, governments and even hijackers. It also operates the clearing house for inter-airline debts arising from inter-airline traffic (carriage of airline passengers or freight on a service holding tickets issued by other airlines).

Airlines also use bilateral agreements, based on the principle of reciprocity (a fair and equal exchange of rights) while pooling agreements exist (except in the USA where US antitrust legislation prohibits such agreements which are viewed as being anti-competitive). Pooling agreements have been used in duopolistic situations to share the market between two airlines. Where business may not be sufficient to justify a two-airline operation, a revenue cost pool may be used where one airline operates the service on behalf of the pool partners. Airlines may also enter into inter-airline royalty agreements where airlines wish to pick up 'fifth freedom' traffic (see Table 5.4) where they do not have such rights. By making royalty payments to the airline of the country involved, it may gain such rights.

Such a range of regulatory measures ensures that the management of airlines is a complex process when dealing with the international aviation market. A further change to this regulatory environment was the decision of the US government in 1978 to deregulate its domestic airline industry. A more recent development is the evolution of 'open skies' policies since 1992. These have emerged because of:

- increasing concentration in the US airline market following deregulation, with former domestic airlines emerging as major international carriers
- international airlines searching for marketing benefits from mergers in their home country and minority share purchases/strategic alliances to operate in other markets (which are discussed further below)
- the growing trend towards privatization of national flag carriers
- trade agreements associated with trading blocs such as Asean that have encouraged open skies agreements.

Open skies policies involve bilateral air service agreements where market access and price controls are removed, with over 50 per cent of the world's airline traffic now based on open skies agreements, illustrating the scale of change in just over a decade.

One of the most recent open skies agreements was the second stage of the US–EU agreement concluded in 2010. This permits new entrants to the transatlantic airline market thereby creating more competition than previously existed.

Deregulation in the USA aimed to achieve greater competition, and resulted in a 62 per cent increase in domestic passenger traffic between 1978 and 1990 followed by greater integration and concentration within the industry. It led to a new business environment where airline companies reorganized their activities to achieve cost reductions, least-cost solutions and network maximization with the intention of making operations more cost effective. Hub and spoke operations (see Figure 5.2) allowed airlines to develop a network to serve a large number of people over a wide area, with the hub acting as a switching point for passengers travelling on feeder routes along the spokes which cannot sustain a trunk route. This has resulted in the geographical concentration of hubs in major US cities and the six largest US airlines developing four major hub

Table 5.4 Air rights

Aviation rights

First freedom rights grant a foreign carrier the right to fly over the home country without landing.

Second freedom rights grant a foreign carrier the right to land at specified points in the home country, for purposes of refuelling and maintenance, but not to pick up or disembark traffic (passengers, cargo or mail).

Third freedom rights allow for traffic that was picked up by a foreign carrier outside the home country to be disembarked at specified destinations in the home country.

Fourth freedom rights allow a foreign carrier to pick up originating traffic in the home country, for transport to the foreign country in which the carrier is based.

Fifth freedom rights (also called beyond rights) permit the foreign carrier to pick up or disembark traffic en route.

1st Freedom: Right of transit without landing.

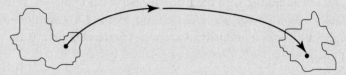

2nd Freedom: Right of technical stop (e.g. refuelling).

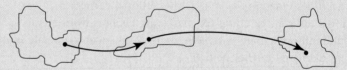

3rd Freedom: Right to set down traffic from home state.

4th Freedom: Right to pick up traffic bound for home state.

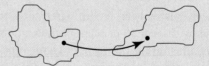

cities – Atlanta, Chicago, Dallas and Denver. The more competitive and unregulated the market, the greater the degree of planning and adjustment needed to match supply and demand. This is normally undertaken under the auspices of the marketing process.

Airline marketing: Its role and recent innovations

Growing global competition in the air travel market has meant that the 1990s were the decade of the air traveller as a consumer, usually seeking enhanced service quality. This has gone a stage further in the new millennium as the price-sensitive customer is a

Table 5.4 *continued*

5th Freedom: Right to pick up and put down traffic between two foreign states as an extension of routes to/from home state.

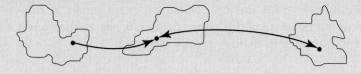

6th Freedom: Unofficial right to pick up and put down traffic between foreign states via home state (by combining 3rd and 4th Freedom rights).

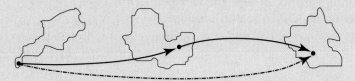

7th Freedom: Right to pick up and put down traffic between two foreign states.

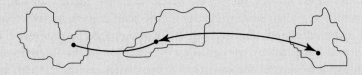

Sixth freedom rights allow the unofficial right to pick up and put down traffic between foreign states via home state (by combining third and fourth freedom rights).

Seventh freedom rights grant the right to pick up and put down traffic between two foreign states.

Source: redrawn from Figure G.1: Air transport freedom rights, which first appeared in *Asia Pacific Air Transport: Challenges and Policy Reforms*, edited by Christopher Findlay, Chia Lin Sien and Karmjit Singh, p. 193, with the kind permission of the publisher, Institute of Southeast Asian Studies, Singapore, http://bookshop.iseas.edu.sg

dominant element, especially in domestic air travel, and concerned with a minimum standard of service. Airlines have been forced not only to reduce operating costs and compete aggressively for business, but also to focus on the needs of their customers. Airline marketing is now more complex as it is vital to the management process of deciding what to produce and how it should be sold. Thus, 'the role of airline marketing is to bring together the supply of air services, which each airline can largely control, with the demand, which it can influence but not control, and to do this in a way which is both profitable and meets the airline's corporate objectives' (Doganis 1991: 202). BA explained its financial turnaround from a loss of £544 million in 1981–1982 to a profit of £272 million in 1983–1984 in terms of a more focused marketing orientation involving recognizing customers' needs and setting about satisfying them. This has now come full circle, with a re-evaluation of the company's core business and marketing focus as its business has been significantly affected by the rise of low-cost carriers on short-haul domestic and European routes.

BA's strategy amid financial pressures induced by losses of £530 million in 2010 was to seek to reinvigorate its international brand and image amid cost cutting with a new vision to become a premium airline where passengers pay a little more for that special service. Its five-fold focus in its new strategy was to:

- be the airline of choice for long-haul and premium passengers
- deliver an outstanding level of service for its customers at every point where they interact with the organization
- grow its presence in new and emerging global cities
- build on its leading role in London
- meet customers' needs and improve profit margins through new revenue streams.

Source: BA (2010) *Annual Report* 2009/10

This strategy involves putting the customer at the heart of the airline industry and an ability to communicate with its customers through enhancements to its online medium (i.e. BA.com). BA also acknowledged the uncertainty and risks which the global aviation market faces. Among these were access to global finance to reinvest in new capital assets such as aircraft since the onset of the credit crunch, increased competition, the fragility of a brand reputation that can easily be damaged by unforeseen events (e.g. strikes and service breakdowns) and growing deregulation of the international aviation market. BA's goal is to become the world's most responsible airline through its acclaimed environmental responsibility programme (see BA.com).

How airlines use marketing functions

The role of marketing in the management of airline services can be summarized as a four-stage process:

1 identify markets and market segments using research methods and existing data sources and traffic forecasts
2 use the market analysis to assess which products to offer, known as product planning. At this stage, price becomes a critical factor. Therefore product planning is related to:

(a) market needs identified from market research
(b) the current and future product features of competing airlines and the cost of different product features
(c) assessing what price the customers can be expected to pay for the product.

2 develop a marketing plan to plan and organize the selling of the products. Sales and distribution outlets need to be considered together with a detailed programme of advertising and promotion, such as the impact and effect which adverts on the side of taxis may have for the travelling public

3   monitor and review the airline's ability to meet service standards, assessed through sales figures, customer surveys, analysis of complaints and long-term planning to develop new service and product features.

Source: after Page (2002)

The role of marketing, particularly advertising, has also assumed an increasingly important role in the evolution of the low-cost carrier market, which has embraced technology and electronic marketing tools (e.g. web booking) to revolutionize the process of air travel from looking to booking to check-in and boarding.

The low-cost carriers: Aligning service provision to demand

Airlines traditionally targeted service quality in the business travel and luxury market for first-class travel. This is because it is the most profitable segment of the market for scheduled airlines, with premium pricing and high profit margins per seat; the yields of economy class are lower and profitability is attained by achieving high load factors. However, this traditional strategy has been significantly challenged in many markets that have allowed liberalization of services – in the USA in the 1980s, Europe in the 1990s (see Web Case 5.2) and elsewhere in the new millennium (i.e. Brazil and South Africa in 2001; the Middle East in 2003 and China in 2005) – allowing new entrants to compete for business – notably low-cost carriers, since more travellers now seek budget fares. By 2011 low-cost carriers were a ubiquitous feature within the global aviation market, as illustrated by Figure 5.3.

What makes the low-cost model interesting is the way the carriers start up new routes, offer massive incentives to build the market and then create long-term demand, often developing lesser-known airports and destinations. For example, the cost savings

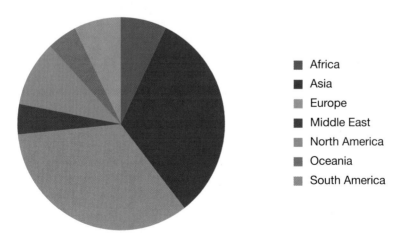

Figure 5.3
Distribution of low-cost carriers by continent in 2011

Source: data from Gross, S. and Luck, M. (2013) *The Low Cost Carrier Worldwide*. Aldershot: Ashgate.

CASE STUDY 5.3
THE LOW-COST CARRIER: THE SOUTHWEST PHENOMENON

Low-cost air travel, often termed no-frills or budget airline travel, is a relatively new phenomenon in Europe – despite the ill-fated attempt in the 1970s by Freddie Laker and his Skytrain concept, which sought to compete on the North Atlantic market. In fact some analysts point to the establishment in 1949 of Pacific Southwest Airlines as the pioneer low-cost airline. Yet low-cost air travel was well established in the USA long before deregulation, with certain airlines specializing in this niche market. Indeed, the growth of Southwest Airlines in the USA since 1971 epitomizes the traits of the low-cost carrier and established many of the basic business principles of streamlined airline operations (see Table 5.5 for key data on Southwest).

Southwest entered new markets at a low price, using lesser-known secondary airports, and demand outstripped supply. Following deregulation in 1978, Southwest expanded across the USA in a cautious manner as many other carriers went bankrupt or were taken over. It avoided head-on competition with the major carriers, though when it had to face such competition (such as when United launched its shuttle services in California) it initially saw market share drop; business then recovered (as United could not operate services viably) to the point where Southwest is the dominant intra-state carrier in California. *So how does Southwest manage to operate a viable business where competitors fail?*

In terms of the economics of airline operation (see Figure 5.4 for an illustration of the main costs in airline operation), it manages to operate at a cost structure well below its revenue. This means it can operate at a cost base that is often 25–40 per cent below that of its competitors where unrestricted fares are low. In 2003, the airline cut all commission for travel agent bookings, following on from a decision by Delta Airlines in March 2002. Many of Southwest's flight sectors are short and so revenue per kilometre flown is relatively high; the company has a simple fare structure, high levels of punctuality and correspondingly high levels of customer satisfaction. Southwest usually attracted a good mix of business and leisure travellers, despite being no-frills, high-density, one-class seating. There is no seat allocation and to keep costs down only snacks are offered to passengers. Pilots entered into a ten-year agreement on remuneration levels, which are a key element of operation for the airline, in return for share options to help stabilize costs. By standardizing its fleet type with only Boeing 737s, Southwest keeps maintenance and staff training costs low. Using fifteen- to twenty-minute turnaround times at terminals can increase the number of flight sectors an aircraft can fly in a day: on average 6.5 per day and over 12 hours' flying time. In 2010, Southwest acquired Air Trans, a successful LCA and operated it as a subsidiary. Air Trans (previously called ValuJet) was established in 1992 and by 2013 was operating 600 flights to 54 destinations. The company is also rated as one of the most successful airline companies internationally, flying 108 million passengers a year. Part of its corporate success is attributed to its team-based approach to management, high level of supervisory staff to teams and corporate ethos, with few internal barriers to its operations. As a result, the airline has around 30 per cent of the USA's low-cost airline capacity, which is estimated to be around 25–30 per cent of the domestic market. Low-cost carriers are estimated to compete on 70 per cent of US domestic air routes. Southwest is a market leader due its constant innovation, such as not charging any baggage fee. The airline constantly seeks new ways of providing consumers with more choice when flying. The underlying motivation is to further enhance customer satisfaction and to increase revenue per departure. These initiatives further support the airline's position as a market leader in customer satisfaction, with one of the lowest levels of complaints in the US airline industry.

Table 5.5 Key facts on Southwest Airlines' operations

- In 2009, the airline served 65 cities in 30 US states, with a fleet of Boeing 737s. By 2013, it was serving 96 destinations in 41 US states. It also offered international flights to Colombia, Puerto Rico and five other countries
- It had a net income of US$99 million in 2009 on a turnover of US$10 billion
- It carried 64.4 million passengers in 2001, 88 million paying passengers in 2009 and 108 million in 2013
- In 2002, its average fare was US$82.84 for a one-way trip on an average flight length of 715 miles; in 2009, the average fare was US$124.90 on a 859 mile one-way trip
- In 2009, the airline paid US$2.44 per gallon for aviation fuel and consumed 1.4 billion gallons
- In 2009, it had the lowest ratio of complaints per passenger carried on US airlines
- The airline's average load factor in 2013 was 80 per cent and average route length of trip 966 miles
- The airline was ranked among the top five US airlines in the National Airline Quality Ratings in 2010 and the top low-cost airline (LCA) after JetBlue
- Southwest was the first airline company to establish a home page on the internet (www.southwest.com)
- According to search engines such as Lycos, Southwest is one of the most commonly searched airlines on the web with 81 per cent of bookings made online in 2009, up from 78 per cent in 2008; 78 per cent of passengers check-in online or at a self-service kiosk
- It had 3000 departures a day in 2007 and 3300 in 2009
- The airline seeks to remain ahead of the competition and does not charge for carrying baggage
- The year 2009 marked 37 consecutive years of profit for the airline
- The company employs around 46 000 staff, nearly 14 000 as flight crew
- In April 2010, the airline was ranked by FORTUNE magazine as one of the world's most admired companies.

Source: based on data from www.southwest.com

by low-cost carriers versus full-service carriers are around 70 per cent on ground services, 74 per cent on crewing costs, over 60 per cent on publicity and marketing and over 100 per cent on catering. This means that, overall, low-cost carriers may have more than 50 per cent cost savings compared with full-cost/established carriers, as exemplified by Case Study 5.3 on Southwest Airlines.

These innovations in low-cost flying have been translated into the low-cost revolution that has permeated the UK and mainland Europe since the last wave of deregulation after 1997. Companies in Australasia (e.g. Virgin Blue, OzJet, JetStar) and Asia (Air Asia, JetStar Asia, Valuair) are following this pattern. For example, Air Asia established a long-haul division (Air Asia X) in 2007 and has low-cost subsidiaries in Thailand and Indonesia

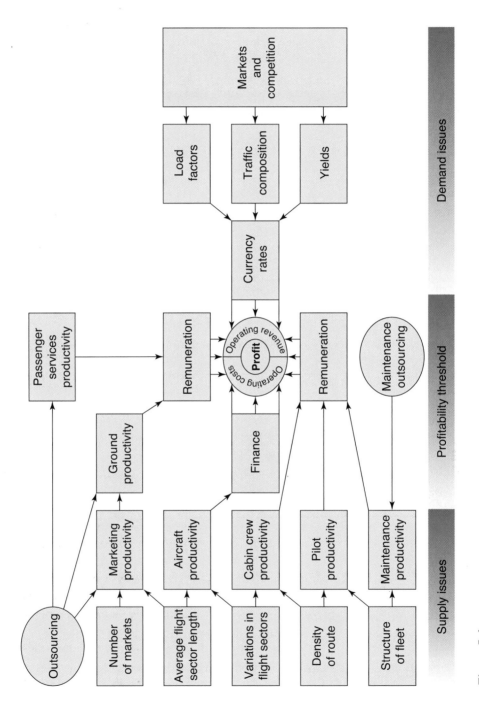

Figure 5.4

The main costs in operating an airline

Source: modified from Page (2005); reprinted in the *Journal of Air Transport Management*, 3; Seristö and Vepsäläinen, *Airline Cost Drivers*, 11–22, © 1997

with 82 aircraft serving 30 countries, 7000 staff and a 21 per cent growth in passenger volumes in 2009 in spite of a global recession. There are also examples of low-cost entrants in Brazil (Gol) though none rival the most cost-competitive model of Air Asia, based in Malaysia, which has generated a great deal of first-time fliers. In Bolivia, the formation of a low-cost carrier –Boliviana de Aviacion (BoA) – as a state run enterprise has almost doubled the volume of seats available to 2 million to democratize air travel. Air Asia has the enviable reputation of having the lowest production costs of any low-cost airline globally. In 2008, the airline entered the Vietnamese market, serving Ho Chi Minh city from its Bangkok hub, adding to its expansion into Indo China (i.e. Cambodia, Laos, Vietnam, Myanmar). The airline was providing 101 routes to 53 destinations. However, the most visible impact has been the massive expansion of low-cost carriers in Europe.

Low-cost carriers in Europe

There has been a sustained debate among industry analysts, the media and academic researchers on the rise of LCAs in the UK and Europe. Airbus documented the scale of such airline development where 13 airlines controlled 25 per cent of the market in the USA in 2007, while in Europe 44 airlines controlled 30 per cent of the market, 10 controlled 20 per cent of the market in Latin America and 43 in Asia controlled only 12 per cent of the market. By 2012, LCAs in Europe controlled 31 per cent of the flights undertaken within Europe. From a tourism perspective, there has been interest in how these airlines have impacted on tourist travel behaviour, destination development and competitive behaviour within the aviation sector. Bel (2009) highlighted the impact of Ryanair on Girona-Costa Brava airport in Spain which saw passenger traffic grow from 500 000 in 2002 to nearly 5 million in 2007, a 770 per cent increase. Ryanair accounted for almost 88 per cent of the airport's passenger traffic, reflecting its corporate strategy of focusing on secondary airports which their business model for flight operation is based upon. The Civil Aviation Authority (CAA) (2006) report *No Frills Carriers: Revolution or Evolution?* summarized the main issues associated with the growth of LCAs, which the CAA entitled 'no frills' due to the low-cost model they employed.

The use of yield management systems to maximize review and profitability, load factors and the business mix combined with direct sales by phone and the internet generated a wide range of new travel options as well as encouraged passengers to switch from full-service carriers on domestic routes. Regulation in the European Union up until 1986 (when the UK–Ireland routes were deregulated to allow more competition) limited the potential for LCAs to begin operation. It was not until the European Union introduced the 'Third Package' or airline deregulation in 1992, which facilitated carriers from any member state to fly any route throughout the EU, frequency restrictions on routes and obstacles to where airlines could operate that were removed, as well as liberalized fares. Whilst Ryanair began operation in 1986 on UK–Ireland routes, much of the expansion in the UK and EU market for LCAs dates post-1992.

The significance of the rapid internal growth LCA in the UK–EU market is reflected in the following CAA statistics:

Plate 5.1
The low-cost airline revolution has been spearheaded by innovators such as easyJet

Source: easyJet

- in 1996, no frills airlines comprised 3.1 million passengers on UK–EU traffic whilst full-service carriers comprised 42.2 million and the charter market 23.8 million
- by 2005, no frills airlines comprised 51.5 million passengers on the UK–EU market, followed by full-service carriers with 47.2 million and the charter airlines with 25 million passengers
- in 1996, no frills airlines carried 1.2 million domestic passengers in the UK domestic market whilst full-service carriers had 30.9 million (the charter airlines share was negligible)
- by 2005, no frills airlines carried 26 million domestic passengers in the UK, with full-service carriers 26.1 million passengers
- for 2005, no frills airlines carried 77.5 million passengers from UK airports, capturing 42 per cent of the UK–EU traffic and 49 per cent of the domestic market.

One illustration of this growth is that regional airports such as Bristol in the UK saw passenger numbers rise from 2 million in 2000 to 6 million in 2008. Even so, the market for LCAs is extremely fluid as, between 1992 and 2012, Budd *et al.* (2014) found that, of 43 LCAs which began operation in Europe, only 10 remained operational. The failure rate of 77 per cent can be attributed to a wide range of factors, a number of which are illustrated in Figure 5.5. Whilst Figure 5.5 pertains to Europe, these factors were also evident in the USA which experienced deregulation prior to Europe and saw LCAs set up, develop and prosper, or collapse, or be subject to corporate takeover.

Figure 5.5
Selected factors contributing to LCA failure in Europe

Source: developed from Budd *et al.* (2014)

LCAs have overtaken the full-service carriers in many parts of Europe and their competitive edge is best summarized by their price competitiveness through cost savings as illustrated in Table 5.6. This shows how LCAs have grown at the expense of full-service and charter airlines with operating margins of up to 22 per cent compared to much lower margins for full-service carriers, which corresponds with high growth rates of around 10 per cent annum in the UK in recent years despite a recession (see Figure 5.6 on future competition issues for airlines in Europe). After a route is launched, high growth rates are achieved by a cheap lead in fares which is then followed by passenger increases of 4–5 per cent per annum and these airlines have also taken market share from charter airlines on popular routes.

Table 5.6 Key characteristics of low-cost carriers which make them more competitive than other carriers

- Some carriers have introduced single/one-way fares not requiring stopovers or Saturday night stays to get advanced purchase (APEX) prices

- No complimentary in-flight service (no frills) often reduces operating costs by 6–7 per cent

- One-class cabins (in most cases)

- No pre-assigned seating (in most cases)

- Ticketless travel – up to 98 per cent of bookings (e.g. Ryanair in 2005) made online at travellers' convenience

- High-frequency routes to compete with other airlines for popular destinations and up to three flights a day on low-density routes

- Short turnarounds that are often less than half an hour, with higher aircraft rotations (i.e. the level of utilization is higher than other airlines) and less time charged on the airport apron and runway

- The use of secondary airports where feasible (including the provision of public transport where none exists)

- Point-to-point flights

- Lower staffing costs, with fewer cabin crew (since there is no complimentary in-flight service; having no food service and thus no cleaning also reduces turnaround times)

- Flexibility in staff rostering, no overnight stays for staff at non-base locations and streamlined operations (e.g. on some airlines toilets on domestic flights are only emptied at cabin crew request and not at each turnaround, thus reducing costs)

- Many of the aircraft are leased, reducing the level of depreciation and standardizing costs

- Many airline functions, such as ground staff and check-in, are outsourced, reducing overhead costs by 11–15 per cent

- Standardized aircraft types (e.g. Boeing 737s) reduce maintenance costs and the range of spare parts which need to be held for repairs

- Limited office space at the airports

- Heavy emphasis on advertising, especially billboards, to offset the declining use of travel agents as the main source of bookings

- Heavy dependence upon the internet and telephone for bookings

- Small administrative staff, with many sales-related staff (as well as pilots in some cases) on commission to improve performance

- Narrower seating on Boeing 737s (148 seats on Ryanair's 737s as opposed to the standard 126 on full-cost carrier configurations)

- Multi-skilled staff (can handle check-in and departure gate)

- Innovation (e.g. New-York-based JetBlue has introduced live television on board to add greater perceived value to the product, shifting the attention away from competition just on price; in 2005, Air Asia moved into more flexible mobile technology for expanding its distribution channels, introducing a mobile phone booking service for tickets)

- Higher yield per passenger and innovative means of securing additional passenger revenue (e.g. in 2003, Ryanair derived 16 per cent of revenue from non-passenger sources other than tickets: 28 million euros from car hire; 23 million euros from in-flight sales; 12 million euros from internet revenue; 35 million euros from non-flight revenue). It aims to increase non-flight revenue from commission on accommodation bookings and areas of activity. The company aims to increase its proportion of free seats (taxes only) from 20 per cent in 2004 to 50 per cent by 2009

- Ongoing cost cutting, with Ryanair considering taking out window shades, seatback pockets and seat reclines

- Diversification into full-cost carrier markets (e.g. German Wings has 40 per cent of its market as business travellers with 500 company accounts) and Air Berlin offers hot meals on flights over 3.5 hours

- Ryanair introduced web check-in to reduce queues at airports and for passengers to only pay for the luggage services they use

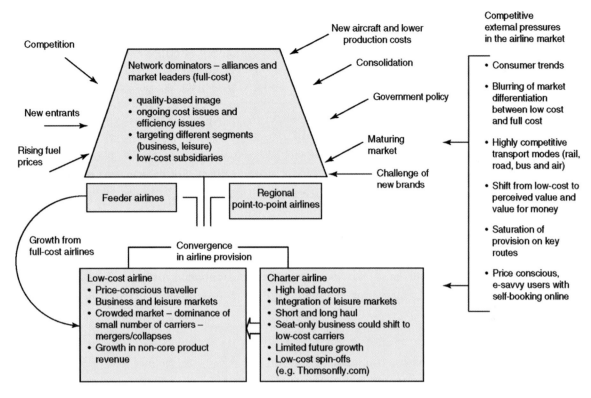

Figure 5.6
The competitive environment for airlines in Europe to 2015

Source: author

Airline marketing and developing client relationships: Frequent flyer programmes and alliances

To continually build and develop the market for air travel, whilst competing with low-cost carriers, full-cost airlines have begun to recognize the benefits of collaboration and joint working in terms of alliances to address the competition. The concept of frequent flyer programmes (FFPs) is one example of building good client relationships to encourage customer loyalty as part of customer relationship management. These programmes were originally developed in the USA in May 1981 by American Airlines (AA). FFPs were developed to attract business following deregulation. AA used its database of passengers to identify frequent flyers who were enrolled into a Very Important Travellers Club. The reward for loyalty was free air travel on a route that consistently had a high ratio of unsold seats – Hawaii. AA's Advantage FFP aimed to maximize revenue yield and its load factor, it helped to develop Dallas as a logical hub and it captured business from AA's competitors' airlines. Other companies (e.g. United, TWA and Delta) soon launched similar schemes. To broaden the marketing appeal of FFPs, non-airline travel services (car rental companies, tour operators and hotel chains), airline-affiliated credit card purchases (mileage credits added according to the volume of spending) and other services now attract FFP points. It is a basic element of airline marketing strategy in the USA, and European and other global carriers have also introduced it.

British Airways was added to the AA FFP to give it an international dimension; soon Qantas joined. This became the Oneworld global alliance in 1999, which now comprises Mexicana, Qantas, British Airways, Cathay Pacific, Iberia, Lan Chile, Finnair, Royal Jordanian, Malév in Hungary and JAL. The Star Alliance is a major airline alliance and was formed in the Asia-Pacific region to challenge the Oneworld alliance. It is a combination of 28 airlines including Air New Zealand, Air China, United, Lufthansa, Thai Airways International, SAS, Swiss, ANA, Asiana Airlines, bmi (British Midland), LOT Polish Airlines, Singapore Airlines, Turkish Airlines, Adria Airways, Croatia Airlines, Egypt Air, Spanair, TAP Air Portugal, US Airways, Austrian Airlines, Blue1, Air Canada, Aegan, brussels airlines, Continental, SAS, South African Airways, Shanghai Airlines, TAM; it offers services to over 1077 airports with 19 700 daily flights and 1000 destinations (with their capacity linked together by the StarNet computer to allow them to talk to each other). There is also a smaller alliance, Skyteam, comprising Aeroflot, Aeroméxico, Air France, Alitalia, China Southern Airlines, Continental Airlines, CZA Czech Airlines, Delta, KLM, Korean Air, Vietnam Airlines and TAROM. This network serves 841 destinations in 162 countries and carries over 420 million passengers a year. Over half of the world airline capacity is linked to airline marketing alliances and this reflects a growing consolidation in the market. Alliances allow partner airlines to grow their network; achieve economies of scale in ticketing, maintenance and purchasing; and provide the consumer with seamless travel.

Doganis (2001) identified two types of airline alliance in existence:

1   commercial alliances, which are operationally driven and focused on the early stages of alliance development
2   strategic alliances, leading towards full merger of airlines.

This is reflected in the three stages to alliance development. The first phase is revenue generation, where partners can enter and exit easily, and involves a series of code shares, joint FFPs, network coordination, joint sales, shared business lounges and an alliance logo. In the second phase, the alliance is cemented together in order to make cost savings for its members from common ground handling, joint maintenance, sales and call centres, purchasing and fleet harmonization. Exit is difficult at this stage. In the last phase, a joint venture situation, exit is almost impossible as it involves franchising, joint product development, sharing aircraft and crews and a single alliance brand. The emergence of alliances reflects a more sophisticated business approach to airline development, although some airlines still seek to differentiate themselves on the basis of unique selling features or propositions – especially in the luxury market, through in-flight food provision.

In-flight catering: A marketing opportunity?

Food provision is estimated to account for 5–10 per cent of the total cost of the fare and some airlines recognize that it is an important element of the in-flight experience, particularly in business and first class where customer expectations are high as a result of advertising campaigns. In contrast, economy travellers often view in-flight food as a sign of value for money although food critics have questioned the need for food as a sign of service quality. With the growth of low-cost airlines, many have decided to remove this element of their cost structures and to charge for in-flight catering. However, airline managers have universally endorsed the role of food as a vital element in airline marketing as recent advertising campaigns have attempted to differentiate airline service. Indeed, Concorde was the first airline service to introduce a vegetarian option in the 1970s and now there are an estimated 19 special meal types. British Airways champions high-quality culinary experiences on board its aircraft as promoted on BA.com:

> British Airways seeks to take the best of world cuisine, finding inspiration from culinary circles, trends, fashion and art and then adapting these for delivery and presentation in an aircraft environment. The British Airways 'Signature Style' offers a clear directional message for our in-flight food strategy. It illustrates our commitment, passion and dedication to creating new standards in an exciting, challenging and continually progressive industry.
>
> (BA.com, accessed 23 December 2005)

To steer this strategy, BA has a range of leading chefs and advisers as part of its Culinary Council, to advise, inspire and lead their 'Signature Dishes' (unique dishes that are associated with an individual chef or restaurant). This is a completely different approach to that of the low-cost airlines, which have downgraded food provision, in many cases, to snacks which are free or to be purchased.

Some airlines perceive food provision as more than a simple element of their product or service and it may explain why customers focus on it as a source of dissatisfaction when their expectations are not met. Yet catering at 30 000 feet is not easy since the tastebuds of passengers change due to pressurization, and their digestive systems become sluggish due to humidity levels and dehydration. Airline meals often come in for very bad press for their poor flavour, although in business and first class meals are often of a gourmet standard to add value to the in-flight experience. Airline meals are often prepared on the ground and frozen then reheated prior to take-off, and this can affect their quality; changes to our tastebuds in the air compound complaints that airline food can sometimes seem very bland. Whilst many short-haul budget airlines do not offer in-flight meals to save costs of £5–6 per passenger (passengers can purchase snacks and sandwiches), food provision on long-haul flights is seen as a way of occupying the travellers' time to create the illusion that the flight is shorter than it actually is. Even so, with a passenger's limited ability to move around and exercise, meals must be easily digestible. In the USA, in 2005 Northwest Airlines replaced its domestic in-flight food provision with a range of snacks for US$3 (a smartsnack snack box) and a US$5 breakfast or lunch/dinner. The airline estimated that this would save it US$20–30 million a year, at a time it was seeking to cut costs.

The growth in contract catering (for example, Lufthansa's LSG Sky Chefs in Europe) has removed the problem of food provision from the immediate remit of airline managers and has created a new business activity for large companies able to meet the exacting requirements of airlines (for example, on a Boeing 747 50 000 catering items are required per flight). Despite the logistical and technical problems of providing quality food on board aircraft, it remains essential in the expectations of consumers on full-cost carriers, and continues to assist airline managers in the perceived differentiation of their products and services, especially in the premium sector of the market (i.e. full economy fares, business and first class). Major advertising campaigns have been designed around these very attributes in an attempt to nurture the high-value business traveller.

The food service sector for the airline industry is estimated to be worth US$15 billion a year globally. LSG Sky Chefs' group of 130 companies in 51 countries has a market share of around 30 per cent, with a turnover of 2.3 billion euros a year. The scale of these catering operations are reflected in LSG Sky Chefs' provision of around 405 million airline meals a year for 300 airlines in 49 countries at 200 locations. Individual markets, such as India, are estimated to be worth US$50 million a year and companies such as Gate Gourmet offer services to 200 airlines worldwide. Much of the growth in this sector of the industry is due to the outsourcing of the airline meals provision as airlines sell off these operations in a bid to reduce costs. In the UK, analysts have indicated that around half of the companies servicing the airline catering market are not operating in profit, highlighting the cost pressures which are being placed on their operations by airlines in terms of the service they require and the prices they are prepared to pay.

Future trends

Airlines are a complex industry to understand, especially as they are working in a constant state of flux and change. As Page (2005) indicated, the main challenges for airline managers in the new millennium are:

- technical change (that is, the greater use of technology such as computer reservation systems (CRS) and global distribution systems which are more complex and all-embracing than the former CRS)
- regional change, where new trading blocs (for example, the Association of Southeast Asian Nations or ASEAN) are posing new challenges for patterns of trade and business travel.

For the traveller, air travel poses ongoing health risks, especially highlighted by the recent concern over deep vein thrombosis (DVT) on long-haul flights where cramped conditions and a lack of movement by passengers in flight can aggravate the situation. Research by the Aviation Health Institute (www.aviation-health.com) examined 447 examples of DVT, of which 67 led to death. The profile of deaths were:

- one third male; two thirds female
- just under half were aged 20 to 49
- 83 per cent occurred on long-haul flights, the bulk of which were in economy class (12.5 per cent in business class)
- the onset of DVT is after the flight.

In addition, there has been a worrying growth in disruptive behaviour on board flights known more commonly as 'air rage'. In the UK, it is estimated that over 3500 incidents of air rage occur each year. This was estimated to be growing at 10 per cent a year. Some of the explanations of the causes of air rage offered by travel medicine research included:

- a lack of oxygen on board; if airlines reduce fuel costs by using recirculated rather than fresh air, passenger belligerence is increased and compliant behaviour reduced
- lack of training for staff to deal with difficult travellers as low-cost travel is not accompanied by reduced expectations.

The Department for Transport (2009) in the UK indicate that whilst this is not a widespread problem, violence occurred in 7 per cent of cases, with alcohol involved in a further 45 per cent of cases, and smoking (which is banned on most European flights) in toilets also being a problem. Although air rage is downplayed by airlines and the CAA, it is nonetheless very disruptive and potentially dangerous; this is exacerbated when drunk passengers are carried by airlines despite guidelines that are supposed to prevent them from boarding. The majority of such offences are committed by males (73 per cent of cases), largely 20 to 40 years of age, with only 5 per cent of cases occurring in first or business class. Typical problems included disruptive passengers using verbal abuse and being unruly because they were offended by airline regulations including use of a mobile phone, laptop and arguments among passengers over seating and rowdy behaviour. Only a small number of incidents led to physical restraints being used or an aircraft being diverted. The likelihood of an offence occurring in UK airspace or on an UK outbound/inbound flight was 1:24 000 for a serious incident on a flight. Greater risks were encountered in the quality of recirculated cabin air provided to passengers in flight and the ongoing debates over the problems of dehydration due to dry air.

Conclusion

The future global aviation industry is likely to contain a limited number of global mega-carriers, with smaller airlines integrated into their operations by strategic alliances and other devices (for example, part ownership by the larger carriers).

The major constraint on this rapidly evolving business activity for airline managers will be the availability of uncongested airspace and airports with sufficient capacity, a feature which the low-cost carriers have addressed through the use of secondary airports. This is already affecting air travel in Europe and the USA, while the environmental lobby regularly opposes airport expansion near to major urban centres. Trying to understand the future for travel is always a challenge as so many factors cannot be anticipated. However, a project funded by the EU (see Peeters *et al.* 2007) sought to model traffic growth for 29 states and Europe to 2020. Figures 5.7 and 5.8 show one aspect of the growth in the air transport market and its impact on CO_2 emissions, which is Greenhouse Gas (GHG). This reflects the expected growth in the volume of tourism

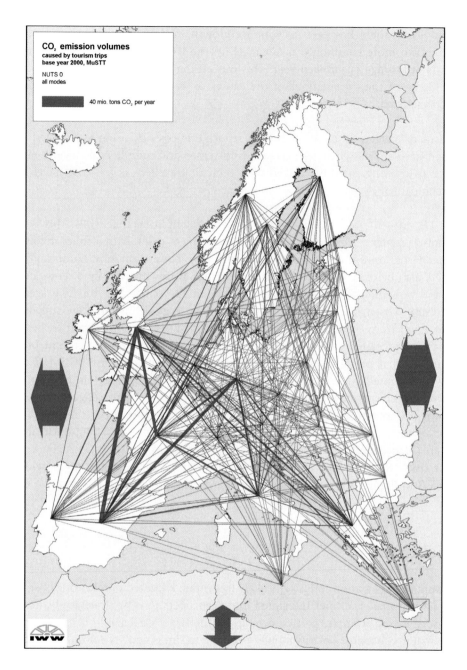

Figure 5.7

Total international tourism origin/destination transport volume GHG emissions (in tons of CO_2-eq.) in 2000. The western arrow represents GHG emissions from tourism flows to America, the southern one to Africa and the eastern one to Asia and the Pacific

Source: reprinted from Paul Peeters, Eckhard Szimba and Marco Duijnisveld (2007) Major environmental impacts of European tourist transport. *Journal of Transport Geography*, 15(2): 83–93, with permission from Elsevier

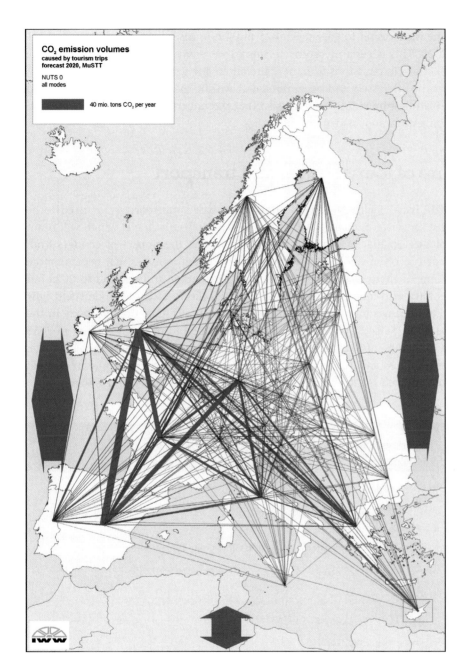

Figure 5.8

Total international tourism origin/destination transport volume GHG emissions (in tons of CO$_2$-eq.) in 2020. The western arrow represents GHG emissions from tourism flows to America, the southern one to Africa and the eastern one to Asia and the Pacific

Source: reprinted from Paul Peeters, Eckhard Szimba and Marco Duijnisveld (2007) Major environmental impacts of European tourist transport. *Journal of Transport Geography*, 15(2): 83–93, with permission from Elsevier

trips in Europe which is set to grow from 875 million tourism journeys in 2000 to 1371 million in 2020. This is certainly going to impact on environmental pollution despite expected reductions in emissions from new aircraft engine technology. These managerial issues have to be addressed and accommodated within the day-to-day operation and longer-term planning by airline managers so that passengers are not adversely affected by delays, congestion and inadequate planning.

The future of tourist travel and transport

The immediate issues facing the aviation and land-based transport sector need to be viewed against longer-term changes which may evolve in tourist travel which will result from technological changes to the way people travel and the impact of changes from an oil-dependent economy to one where alternative energy sources will become more dominant. Some of these changes were identified in Chapter 3 in relation to 2025 but other studies have also looked much further into the future to try to understand how current and future issues may coalesce to shape tourist travel. One notable study in the UK, summarized in Table 5.7, looked at the issues of intelligent infrastructure to 2055 and pointed to a range of likely trends and questions over what travel might look like. Whilst this is informed analysis by futurologists, it does reinforce the long-term changes which will be enforced on the tourist as a traveller as oil dependence declines.

Table 5.7 Critical issues for intelligent infrastructure towards 2055 in the UK

- Carbon emissions/carbon trading
- Waste footprint of energy use by transport
- Social impact on the community
- The future shape and land use patterns associated with human settlement
- Nature of future business activity, its location and method of engaging with other businesses and consumers
- The future of hydrogen as a fuel source for transport
- Mobility – the end of car dependency?
- Leisure activity – its form and nature
- Air travel – will it still exist? If so, in what form – will it be the privilege of the few?
- Will a new world emerge based on a technological future or will technology fail, and if so, what will transport that replaces it be like?

Source: adapted and developed from Office of Science and Technology (2006) *Intelligent Infrastructure Futures. The Scenarios – Towards 2055*

CHAPTER REVIEW

References

Ashford, H., Stanton, H., and Moore, C. (1991) *Airport Operations*. London: Pitman.

BA (2010) *Annual Report*. London: BA.

Barlay, S. (1995) *Cleared for Take-off: Behind the Scenes of Air Travel*. London: Kyle Cathie Limited.

Bel, G. (2009) How to compete for a place in the world with a hand tied behind your back: The case of air transport services in Girona. *Tourism Management*, 30(2): 522–529.

Boeing Commercial Airplane Group (2002) *2002 Current Market Outlook*. Seattle: Boeing Commercial Airplane Group.

Boeing Commercial Airplane Group (2004) *Current Market Outlook 2004*. Seattle: Boeing Commercial Airplane Group.

Boeing Commercial Airplane Group (2010) *Current Market Outlook 2010*. Seattle: Boeing Commercial Airplane Group.

Budd, L., Francis, G., Humphreys, I. and Ison, S. (2014) Grounded: Characterising the market exit of European low cost airlines. *Journal of Air Transport Management*, 34: 78–85.

CAA (2006) *No Frills Carriers: Revolution or Evolution?* London: CAA.

Department for Transport (2009) *Disruptive Behaviour on Board Aircraft*. London: Department for Transport.

Doganis, R. (1991) *Flying Off Course: The Economics of International Airlines*. London: Routledge.

Doganis, R. (1992) *The Airport Business*. London: Routledge.

Doganis, R. (2001) *The Airline Business in the Twenty-First Century*. London: Routledge.

Environmental Change Institute (ECI) (2006) *Predict and Decide: Aviation Climate Change and UK Policy*. Oxford: ECI.

European Low Fares Airline Association (ELFAA) (2002) *Liberalisation of European Air Transport: The Benefits of Low Fare Airlines to Consumers: Airports, Regions and the Environment*. Belgium: ELFAA.

Page, S. J. (2002) Airline management. In M. Warner (ed.) *Encyclopaedia of Business and Management*, Vol. 1, 2nd edn. London: Thomson Learning (online version).

Page, S. J. (2005) *Transport and Tourism: Global Perspectives*, 2nd edn. Harlow: Pearson Education.

Page, S. J. (2009) *Transport and Tourism: Global Perspectives*, 3rd edn. Harlow: Pearson Education.

Peeters, P., Szimba, E. and Duinjnisveld, M. (2007) Major environmental impacts of European tourist transport. *Journal of Transport Geography*, 15(2): 83–93.

Further reading

The following are very good sources and accessible as well as easy to read:

Chang, H. and Yang, C. (2008) Do airline self-service check-in kiosks meet the needs of passengers? *Tourism Management*, 29(5): 980–993.

Doganis, R. (1992) *The Airport Business*. London: Routledge.

Doganis, R. (2001) *The Airline Business in the Twenty-First Century*. London: Routledge.

Graham, A. (2013) *Managing Airports*, 4th edn. London: Routledge.

Graham, B. (2008) New air services: Tourism and economic development. In A. Graham, A. Papatheodorou and P. Forsyth (eds) *Aviation and Tourism: Implications for Leisure Travel*. Aldershot: Ashgate, 227–238.

Halpern, N. and Graham, A. (2013) *Airport Marketing*. London: Routledge.

Morley, C. (2006) Airline alliances. In L. Dwyer and P. Forsyth (eds) *International Handbook on the Economics of Tourism*. Cheltenham: Edward Elgar, 209–223.

Page, S. J. (2009) *Transport and Tourism: Global Perspectives*, 3rd edn. Harlow: Pearson Education.

Warnock-Smith, D. and Morrell, P. (2008) Air transport liberalisation and traffic growth in tourism-dependent economies: A case-history of some US–Caribbean markets. *Journal of Air Transport Management*, 14(2): 82–91.

Questions

1 Why are airports so important as staging points for international travel?
2 What range of issues would you have to deal with as an airport manager?
3 Why is the US airline industry facing a crisis?
4 How have the low-cost carriers affected the business of leisure travel?

Access additional resources

- For students: Multiple choice questions for each chapter, video links and further reading.
- For instructors: PowerPoint slides with tables and diagrams, additional case studies, video links and further reading.

Accommodation and hospitality services

Learning outcomes

This chapter examines the significance of the tourist accommodation product and hospitality services consumed by tourists. The chapter will outline the diversity of accommodation types and a number of current trends in the accommodation sector. On completion of the chapter, you should be able to understand:

* the scope and nature of tourist accommodation and hospitality services
* the range of operational issues affecting the accommodation sector
* the differences between serviced and non-serviced accommodation
* the importance of environmental issues in the management of hotels.

Introduction

Accommodation provides the base from which tourists can engage in the process of staying at a destination. It is an element of the wider hospitality sector that is used by tourists. Accommodation has emerged as the focal point for the hosting of guests and visitors through the ages: a guest pays a fee in return for a specified service and grade of accommodation, and associated services such as food and beverages. The accommodation establishment as a commercial venture, especially the evolution of the commercial hotel in the Victorian period, has dominated the literature on accommodation, as entrepreneurs responded to the demand for serviced accommodation of a high standard. The development of accommodation has normally accompanied the growth of resorts, areas of tourism activity and the demand to visit specific areas. Like the tourist, accommodation assumes many forms, and not all of them fit the conventional image of the hotel (Plates 6.1 and 6.2).

This chapter examines the scope and nature of accommodation, the impact of globalization and the operational issues that affect the accommodation sector. To understand the wider context of accommodation as a hospitality service, the hospitality industry is examined. The discussion then turns to the growing differentiation of accommodation in the serviced and non-serviced sector. The accommodation sector is part of the capital-intensive infrastructure that tourists utilize, and is very labour intensive in servicing visitors' needs.

The hospitality sector

Hospitality is the very essence of tourism, involving the consumption of food, drink and accommodation in an environment away from the normal home base. The very nature of hospitality involves hosting and hospitality provided by a host and involving a guest. Historically, hospitality was not necessarily a commercial endeavour, as you might host someone with the expectation they might host you at a later stage (as is the case with visiting friends and relatives). In modern-day society (although not necessarily in traditional societies) hospitality has become a commercialized experience, where the guest pays for the services/goods they consume via a bill. This commercialized transaction has its historical roots in the ale houses of medieval times, which were followed by the emergence of coaching inns on long-distance journeys and public houses. It was not until the mid-seventeenth century that the idea of a hotel developed in Paris, and this subsequently continued in eighteenth-century London. Much of the subsequent growth in Victorian and Edwardian times saw hotels developed at major transport nodes, such as railway termini in cities, and around commercial districts to cater for business travellers. Certain districts of cities also began to develop different reputations for tourist accommodation at this time, as high-class establishments aimed at the luxury market were developed (e.g. in London's West End) whilst other districts developed a reputation for lower grades of accommodation.

Plate 6.1
Resort Hotel, Denarau Island, Fiji

Source: author

Plate 6.2
Bodmin Jail, Cornwall, a former jail now operating as a restaurant, accommodation facility and attraction

Source: author

Accommodation is only one component of the hospitality sector, as Figure 6.1 shows, which outlines a typology of establishments providing hospitality services.

Hotels

Restaurants

Cafes and catering places

Night clubs and licensed clubs

Take-away food bars

Public houses

Canteens

Camping and caravaning sites

Holiday camps

Short-stay tourist accommodation

University and higher education accommodation provision

Catering services to educational establishments

Contract caterers (e.g. Compass Catering and Brake Brothers in the UK)

Figure 6.1
Typology of hospitality establishments
Source: author

In the UK, an indication of the scale of the hospitality sector can be gauged from the following statistics – there are over:

*   4700 hotels
*   122 000 restaurants
*   110 000 public houses, clubs and bars
*   25 000 contract catering companies; and
*   it generates £4.2 billion in revenue.

The tourism industry more generally employs 2.7 million people in the UK, of which 347 000 are associated with accommodation and 1.1 million with food and beverage servicing, these being the two largest categories of employment (Table 6.1).

The scale of employment illustrates the labour-intensive nature of these businesses in servicing visitor hospitality needs. The geographical distribution of hospitality employment in the UK is dominated by London, particularly the City of Westminster

Table 6.1 UK employment by tourism industry (2011)

	Industry group	Employment in main and second jobs 2011 (1000s)	Percentage of total for all industries
1	Accommodation for visitors	347	1.2
2	Food- and beverage-serving activities	1179	3.9
3	Railway passenger transport	71	0.2
4	Road passenger transport	235	0.8
5	Water passenger transport	13	0
6	Air passenger transport	51	0.2
7	Transport equipment rental	26	0.1
8	Travel agencies and other reservation services activities	104	0.3
9	Cultural activities	226	0.8
10	Sports and recreational activities	442	1.5
11	Exhibition and conference activities	27	0.1
	Subtotal: Tourism industries	**2722**	**9.1**
	Subtotal: Non-tourism industries	**27 213**	**90.9**
	Total: All industries	**29 935**	**100**

Source: ONS (2012) *Geography of Tourism Employment*. ONS: London

with over 86 000 hospitality jobs, and nine other key locations (i.e. Birmingham, Glasgow, Edinburgh, Manchester, Leeds, Cornwall, Camden in London, Liverpool, and Kensington and Chelsea in London) according to the British Hospitality Association report in 2011, *Hospitality Driving Local Economies*. The study also identified the growth potential of the sector which could generate a further 236 000 jobs by 2015 and a further 239 000 jobs by 2020 to create a visitor economy with a £90 billion turnover.

But it is the accommodation sector which tends to attract a great deal of interest due to its role in housing tourists during their stay at a destination. Globally, the International Hotel and Restaurant Association estimates that there are 300 000 hotels and 8 million restaurants employing 60 million people and generating US$90 billion.

In contrast, in the 27 countries of the EU, in 2010 accommodation and food services contributed €195 billion to the economy. The sector employed 10.1 million people, with 42 per cent employed in businesses with fewer than ten employees. By comparison, hotels licensed in India by the Ministry of Tourism numbered 1376 in 2012 with 76 000 rooms.

The accommodation sector

It is the scope and significance of the accommodation sector which is of interest to tourism analysts, not least because it often comprises the largest element of tourist expenditure during a trip (excluding visiting friends and relatives) (see Table 6.2 for a list of key studies of tourism and accommodation). More specifically, hotels provide a base for business travel, meetings and conferences and these are also lucrative, high-yielding business (i.e. they attract high profit margins due to the expenditure by business travellers and delegates), with rooms being hired for meetings, and functions being provided along with entertainment. Both business travellers and leisure travellers staying in hotel accommodation have a higher propensity to spend whilst they are away than when they are at home. Therefore, hotels not only meet the visitor's basic requirement – of shelter for the night – but also add value to the experience by providing ancillary services and products. Hotels also have the advantage that hosting guests has the potential to generate additional revenue from food and beverage services.

Table 6.2 Key studies on accommodation and hospitality

Brotherton, B. (ed.) (2003) *International Hospitality Industry: Structure, Characteristics and Issues*. Oxford: Elsevier.

Davis, B., Lockwood, A., Pantelidis, I. and Alcott, P. (2008) *Food and Beverage Management*. Oxford: Elsevier.

Kaufman, T., Lashley, C. and Schreier, L. (2009) *Timeshare Management*. Oxford: Elsevier.

Rutherford, D. and O'Fallon, H. (2010) *Hotel Management and Operations*. Oxford: Elsevier.

Timothy, D. and Teye, V. (2009) *Tourism and the Lodging Sector*. Oxford: Elsevier.

The accommodation sector as a global phenomenon and operational issues

In Chapter 1, the growing globalization of the tourism sector was briefly introduced, with global companies responding to consumer trends. Globalization has resulted in various forms of company that operate in a globalized or transnational manner. These comprise:

- global corporations which operate throughout the world, such as the International Hotel Group which franchises its brand across the world (see Table 6.3)
- multinational corporations, with operations in countries outside their main base or headquarters
- smaller multinationals, which operate in a limited number of countries.

Table 6.3 Operational characteristics of the IHC Group: A global organization

The IHC Group operates in 100 countries, has 674 000 rooms and had a $614 million operating profit in 2012. Key features of the IHC accommodation offer include preferred brands, comprising:

- Intercontinental Hotels and Resorts with 170 hotels
- Crowne Plaza with 372 hotels
- Hotel Indigo with 50 hotels
- Holiday Inn with 1200 properties, with a further 10 Holiday Inn Club Vacations properties, 37 Holiday Inn resorts
- Holiday Inn Express, with 2172 properties
- EVEN Hotels (1 property under development in 2012)
- Staybridge with 187 properties
- Candleford Suites with 277 properties.

The company operates 3934 franchised properties, 658 are managed and 10 are owned/leased.

The company's global operations are evident from its regional distribution of properties it operates (and those in the pipeline):

- The Americas, 3555 properties (670 pipeline)
- Europe, 628 properties (51 pipeline)
- Asia, Middle East and Africa, 232 properties (292 pipeline)
- Greater China, 187 properties (160 pipeline).

Source: developed from the IHC 2012 Annual Report

A company can adopt transnational strategies by:

- franchising its operation to other businesses in other countries
- licensing other companies or premises to operate using its brand, logo or trademark
- entering into non-investment management agreements
- acquiring overseas properties and interests
- pursuing mergers to integrate business interests horizontally to operate in a number of countries.

These provide businesses with a number of options when deciding on the best mode of entering a market in another country (known as entry mode).

These changes have led to nearly 30 per cent of all of the world's accommodation stock being chain controlled (chains in this case are international businesses operating globally) although the IHC argued that it controlled around 9 per cent of branded rooms globally. Chain hotels often expropriate profits back to the country in which the hotel chain is based. In addition, many of the chains have highly developed distribution channels, being affiliated to major global distribution systems that distribute the product electronically to travel agents. The Horwarth and Horwarth Worldwide Hotel Industry report predicted that by 2050 up to 60 per cent of hotels will be affiliated to global chains, continuing the consolidation trend.

According to the World Tourism Organization (UNWTO), global hotel rooms have increased from 14 million rooms in 1997 to around 17 million in 2008 and this growth has been pivotal to countries increasing their capacity to accommodate continued growth in domestic and international tourism. The majority of investment has arisen from private sector finance, although some governments provide incentives to hotel developers (e.g. tax breaks and tax holidays) to encourage investment in this sector. With hotel room construction costs now in excess of £100 000 (e.g. costing over £1000 a square foot) in London, one can see the enormous capital costs of development. Add to this the cost of land, and one immediately sees why some modest London hotels command resale values in excess of £100 million. However, budget hotel rooms can be built for £35 000.

Growth in chain-owned hotels is a fast-changing area of activity in tourism, as groups acquire, takeover and divest themselves of properties (as the example of IHC in Further Reading 1 indicated). The major areas of activity are often in the key tourist locations (e.g. resorts and cities), which is evident from a brief analysis of VisitLondon's monitor of hotel activity. Much of the UK activity has traditionally occurred in and around London as the country's main tourist gateway and business centre. A lack of development land and restriction on new projects in the West End of London has pushed development to the east, south and north of London's traditional central tourist district in the boroughs of Kensington and Chelsea, Hammersmith, Camden and Westminster. Whilst the main tourist market (i.e. domestic and international tourists undertaking leisure travel) provide a base for the accommodation sector, Horwarth and Horwarth also highlighted a number of other markets for hotel accommodation including:

- airline crews on layovers in between flight schedules, resting before continuing their duties
- conference delegates
- tour groups
- government officials
- other categories of travellers.

The business traveller remains the premium market for hotels, since they stay shorter periods than leisure travellers, but spend higher sums per visit. Many budget chains such as Travelodge have also developed a two pronged strategy to be the number one budget chain: expansion in London and in other smaller urban centres in the UK. The Horwarth and Horwarth study also found that the balance of domestic to international visitors in chain hotels were 48:52 per cent compared to 51:49 per cent in independent hotels. In this respect, the Horwarth and Horwarth study highlights the diversity of markets which hotels serve, although some accommodation may specialize in certain markets as we will see in the discussion of boutique hotels later in this chapter. One indication of the scale of tourist use of global hotel accommodation is provided by UNWTO data which shows that in 2008, the USA had the largest volume of rooms (4.6 million). In terms of domestic tourist use, UNWTO illustrated the scale of demand in 2008: China had 1.5 million rooms with 437 million domestic tourist nights spent in accommodation followed by Italy with 1 million rooms and 141 million domestic tourist nights spent in 2008 followed by Germany with 900 000 rooms and 180 million nights spent and Spain with 838 000 rooms and 113 million nights spent by domestic tourists. By 2012, the IHC Annual Report highlighted that global hotel capacity had reached approximately 21.5 million rooms, with around a third being branded. In a European context, private accommodation still remains the most important for certain markets such as Greece, Spain, Italy, Portugal, Finland, Sweden and the UK. In contrast, Danes, Germans, Irish, Austrians and visitors from Luxembourg have a propensity to use hotels for domestic and international travel. This highlights the divergence among different countries and illustrates the appeal of different elements in the accommodation industry.

The characteristics of the accommodation industry

Accommodation has been conceptualized by some researchers as a product and this is illustrated in Figure 6.2 which depicts the principal factors that can impact upon the way the product is constructed, portrayed and sold to customers. For example, large luxury hotels will emphasize facilities, service and image to certain market segments, such as business travellers, to secure business. In contrast, economy hotels will ultimately emphasize price as the key determinant of the product formulation. In each case, the accommodation product is a complex amalgam of factors that combine to provide the tourist with something they wish to consume. Tourist accommodation is also characterized by a number of features described in Table 6.4.

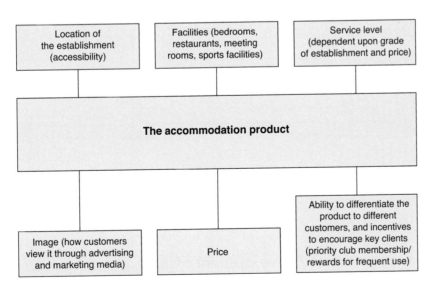

Figure 6.2
Accommodation as a product

Source: author

Table 6.4 Forms of tourist accommodation

	Usage	
	Business	Leisure
Serviced accommodation		
Hotels	X	X
Resort hotels		X
Educational establishments	X	X
Airport hotels	X	X
Motels	X	X
Inns	X	X
State-run hotels	X	X
Bed and breakfast		X
Apartment hotels	X	X
Non-serviced accommodation		
Holiday villages/centres/camps		X
Caravans		X
Camp sites		X
Gîtes		X
Holiday cottages		X
Villas		X
Youth hostels		X
Backpacker hostels		X
Recreational vehicles		X
Other		
Staying with friends/relatives	X	X
House swaps		X

The diversity of accommodation types which exist means that there is scope for the accommodation sector to adapt and develop its product base to meet changing consumer needs.

The management and development of the accommodation sector

The sector's management and development are dependent upon a wide range of factors, not least are the diverse range of key stakeholders and interest groups which shape the

Figure 6.3
Scope of the accommodation stakeholders in Scotland

Source: author

way the sector is managed and directed on a day-to-day as well as strategic level, illustrated in Figure 6.3. This shows that aside from the owners and managers who are responsible for delivering accommodation products and experiences to visitors on a daily basis, a wide range of other stakeholders interact with the sector to shape its development. This model of stakeholder involvement is fairly typical of most countries: it is predominantly a private sector activity with public sector involvement to consider the long-term development needs of the industry (i.e. investment needs in relation to its objectives for developing key destinations). For example, in Scotland, the creation of a national investment plan for tourism will have accommodation development as a key priority because of the need to invest in further development of the sector given the wide range of consumer-led and supply-led issues shaping the sector to 2015. As Table 6.5 shows, these issues (which are fairly typical of many other countries) highlight key trends and developments that the sector will need to address in terms of strategic planning and investment which affect the demand for different types of accommodation. One of the most notable examples of state-led promotion of the accommodation sector, where all the stakeholder interests have been coordinated to create a new destination product, is Dubai as shown in Web Case 6.1.

Types of tourist accommodation

The accommodation sector, like the tourism industry, has undergone profound changes since 1945, as the sector has been characterized by constant innovation, evolution and diversification of the product range (see Table 6.4). The pre-1945 pattern of tourist accommodation was dominated by serviced accommodation, with a rapid growth in non-serviced types of accommodation after 1945. Yet even the distinction between serviced

Table 6.5 Future demand and supply issues for the Scottish accommodation sector to 2015

Demand issues	Supply issues
• Experience you provide rather than the tangible features will be important	• Rise of timeshare/shared ownership/fractional use
• Dynamic packaging	• Seasonality may be addressed more fully in urban locations following Glasgow's success in the area to fill capacity
• Further segmentation into niche groups	
• Grey market continues to grow	
• Technology usage increases	• Rural version of boutique hotel is beginning to show evidence of development
• Individualism in the requirements of guests	• Second homes and new models of ownership
• Standards required will be higher	• Large number of small operators due to retire and exit the industry by 2015
• Internet as primary booking source	
• Value for money will continue to grow in importance	• Investment in technology
• Need for compulsory registration of premises as consumers seek guarantee of what they will get for their money	• Continuation of budget model
	• Building costs – cheaper to build new than refurbish but will depend on future labour availability and resources
• Visitor experience develops more fully around the accommodation and other features as opposed to being focused on other elements of the visit	
• More experienced customers; customer journey is more important – life histories of travel more complex	

Source: Page *et al.* (2007)

and non-serviced accommodation is blurring, with the growth of apartment hotels which permit self-catering but also have arrangements so that guests can enjoy food and beverage services at local restaurants and have them charged back to their account. However, the two sectors will be considered separately here.

Serviced accommodation sector: Hotels

Throughout this chapter, much of the discussion has been on the most recognizable element of the serviced accommodation sector – the hotel. Yet even though it was argued above that the greatest changes have occurred in the non-serviced sector, hotels have not been immune to change. A hotel is not simply a premises with rooms, food and beverage services, but a business oriented towards a constantly changing clientele. In some countries, there has been a rapid expansion of hotels into the fast-growing health resort market (e.g. Iceland and Estonia). In other cases, the business of hotels has become highly competitive and independent. Small hotels of fewer than 50 rooms of one- to three-star status have become much more prone to insolvency (i.e. likely to

Table 6.6 Characteristics of tourist accommodation

- Seasonality – periods of demand are typically buoyant in the peak season (i.e. the summer season) with a drop in the low season, usually winter (except for accommodation located in ski resorts)

- Occupancy levels – demand for rooms is spread across seasons, but more precisely according to weeks and days. Accommodation seeks to sell its rooms; they are a perishable product that cannot be stored or sold at a later stage

- Location, which often determines the appeal and accessibility of properties. Typically, a distance-decay principle exists in accommodation locations, with the luxury properties located in the prime in-town sites with greater access to attractions and facilities. Similar micro-locational factors also operate at airports, with the most accessible and prestigious properties in easy reach of the airport

- Different grading systems exist, which may be statutory or voluntary, using a star rating to denote the quality of the establishment

- Properties can range from complex business ventures at the luxury end of the market through to basic hostel accommodation. Accommodation has a high capital asset value relative to the prices charged to customers, with yield per client relatively modest in relation to cost structures

- Accommodation has high fixed costs to service and owners/managers seek to optimize occupancy levels to cover costs

- Accommodation provision is subject to numerous regulatory codes and laws in terms of the fixed plant (i.e. health and safety legislation) as well as specialist laws governing food safety where food is served. Larger premises require a wide range of skilled staff to operate key departments such as front office functions, food and beverage services, housekeeping services, and concierge and portering staff. In some cases, unskilled staff are employed in menial roles, but skilled staff are needed to operate and manage each department.

run into financial difficulty), typically due to cash-flow problems, where inadequate revenue cannot cover fixed costs. Owners need to plan for regular refurbishment and investment to remain competitive, and such costs are often deferred due to poor financial performance. Some luxury hotels will refurbish their properties every five to ten years. Hotel managers need to understand how the operation of their establishment(s) generates revenue, and the scale of costs. It is important to understand other causes of low profitability: employee costs, the cost of staff per room, restaurant costs, supply costs and costs of debt that have to be serviced. How the hotels generate their business is also significant for the hotel manager, particularly when underlying issues of seasonality are considered. Hotels located in city areas suffer less seasonality in occupancy levels than those located in mountain areas where unreliable weather may impact upon the levels of business they can generate.

One important consideration for hotel managers is the global demand and the resources and marketing efforts needed to generate business. The location of the hotel and its size are important determinants of profitability, and affiliation to distribution channels can offer global booking systems (e.g. global distribution systems) as well as a website.

CASE STUDY 6.1
SPA HOTEL DEVELOPMENT IN AUSTRALIA

In the UK and USA, health resorts developed to service the needs of the emerging market for health tourism. This area of the market waned in many countries in the inter-war and post-war period but regained popularity in the 1980s and 1990s as many luxury hotels began to add on-site health spas to attract the market for relaxing breaks as a welcome rest from the stresses and strains of everyday life. This reflects a growing focus among some visitors for improvements to their life-style. It has been estimated that the spa tourism industry is worth US$274 million a year and is growing and is part of the wider market for medical tourism that is expected to have exceeded 4 per cent of global tourism in 2010. The Australasian Spa Association has identified the diversity of spa experiences and products available, dividing the market into: day spa, destination spas (e.g. resorts and individual hotels), natural bathing spas and related spas. The whole ethos of spa tourism is to pamper the guest (as opposed to the more focused health spas which seek to help people address health and nutritional issues). Hotels have begun to recognize the high yielding nature of such treatments and guest stays. Some spas offer holistic treatments and new age activities such as yoga, meditation and complementary medicine treatments. This is a stage on from the 1980s trend of hotels adding health and fitness centres.

In Australia, the state of Victoria has developed a strategy to promote spa and wellness tourism focused on hotels specializing in such treatments to take advantage of the state's natural resources (e.g. geothermal areas and existing hotels). One strand of the strategy is to improve the marketing of this activity to domestic markets, given that the state capital – Melbourne accounts for 70 per cent of all spa tourism. Queensland also contains three of Australia's top 15 destinations for spa tourism with the largest cluster occurring in New South Wales. The activity is largely focused on mineral and geothermal spring areas providing spa and wellness tourism facilities. Hotel groups specializing in these products in Australia include Accor, Crown, Hyatt and Australian owned private hotels. One of the key priorities in marketing these experiences is to differentiate the types of products each hotel offers, so a diversity of products can be assembled for the prospective tourist to choose from. A number of hotels and resorts also specialize in wellness where diet control, stress management, detoxification and exercise programmes are offered such as in Queensland and New South Wales. This will be a growing market segment in the near future, which is currently attracting the more affluent over 50-year-old female visitor. In 2010, Tourism Australia also pointed to potential growth markets such as long-haul German visitors to Australia who were interested in such products and experiences.

Further reading

McNeil, K. and Ragins, E. (2005) Staying in the spa marketing game: Trends, challenges and techniques. *Journal of Vacation Marketing*, 11(1): 30–31.

Pearce P., Filep S. and Ross G. (2010) *Tourists, Tourism and the Good Life*. London: Routledge.

These affiliations help to generate business that is supported by promotions, loyalty programmes, links to other tourism businesses and services as part of the distribution system. For example, the IMC has 48 million members in its Priority Club Rewards Scheme globally. Two basic types of affiliations exist for hotels:

1 *voluntary chain associations*, which have limited marketing activities for members with low fees and shorter member contracts; they are aimed at smaller independent hotels
2 *franchised products* run by the larger integrated hotel chains, with complex purchasing facilities, but higher fees for members. The participating companies often have ten- to fifteen-year contracts.

Among the voluntary chain associations, the most well known is Best Western which has a non-profit approach, being American-based but organized on a country-by-country basis. It has a global brand recognition and charges an initial entrance fee to members. It then charges a yearly flat fee, plus a fee per room booked. Up to 10 per cent of its business is generated by company reservation systems and Best Western charges a reservation fee from call-centre bookings. Other voluntary associations tend to operate in a country or across a number of countries (e.g. Alpine Classic, which operates in Austria, France, Germany, Switzerland and Italy). In contrast, franchise chains are more global. Notable examples include Holiday Inn, which is the largest global hotel brand based on room capacity, and the Comfort Inn chain owned by Choice in the USA, which is the second largest. The Holiday Inn chain charges an initial fee based on the number of rooms in an establishment then a number of other charges including:

• a 5 per cent royalty based on an establishment's gross room revenue
• a 2.5 per cent royalty based on gross room revenue to cover marketing costs
• a reservation charge per room per month.

Joining a chain not only generates business from reservation systems; the image of the chain is important, as well as client relationships. As a recognizable brand it also receives a large proportion of bookings by telephone and email as well as in person, known as 'walk-ins'. Around 68 per cent of IHC bookings are now made online.

To develop profitability, larger hotels have also adopted revenue or yield management strategies, pioneered in the airline industry. By identifying peaks and troughs in hotel bookings from previous years, hotels can provide a predicted pattern of demand based on experience. Using such models, hotels can then charge prices based on likely demand and future room capacity and seek to balance supply with demand to maximize occupancy. The hotel monitors the booking rate and can adjust prices according to future demand, flexibly responding to market conditions. This will take into account the expected business mix, and the profitability of each segment, since filling a hotel with low-yielding business such as air crews is unviable – this sort of business needs to be mixed with full-price and discounted business. Investment in yield management computer systems (as well as the training and know-how) may not have been attractive to smaller hotels but these systems can now be accessed by non-chain hotels via the internet for a monthly fee. Yield management has been widely used in the larger urban-based and resort hotels.

Trends in hotel development have indicated that mega-hotels with over 5000 rooms have also been constructed (examples are the MGM Grand Hotel and Casino in Las Vegas). Yet estimates by tourism authorities in Las Vegas indicated that each new 1000 rooms opened need an additional 275 000 tourists a year to fill them. This in turn needs significant investment in transportation to allow visitors to access Las Vegas, and increased marketing efforts to attract the visitor. Therefore, the hotel manager, hotel chain and developer must be aware of existing levels of supply so that markets do not become saturated and occupancy does not drop, impacting upon profitability. Tourism markets do not operate in an ideal competitive environment owing to the development process, which can lead to shortages in capacity then oversupply. Much of the discussion of hotels and trends has indicated that larger chain properties are the future direction for profitability, given the process of consolidation. Consolidation is one of many trends occurring internationally, as hotel capacity growth has been directly affected by high fixed investment costs in the sector and new modes of management (e.g. Holiday Inn now part of IHC moving from a hotel owner/operator to a management company – see Further Reading 1) as well as the competition in many locations between tourism and commercial offices for land. Other key trends affecting the sector include:

- internationalization of many hotel and accommodation chains (e.g. represented in the three- to five-star category: see Case Study 6.2)
- greater product differentiation and the use of brands by larger operators (and multiple brands by some hotel companies)
- the growth of the non-serviced sector internationally with serviced apartments and self-catering providing greater flexibility and individuality for tourists
- new ownership models (e.g. franchising and management contracting, joint ventures) as well as the rise of investment portfolios in the self-catering market as it has grown in popularity
- the growing importance of second homes in domestic and international settings as greater affluence has created new opportunities for developers and investors
- increasing use of technology, such as the world wide web for marketing and purchasing by consumers which has reduced the time horizon for booking. It has also created new tools for the discerning consumer to track the rating of accommodation by consumers
- the creation of new forms of demand (e.g. the growth of short breaks induced by the introduction of low-cost airlines serving a wider range of destinations)
- the expansion of niche and novelty forms of accommodation (see Table 6.9)
- increased competition between accommodation providers in different destinations and within destinations as epitomized by the shifting trend towards self-catering in some locations, such as the Lake District National Park, where it has begun to outperform serviced accommodation
- a perception that some sectors of the market for accommodation are being displaced (e.g. bed and breakfasts) by budget brands and changes in hostel accommodation

- a more discerning consumer, seeking more for less from accommodation products in the low to mid range
- growth in social media-informed consumers who increasingly review brands, products and services using social media. These consumers review products, services and experiences post-purchase, which is described as e-word of mouth or *eWoM*. *eWoM* increasingly reviews service experiences such as service failures (e.g. this may be presented to a service provider as a complaint) via online travel communities (i.e. TripAdvisor). Research on *eWoM*, reviewing the responses and approaches adopted by companies to *eWOM*, especially in the hospitality sector, illustrates its value in engaging with consumers. This type of engagement can be viewed as a tool to aid in service recovery (i.e. putting things right after a poor experience or at least apologizing for the poor experience). Such approaches are increasingly being used as part of a corporate marketing strategy to help develop greater consumer loyalty through the expanding use of social media to target communities of consumers. A useful review of this expanding area of research within tourism and marketing can be found in Nieto *et al.* (2014)
- a demand for luxury in accommodation experiences by some consumers, for which they will pay a premium (e.g. being pampered with chocolate, flowers and champagne in a top-of-the-range hotel suite)
- a greater use of yield management among hotels to increase profitability
- mixed development where a hotel project incorporates an office or residential development as well as further splitting of the brand and property – a *bricks and brains* split which will lead to divestment in the hotel sector.

In the UK, budget hotels form a fast-growing sub-sector, and key trends affecting the market include:

- an increase in amenities and costs at properties, termed *amenities creep*
- a drop in the number of business travellers using budget hotels
- the necessity of attracting more leisure business
- a growing average size of budget properties
- greater pressure on room rates, due to more flexibility in pricing policies by operators such as Travelodge (e.g. £25 a night for bookings up to a year ahead)
- improvements in full-service hotels which have put pressure on budget hotels to cut prices
- the market leader, Premier Travel Inn (650 properties), was closely followed by Travelodge with 500 properties (after acquiring Mitchell and Butler Innkeepers)
- 'breakfast included in the price' is the single greatest attractor in guest stays (despite the market leaders not offering this), with Express by Holiday Inn providing free breakfast.

The market for budget hotel development in the UK has become fiercely contested with major expansion in budget property development in non-central city locations on cheaper land. In the UK, Premier Inn and Travelodge are seeking to also be the number one provider of budget accommodation in London with Premier Inn set to launch a new low-cost brand in major cities.

CASE STUDY 6.2
THE CHINESE HOTEL SECTOR

China is a good illustration of many of the trends affecting the global accommodation sector, experiencing growth rates of 20 per cent per annum in its hotel sector, which far exceeds the impressive rate of GDP growth. China is a relative newcomer to tourism development, given that the economic reform after 1978 gradually opened the country to international and increased domestic tourism growth. As Gu *et al.* (2012) indicated, the period 1978–88 was associated with growing international arrivals, which numbered 716 000 in 1978 rising to almost 60 million over 30 years later. After 1994, domestic tourism growth expanded from 524 million to over 2.1 billion in 2010. Therefore the combined growth of international and domestic tourism has fuelled the growth for hotel accommodation, as illustrated in Figure 6.4. Figure 6.4 illustrates the dominance of the major cities and South Eastern Seaboard based on data from UNWTO (2012) *Report on Urban Tourism Development in China*.

The accommodation sector has grown, initially from joint ventures between government agencies and Chinese overseas investors. International hotel corporations also entered the market in the 1980s, through management contracts and joint ventures (Gu *et al.* 2012). The high-quality brands initially focused on the cities of Shanghai, Guangzhou and Beijing. This was followed by growth in smaller cities and major tourist destinations with a wide range of hotel groups operating in the

Table 6.7 Major hotel groups operating in China in 2010

Rank	Hotel name	Hotels (worldwide)	Rooms (worldwide)	Hotels (China)	Rooms (China)
1	IHG (Inter-Continental Hotels Group)	4432	643 787	227	50 440
2	Wyndham Hotel Group	7112	597 674	326	48 821
3	Hilton Hotel Corp	3526	587 813	24	8695
4	Marriott International	3329	580 876	58	21 970
5	Accor	4111	492 675	107	28 002
6	Choice Hotels	6021	487 410	3	455
7	Best Western International	4048	308 477	34	6396
8	Starwood Hotels and Resorts Worldwide	979	291 638	72	26 704
9	Carlson Hotels Worldwide/Rezidor	1059	159 756	9	3817
10	Global Hyatt Group	399	120 031	17	NA
11	Shangri-La	72	30 000	36	NA
12	Banyan Tree	30	NA	5	502
13	Ascott	NA	NA	40	7000

Source: H. Gu, C. Ryan and L. Yu (2012) The changing structure of the Chinese hotel industry: 1980–2012. *Tourism Management Perspectives*, 2(1): © Elsevier

NA = Not Available

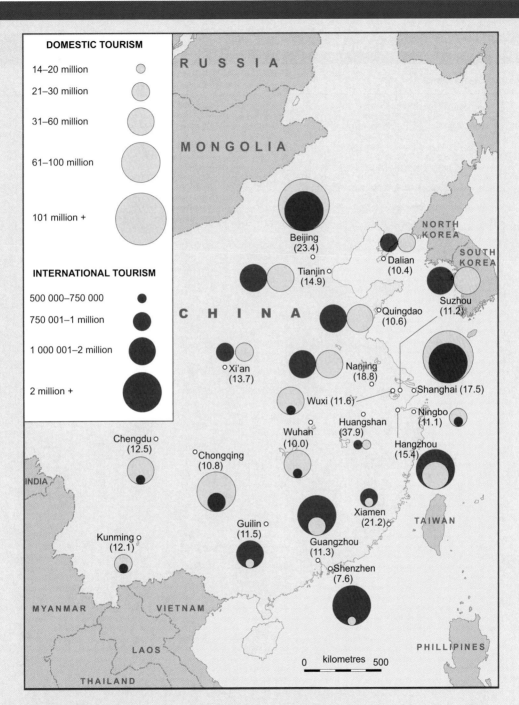

Figure 6.4
The geographical distribution of domestic and international tourism by major cities in China in 2010–2011

Source: data derived from UNWTO (2012) report on *Urban Tourism Development in China*

Table 6.8 Top 30 Chinese hotel brands (2011)

Rank	Group name	Rooms	Hotels
1	Jin Jiang Hotels	105 149	703
2	New Century Hotels & Resorts	24 610	83
3	CTS HK Metro Park Hotels	23 964	74
4	Jinling Hotels & Resorts	23 057	92
5	BTG-Jianguo Hotels & Resorts	20 283	67
6	Blue Horizon Hotels Group	16 239	51
7	Biguiyuan Phoenix	15 707	50
8	Guangzhou Lignan International	14 511	55
9	Ladison	13 782	70
10	Hunan Huatian Hotel Group	13 266	63
11	SGF International Hotels	12 346	37
12	Zhejiang Narada Hospitality Services	12 032	42
13	Guangdong (International) Hotels	12 024	41
14	Plains Hotel Henan	11 998	62
15	Minshan Hotel	10 132	69
16	Soluxe Hotel Group	9698	53
17	Nanyuan Hotel Group	9566	69
18	Shandong Silver	8585	66
19	Shaanxi Provincial Tourism	7810	46
20	Centuries	7400	16
21	Tianlun Hotels International	7105	28
22	Gloria Plaza	6754	27
23	Shanghai Hengshan	6504	26
24	Oriental Jasper Hotels	5606	18
25	CTS Fujian	5580	29
26	Hangzhou Tourism	5121	31
27	Shenzhen Airlines Hotel	4983	24
28	Fuzhou Westlake	4496	24
29	Sichuan Jinjiang	4298	15
30	Zhejiang Tourism	4041	18
	Total	426 647	2049

Source: H. Gu, C. Ryan and L. Yu (2012) The changing structure of the Chinese hotel industry: 1980–2012. *Tourism Management Perspectives*, 2(1): © Elsevier

country by 2010 (Table 6.7). Alongside the internationalization of China's hotel industry has been the development of Chinese hotel brands, the largest of which – Jin Jiang Hotels – is among the top 13 hotel brands globally (Table 6.8), in common with developments in Europe and North America.

As a result, China's rapid growth in the supply of hotel capacity has seen continued competition with domestic and budget brands entering the market to drive expansion.

Further reading

Gu, H., Ryan, C. and Yu, L. (2012) The changing structure of the Chinese hotel industry 1980–2012. *Tourism Management Perspectives*, 2(1): 56–63.

Table 6.9 Niche and novelty forms of tourist accommodation

- Ice hotels
- Ecolodges
- Tree houses
- Caves and underground lodges
- Underwater hotels
- Historic buildings
- Capsule hotels
- Pilgrim rest homes and retreats
- Outer space experiences
- Cruises
- Lighthouses
- Plastic surgery/medical tourism venues (e.g. luxury hospitals)

Source: based on Timothy and Teye (2009)

But one interesting new trend that has challenged this is the growth of boutique hotels.

The boutique hotel

Boutique hotels are a new category of property in the hotel sector which have been described as townhouses or small style-led properties that are fashion-conscious and are modelled on the concept of a 1960s clothing boutique, based on unique products and goods. Such properties defy conventional star ratings, their attraction being the consumer who seeks a unique experience, different to that provided by the conventional chain hotel. In this respect, the boutique hotel is a lifestyle product, with unique architectural or style features such as individually decorated rooms. In the USA, the operators in this market are Ian Schrager, Kimpton, Joie de Vivre, Starwood and the South Beach Group. Such operators have styled their properties as fashionable properties to stay in, and they are associated with consumers who are trendsetters in the music, media and film industry. The Design Hotels marketing consortium now has 150 'unique' hotels in 35 countries where key characteristics include:

- *design*, where fashionable interior design is the attraction with Armani, Lauren, Bulgari and Versace associated with these elements in some unique properties
- *tasteful*, cool or minimalist design features, emphasized in some locations
- the properties being typically *smaller properties*, with the first generation of them converted from historic buildings. This trend has now spread to resort locations and also exists in the budget range too – cheap and chic.

The designer hotel has also evolved into a chain proposition in upmarket segments (e.g. W Hotels (Starwood) and Bulgari Hotels (Ritz-Carlton)) pitched at lifestyle travellers, interested in the latest trends, and business leaders. In the USA, 45 000 rooms in boutique hotels saw their premium value in room rates and revenue per average room rate almost double the luxury segment of the hotel market. Boutique hotels do not have standardized maintenance and repair costs but the positive features normally outweigh operational costs.

In some boutique hotels (such as the Malmaison chain in the UK) there is no room service and few frills in the eating establishments. Some owners have even reduced the fitting-out costs of hotels by adopting a minimalist strategy. In the USA, occupancy levels in boutique properties have grown steadily from 69 per cent in 1995 to 71 per cent in 2000 – a good performance. In some instances, boutique hotels have reduced costs by reducing service levels, compensating for this with their style features and their marketing of the limited services as positive elements. For example, the property owned by Firmdale in Knightsbridge, London, does not have a restaurant and so has marketed itself as an exclusive bed-and-breakfast hotel. Many boutique operators are also responding to the market more flexibly than are larger chain hotels, through a process of continuous improvement. A number of factors that are promoting a continued growth in boutique hotels include:

- the internet, making it simpler for customers to access this new form of hotel
- a number of larger hotel chains entering this market, such as the Hilton Group and Marriott International.

The entry of chains to the boutique market may be a contradiction in that the individuality of each hotel could be compromised by the homogeneity of chain principles (i.e. the experience should be uniform in each property regardless of location). For example, in 2010, Marriot were to launch a new boutique brand developed in conjunction with Ian Schrager called edition in Hawaii and then Istanbul, which it will manage on behalf of a consortium of real estate developers who will own the properties. Further expansion is expected with up to 100 hotels planned for the future. Some analysts have seen larger chains moving into this market segment due to its profitability and prestige factor and they have tended to be successful ventures in mature holiday markets. There has also been expansion of boutique hotels in the Middle East with 10 opening in 2007–2009 in a market where the boutique hotel was relatively unknown. However, the principles of boutique hotels are being embodied to emphasize the individuality of the property.

There are also properties that are small and family run with fewer than 12 rooms; they dominate the bed-and-breakfast/small hotel sector. This form of serviced accommodation has also been developed into the home-stay concept (the visitor stays on the farm or in the home of a family who act as hosts and allow the visitor to experience the local way of life) in countries such as New Zealand where it enables rural farmers to supplement their income. At the other extreme are the resort hotel complexes popularized by Club Med, where all tourist services are included and paid for at the time the holiday is purchased. At the same time, a trend towards luxury travel has caused a rise in luxury accommodation as a significant growth market. The significance of the luxury hotel market is illustrated by the following examples of the cost of staying in some of the world's most expensive accommodation: the Bridge Suite in the Atlantis (Bahamas) £14 500 a night; the Royal Suite in the six-star Burj Al Arab (Dubai) £11 800 a night and the Ritz Carlton Suite (Moscow) £10 500; and there are examples of even more expensive suites in other popular locations.

These developments in the luxury market, however, have also been overshadowed by one further trend – the rise of the budget accommodation market.

Budget accommodation and hotels

The North American market, with its large car-based domestic tourism traffic, saw the motel evolve as a cheaper, more flexible form of accommodation. Normally located on principal routeways and roads, motels evolved as a cost-effective way to accommodate a range of budget-conscious travellers who did not want to pay hotel prices. Motels have developed outside North America, particularly in Australia and New Zealand, and have become a ubiquitous feature of the accommodation sector in these countries, filling a niche for budget serviced accommodation. Motels often provide catering facilities for travellers. They are typically smaller than the average 50-room hotel, being run or managed as family businesses, although some may be affiliated to chains such as Best Western.

In Europe, other forms of budget accommodation exist such as youth hostels. In the UK, youth hostels began in 1931. They now operate at 230 locations in England and Wales, and there are 4500 globally. There has also been investment in new forms of youth-oriented hostel accommodation in the form of backpacker hostels. The traditional market for budget accommodation has been challenged in recent years by the rise of the budget hostels, but most notably by the expansion of budget hotels. For example, the Edinburgh SmartCity Hostel in Edinburgh, which opened in 2005 at a cost of £10 million, is a 132-room five-star hostel with en-suite accommodation. This is blurring the traditional differentiation in the market between what is budget as the hostel has a range from large dormitory style rooms through to private hotel style rooms.

The budget hotel industry is most highly developed in France where two main companies dominate the market – Accor and Group Envergure, the latter which focuses on France and budget brands such as Campanile. For example, Accor had 21 per cent of its hotel business located in France based on popular brands such as Ibis, All Seasons, Etap and Hotel F1. In contrast, it had 22 per cent of its properties in the US and Canadian budget market based on its Motel 6 and Studio 6 brands. Accor was in the process of splitting its hotel and services businesses in 2010 and refocusing its strategy in line with the IHC – to primarily be a hotel management company so it manages its 4100 hotels in 90 countries with an active expansion strategy to grow capacity by a further 200 000 rooms by 2015. The UK has also embraced the budget hotel market which has rapidly expanded since the 1990s as major players have entered and developed the market (e.g. Travelodge owned by Dubai International Capital, Premier Inn owned by Whitbread and Holiday Inn Express which is an IHC brand). Travelodge first developed its presence in the UK market in 1985. In 2010, the two major players were Travelodge and Premier Inn in the UK. The third player is Holiday Inn Express which launched its first budget hotel in the UK in 1996 after developing the concept in the USA in 1991.

The hotel-chain domination of the European budget sector reflects its profitability, with low staffing requirements (i.e. a full-time staff of 20 can operate a 100-room hotel) and the costs of construction are modest: modular construction techniques allow prefabricated rooms to be built and fitted out relatively cheaply at a fraction of the cost of building an in-town luxury hotel. Many new-build budget hotels are located at out-of-town sites, or adjacent to motorway junctions to meet the needs of car-borne traffic. Major city budget hotels have often converted older properties, with low fit-out costs per room of typically £5000 in the UK, since the accommodation offered is of a basic standard. This expanding segment is taking business away from existing budget providers such as the youth hostel market and from the mid-range hotels (three-star hotels) since prices are competitively priced per room (i.e. £39–45), mirroring the North American and Australasian motel sector. The success in Europe of the budget hotel market can be related to the guarantee of quality and minimum standards through the involvement of credible consumer brands, convenience of car parking and location (adjacent to intersections or out-of-town sites) and value for money. Budget hotels also attract mid-week business travellers, leisure travellers and weekend breakers to keep occupancy levels high.

Another trend is towards the unique and more authentic 'hip' budget hotel market. According to Ypma (2001), what makes a hip hotel is fantasy, originality, location, style and authenticity. Ypma's *Hip Hotels: Budget* (2001) outlines the characteristics of some of these trendy locations and unusual properties. The phenomenon of the Hip Hotels range has been a runaway success, selling with around 2 million copies. Around two new titles are launched each year and over 14 titles have been published to date. The website Hiphotels.com has over 400 hotels and 25 000 rooms now listed worldwide.

The non-serviced accommodation sector

Whilst the budget market has experienced considerable growth in recent years, the non-serviced sector has also seen major changes. In the Victorian and Edwardian period, coastal seaside resorts grew and so did commercial accommodation such as hotels, guesthouses and boarding houses. The seaside landlady, with her rules and conventions for guests (i.e. set mealtimes and the need to vacate the room each day) heralded an age when regimentation and rigid social rules dominated. In the post-war period, these accommodation forms began to be replaced by innovations in the non-serviced sector. In the inter-war period, holiday homes developed in many countries throughout the world as the new middle classes developed leisure habits. Yet in the post-war period, a new genre of accommodation developed from caravan parks to self-catering villages and, more recently, holiday parks (e.g. Center Parcs which is now owned by its former competitor, Oasis, in the UK). Since the 1970s, Mediterranean apartments in Spain and other destinations have been developed for self-catering holidays, along with timeshare developments as a new form of limited-ownership 'second home'. *Gîte* holidays are a time-honoured tradition for urban French workers in southern France, and novels such as Peter Mayle's *A Year in Provence* have portrayed the virtues of such holidays. The self-catering market is characterized by high levels of seasonality and a desire for home from home facilities and a shift towards more luxury provision.

The strengths of the self-catering product include: flexibility, authenticity, an ability to manage one's own carbon footprint and impact, and an appeal to the higher socio-economic groups. In contrast, the weaknesses of the self-catering product include: limited quality control, and the perception of it being hard work among visitors and family-centric (only for families). The holiday length is also perceived as very inflexible and based on a model of seven- and 14-day booking patterns so a need for more flexibility is evident, although there is evidence of operators already moving away from such models. In Scotland, the sector was experiencing the following changes: diversification in the sector into timeshare, holiday lodge development, aparthotels, new cottages/residential conversions, university accommodation (to let outside term-time) and alternative properties. What this suggests is that the self-catering sector is innovating and adapting to tourist demand and in some cases, out-performing the serviced accommodation sector, as Web Case 6.2 shows in the case of England's Lake District.

In each category of non-serviced accommodation, specialist operators have nurtured this niche (examples being Eurocamps' sited tents and caravans and Hoseasons' boating holidays on canals and waterways). What is also notable is that major capital investment and large corporations have also entered this market. Each leisure company has other tourism interests: the Rank Group which operate holiday camps/villages using their original brand names (Butlins, Haven and Warner) in the UK was sold to Bourne Leisure who continues to operate these as individual businesses. Haven and its sister company, British Holidays, operate 40 sites as Holiday Parks in the UK. A further development in the non-serviced sector is the rise in the use of university campuses in holiday letting in addition to their well-developed conference businesses.

The caravan and motor home sector

One sector that has seen substantial growth in recent years is the caravan sector. In the UK, Caravan Club membership in 2010 was over one million (380 000 owners), a 200 000 increase since 2005 and these people use the 7000 or more campsites in the UK. Yet an increasing number are using caravans that cost anything from £8000 to £30 000 to purchase new. The image of caravanning as being a low-status and low-quality holiday market business has been rectified by the higher standards of comfort now provided by fixed and touring caravans. They are very popular among young families and the retired. Since the first caravan, the *Wanderer*, was built in 1885 in Bristol, the use of caravans has developed into a substantial element of the European holiday industry. In the UK, this generates around £3 billion as an industry through retail sales, products and holidays, employing 90 000 people (many on a seasonal basis). In Wales the impact of caravan tourism is £22 million. The major expansion of sites since the 1930s pre-dates many planning restrictions and the sites are often near to or in coastal areas as well as in forest and valley areas. Some of the fixed caravans – known as holiday homes – are located in the UK's 2700 holiday parks.

Registrations of motorhomes, which are dominant in the USA and Australia, have increased in the UK and this is part of the wider growth in caravans, motorhomes and holiday homes from a total stock of 710 000 units in 1975 to 1 054 000 units in 2000; growth continued until 2004 and then began to slow down in 2005 and growth returned in 2006–2007. As a result, 62 million nights were spent in such accommodation in the UK making it the most popular form of accommodation after VFR. It accounts for around £2.2 billion of holiday spend in the UK, the majority of nights being spent in England and Wales. In Europe, there are approximately 4 275 000 touring caravans and 920 000 motorhomes in use, being most popular in Germany, the Netherlands, France, Italy and Finland. The market for caravanning in Europe led the European Caravan Federation to estimate that the camping tourism sector generates £15.33 billion a year, based on 375 million overnight stays at 25 000 campgrounds in Europe. Estimates for Eastern Europe suggest these are 18.75 million campsite stays a year by caravanners generating 600 million euros a year. Around £5.5 billion a year is spent on new leisure vehicles with 154 000 new leisure vehicle registrations a year. Many analysts tend to overlook this sector even though it has seen a massive re-imaging and development since the 1970s, with flexibility and less need for planning cited as key reasons for using such accommodation.

A recent UK government Select Committee report on Northern Ireland Affairs provided an in-depth review of the importance of the caravan sector on the economy, highlighting the problems of collating accurate statistics on the size and value of the industry. As a result the enquiry generated the following statistical insights on the sector's significance to the tourism sector in the UK:

*   it employed 90 000 people (including seasonal and part-time staff)
*   11 per cent of all UK holiday spend is on caravan holidays
*   the UK now represents the largest market in Europe for touring caravans as there are around 500 000 touring caravans, 330 000 caravan holiday homes and 120 000 motor homes.

An interesting trend was observed by the National Caravan Council of the UK that thefts of touring caravans had dropped from 5400 a year a few years ago to just under 1000 a year in 2007 following the implementation of a Caravan Registration and Identification System. The NCC is also sponsoring an industry-led initiative to promote the 'Go Green Go Caravanning' website which extols the virtues of towing a caravan versus other holiday alternatives based on carbon output (especially versus flying).

Other issues for the accommodation sector

According to Timothy and Teye (2009), other important sources of revenue for accommodation providers can be found in the food and beverage market (F&B), gaming (i.e. casino operation) as well as conferences and convention market in the USA. Casinos have been highly successful and are relatively recession proof in generating additional income while conferences and conventions can help to fill room capacity in the off-peak season as well as generating high spending visitors.

Eating out

Whilst accommodation establishments provide the focus for hosting and hospitality for guests, not all accommodation premises/sites have hospitality services. These are often provided by restaurants, fast-food establishments, cafes, bars, clubs and canteens. For example, the catering sector generates around £30 billion a year in the UK and employment is around 114 000 businesses. Some parts of the fast-food sector have a very long history of provision for tourism and leisure markets (e.g. the fish and chip shop at coastal resorts in the UK). Recently some chains such as Harry Ramsden's have entered this market. The fast-food market uses contract catering and portion-control techniques to keep their prices down and their delivery is fast to increase the volume of sales; this poses a challenge to independent cafes and restaurants. As in the hotel sector, trends towards consolidation can be observed in the hospitality sector with the rise of contract caterers (e.g. Compass Catering in the UK) and franchises in the fast-food market (McDonald's, KFC, Burger King, Wendy's and Pizza Hut). These outlets pose a threat to conventional food retailing. For example, in the UK in 2010, there were 1193 branches of McDonald's, 700 of Burger King, 650 of Pizza Hut, 300 of Pizza Express and 700 of KFC (in the UK and Ireland), 214 of Wimpy and 170 of Harry Ramsden's fish and chips outlets, plus numerous other small chains such as 173 Little Chefs on major routeways in the UK. Restaurants and cafes have had to respond with innovative marketing. Formula-style cafes such as Starbucks have emphasized the pleasures of quality coffee consumption and relaxation in contrast to the fast-food experience. In 2007, Starbucks had over 530 outlets, Costa over 400, Caffè Nero 290 and Coffee Republic 44 outlets, reflecting the massive expansion in coffee/cafes in the UK market by chains. This is a growth in chain cafes from 885 outlets in 2004 to 1264 in 2007 as the market becames more chain-dominated.

Many of these chain hospitality businesses have global operations and are managed by large corporations. For example, Yum Brands, which was a spin off from the PepsiCo corporation in 1997, owns KFC, Pizza Hut, Taco Bell and the Long John Silvers chain which is based in the USA. They operate in 110 countries, have 37 000 restaurants and employ 1 million people and had a net income in 2009 of US$1 billion.

At a country level, the example of one of the UK's major public house chains – J D Wetherspoon illustrates how a company can seize a commercial opportunity, such as the government's decision to force breweries to sell some of their tied pubs (i.e. those attached to breweries and could only buy and sell brewery approved supplies). Wetherspoon entered the market in the 1990s and purchased existing public houses as well as converted former public buildings (e.g. banks) that were surplus to requirements and turned them into public houses in high street locations operating throughout the day. The scale of the company's operations is shown in Figure 6.5 which depicts the growth and geographical distribution of public houses by 2009. What is apparent from the geographical strategy of the company is that they have grown the number of premises in absolute terms, but reduced the number of premises in the highly competitive London market. In addition, since 2004 the company has expanded the number of premises in Scotland while downsizing in Dorset, Suffolk and South Wales. In contrast, it has extended its geographical reach by expanding the number of premises in Leicestershire, Essex, Kent, Hampshire, Merseyside and Surrey. What this example illustrates is that the hospitality sector is in a constant state of development as corporate strategy determines how, where and when companies decide to expand, contract or stay with the status quo in their business operations and portfolio of businesses.

Food festivals

In more innovative forms of marketing of cities, regions and districts, food consumption has been heralded as the main attraction or theme for the tourism sector. For example, regional food and wine festivals have been used to pump-prime the tourism sector, yielding business for the accommodation sector, and promoting and showcasing local products. In Perth, Scotland, an annual food festival is used to promote the district's tourism industry; this is supported by VisitScotland's area office and public sector funds as a means of encouraging visitor activity. Rolling events, such as the French market it hosts which tours different UK locations, have had a similar impact on Perth as an attraction for visitors. This follows the highly visible and distinctive growth of farmers' markets in many small towns and similar locations in Europe which have acted as a nucleus for visitor activity. In Wales, Abergavenny, a small town north of Cardiff, has an annual food festival funded by the Welsh Development Agency, Welsh Assembly, VisitWales and Monmouthshire County Council. This attracts around 25 000 visitors a year, with 67 per cent of visitors from Wales and 38 per cent from the UK, to a little-known tourist destination. Interestingly, two thirds of the visitors state that the food festival is the main reason for visiting, yet this has raised the town's profile and led to repeat visits. Thus we see that hospitality services can in fact be developed as the prime attraction for a region when they are carefully developed around a unique theme, utilizing local produce, famous chefs and celebrities, as well as high-quality public relations and media coverage. This was certainly the case for Abergavenny, which was featured on the BBC's Rick Stein's *Food Heroes* series and in the accompanying book.

Number of public houses

○ 1–2
○ 3–4
○ 5–10
◯ 11–20
◯ 21–38

Highland

Grampian

Tayside

Central Scotland

Fife

Lothian

Strathclyde

Borders

Northumberland

Dumfriesshire

Tyne and Wear

Cleveland

Londonderry

Antrim

Durham

Cumbria

North Yorkshire

Fermanagh

Down

Lancashire

Humberside

West Yorks

Merseyside

Greater Manchester

South Yorks

Clwyd

Cheshire

Derbyshire

Lincolnshire

Gwynedd

Notts

Staffordshire

Norfolk

Shropshire

Leicestershire

West Midlands

Cambridgeshire

Worcestershire

Warwicks

Northants

Suffolk

Dyfed

Herefordshire

Beds.

Essex

Gwent

Gloucestershire

Bucks

Herts

Glamorgan

Oxfordshire

106

Avon

Berkshire

Kent

Wiltshire

Surrey

Somerset

Hampshire

West Sussex

East Sussex

Cornwall

Devon

Dorset

Greater London/ M25 area

100 km

© SJ Page

215

An interesting example of this approach contributing to a destination becoming over-popular is the small harbour town of Padstow in north Cornwall, which is still a working port. It is the location for many of the celebrity chef Rick Stein's ventures. His success has led to this small town becoming so saturated in the peak season that it is no longer pleasurable to visit. The boom in visiting (including a growth in second-home ownership and massive increases in property prices) followed the filming of Stein's first BBC television series which featured his Padstow seafood restaurant and provided the main stimulus to the destination's redevelopment. Increased visitor volumes have been added to by the success of the Camel Trail, a cycle route in north Cornwall which follows the estuary to Padstow in a highly scenic and attractive area. However, the town's historic form is small and it needs drastically to restrict tourist access by car to deal with the major problems of congestion in the peak season: a problem faced by many small historic cities in Europe. Measures such as those discussed in Case Study 11.2 in Venice are needed to manage the major influx of day trippers to Padstow. Nearby resorts such as Newquay in north Cornwall routinely have visitor numbers in excess of 31 times the resident population in a county where tourism is now estimated to comprise 24 per cent of GDP. The combination of economic generation by the successful repositioning of a locality such as Padstow, combined with the investment by North Cornwall District Council to stimulate economic development around tourism and marine activities, now needs to be accompanied by measures of visitor management due to the major success it has achieved (see Chapter 11 for more detail on this issue).

Environmental issues

Many accommodation providers have also had to respond to global concerns associated with environmental issues and sustainability. Some hotels have embraced the principles of sustainable development to mirror customer concerns with the energy consumed by their stay, and three distinct strands of management practices can be discerned (Figure 6.6). For example, recycling (Plate 6.3), and re-using linen and towels, are minor measures that hotels have introduced. Much more major measures have been undertaken by small hotels, which have run environmental audits to assess the environmental costs of their activities in relation to:

* energy consumption
* transport
* waste
* purchasing
* health
* the local environment, and these are summarised in Figure 6.7.

As Figure 6.7 shows, there are three principal areas where accommodation providers can embrace the principles of sustainability to make environmental improvements to their operations: in terms of tourist activities and their consumption behaviour; in purchasing; and through a commitment by management to drive forward these agendas. This is crucial given that around 21 per cent of all CO_2 emissions in tourism are from

At a practical level the sustainability agenda is addressed through management processes focused on these three areas of company activity

Figure 6.6
The scope of sustainability activity within businesses

Source: author

Plate 6.3
Recycling is a key element of educating the tourist about sustainability as illustrated at an attraction where these recycling bins allow the separation of waste

Source: author

Educating the tourist

- Less towels
- Using less water
- Ecotaxes
- Information for guests on green days out

Purchasing

- Buying green in the supply chain
- Certified suppliers
- Championing green and organic products
- Using local products so as to reduce food miles

Management

- Training and educating staff
- Waste management
- Energy reduction (e.g. solar power)
- Water conservation
- Sustainable building technology
- Environmental certification

Figure 6.7

Environmental issues affecting accommodation businesses: Education – mitigation and reduction strategies

Source: author

the accommodation sector. Much of the stimulus from the sector to be more environmentally sustainable can be traced to 1991 when the Inter-Continental Hotels Group developed an Environmental Reference Manual to guide staff on environmental management measures. In 1992, the International Hotels Environment Initiative developed *Environmental Management for Hotels: The Industry Guide to Best Practice*.

One of the market leaders in the hotel sector for environmental improvements is Scandic Hotels, which is outlined in Innovation in Sustainability 6.1.

In Scotland, the Green Tourism Business Scheme, operated on behalf of VisitScotland, has embraced the hotel sector and other accommodation providers, as part of Visit-Scotland's Quality Assurance Scheme. To join the scheme, a business needs to undergo voluntary accreditation based on an assessment by an independent environmental assessor. The scheme is based upon the implementation measures a business applies and can help raise market appeal for the business's products. Some examples cited by the scheme include making savings of up to £3000 in large hotels through using a compactor for waste disposal, and saving £300 a year in family-run hotels by installing low energy candle bulbs in chandeliers. It is estimated that businesses can save between 10 per cent and 20 per cent of operating costs by using such measures (see www. greenbusiness.org.uk). This is part of a global trend towards embracing more green and sustainable business principles to attract the green consumer. The Green Tourism Business Scheme is one of the most successful worldwide and part of a growing range of environmental accreditation schemes. In 2010, Whitbread announced it was spending £7 million on environmental measures to reduce its energy use by 26 per cent and water use by 20 per cent by 2020 with additional investments in infrastructure to reduce these major resource inputs through solar panels, better insulation and installing low-energy light bulbs.

INNOVATION IN SUSTAINABILITY 6.1
SCANDIC HOTELS AND ENVIRONMENTAL ISSUES –
A PIONEER IN SUSTAINABLE BUSINESS PRACTICES

The Scandinavian hotel chain, Scandic, embarked on its journey towards becoming a sustainable operator in 1993, initially with training materials for staff. In 1994 it pioneered the campaign 'Are you happy to use your towels more than once?', now adopted as an environmental principle globally amongst hotel operators. Such action was designed to reduce energy, water and chemical use in laundering towels which are changed daily in hotels. In the same year Scandic encouraged employees to develop suggestions on how to become a more sustainable company, resulting in 1500 ideas. In 1995 the company introduced more water-efficient measures, aiming to cut its consumption by 14 per cent in 2006. Further measures around waste management culminated in 1996 with each hotel reporting their resource use to monitor water, waste, CO_2 and unsorted waste so as to further reduce resource use. The company also discontinued use of disposable packaging for shampoo.

In 1998, Scandic introduced its 'Omtanke' vision (caring for our guests and each other whilst caring for the environment), which was focused on its sustainability compass (see Scandic.com) emphasizing economic sustainability (i.e. the need to be profitable); ecological sustainability (caring for the environment); and ethical sustainability (embodied in its Scandic in Society programme). This was followed in 1999 with its Swan labelling scheme to identify properties that were lowering their impact on the environment. The same year also marked a redesign of its building and architectural standards, using natural and sustainable materials to meet the aesthetic needs of guests. In 2001, more sustainable supply chain systems were introduced to source an ecologically labelled breakfast so as to reduce pesticide use in agriculture, emphasizing the chain's use of eco-labelled products.

Constant innovation and investment in the company led to its e-learning programme in 2002 for its team members, and in 2004 it introduced a new Disability Coordinator to make its properties more accessible. By 2007, Scandic had educated 5700 employees in sustainability principles and it continues to promote constant environmental innovation as a corporate philosophy with the enviable reputation that a stay at a Scandic Hotel will have a low environmental impact.

Further reading

www.scandic.com

Despite these laudable attempts by larger corporations, the small to medium-sized hotel enterprises (SMEs) still play a major role in the supply of accommodation and hospitality services. As Figure 6.8 shows, some SMEs' awareness of environmental management systems (EMS) was low for a range of reasons. In Chan's (2011) study of Hong Kong SMEs, over 60 per cent of respondents had a limited understanding of EMS, with many not planning to implement this in the near future. The barriers to implementation were reviewed by Chan (2011) who advocated a number of possible solutions to overcome the barriers:

- working with SMEs in the hotel sector to exchange EMS experiences and to share resources
- identifying and selecting suitable partners to assist in EMS implementation, such as green associations and government departments.

These obstacles reinforce the importance of human resource policies to embed environmental values in corporate culture, promoting better education and training for employees.

Figure 6.8
Typical obstacles to implementing EMS in small and medium-sized hotels

Source: developed from Chan (2011) and Kasim (2009)

Human resources issues

Human resource issues have also assumed a growing significance for the hotel and hospitality sector, which has a poor image as an employer. This poor image is partly linked to pay and financial rewards but also highlights cultural issues – where images of servility are conveyed by perceptions of what hotel work involves. Problems in training, shortages of skilled senior and technical staff as well as managerial concerns over service and product quality dominate the ongoing debates over the continued problems this sector faces. Recruiting and retaining good staff remains a perennial problem for the global accommodation sector, in a business where high levels of staff-to-guest interaction not only determine the levels of the guest's satisfaction with the accommodation product, but can impact upon their images of the product and the levels of repeat visitation.

The UK agency People First reported that 1 in 8 hospitality businesses had problems in filling vacancies, with skill shortages for managers and chefs and staff turnover rates of 31 per cent, which costs the sector £414 million a year given the initial recruitment and training costs per employee of £514. This does not include the cost of retention in a sector which has notoriously high rates of staff turnover. Add to this the difficulty of recruiting staff to work in the hospitality sector, and it is not surprising to find major hotels in the UK recruiting workers from Eastern Europe after those countries acceded to the EU. Poland, Latvia, the Czech Republic, Estonia, Hungary and other new EU member states are providing a much-needed workforce for the hospitality sector.

Aside from these operational issues, future trends and developments will also be important in shaping the future form of the accommodation sector. According to the 2004 Future Holiday Forum, assembled by Thomson Holidays, in 2024 we will be enjoying vacations in transportable pre-fabricated packs which can be located anywhere. Other futurists point to airship and underwater hotels as well as the prospects of a space hotel. The holiday pod idea, a 17-storey gherkin-shaped structure, would have the lowest impact on the environment and rooms with changeable images and colours to suit the visitor's mood. In London, the YoTEL concept in South Kensington has many of these features in a 10 m² space, turning underground subterranean locations into profitable hotel sites. Other trends in alternative forms of hotel accommodation can also be discerned. They can be categorized into:

- adapted former buildings such as prisons (e.g. Bodmin Jail in Cornwall – see Plate 6.2), lighthouses, churches and monasteries
- purpose-built structures with very unusual settings or appeal such as cave hotels, houseboats, tree houses which have permanent structures as well as those with more temporary structures (e.g. ice hotels, yurts and igloos) as shown earlier in Table 6.9.

Conclusion

The accommodation sector is a central element of the tourist experience of a place. Indeed it is often purchased in a package holiday and is one of the most frequent areas of disquiet when consumer complaints are made. Yet the international growth in chain activity in the accommodation sector highlights the potential profitability in this market when the product mix, visitor mix and supply–demand interactions are well managed. Accommodation provides a containing context for the visitor and one where tourism managerial skills need to be harnessed at two levels:

1   within the organization, so that operational issues are addressed to maintain profit-ability. The accommodation manager needs a good understanding of business issues (i.e. hotel operations, finance, accounting, food and beverage issues and marketing)

2   in a customer-focused role so that the guest is satisfied with their visit and can be a good ambassador for the hotel product.

Increasingly, accommodation managers need to be aware of competitive pressures in a rapidly evolving marketplace, as reflected in the case of budget and boutique hotels. Customer attitudes and needs are also important, and the growth of environmental awareness among hotel chains – some of which have recognized the cost savings which greater environmental responsibility can confer – reflects this. One thing is certain in the accommodation sector – the consumer's tastes and needs are constantly evolving, and this is reflected in recent trends and developments. Managers and property owners unable to respond to change will find that they will be passed by, as innovations, market changes and price competition redefine the business environment for accommodation providers.

CHAPTER REVIEW

 ## References

Chan, E. S. W. (2011) Implementing environmental management systems in small and medium-sized hotels: Obstacles. *Journal of Hospitality & Tourism Research*, 35: 3–23.

Kasim, A. (2009) Managerial attitudes towards environmental management among small and medium hotels in Kuala Lumpur. *Journal of Sustainable Tourism*, 17(6): 709–725.

Nieto, J., Hernández-Maestro, R. M. and Muñoz-Gallego, P. A. (2014) Marketing decisions, customer reviews, and business performance: The use of the Toprural website by Spanish rural lodging establishments. *Tourism Management*, 45: 115–123.

Timothy, D. and Teye, V. (2009) *Tourism and the Lodging Sector*. Oxford: Butterworth-Heinemann.

Ypma, A. (2001) *Hip Hotels: Budget*. London: Thames and Hudson.

 ## Further reading

The most accessible sources on this topic are:

Cantallops, A. and Salvi, F. (2014) New consumer behaviour: A review of research on eWOM and hotels. *International Journal of Hospitality Management*, 30: 41–51.

Verginis, C. and Wood, R. (eds) (1999) *Accommodation Management: Perspectives for the International Hotel Industry*. London: Thomson Learning.

Yu, L. (1999) *The International Hospitality Business: Management and Operations*. New York: Haworth Press.

Questions

1   Why does hotel accommodation play such an important role in the business travel market?
2   What is the wide range of forms of serviced accommodation?
3   How has the non-serviced accommodation sector developed since 1945? What are the main explanations for growth in certain sections of this market?
4   What is the future for boutique hotels?

 Access additional resources

- For students: Multiple choice questions for each chapter, video links and further reading.
- For instructors: PowerPoint slides with tables and diagrams, additional case studies, video links and further reading.

7 Tour operating and travel retailing

Learning outcomes

This chapter examines the way in which tourism products and services are sold to the consumer. The role of the tour operator and the travel agent are evaluated in terms of their respective roles in the supply chain. On completion of this chapter, you should be able to understand:

- how the distribution chain operates in tourism
- how tour operators package holidays
- the role of travel agents in retail operations
- the use of information communication technology (ICT) in travel retailing
- the managerial skills needed to manage a travel agency and to present holiday products to consumers.

Introduction

For tourism to occur, consumers need to purchase, arrange or acquire the means by which they can travel from their home area and (origin area) to a destination. One element in this process is tour operators and travel retailers. Tour operating and retailing tourism products to consumers are key parts in the production, selling and distribution of tourism services. The organizations that do this link the supply to the source of demand. Yet tourism is not like many other products or services. It is intangible; it is often an experience or product that cannot be stored, tried or tested before purchase, and so the consumer often buys as an act of faith, in the belief that what the tourism industry supplies is in line with their expectations and needs. This is epitomized in the following quotation:

> The travel industry, according to everybody outside it, is run by cowboys. Despite the abundance of professionally run companies, both big and small, the perception is still that holiday firms rip off unsuspecting customers ... ABTA fights gamely to defend the industry, but it's like pushing water uphill. Even though a lot of criticism is unfair, you can't help thinking that the industry has brought a lot on itself ... But the biggest problem is that operators are often selling a product where the gap between perception and reality is huge. Mass-market holidays are often sold as a dream vacation when they are often anything but.
>
> (www.travelmole.com, Issue 226, 17 September 2002: Comment)

One of the main ways in which the tourism industry communicates, trades and interacts with the tourist is through the distribution chain (i.e. the way in which the product is sold to the consumer) using intermediaries – agents that sell products for the industry. Historically, tourism products were retailed through travel agents who offered products from tour operators, known as 'principals'. The tour operator and travel agency sector is highly developed in the EU with approximately 190 million package holidays sold annually. The sector employs 409 000 in 90 enterprises, generating gross revenue of £150 billion. The UK and Germany dominate the market, employing 21 per cent and 11 per cent of the workforce, respectively, although many of these jobs are within large integrated tour operating companies such as TUI. There are 145 companies employing over 250 employees and the average profit margin for the business transacted is relatively low at 7 per cent.

These traditional patterns of purchasing have been challenged by trends such as direct selling. Portland Holidays was one of the companies that began to change the relationship between the tourism sector and the public in the 1980s, by selling direct to the customer and cutting out the travel agent (Plate 7.1). More recently, this relationship has changed again with the impact of information communication technologies (ICT) such as the worldwide web, and ease of communication by email, to create a new form of distribution – a virtual distribution channel. The last five years have seen dramatic changes in the tourism sector as technological advances have revolutionized the way in which the tourism industry communicates and interacts with its consumers. Chapter 5 illustrated the significance of technology as one element in the growth strategy and expansion of

Plate 7.1
A traditional high-street travel agent, located in a shopping mall where the throughput of people is high

Source: author

low-cost airlines. Selling online holidays and the rise of e-travel agents, as well as direct selling to bypass existing distribution channels, have created a high degree of change and uncertainty within the tourism sector. For example, in February 2006 Travelsupermarket. com in the UK launched a package holiday price check site, where holidays from 120 travel websites can be compared to provide the most competitive prices. The site received around 2 million hits a month and was positioned to attract those people who do not want to self-package online: instead, it will direct clients to the best options. This comes at a time when new technological advances, such as *dynamic packaging* (the availability of software that allows a client to organize and purchase the elements of a holiday online), have made major inroads. In the UK, it is estimated that a significant proportion of travellers have used such software to avoid visiting travel agents.

These changes have provided major challenges to the way the travel agent and tour operator distribute their products through various distribution channels (see Figure 7.1). However, as Figure 7.1 shows, the travel agent and tour operator still have a role to play, as this chapter will show (see Table 7.1 for a number of recent academic studies of tour operators and travel agents).

The tour operator

Defining the tour operator is a far from easy process because its role, activities and form have changed dramatically from the early days when Thomas Cook first organized a package trip by rail in the 1840s. One useful approach is to identify what a tour operator

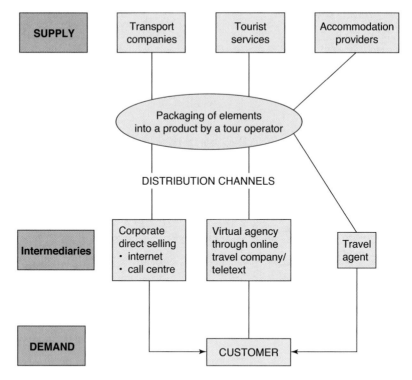

Figure 7.1
How tour operators link the elements of a holiday together to produce, assemble and distribute the package to the consumer

Source: author

does as a means of establishing its characteristics and form. In simple terms a tour operator will organize, package together different elements of the tourism experience (as shown in Figure 7.1) and offer them for sale to the public either through the medium of a brochure, leaflet or advertisement, or using ICT. If a tour operator is to offer a package, also known as an inclusive tour, it will normally have to include at least two elements that are offered for sale at the inclusive sale price, and will involve a stay of more than 24 hours in overnight accommodation. These elements normally include transport, accommodation and other tourist services (see Table 7.2).

The type and range of packages sold by the tourism industry can normally be divided into two types: those using the traditional charter flight and those using scheduled flights, where it is uneconomic for the tour operator to purchase charter flights.

The type of packages are often segmented according to:

- mode of travel, such as ferry or coach holiday (typified in the UK by Shearings). It may also be based on twin-transport packages such as fly–drive, which are very popular with inbound tourists in the USA
- mode of accommodation, where hotel chains become tour operators by packaging their surplus capacity to offer weekend or short-breaks in business-oriented hotels, selling rail or air transport and visits to attractions as an all-inclusive package

- whether they are international or domestic packages
- length of holiday (whether a short break, i.e. fewer than four nights away, or a long holiday, i.e. more than four nights, is offered)
- distance, where the market is divided into short-haul and long-haul; over 90 per cent of UK outbound packages are short-haul
- destination type (e.g. city breaks, beach holidays, adventure holidays).

These tours may be organized by small independent tour operators, who specialize in certain segments (e.g. youth operators such as PGL in the UK); larger operators, such as TUI, which have trans-European or global operations. In addition, there are over 300 tour operators who organize the itineraries, activities and logistics of inbound visitors

---

Table 7.1 Recent studies on tour operators, travel agents and tourism

Tour operators

Hudson, S., Hudson, P. and Miller, G. (2004) The measurement of service quality in the tour operating sector: A methodological comparison. *Journal of Travel Research*, 42(3): 305–312.

He, Y. and Song, H. (2009) A mediation model of tourists' repurchase intentions for packaged tour services. *Journal of Travel Research*, 47(3): 317–331.

Budeanu, A. (2005) Impacts and responsibilities for sustainable tourism: A tour operator's perspective. *Journal of Cleaner Production*, 13(2): 89–97.

Tepelus, C. (2005) Aiming for sustainability in the tour operating business. *Journal of Cleaner Production*, 13(2): 99–107.

Takedaa, K. and Carda, J. (2002) U.S. tour operators and travel agencies: Barriers encountered when providing package tours to people who have difficulty walking. *Journal of Travel & Tourism Marketing*, 12(1): 47–61.

Travel agents

Ahluwalia, D. (2009) *Disintermediation of Tourism Intermediaries and Related Association*. Saarbrucken: VDM Verlag.

Garvenko, V. (2009) *New Zealand Travel Agents in the Internet Era: Impacts, Responses, and Relationships*. Saarbrucken: VDM Verlag.

Tse, A. (2003) Disintermediation of travel agents in the hotel industry. *International Journal of Hospitality Management*, 22(4): 453–460.

Barnett, M. and Standing, C. (2001) Repositioning travel agencies on the Internet. *Journal of Vacation Marketing*, 7(2): 143–152.

Huang, L. (2006) Building up a B2B e-commerce strategic alliance model under an uncertain environment for Taiwan's travel agencies. *Tourism Management*, 27(6): 1308–1320.

Buhalis, D. and Licata, M. (2002) The future eTourism intermediaries. *Tourism Management*, 23(2): 207–220.

Frias, D., Rodrígueza, M. and Castañedaa, A. (2008) Internet vs. travel agencies on pre-visit destination image formation: An information processing view. *Tourism Management*, 29(1): 163–179.

to countries such as the UK and who are represented by their trade organization – the British Incoming Tour Operators Association (BITOA). But why do tour operators exist, and why do people use them? The answers lie in the way they operate and the economic benefits that they provide to the customer.

Economics of tour operation: Managing for profit

Tour operators have the ability to purchase services and elements of the tourism experience from other principals or suppliers at significant discounts by buying in bulk. They fulfil a major role in the tourism sector as they allow the different tourism sectors in Figure 7.1 to sell their capacity in advance – often a long time in advance as contracts are drawn up a year prior to tourists using accommodation or services. This obviates the

	January	April	June	September	December
Year 1			Research	Research	
Research and planning			• Package holiday prospects • Destination selection	• Analysis of competing choice of destination	
Year 2	Select destination	Brochure production (Design, development, printing contracts agreed)	Printing of brochure proofs		
Negotiation	• Hotel capacity determined • Departure dates identified • Brochure production decisions	• Negotiate with airlines for charter seats, transfers and hotel rooms	• Contracts concluded		
Administration			• Determine exchange rates • Estimate selling prices • Proofs of brochures from printers • Recruit booking staff	• Final tour prices added to brochure • Printing of brochure	
Marketing				• Brochure distributed to agents and launched • Publicize to press and media	
Year 3	January	April	May	September	December
	Peak advertising Recruitment and training of holiday reps		First tour departs		

Figure 7.2
Planning horizon for a tour operator's summer programme
Source: modified from Holloway (2001)

need for smaller, specialized businesses to market and distribute their product to a wide range of potential retailers, hoping that customers will choose their product or service over and above others. The bulk purchase agreements in large resorts areas mean that, in the summer season, the complete capacity of hotels, self-catering and other forms of accommodation may be block booked, leaving the business free to develop its own expertise in running or managing its business. Similarly, the tour operator connects together with all the ancillary services to negotiate contracts and deals that will allow a holiday to be sold and be delivered on the ground.

So, as Chapters 4 and 5 showed in terms of transport, the tour operator will bulk purchase airline seats, airport transfer services from coach operators, and taxis in the destination area, as well as a whole host of local entertainment and visitor attraction opportunities to be sold to clients at the booking stage or in the destination. The result is that tour operators traditionally provided a guaranteed level of sales which allowed principals to fix their costs in advance and operators to achieve economies of scale by gaining heavily discounted rates on their purchases. The outcome is a business opportunity for the tour operator, which creates a package, product or experience through assembling the elements together, advertising and selling them, and using third-party agents to deliver each element on the ground. It is obvious that tourists may experience dissatisfaction if there are service interruptions or breakdowns in the delivery and the seamless experience does not occur. Therefore, ensuring the holiday experience is an enjoyable and rewarding one is a key element of customer care for tour operators. The tour operator will often add a mark-up on the product it is selling by calculating all the input costs and their overheads and adding a profit margin to produce a price.

The process of establishing a tour through from the initial idea to its sale and delivery to the client is shown in Figure 7.2, a schematic illustration using a time line to highlight the long time frames involved in researching, planning, developing, administering and implementing a tour programme. Figure 7.2 also illustrates the vast range of risks that the tour operator takes in planning a holiday, including:

- estimating the likely market
- competing with long-established tour operators in a destination with a recognizable brand
- investing heavily in human resources and infrastructure to set up a destination.

Given these major risks, it is important for tour operators to recognize how important it is to set up and operate their business in a competitive and sustainable manner so that the investment pays a dividend over and above the costs of operation.

Tour operating business performance

Tour operating business performance is determined by the skill of the company in buying its product components (e.g. aircraft seats, accommodation and transfers) at a competitive price, and reselling at a price that is lower than that for which a consumer could assemble the same product. One consequence is that tour operators standardize packages (which differ little between destinations) to keep prices low.

Table 7.2 Elements of an inclusive tour (a package)

Basic elements:

- Aircraft seat
- Accommodation at destination
- Return transfer from airport to accommodation
- Services of a tour operator representative
- Insurance

Optional add-ins:

- Car hire
- Excursions

Alternative forms:

- Multi-destination packages that visit more than one destination/country
- Optional extensions to the package to extend the itinerary
- Linear tours by coach operators

Tour operators may keep their prices low by:

- negotiating low prices from suppliers
- reducing profit margins
- cutting their cost structures.

Tour operators that have become integrated tourism companies and operate aircraft can reduce the prices for air travel through heavy usage of an aircraft (i.e. increasing the number of flights it can achieve each day). This will typically involve flying from a base in the UK to another destination, bringing a plane-load of passengers back to a return destination in the UK, and then flying to the same destination again and then back again to the original base; this is known as a W pattern (see Figure 7.3). This flight scheduling is very efficient until flight delays (e.g. due to air traffic control) occur; these throw the entire schedule back and cause knock-on effects for passengers on other flights.

To achieve cost reductions, charter flights must have high load factors to break even, typically 80–90 per cent, compared to 50–70 per cent for scheduled flights (this depends on the cost base of the carrier and typically around 70 per cent or more for low-cost-airlines). Any unsold seats therefore may be unloaded onto the market at cost or less to fill the aircraft, either as seat-only sales/cheap holidays.

Costing charter operators' prices is a complex process, as 'dead legs' at the beginning and end of a season have to be incorporated. At the beginning of a season, an aircraft on a W pattern will fly out with tourists but return empty and vice versa at the end of the season. To extend the season, operators may provide inducements such as low-cost

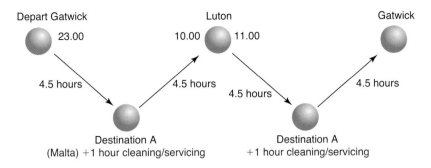

Figure 7.3
A hypothetical W flight pattern for a charter aircraft

Source: author

accommodation to attract low-season business to fill capacity. One such example is the winter flows of elderly people from northern Europe wintering in the Mediterranean. Hotels discount their rates hoping guests will spend money in their premises to compensate for discounts given. Yet, the future growth in the package holiday market in the UK is likely to limit the scope for further development of the charter airline and the use of seat-only sales, as the low-cost airline companies have begun to challenge this sector's cost competitiveness. The response is likely to be continued innovation by tour operators and principals to adapt tour supply to the needs of ever-changing customers. This is why companies such as Thomson Holidays have introduced the concept of dynamic packaging for clients as well as rebranding its charter airline from Britannia to Thomsonfly.com and again in 2009 to Thomson Airways (incorporating Thomsonfly and First Choice), with an associated low-cost airline element. Businesses have to constantly adapt and respond to changes in the market and the most adept and strategic businesses often anticipate or shape consumer tastes in the holiday market through their product offerings.

Regulating tour operating

Like any other form of business, tour operating is regulated in many countries. Since the 1960s, the UK has seen a number of massive tour operator collapses, and this led ABTA, the Association of British Travel Agents (now renamed the Travel Association), to set up its bonding scheme in the 1970s. In 1975, the government made it compulsory for operators to contribute 2 per cent of their turnover to ABTA's bonding scheme. This is to safeguard tourists from company insolvencies and being stranded overseas – as happened in the 1990s with the collapse of the International Leisure Group, which severely depleted ABTA's fund. This situation has persisted with a number of notable collapses (e.g. XL in 2008).The ATOL bonding scheme requires any company wishing to run packages overseas to obtain an Air Travel Organiser's Licence from the Civil Aviation Authority (CAA) so that if the company goes bankrupt any stranded customers are brought home by the ATOL fund. In 2008 the ATOL bond was replaced by a

£1 passenger levy to provide protection in the event of collapse. In 2009–2010 the scheme was also put under increased pressure by the collapse of several tour operators.

The European holiday market

The European market is one of the most highly developed and complex areas of activity globally in relation to the development of tour operators. It has seen a great deal of activity in terms of investment, acquisitions and mergers. This is reflected in the scale of tourism activity. Since the expansion of the EU from 15 to 25 and then 27 member states, domestic tourism has been the main driver of tourism demand. In terms of inbound tourism to EU countries, 74 per cent of the accommodation nights spent by non-residents (i.e. tourists) in hotels and similar establishments was by travellers from within the EU. This illustrates the importance of intra-regional tourist flows (i.e. travel within the region) in the EU. For the majority of EU countries, either Germany or the UK is their main holiday market. For example:

- in the Czech Republic, Greece, Italy, Latvia, Lithuania, Hungary, Austria and Poland, German tourists are the most important source market
- in Belgium, Spain, France, Ireland, Cyprus, the Netherlands and Portugal, British tourists are the most important source market.

In addition to the UK and Germany, Scandinavia has been a major driver of demand in the package holiday market. Much of the traffic from these source countries has been destined for coastal locations in Mediterranean Europe.

The demand for package holidays and outbound travel in Norway is examined in Web Case 7.1, the case study of one country as a generating market. Norway is a lesser-known market. It is distinctive as Norwegians have a high propensity for holidaytaking. The web case study also helps to explain the dynamics of holiday traffic emanating from one country, and how the choice of destination is influenced by what tour operators offer.

ATOL trends

In a UK context, a range of data exists in the ATOL database (ATOL.org.uk). It lists the number of passengers whom tour operators are allowed to carry, which dropped betwen 2007 and 2008 from 26.4 million to 24.5 million, and again to 18.9 million in 2013. At the same time, the number of ATOL licensed businesses dropped from 2516 in 2007 to 2438 in 2008, in part reflecting the tighter financial criteria to be bonded given the collapse of operators and the rise of dynamic packing (no data are available for later years). The top 20 operators' licences by ATOL in 2013 are shown in Table 7.3, which illustrates the control of the market by the larger integrated operators as well as the growth of online provision (e.g. Expedia) in the UK. Previous data (no longer published by ATOL) highlighted the seasonality of passenger trips with a steep rise in the summer season and a second rise in winter holidays. A notable trend up to 2007 when comparing the summer and winter seasons was the relative growth in revenue in the winter market. As more consumers are booking direct than through ATOL-bonded travel organizations this has led to warnings over the dangers of self-booking with the rise of holiday company insolvencies that have led to consumers having to look at alternative forms of compensation such as holiday insurance.

A more detailed insight into the volume of business licensed since 2002 shows that online specialists (e.g. Expedia Inc. and Flightbookers) have entered the top 50 rankings. In 2002, no online specialists were prominent in the rankings. This confirms the rapid rise of the online operators in the UK. The four major licensees (TUI UK Ltd, Thomas Cook Tour Operations, Jet2holidays and Travel Republic Ltd) are a mix of established and online players. The online companies have challenged the large integrated operators (e.g. TUI and Thomas Cook), with Travel Republic reporting over 2 million online bookings a year and Jet2holidays over 1 million a year in 2013. Yet the indisputable

Table 7.3 Top 20 ATOL holders 2013

Rank	Licence holder	ATOL number	Passengers licensed
1	TUI UK Ltd	2524	4 418 145
2	Thomas Cook Tour Operations Ltd	1179	3 694 002
3	Jet2holidays Ltd	9618	1 186 579
4	Travel Republic Ltd	10 581	798 805
5	Expedia, Inc	5788	778 418
6	On The Beach Ltd	10 017	638 673
7	Avro Ltd	1939	498 000
8	British Airways Holidays Ltd	5985	468 200
9	Travelworld Vacations Ltd	4108	399 500
10	Virgin Holidays Ltd	2358	329 912
11	Cosmos Holidays Ltd	2275	324 700
12	Southall Travel Ltd	5553	310 000
13	Trailfinders Ltd	1458	307 921
14	Gold Medal Travel Group PLC	2916	267 846
15	Hays Travel Ltd	5534	211 000
16	Carnival PLC	6294	209 595
17	The Global Travel Group Ltd	3973	201 430
18	LM Travel Services Ltd	3970	200 207
19	The Airline Seat Company Ltd	3971	190 655
20	Hotelplan Ltd	0025	183 850

Source: CAA

fact is that in 2013 two companies dominate. In other words, the competitive behaviour of organizations has reallocated capacity whilst placing pressure on the smaller companies. Competition from medium and large corporations combined with the challenge of dynamic packaging and low-cost airlines has begun to redefine the business environment and affect profit levels for the smaller ATOL businesses.

With continued consolidation in the tour operator sector in the UK and Europe (such as TUI's growth as the largest integrated tourism company), it is interesting to consider how the larger transnational and smaller businesses compete.

How do these companies compete for business?

In June 2002, MyTravel initiated a price war over its 2003 summer holiday brochure by claiming its prices in its first edition brochure were lower (306 were priced lower) than its rivals (i.e. Thomson and First Choice). This is a very characteristic action from the tour operator sector, especially the larger companies, for the following reasons as shown by Figure 7.4.

In some cases, such predatory behaviour has not effected dramatic change. For example, following the collapse of the ILG group, other companies were formed to fill market niches, as business opportunities emerged. In addition, more complex economic forces such as currency fluctuations and changing consumer behaviour have led to companies rethinking how they operate and compete. An example is the practice of most tour operators of issuing holiday brochures in multiple editions. In the 1970s and 1980s, consumers were encouraged to book early for discounts and price guarantees. In the late 1980s, the traditional booking period was in late December (after Christmas), when

> They seek to expand their market share, market dominance and position in consumers' minds

> They seek to convert domestic holiday taking to outbound travel by conveying images of low-cost holidays

> They acquire smaller or equivalent businesses in competing businesses and expand into new areas

> They drive down the cost from suppliers and by repackaging the product, so that no frills packages (i.e. no airport transfers, no holiday representative or in-flight meals) are provided in the market appealing to the lower end of the comsumer spectrum

> They drive out the smaller operators in the long term, to consolidate further their market dominance

> The have recently started to establish online direct selling or have purchased an online company/enter into a strategic alliance with an online distribution channel

Figure 7.4
How large tour operators compete

Source: author

much of the tour operators' advertising on television and in the press was mobilized to stimulate consumer activity (as the AIDA model in Chapter 3 indicated). This provided operators with client funds from early in the year until bills were due from suppliers, often as late as September, providing up to nine months' interest-bearing income. With increased ICT, clients recognized the value of late bookings as supply normally exceeded demand in most years for outbound inclusive tours from the UK and many European countries. Most notable in the last five years has been the switch to massive investment in online technology by the four leading ATOL groups in the UK, as competition has intensified.

Tour operators responded to the loss of investment income from banking clients' money prior to their paying suppliers for the holiday and services by introducing fluid pricing. Larger discounts for early booking and price increases were provided in later brochure reissues; a second edition relaunch for its summer 2003 programme cost MyTravel an estimated £5 million in 2002. Other strategies have been to develop new markets, such as long-haul markets (which now exceed 20 per cent of outbound UK business). Seat-only sales on charter flights have also seen some operators expand their business. More common strategies are to seek new, cheaper destinations as the European industry did in the 1980s with Greece then Turkey, as sun, sea and sand packages remain popular. This was replicated in the period since 2000 with the opening up of Eastern Europe's holiday potential as the new Mediterranean for package holidays. With over 50 per cent of UK holidaymakers choosing packages when travelling overseas abroad at some time, it is evident that operators have had to switch attention from first-time, novice travellers (i.e. the 1950s and 1960s) to repeat travellers. The result has been product diversification to grow the range of possible holiday options, including:

- city breaks and additional short breaks as secondary airports open up new potential destinations (such as Iceland Air's service to Reykjavik)
- long-haul and adventure travel such as ecotourism and nature holidays
- greater flexibility and tailoring of the packages to the client's needs, and new pick- and-mix technology such as dynamic packaging.

Increased competition is likely to lead to further consolidation in the marketplace among tour operators, especially as virtual tour operators sell more capacity on the worldwide web as part of a growing e-business strategy, as shown by the Thomas Cook–MyTravel merger (Web Case 7.2).

By 2013, Thomas Cook Group plc was established as a major global operator, undertaking business in 19 countries with a £9.5 billion turnover and 23 million customers. But the tour operating sector is not simply characterized by constant growth and profitability among the businesses working within the sector. For example, in 2001, 23 ATOL-licensed companies went bankrupt and £3 million in compensation was awarded to travellers. In the period 1985–2001, £159 million was paid from the bond ATOL retains from tour operators to 190 000 people for 30 ATOL operators failing. The CAA pays any shortfalls in compensation from the bond from its Air Travel Trust Fund, which in 2002 was reportedly £8 million in debt, highlighting the need to re-evaluate the role of bonds and tour operators' solvency in 2005. In 2005, Experian in the UK reported that 492 businesses in the leisure and hotel sector (including caravan parks) went bankrupt out of a total of 18 122 companies while 581 in the transport sector also endured the same fate. With the impact of the credit crunch, tougher trading conditions saw a number of high profile collapses (e.g. XL in September 2008 stranded 85 000 passengers overseas; Globespan in December 2009 who cancelled 27 000 bookings; Goldtrail in July 2010 which stranded 20 000 overseas and led to 112 000 cancelled holidays). Research on the efficiency of travel agencies and tour operators has highlighted how the large integrated operators control costs and the market.

However, much of the activity in further integration and consolidation is likely to focus upon a number of key themes:

- expansion via acquisitions (e.g. Cendant Corporation's Strategy in 2004–2005 prior to its sale to the Blackstone Group)
- integration of air and hotel businesses (e.g. low-cost airlines and hotel companies)
- further widening of distribution channels (e.g. online; possible new mobile phone booking technology using social media)
- widening geographical coverage of markets and tour operators merge/enter into strategic alliances
- the impact of the euro, which may allow operators to buy capacity cheaper from weaker currencies providing lower-priced holidays (e.g. UK purchasing of cheap Eastern European capacity)
- a gradual levelling of package holiday prices across the EU
- greater cost controls and more sophisticated yield management systems to derive revenue according to demand
- new business strategies towards products (i.e. focus on core business versus diversification)
- a greater alignment of business activity towards changing consumer behaviour, as markets for products become more specialized, tailored and tourist focused.

Consumer trends affecting the future of tour operating

For the travel retailer, one of the principal changes observed over the last decade has been a diversification away from the preoccupation with mass tourism as the market (i.e. the demand) for tourism products has changed. Industry commentators such as Auliana Poon described this as a transition in tourism retailing from 'old' to 'new' forms of tourism and many industry analysts believe we are in an age where the combined impact of consumer tastes, technology and the influence of the media is rapidly changing the nature of tourism trends and behaviour. The globalized media now provides 24-hour coverage of world affairs and the instant nature of broadcasting, the internet and other media sources plays an important role in portraying global tourism and its development in different destinations.

Old tourism was best described as driven by consumers who were inexperienced travellers satisfied with homogenous tourism products (i.e. similar mass-produced packages) which were predictable and based on sun-based destinations (i.e. the Mediterranean resorts) seeking escape from the routine of everyday life, especially work. In contrast, 'new' tourism is characterized by more experienced travellers who have a growing concern about the environmental impact of their holidays on the places they visit. Yet interestingly, an industry report in 2005 by Thomson Holidays found that 30 per cent of UK tourists were uninterested in sustainable tourism and their impact on the environment, implying that 'old' forms of tourism remain the cornerstone of the package holiday market, and other studies have reinforced this point. In contrast, the 'new' tourist seeks more individualized products rather than the mass products that are less predictable, full of surprise, discovery and a memorable experience rather than simply a repetition of last year's beach holiday. The 'new' tourist is looking for something different; the holiday is an extension of their life rather than simple escape. In contrast to 'old' tourism, which was very much supply driven, as the history of mass package holidays has shown, the 'new' tourist is seeking to define what they want. Whilst 'old' and 'new' tourism co-exist, 'new' tourism offers the tourism industry many growth opportunities, given that tourism businesses can react to the demand for increased flexibility through greater use of information technology. In particular, marketing techniques (e.g. market segmentation to break demand up into discrete components) can be applied to create a move towards niche products.

As Chapter 6 illustrated, environmental issues have also become a theme affecting consumer attitudes and businesses. One recent innovation in sustainable behavior by tour operators has been the growth in corporate social responsible behaviour as shown in Innovation in Sustainability 7.1.

INNOVATION IN SUSTAINABILITY 7.1
CORPORATE SOCIAL RESPONSIBILITY AND TOUR OPERATORS

Increasing interest has been shown in the expanding role of transnational tourism corporations operating globally, with considerable power and control over 80 per cent of the mass holiday market. At a corporate level this concern has been translated into the extent to which these global companies have embedded sustainability into their operations. As Chapter 6 indicated, concerns over green washing by companies exists, but the analysis of the actions, philosophy and scope of their impact has arisen through the field known as Corporate Social Responsibility (CSR). The underlying principles and rationale of CSR are outlined in Figure 7.5 and the academic study of CSR has been framed around three distinct approaches:

- the shareholder approach, outlining the main responsibilities of business to maximize shareholder profit
- the stakeholder approach, where a business has a responsibility to a wider range of stakeholders than just its shareholders

An organization's responsibility for the impacts it creates

Focused on activities designed to improve or contribute to environmental, social and ethical impacts created

Sometimes undertaken for altruistic reasons and/or for business reasons

Based upon the notion that reporting is designed to go beyond the need to report to shareholders by recognizing wider range of stakeholders affected by company activities

ISO 26000 indicates that CSR accountability should be based upon principles of: transparency; ethical behaviour; respect for stakeholder interests; respect for the international norms of behaviour; respect for human rights

Figure 7.5
Corporate Social Responsibility (CSR)

Source: author

- the societal approach, where the underlying assumption is that business has a wide responsibility within society.

Source: Van Marrewijk (2003)

The analysis of CSR in tourism has grown in recent years but, in the case of European tour operators, the concern has been about the large integrated companies with huge turnovers (e.g. TUI, £15 billion; Thomas Cook, £7 billion; Rewe, £4.6 billion; MyTravel, £4.3 billion; First Choice, £3.8 billion). Within the northern European markets in which they dominate (i.e. the UK, Germany and Scandinavia), the businesses have achieved major economies of scale and control of the market, prices and tourist choice of destination. Given the size and market prominence of these companies, they have considerable potential to adopt a more responsible attitude to the environment through their CSR activities, as illustrated by TUI's key role (Table 7.4).

Other large organizations such as British Airways have pioneered CSR since the early 1990s, epitomized in its environmental reporting. The key question that many critics of the large tour operators pose is: How do they embed responsible tourism actions within the business model and operations?

Whilst many examples exist for individual operators supporting community projects in destinations, recent progress has been made in more environmentally led supply chain management across these large organizations (see Chapter 1 for more detail on supply chain management in tourism). This has meant looking at all aspects of the supply chain, including the activities and products sourced from suppliers both upstream and downstream in the supply chain. A study by Budeanu (2009) found that a sustainability ethos was less important than market drivers (i.e. being ahead of regulation). Although many of the larger tour operators have embraced a CSR philosophy, it has lagged behind the CSR reporting in the aviation industry over the last 20 years.

Table 7.4 Profile of TUI Travel plc: A global brand and sustainability champion

In 2013, the company had revenues of £15.1 billion, with a profit of £589 million and a market capitalization (ie: capital value of the company) of £4.8 billion.

In 2013:

- it had 30 million customers spread across 31 source markets (i.e. the origin of the visitors)
- it operated 138 aircraft
- it ran 1800 retail shops in Europe
- it employed 55 000 staff.

It focused its product portfolio on three key sectors – Mainstream; Accommodation and Destinations; and Specialist and Activity

- its sustainability plan 2012–2014 outlines four major goals:
  - o taking care in destinations, via 10 million greener holidays
  - o reducing carbon emissions, operating Europe's most fuel efficient aircraft
  - o employees embrace the sustainability ethos as an exemplar of best practice
  - o among consumers, it aims to develop an awareness of TUI Travel as a leader in developing sustainable holidays.

Source: developed from TUI Travel plc (www.tuitravelplc.com)

However, collaboration of the United Nations organizations (i.e. UNEP, UNESCO and UNWTO) combined with leading tour operators led to the development of the Tour Operators Initiative for Sustainable Tourism Development. This was a stimulus for improved sustainability reporting, cooperation between tour operators and destinations, and supply chain management, and a spin off was the establishment in 2003 of the Travel Foundation (thetravelfoundation.org.uk) funded by partner companies and other bodies to pursue more sustainable and fairer tourism.

One of the principal outcomes of the Travel Foundation has been the establishment and testing of projects to enhance its dual aim of sustainable and fairer tourism. The projects serve as a basis for practical tools and training to help individual businesses to develop more sustainable business practices. Therefore a partnership approach between tour operators and a non-government organization, the Travel Foundation has assisted in tour operators pursuing much greener approaches to business, whilst embarking on a journey towards greater responsibility and ethical approaches to business.

Further reading

www.toinitiative.org

Budeanu, A. (2009) Environmental supply chain management in tourism: The case of large tour operators. *Journal of Cleaner Production*, 17(16): 1385–1392.

Van Marrewijk, M. (2003) Concepts and definitions of CSR and corporate sustainability: Between agency and communion. *Journal of Business Ethics*, 44(2–3): 95–105.

Demographic factors

One very visible factor characterizing most Western countries is the ageing population, with a growth in the segment of the population aged 50 to 70. This is often labelled the rise of the 'senior' or 'grey' or 'third age' market. Many of these people now enjoy a higher standard of health care, are less sedentary and have experience of travel. What is also notable about this section of the travelling population is that they tend to spend up to 30 per cent more on travel than other age groups, given their greater disposable income. Many people in these age groups are described by marketers as 'empty nesters': their children have grown up and left home, and many are taking early retirement, are mortgage free and have more free time translating into a greater propensity to travel. In many Western countries with well-funded state and private pension schemes, this has been a key element of growth, although concerns over the sustainability of pensions funded by a declining pool of people of working age raises many questions over how this will translate into long-term growth. In France, senior travellers comprise approximately 30 per cent of the population; this is 28 per cent in Canada, 27 per cent in Japan, 27 per cent in the USA and 20 per cent in Germany. In many countries, tour operators, visitor attractions and accommodation providers have experienced continued increases in the mature market. Indeed, some tour operators who direct-sell specialize in this market (such as Saga in the UK and Elderhost in the USA). In the USA alone, the forecasts of the growth of the mature market aged between 55 and 74 years of age will increase from around 40 million in 2001 to 74 million in 2031. The implications for tourism managers are that not only will the market for mature tourists continue to grow (also see Case Study 3.3 on dementia), but that they will potentially be tourists for much longer due to increases in longevity. The conventional view among the tourism industry is that this age group is less technologically able, and so more prepared to rely on travel agents as holiday organizers. However, there is growing evidence in consumer surveys of e-preparedness and that these groups are embracing the internet.

Consumer issues in tour operating

With the growing expansion of the holiday market, reduced costs and the continued growth in the package market a number of trends have become evident. The growing variety of destinations has meant that competition between countries has intensified cost pressures. For example, in 2002 Spain experienced a 20 per cent drop in visitor arrivals up to July, the first decline since its growth in the 1960s; this is attributed to cost and wider issues such as image and the availability of cheaper alternatives such as Morocco, Bulgaria, Croatia, Turkey and Tunisia. But by 2004, growth had resumed, and in 2005, the 6 per cent growth in visitor arrivals was attributed to a 31 per cent increase in low-cost airline arrivals in Spain. At the same time, reduced prices and increased numbers of people taking budget holidays has been accompanied by growing numbers of complaints. According to ABTA, in 2000 almost 5 per cent of the UK's 20 million package holidaytakers were fairly or very dissatisfied with their holidays. In 2009, 9000 package holidaymakers complained to the UK government body – Consumer Direct. This reflected dissatisfaction with the quality of accommodation, perceived safety standards of overseas chartered aircraft, surcharges and failure to provide what was advertised. The actual official complaints made to ABTA (now the Travel Association) are relatively low, at around 17 916 in 2005, although legal recourse and litigation is growing in popularity as a small minority seek legal redress; an example is the deep vein thrombosis claims against airlines in recent years with law firms specializing with No Win No Fee actions.

In the EU, the 1993 EC Directive on Package Travel has brought a greater degree of precision into the roles and responsibilities of the tour operator. The response of the then Department for Trade and Industry (DTI) led to the following measures being implemented:

- all tours must be licensed
- a greater degree of honesty is required in holiday brochure descriptions
- an obligation has been placed on travel agents to take responsibility for the information contained in brochures they stock and to ensure adequate advice to clients on:

    o   health
    o   passport and visa requirements
    o   insurance needs.

In addition, the tour operator is liable for losses resulting from misleading information or where suppliers do not provide the services paid for and contracted. The growing litigation towards tour operators by holidaymakers has continued apace, as the EC Directive encourages a greater duty of care for visitors. In 2010, the EU were reviewing the Directive.

This also highlights the greater onus on the tour operator in terms of the provision of support staff in the destination, namely the holiday representative ('the rep'). Reps are useful trouble-shooters who can often remedy problems or complaints *in situ*. The job is very demanding and involves being the public relations agent of the company, often on call twenty-four hours a day, seven days a week in the peak season. Reps typically intersperse a number of roles as illustrated in Figure 7.6.

Typical roles in terms of safeguarding tourists' well-being include locating lost baggage, calling doctors when clients get ill, or (on rare occasions) die and in extreme cases liaising with police and authorities, as well as rebooking flights when emergencies arise. At airports, when flight delays occur holiday reps may have to deal with disgruntled passengers and offer company refreshment vouchers. They also address complaints about the accommodation. A recognizable human face in a strange environment, able to offer tourists local advice on health and safety issues, is paramount in ensuring their well-being. Whilst the role, character and ability of the holiday rep will be critical in undertaking this key client liaison role, training and excellent interpersonal skills (i.e. the ability to empathize with people and their problems) is essential as the tourist experience and client satisfaction are critical in gaining repeat business. In the UK,

| Meeting and greeting incoming and departing passengers at the airport to ensure airport transfers drop the right passengers at the correct accommodation | Handling a wide range of destination-specific enquiries and requests and providing social events | Publicizing company-endorsed tours and services for which a commission is received by the company | Dealing with special requests (e.g. arrangements for disabled guests) and acting as a go-between for the tourist and hotel, local police, medical services and other agencies when required |

At the destination

Figure 7.6
The role of the holiday rep
Source: author

Thomson Holidays has an enviable reputation for generating repeat business as its in-flight customer satisfaction scores frequently show. Yet the demand for budget, cost-conscious holidays has led some tour operators to remove holiday reps, replacing them with a 24 hour call centre to provide advice and help to tourists. In contrast, Thomas Cook has introduced its 'Connected' initiative to enhance rep services (see Case Study 7.1).

A recent European Court of Justice ruling in January 2006 has also upheld EC legislation that provides compensation for passengers delayed on airlines who purchased seat-only (these seats are a growing trend on low-cost airlines). The ruling meant that passengers could have to be compensated £172 for delays outside the airline's control and this may impact on airlines such as Ryanair and easyJet where average fares paid are around £42. This further extension of consumer protection for travel in the EU provides support for the argument that travel is now being more heavily regulated.

CASE STUDY 7.1
NEW TECHNOLOGY AND THE HOLIDAY REP

In 2013, Thomas Cook Group introduced a new service, 'Connected', to expand the opportunities for customers to stay in touch with a rep via a free online service or by phone, e-mail, SMS, Blackberry, Facetime, Skype and WhatsApp. This enables customers, who, on arrival, do not wish to attend the customary welcome meeting, to retrieve the same information as presented at the welcome meeting. It also removes the time that new customers need to wait on arrival, to meet their rep. Thomas Cook stress that this is a complementary service to the conventional rep service – not a replacement. The additional enhancement to this service is that the company is offering WiFi in 1000 of its hotels in 2013 to allow customers to stay connected around their accommodation via phone or tablet.

The underlying philosophy, to provide greater flexibility and to enhance existing services, allows consumers to choose how they engage with the business. To staff this new style of engagement, Thomas Cook have provided multi-lingual staff within its service teams in resorts to also help with booking ancillary services such as car hire and excursions and to manage hotel transfers. The service was launched in 15 resorts in Spain and Portugal in 2013 and a planned roll-out to other destinations will occur in 2014 with additional multi-media enhancements around video meetings and smart phone-compatible destination guide books. The innovation is indicative of the Thomas Cook Group's desire to stay engaged with their customers across the entire holiday experience at critical 'touchpoints' (Figure 7.7).

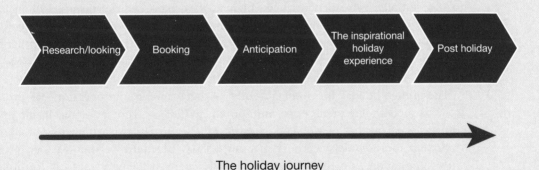

The holiday journey

Figure 7.7
Thomas Cook holiday experience and touch points
Source: Thomas Cook press release 2013

The holiday rep innovation is one aspect of the company's high-technology high-touch transformation to engage with its customers using new technology to build a closer relationship. In technical terms, this approach is a multi-channel approach (i.e. it uses different communications to reach its target audience), both traditional methods (i.e. print, television advertising) and new social media methods.

Marketing and planning the holiday: The holiday brochure

Traditionally the printed holiday brochure has been the tour operator's most powerful marketing tool, since the intangible nature of tourism makes it imperative that the potential customer can read about what they may want to purchase. This has been accompanied by online brochures, websites and virtual tours of destinations, making the places accessible to potential visitors. It is not uncommon for up to 50 per cent of tour operators' marketing budgets to be spent on brochure production although web-based materials have now become a key element of investment. This has to be viewed in the wider context of planning, organizing and implementing a tour programme. In the hypothetical example shown in Figure 7.2 the tour operator has to undertake a series of stages of work including:

- research and planning
- negotiation with suppliers
- administration
- marketing.

With the exception of the initial research stage, the holiday brochure is an integral part of the planning and marketing process. Figure 7.2 highlights the time frames involved in brochure production and distribution, with many holiday brochures costing as much as £1 a copy and print runs of millions for large operators where they may publish up to five editions. Yet brochures have high wastage rates and are disposed of in large numbers. Of 120 million printed in the UK, nearly 48 million were never used according to data provided by Green Flag International (Holloway 2001). It is estimated that this adds up to £20 to the average cost of a package holiday although these costs are reducing with the use of digital online brochures.

The printed holiday brochure currently in vogue among tour operators has evolved from its modern-day predecessor, introduced in 1953 by Thomas Cook. It adopted a similar format to that of women's magazines, reflecting the important role of women as holiday decision-makers. The 1960s saw holiday brochures become glossier, packed with information, and their role has gradually changed to its present one of holiday catalogue (Plate 7.2).

Holiday brochures distributed through travel agents or online seek to achieve a number of objectives:

- to obtain sales
- to provide information to assist in decision-making by purchasers in relation to the destination, product offerings, timing (summer/winter), price and ancillary services
- to afford cost-effective distribution for the tour operator, by having an attractive cover, being prominently racked in travel agents and generating business among agents
- to provide an effective tool to allow agents to sell holidays with detailed products/booking codes

Plate 7.2
These two brochures illustrate the changing design of
brochures within Thomas Cook between 1969 and 1978

Source: Thomas Cook

- to allow a contract to be agreed between the tour operator and customer, providing information on procedures for changing the booking, complaints, refunds, the details of the product purchased, the client's details and the insurance premium paid.

In the case of direct mail, the brochure seeks to fill some of the objectives above, but places more emphasis on the customer to decide on the product offering. It also seeks to appeal to the market segment it is targeted at and needs to be easy to use.

A brochure will typically comprise the elements embodied in Figure 7.8 and involve a complex process of design including:

- identifying the market audience and product
- utilizing an appropriate company brand
- designing a mock-up, using a computer, with illustrations and professional photographs of the hotel, destination, product offerings and services
- using a desktop publishing system that will help with brochure layout and design
- producing a proof, which is checked so that inaccuracies can be identified and rectified prior to printing.

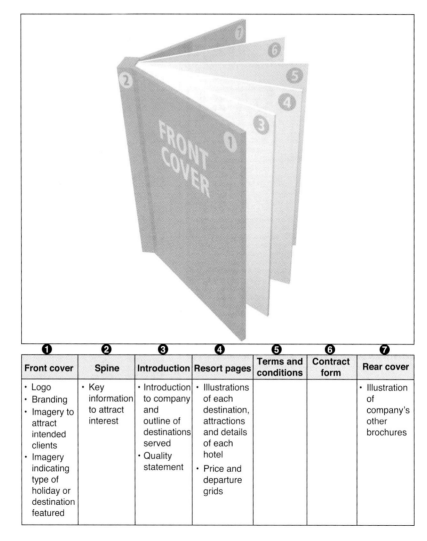

1	**2**	**3**	**4**	**5**	**6**	**7**
Front cover	**Spine**	**Introduction**	**Resort pages**	**Terms and conditions**	**Contract form**	**Rear cover**
• Logo • Branding • Imagery to attract intended clients • Imagery indicating type of holiday or destination featured	• Key information to attract interest	• Introduction to company and outline of destinations served • Quality statement	• Illustrations of each destination, attractions and details of each hotel • Price and departure grids			• Illustration of company's other brochures

Figure 7.8
Structure of inclusive holiday brochure

Source: © Eric Laws (1997); redrawn and reproduced with the author's permission

With increasing consumer regulation in most countries, holiday brochures must get potential tourists to book a holiday, advertising dreams or images of their ideal holiday, but must also be honest, truthful and accurate. Above all they must not make false statements that can be prosecuted in many countries under trade descriptions legislation. This is now a more stringent requirement since the EU Directive on Package Travel has made it easier for the tourist to litigate against the tour operator who is responsible for the supplier abroad. The need for truth and honesty is endorsed by ABTA in its Code of Conduct for Tour Operators, making the brochure a legal document to which complaints may refer in future claims for compensation.

To meet the obligations of a tour operator's licence, Holloway (2001) identifies the following information as being required in a holiday brochure:

- the name of the firm responsible for the inclusive tour
- the means of transport used, including, in the case of air transport, the name of the carrier(s), type and class of aircraft used and whether scheduled or charter aircraft are operated
- full details of destinations, itinerary and times of travel
- the duration of each tour (number of days/nights)
- a full description of the location and type of accommodation provided, including any meals
- whether services or a representative are available abroad
- a clear indication of the price for each tour, including any taxes
- exact details of special arrangements (e.g. if there is a games room in the hotel, whether this is available at all times and whether any charges are made for the use of this equipment)
- full conditions of booking, including details of cancellation conditions
- details of any insurance coverage (clients should have the right to choose their own insurance providing it offers equivalent coverage)
- details of documentation required for travel to the destinations featured, and any health hazards or inoculations recommended.

Source: Holloway (2001: 253–254)

Brochures are normally distributed to travel agents, and operators need to build in wastage costs – operators typically have to distribute twenty brochures to gain one booking even though this may be for a group of two or three people. Many agents operate different policies on distribution including:

- having brochures available on display with open access
- displaying one copy only – consumers need to ask for a copy.

Even these policies are not a guarantee of success. Operators can classify agents in terms of performance, with high-performing agents selling 100 plus holidays a year and low performers selling fewer than 5 a year. This appears to hold true for mass package holidays, although the significance of the number of sales obviously depends on the value of each holiday.

Once a client has decided to make a booking the tour operator will retail the product through a computer reservation system (CRS), direct to the public or via the internet. Whilst a significant proportion of package bookings are still made via travel agents – who use call centres for manual bookings or the company CRS system where a tour operator link is made direct to the travel agent – the internet has become more commonplace as the rise of online companies highlighted earlier shows. In the USA, online bookings now account for around 30 per cent of travel bookings. However, the brochure is usually supported by a marketing campaign (see Case Study 7.2).

CASE STUDY 7.2
THOMAS COOK'S LET'S GO! INTEGRATED MARKETING CAMPAIGN IN 2013/2014

In 2013 Thomas Cook launched an integrated marketing campaign to drive forward its strategic focus on a high-tech, high-touch approach to its customers (see Case Study 7.1) as part of a service-focused organization so that holidays could be booked across various communication channels. To launch this new strategy, a television campaign on UK television in December 2013 rolling into 2014 used celebrity actor James Nesbitt to spearhead the message of the campaign. The advertising was broadcast across different communication channels with a focus on value-for-money holidays and the online capabilities as well as pioneering holiday travel. The campaign on television was the main launch to the public of the new company brand – the Sunny Heart.

The Sunny Heart rebrand sought to unify the company's activity under this one common symbol, replacing the globe that featured as its brand image. The brand aims to promise the high-tech high-touch experience across all the customer touch points (see Figure 7.7) based on a promise – putting customers at the heart of the corporate transformation, with three principal objectives as shown in Figure 7.9.

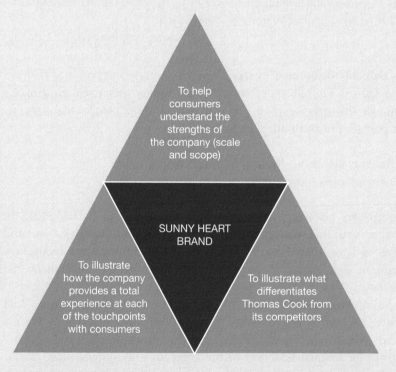

Figure 7.9
Thomas Cook's Sunny Heart brand objectives

Source: Thomas Cook press release 2013

The brand is a powerful approach to reimaging the company, requiring the logo being placed in brochures, on the web, on its aircraft, in its concept hotels and in its retail stores so it is ubiquitous and conveys the message to customers across the touch points with the company. It embodies the notion of the holiday journey with Thomas Cook.

The Let's Go campaign was followed up in 2014 with additional outdoor media coverage in January/February, with online enhancements such as one-search functions to access the destination pages, brands and products. The company's shops preceded the brand launch, with rebranding from October 2013 onwards. To engage existing customer contacts, personalized e-mails to its customer base over the peak booking period of December–February were also undertaken, illustrating the scale and scope of the Let's Go campaign, integrated across all areas of the business designed to sell holidays.

Further reading

Thomas Cook Press Releases, www.ThomasCook.com

As consolidation continues to affect the European holiday market, it is no surprise to find 80 per cent of inclusive tours sold through 20 per cent of agents, with commissions paid to agents, plus an override (1–5 per cent) in addition to the basic 10 per cent for high performance. However, in 1998 Thomson cut commissions to a three-tier level, ranging from 7 per cent to 12 per cent. This has fuelled a lowering of commission levels in 2005 by the leading groups (Thomson and First Choice). The evolution of the worldwide web is placing additional pressure on selling through conventional means. This debate re-emerged in 2005 and 2006 when a number of leading tour operators cut commissions to 7 per cent for agents.

Travel agents

Distributing tourism products is intended to entice customers to purchase an offering, linking the supply with demand. In technical terms, the distribution is a system that links various tourism organizations (e.g. operators and agents) together with the objective of describing, explaining and confirming the travel arrangements to the consumer. Explaining the tourism offering to the consumer requires retailers (and operators through their brochures) to recognize, identify and incorporate the following elements of tourism:

- tourism is intangible, meaning it is a speculative investment and an expensive purchase where the product is usually conveyed to the customer via a brochure
- tourism is perishable, and so can only be sold for the period it is available (it cannot be stored). This highlights the importance of last minute bookings to sell surplus capacity
- tourism is dynamic, meaning that it is forever in a state of flux; a product whose prices can rise and fall

- tourism is heterogenous, meaning it is not a standardized product that is produced and delivered in a homogenous manner. It varies, and interactions can enhance or adversely affect it, since it is dependent upon people and many unknown factors
- tourism is inseparable, meaning that in the consumer's mind, it is purchased and consumed as an overall experience and so communicating what is being offered, its value and scope is important. Since the consumer is transported to the product, it is an unusual form of distribution, where there is a need for timely information on all of the elements as outlined in the brochure.

The traditional package holiday has normally been retailed through agents who have recognized and sold holidays with the above factors in mind. Travel agents remain a key intermediary in the distribution chain, and are characterized by many features. Some have argued that, given the impact of online retailing and home-working (people working flexibly from home to be available to clients outside the usual 9 am to 5 pm shop-based travel retailing times), the travel agent is under threat and this is discussed more fully in Chapter 9.

The evolution of travel agents

When Thomas Cook organized the first tour package by rail from Leicester to Loughborough, the age of travel retailing emerged (see Chapter 2). Travel agents were mainly independent agents, with the exception of the growing Thomas Cook outlets. Their primary role was in acting as agents selling travel tickets for rail, sea and land-based services as well as accommodation. Even in the inter-war years, travel agents retained this brokerage role, receiving a commission on each sale. The 1940s saw the emergence of air-based travel but agents had not reached a mass market. Their travel products were still oriented towards a small section of the international travelling public. The 1960s heralded the greatest changes in travel agencies, with commissions, licensing and greater airline–agency relations, particularly the sale of group travel. By developing increased levels of information, service and specialized products, agents began to become more involved in the tour operation side of travel by organizing tours and selling cruises from block allocations. During the 1970s, these changes saw many travel agents expand with the growth of package travel, basing their business on volume sales. In the 1980s and 1990s, many agencies entered into tour operating, with growing numbers of mergers and acquisitions, and consolidation. Grouping into formal alliances or consortia enabled agencies to seek greater commissions, using increased levels of technology to assist in distribution, while the high street has seen large chains emerge. Many of these changes are documented in Table 7.5, which highlights the relationship between the trading environment in the post-war period and the style of travel retailing which evolved to characterize each era.

Characteristics of travel agents

In the USA, there are over 18 000 travel agents, with American Express operating in over 140 countries and travel sales turnover of US$21.5 billion in 2009. In the US, the

Table 7.5 Changes in travel retailing

Period	Trading environment	Type of travel retailing
1950s	Limited demand for holidays or other travel	Full-service travel specialists located in major urban and business centres
	Reconstruction of war-damaged city centres	Limited competition
1960s	Gradual increase in city centre travel retailers with the development of demand for leisure travel	Coach and other domestic holidays sold by small coach companies and through newsagents
1970s	Rapid expansion in demand for holidays	Successful retailers expand the number of outlets – proliferation of high street retailers
1980s	Development of out-of-town shopping malls and large-scale town centres	First computerized reservations system for inclusive holidays
	Many high streets suffer from shop closures and temporary tenants	Larger travel agency chains grow by acquiring smaller 'miniples', consolidating ownership and putting pressure on independents
		Development of specialized holiday shops and decline of full-service travel agencies
1990s	Increasing financial pressure on travel retailers, increasing rate of acquisition and mergers	Increasingly selective racking policies Technological developments enable customers to create their own holiday packages by booking direct from home

Source: © Eric Laws (1997): 122; reproduced with the author's permission

Association of Travel Agents found 79 per cent of its members belonged to a consortia or franchise, such as Vacation.com, Ensemble Virtuoso or American Express.

In the UK, there are around 5000 travel agency branches and 1890 travel agents, although recent closures/sales and acquisitions means that this figure is often in a state of flux. These are affiliated to their industry body ABTA, the Association of British Travel Agents, who estimated that £31 billion was spent in such agencies on travel services and products. The scale and size of the travel agency market in the EU is shown in Tables 7.6 and 7.7.

The structure of travel agents has changed over the last 20 years: consolidation has led to greater pressure on independent agents and less choice for the consumer, as multiples dominate the retailing of products. Travel agents as businesses carry no stock and act on behalf of the tour operators, so they have little financial risk and do not purchase products themselves. They receive a commission for each sale and, as agents, do not become part of the contract of sale, which is between the tour operator and the customer.

Their role is based upon the products they sell and they can be either generalist agencies selling a wide variety of products or specialist agencies selling a certain type of product. Some agencies, by virtue of their geographical location or appeal, can be

Table 7.6 Number of travel agents' and tour operators' enterprises

	2008	2009	2010	2011	2012
Austria[1]	2.583	2.635	2.895	2.618	2.625
Belgium	1.158	1.839			
Bulgaria	2.068	2.345		2.345	2.579
Cyprus	435	441	430	400	390
Croatia	849	925	899	1.016	1.008
Czech Republic[2]	2.258	2.191	2.167	2.153	2.130
Denmark[3]	594	642			
Estonia		261			
Finland	710	711[4]	724	719	715
France		3.679			3.969
Germany	11.046	10.717	10.370	10.240	9.986
Greece					
Hungary	1.122	1.216	1.115		1.290
Ireland					273
Italy	11.846	*11.000*	*12.272*		*11.167*
Latvia		345			578 [5]
Malta	248[6]				
Montenegro					
The Netherlands		963	951	974	949
Norway		716[7]	*700*	*690*	*690*
Portugal			879	995	1.122
Poland					
Romania	3.200	*3.000*			*2.800*
Serbia					
Slovakia	*650*	*700*	*1.000*	*1.000*	*1.000*
Slovenia		432	458	477	496
Spain	5.100				*6.075* [8]
Sweden[8]	887	869	779	769	*800*
Switzerland	*2.500*	*2.504*	*2.328*	*2.201*	*2.135*
United Kingdom[9]	*7.810*	*7.320*	*6.953*	*6.630*	*6.654*

Source: European Travel Agents and Tour Operators Association

In italic = estimate.

1 Number of sales points

2 Source: Czech statistical office

3 Based on the number of registered tour operators in the Danish 'Rejsegarantifond' (Travel Guarantee Fund)

4 Based on the register of package travel companies maintained by the Finnish Consumer Agency (some of them are banks, associations, bus companies or other entities who occasionally organize package travel; however many of them are not full time travel companies)

5 Source: Latvian Tourism Development Agency is responsible for the registration of travel agents and tour operators in Latvia, data as at August 2013

6 As per licenses issued by Malta Tourism Authority

7 Number of IATA agents: 273. Estimated number including non-IATA: 500 (no registration is required for TAs). Number of tour operators (which may include travel agents included above as well): 716

8 Limited liability companies with employees

9 ABTA member outlets at 31 December, which represent about 75% of the UK market:

	2008	2009	2010	2011	2012
United Kingdom	5.858	5.490	5.215	4.973	4.991

8 Spain: Source Spanish press article based on GDS figures

Table 7.7 Number of persons employed by travel agents and tour operators

	2008	2009	2010	2011	2012
Austria[9]	10.600	10.000	10.100	10.500	9.800
Belgium	8.000	8.000			
Bulgaria					
Croatia	4.455	4.197	4.062	4.502	4.373
Cyprus					
Czech Republic[10]	14.728	13.836	14.875	11.770	
Denmark	6.326	5.900			
Estonia		1.398			1.504
Finland	2.800	2.300	2.250	2.190	2.140
France		33.236		31.117	
Germany[11]	74.000	63.078	62.650	63.890	64.707
Greece		15.000			
Hungary	7.300	7.000	3.000		4.300
Ireland					5.200
Italy	55.000				
Latvia					
Malta					
Montenegro					
The Netherlands		16.860		15.100	
Norway		2.100	1.900	1.800	1.750
Poland					
Portugal			7.000	6.500	6.000
Romania	14.400				12.000
Serbia					
Slovakia	2.800	3.000	2.000	2.000	2.000
Slovenia		1.429	1.206	1.165	
Spain	55.985	55.383	51.355	50.735	49.159
Sweden	8.853	8.791	8.188	8.050	8.008
Switzerland		10.750			
United Kingdom		119.800			105.000

Source: European Travel Agents and Tour Operators Association

In italic = estimate.
9 Without employers
10 Source: Czech statistical office
11 Number reduced due to a change in statistics of Federal Labour Agency (following the new statistics # in 2008 would have been 63.213)

low-cost, low-revenue businesses (selling low-cost packages) whilst others located in more prosperous areas can be high volume, selling high-value cruises and similar products. Other specialist agents, like Austravel, only sell long-haul travel and so are niche agents.

High street agents do not specialize in business and corporate travel, although the market for specialist agents is worth over £10.5 billion a year in the UK. One very controversial area of debate is the process of racking: agents emphasize/display certain businesses' products (perhaps their own company's in the case of integrated businesses) to favour them because of the promise of higher commissions. This perceived favouritism, often described as 'directional selling', has led the independent travel agents in the UK to launch their Campaign for Real Travel Agents, to counter this. They claim their 300 members will offer impartial, objective advice and promote smaller, independent operators' products. In contrast, the dominance of the top three groups (TUI, Thomas Cook and Going Places) highlights their control of UK travel retailing. In 2011, Thomas Cook, Co-operative Travel and the Midlands Co-operative combined into a joint venture in the UK, with a total of 1100 travel agencies and 150 members, including home workers, business travel and websites.

Ultimately, the travel agency is a physical location that offers a convenient place to purchase travel products. It provides a source of information as well as a point of sale, via booking agents. Agents' perceived expert product knowledge (often gained from training and educational trips to the destinations on sale) is seen as offering a competitive advantage, although this is becoming more problematic given the low salaries and young age profile of travel agents as well as the growing product range now available to consumers.

It is evident that travel agents cannot offer a limitless product range, since research indicates that, beyond a certain point, trying to offer too many products erodes agency profitability. As a result, specializing in a limited range of tour operators allows agents to develop product knowledge, tailor them to the markets they serve and recognize their own limitations. With the endless possibilities and knowledge available on the worldwide web, it is apparent that agents are having to compete by developing specialist knowledge and advice to maintain their competitive edge.

The organization of travel agents

Whilst the businesses in this sector can be broadly split into the independent travel agencies and the multiples who are owned and operated by tour operators and other tourism concerns, two basic principles characterize success in each: good quality customer service and management. In terms of management, controlling costs, ensuring highly motivated staff are employed and building upon a customer base through word of mouth are all critical. The independent agencies, which are manager-owned and typically employ fewer than five staff, contrast with the larger chain agencies, located in prominent high street or shopping mall locations, which have high passer-by traffic.

Travel agents typically deal with a diverse range of tasks including:

*   making reservations
*   planning itineraries (including complex round-the-world travel)

- calculating fares and charges
- producing tickets
- advising clients on destinations, resorts, airline companies and a wide range of travel products
- communicating with clients verbally and in writing
- maintaining accurate records on reservations
- ensuring racks are stocked well or supplies are kept in-house
- acting as intermediaries when customer complaints occur.

Not only do travel agency staff need technical skills in reading timetables, calculating fares and an ability to write tickets, they also need good interpersonal skills in closing a sale and in being able to use technology (e.g. CRS). Agents also need to be able to explain the growing complexity of air fares and the conditions attached to them in simple, plain English. An agency manager will have to be able to manage a group of staff and will also be engaged in the financial management of accounts and cash flow, the invoicing of clients and the controlling of expenditure in running the business.

Above all, it is critical to ensure all staff provide a high level of customer service so as to make sales and build the client base. To do this:

- customers must be greeted warmly, typically with a smile
- staff must ensure high standards of dress, appearance and personal grooming as customers are influenced by first impressions; their personal posture, manner and

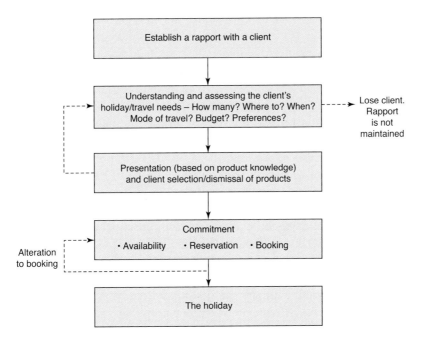

Figure 7.10
The travel agent–client purchase process

Source: author

body language are also important as being alert, attentive and willing to empathize and match client needs with available products is key
- all staff must be polite and able to express themselves clearly, while always maintaining eye contact
- telephones must be answered promptly and courteously.

In selling a product, a set sequence is usually adhered to, as in Figure 7.10. This illustrates the consumer psychology of a holiday purchase, where an agent will need to gradually understand what the consumer wants, how to fulfil that demand and the type of interaction that is sought. In particular, a process of search, evaluation and re-evaluation goes on in the agency or on a return visit if the client takes away brochures to assess product offerings. The agent has a critical role to play, not necessarily in providing definitive answers, but in guiding the consumer, presenting options (and in managing their dismissal) until a suitable product is located. It is clear that this is a time-intensive undertaking and, therefore, it is apparent why many consumers will go through this process using technology such as the worldwide web as well as using a travel agency.

Business travel

The process is somewhat different in the case of business travel, where agencies offer this service. Here the client will be looking for time savings, be less price sensitive (traditionally) and will be very demanding of time and service. Bookings are often made at short notice, sometimes outside office hours, and special help with visas and other documents will be sought. Those agents who offer a business travel service have found this a highly competitive market, and tied arrangements with companies exist. In return for agreements on a certain volume of business, a travel agency may provide a set rate of discount or charge a set management fee for all the business it handles for a company. The latter is proving to be very popular with large companies to reduce business travel costs. Contracts can be constructed in a number of ways, but above all seek to provide companies with greater cost controls on corporate travel and to reduce costs.

Studies of the competitiveness of the travel agent sector point to their key role in business travel. For example, the US Travel Association point to the five key functions of business travel (Figure 7.11), which is reinforced by the estimated value of business travel to the US economy: US$225 billion a year from business travel, with a further US$24 billion derived from spending associated with business trips.

The Guild of Business Travel Agents, with 40 members, represents 75–80 per cent of all business air travel in the UK, which is dominated by the multiples. The key players are American Express, Carlson Wagonlit and The Travel Company (also see Figure 7.11 for the USA example). These multiples can provide substantial discounts by purchasing bulk volumes of air travel. If companies employ travel managers instead of agents, agencies are excluded. This trend is reflected in the growth of a UK professional body, the Institute of Travel Management, and further impacts on the business of travel agents. Direct links between larger businesses and airlines in global alliances are possible; so that discounted travel occurs through volume rebates. In the USA, Topaz International

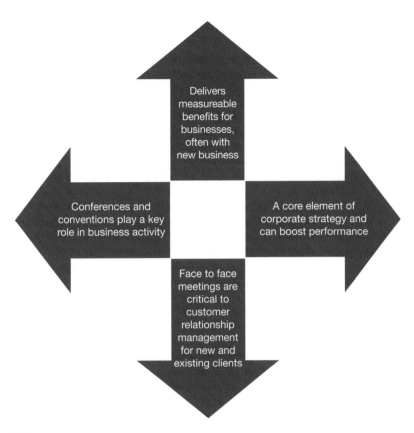

Figure 7.11
The purpose and role of business travel

Source: developed from US Travel Association press release

found business travel agents were the best source for finding cheaper airline fares, typically 19 per cent lower than internet fares. Even so, internet-based Expedia has purchased US business travel management firm Metropolitan Travel as a new IT solution for business travel. Even low-cost airlines such as easyJet have entered into agreements with business travel organizations to grow the business travel market.

Travel agents and information communication technology

In terms of information communication technology (ICT), there are a number of key elements that impact upon travel agents. ICT is designed to allow agents to access the principal's supply of products and services, process bookings and manage corporate performance, but a number of issues are evident:

- CRS are expensive for small and medium agencies to maintain, so internet bookings may be a more cost-effective medium

- CRS do not necessarily provide agents with improved business levels unless used to their full
- there is inherent bias in CRS, with airlines having to pay fees to have a presence
- new forms of technology are overtaking CRS in some market segments, such as the development of electronic agencies (e-travel agencies), the worldwide web, direct-selling operators (known as business to consumer) and a number of operators selling discounted travel (e.g. Expedia, e-bookers and the low-cost airlines online).

E-ticketing has emerged as a new force in global travel markets and this has the potential to bypass the travel agent and the airlines' global distribution systems (GDS). In Europe, Lufthansa led the way by introducing this mode of ticketless travel with ETIX, a concept now adopted by many airlines worldwide. By 2007, all airline tickets were paperless. The system enables passengers with only hand luggage to bypass long check-in counters at airports and allows consumers to buy tickets over the internet without paper coupons. Many of the low-cost airlines adopted paperless e-tickets to reduce administrative costs and this innovation has now permeated global air travel. The GDS company Sabre estimated that almost 70 per cent of its North American tickets are now issued this way, while in the UK, Galileo (the European GDS) reported that in 2001 e-ticketing represented 10 per cent of its business. One response from travel agents according to Sabre is to desire tools that will allow them to access the growing demand for online travel.

Online travel continues to grow in significance and many companies are now expecting to see this as a major driver of their business, which does pose problems for the travel agent if tour operators and airlines now encourage direct booking. This has even begun to hit the new generation of online travel agents created in the late 1990s. British Airways, for example, aimed to grow its bookings online from 22 per cent in 2005 to 50 per cent by 2007, which was backed up by major marketing campaigns that cut out the travel agent and other online agents, steering customers to the BA.com site. In fact, in late 2005, there was evidence to suggest that around 4.5 per cent of all internet traffic was travel-related, an illustration of the rapid growth in this area of activity, and the concerns which the travel agent sector face (also see Chapter 8 on how new forms of agents have developed – notably home workers).

Therefore, given the speed of technological change and its impact on travel retailing, the first decade of internet use largely led to developments associated with:

- reservation systems
- online travel agencies (e.g. Expedia)
- search engines (e.g. Google) and meta-search engines (i.e. those which send a computer user's request to several search engines or databases and display the results as a single list with the source) such as Kayak
- destination management systems (DMSs) such as VisitBritain.com (see discussion later on DMSs)
- price comparison sites (e.g. Kelkoo and travelsupermarket.com)
- individual suppliers' and intermediaries' websites and increasingly the rise of social networking sites, a phenomenon which has seen significant growth in recent years following the rise of Web 2.0 capabilities.

Social networking and tourism

A major revolution has occurred in internet use by consumers, namely the rise of Web 2.0 technology. Since around 2004, Web 2.0 has revolutionized how the second generation of web-based communities and hosted sites have evolved to allow interaction, information sharing and collaboration among users as shown in Figure 7.12. It is these interactions which led to the creation of web-based content. The web technologies associated with Web 2.0 have led to the use of weblogs (commonly called blogs), where entries are displayed in reverse chronological order and where content can be added including commentary, news, images and links to other blogs, web pages and other forms of media such as music-based blogs (mp3 blogs) and audio-based 'podcasts'. Since 2004, blogs have become relatively mainstream on the internet and they can be broadcast not only to personal computers, but also to other mobile devices such as PDAs and

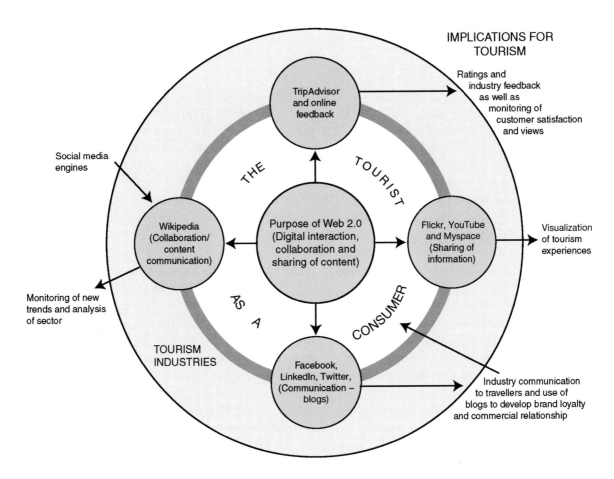

Figure 7.12
Web 2.0 technology and tourism

Source: author

mobile phones (moblogs). In December 2007, the internet search engine for searching blogs, Technorati, was indexing 112 million weblogs with over 500 000 entries under the search term 'holidays'. By 2010, this had expanded to 1.1 million blogs on holidays. For example, in the USA, social media has begun to play a key role in the promotion of business travel by corporate travel agencies to support their travel management programmes to understand clients' travel patterns and to encourage clients to network with each other. Among the main functions they used were real time updates via mobile phones. An indication of the scale of the online revolution in travel is evident from the following statistics:

- over 75 per cent of internet users in the USA actively use social networking sites
- in the EU, 50 per cent of all internet users aged 16–74 used the internet to book travel and accommodation
- there are 50 million Tweets a day on Twitter
- online sales in Europe have grown from €0.2 billion in 1998 to €58.4 billion in 2008, dominated by the UK and Germany as key markets for online travel which comprised 48 per cent of the market.

One of the consequences for consumers and the use of the internet for travel and tourism is that over the last decade there has been a growing overload of information. Consequently, consumers have also been guarded about the bombardment of information on the internet especially junk mail (spam). Consumer-to-consumer (c2c) marketing has emerged through the rise of social networking. This new trend facilitated by Web 2.0 has meant that consumers have begun to trust the comments and feedback of impartial websites (e.g. TripAdvisor) and those of friends and colleagues on social network sites as virtual travel communities with common interests emerge. In fact some analysts have suggested that the majority of internet content in the future will be created by individuals, rather than by companies and organizations. One example of how organizations are now targeting consumers using traditional marketing tools and new forms of social media can be illustrated by Tourism Ireland's 2010 campaign to attract more British visitors to Dublin. The £1 million campaign was targeting 12 million people via radio, online adverting as well as through social media and direct marketing. But one indirect consequence of this technology is that booking a special trip or holiday is no longer a special event as technology has made it routinized, sanitized and lacking human interaction that makes it no different from purchasing any other product, even though it is based on many psychological attributes (see Chapter 3). The technology also passes much of the work to the consumer often for a modest online discount. As Case Study 7.3 suggests, one of the early Web 2.0 developments was TripAdvisor (also see Plate 7.3) with user-generated content which has had a profound impact upon consumer decision-making and search behaviour for tourism products.

Other developments in online social communities relevant to tourism include MySpace.com, which quickly became a teenager site, and Facebook, which developed in 2004 and has over 8 million users in the USA and 18 million worldwide. By 2010 Facebook had 400 million users, 24 million of whom were in the UK. It allows the user to connect with friends and is based on content which is 'click and trust', impacting upon consumer spending. It represents a major source of word-of-mouth advertising for potential travellers based on other travellers' experiences. MySpace, in contrast (owned by News Corporation) had 122 million monthly active users and 70 million users in the USA which was growing at a rate of 10 000 sign ups a day with around 13 billion page views in one month in 2010 equating to 2 hours per person spent on the site.

Ultimately Web 2.0 has enabled greater interaction between travellers and the tourism sectors and it also places greater demands on the tourism industry to undertake corrective action to improve their tourism offering, as complaints and dissatisfaction (as well as praise) may be open to the online community irrespective of industry grading schemes. Indeed chat rooms can be a rapid way of disseminating electronic complaints. There are debates within the public sector, especially tourist boards, that may even lead to the demise of their rating schemes such as stars to denote quality standards, and that the future may be one based on consumer rating schemes such as TripAdvisor. One undesirable example of the impact of this new social media on leisure and tourism is the emergence of flash mobs who can suddenly gather in a public place for a protest or event. The use of mobile phones, viral email and social networking sites has posed several public order concerns at the suddenness with which social media can be used as a communication tool. A consequence of such technology can be seen in a tourism context in the UK with the rise of post-exam chill out holidays among the 16-year-old age group. The resort of Newquay in north Cornwall has been promoted as a surfing and beach resort (alongside less desirable stag and hen party short breaks – see Web Case 3.2 on this market). One of the factors attributed to the growth of this post-exam market is social media (the modern day word of mouth) where a resort population of 20 000 is routinely invaded by 6500 16–18 year olds each summer, often staying in budget accommodation and campsites. A number of high-profile drink-related deaths alongside violence reported in the night-time economy towards young visitors have led to several police campaigns (e.g. Operation Brunel in 2010, where sniffer dogs and police met the incoming trains to search arriving visitors) to reduce drug and drink-induced incidents amongst the under-age population along with the social problems this form of tourism brings to the resort. Whilst part of the problem of the resort stems from the manner in which it was promoted in the late 1990s, it is now compounded by the social networking on Facebook which fuels this form of tourism. So what are the implications for the tourism industry of Web 2.0?

There is no doubt that the Newquay example shows how powerful this form of electronic communication can be and the impact that occurs is difficult to manage. A survey in 2013 for Thomas Cook described the rise of fragging, the use of social media to brag about and show off using technology to outdo one's peers. This has been attributed to the rising popularity and cost of hen and stag parties, birthday celebrations, marriage proposals and life events. The survey found that 70 per cent of respondents like to live for the moment and a third would spend as much as needed to enjoy 'life moments'. The study also pointed to 1:10 of social media users posting updates designed to make

CASE STUDY 7.3
TRIPADVISOR, EWOM AND THE RISE OF INTERNET RATINGS OF TOURISM PRODUCTS AND SERVICES

As Chapter 6 indicated, eWoM (e Word of Mouth) has become a powerful tool in the travel industry and a means by which consumers can rate their holiday experience purchased via travel agents and tour operators as well as the different components of the package/product/services consumed.

TripAdvisor was founded in 2000, operating sites in 42 countries around the world (www.tripadvisor.co.uk). TripAdvisor is arguably the largest online travel community globally, which has grown from 20 million monthly visitors in 2008 to 260 million in 2014. The number of registered users has risen rapidly since its inception, with 5 million registered users in 2008 to 60 million e-mailable members worldwide in 2014. The number of businesses listed on TripAdvisor has increased to over 815 000 accommodation providers, over 420 000 attractions and over 2 200 000 restaurants. The site also features a Hotel Price Comparison tool to check hotel pricing. As of July 2014, TripAdvisor has:

- 4 million businesses listed, of which 815 000 were accommodation providers and hotels; 550 000 vacation rentals; 2.2 million restaurants; and 420 000 attractions
- 100 contributions a minute being posted online and 2800 new topics a day posted on TripAdvisor Forums
- 100 million people who have downloaded the various TripAdvisor apps, with between 10 and 15 per cent of users accessing the site via a tablet or mobile phone, equating to 108 million monthly visits via these communication channels
- around 28 downloads a minute made of the various TripAdvisor apps.

TripAdvisor is constantly innovating with new features such as Trip Journal and Point Me There, linking Social and Global Positioning Technology.

By 2014, the site operated in 42 countries and 25 languages, employing more than 2000 staff. As an online travel tool, it has the most comprehensive advice and information source for destinations on the web (see Plate 7.3 web shot of the company webpage). It allows travellers to create, edit or peruse guide book information with unbiased reviews and opinions of hotels. Reviews of TripAdvisor, such as webuser, have given it a Gold Award, partly for the hotel section with 300–400-word reviews and ratings of hotels in five categories such as cleanliness. In some cases, there are up to 100 reviews of one hotel.

TripAdvisor also produces reports such as that on the top ten castle hotels in Europe in March 2007 (which included two properties in Scotland), which can have an impact on visitor choice of properties. Other reports such as those on the world's ten hippest hotels (October 2006) and the top ten quirkiest hotels (July 2006) are important public relations tools for the destination's tourism sector, with regular use of them in national newspapers such as the *Telegraph* and *Observer*. Similarly, a report, Dirtiest Hotels (February 2007), on the top ten dirtiest hotels in the USA certainly affected tourist use among e-savvy consumers.

The online forum also provides opportunity for customers to receive recommendations from other customers, as extending the networking and word-of-mouth recommendation are so important in tourism. In other words, this acts as a peer review form of quality assurance which is independent of statutory Quality Assurance schemes, but it is highly subjective. In the medium to long term, this is likely to gather momentum as a more impartial judge of quality standards where compulsory registration and lax hotel inspection exist.

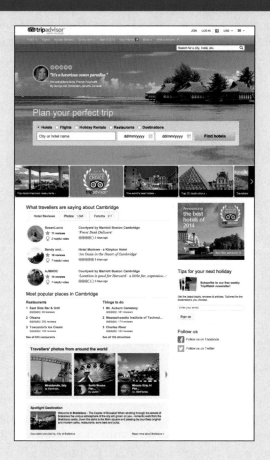

Plate 7.3
TripAdvisor website
Source: © 2014 TripAdvisor

Developments in TripAdvisor include Thomson Holidays in the UK joining the site in October 2007. Thomson Holidays, which sells around 60 per cent of its holidays online, has added 2000 properties to TripAdvisor so the reviews appear when clients search for accommodation. In a similar vein, VisitLondon, the tourism agency for London, has added 2000 hotels and visitor attractions to TripAdvisor to produce London's top ten hotels and attractions based on user reviews and has 2000 hotel and attraction site reviews available.

On VisitLondon.com, the five most recent reviews will be featured (including industry responses) to encourage interaction with visitors so as to further develop the potential to provide better insights for visitors via the new social media. This is the first visitor organization to team up with TripAdvisor. From 2010, TripAdvisor has made it possible to submit reviews from iPhones via an app. However, there have been ongoing debates about people posting fake reviews and, in 2010, the hotel industry in Europe was seeking a review of the EU regulations governing the submission of online reviews to ensure only bona fide guests were able to submit reviews. TripAdvisor has responded that it reviews all submissions and screens them for fake elements.

their peers jealous, with 1:8 feeling pressurized to upload on social media sites when abroad. This means the tourism industry needs to be proactive in the management of social networking information and its implications. According to the UNWTO report in 2008 entitled *Handbook on E-Marketing for Tourism Destinations*, social networking is a powerful tool indicating that many holiday decisions are based on recommendation and the views of online information. So businesses seeking to harness the power of social networking need to:

- find ways to encourage their visitors to write a review about their visit on their favourite social networking site
- create content on key social networking sites (e.g. Flickr, Facebook and YouTube) that supports visual material
- add news items and points of interest about what is happening for visitors
- monitor the key social networking sites and rating sites such as TripAdvisor as well as responding to comments and criticisms on such sites which adopt a light touch and are friendly and positive
- experiment with other mediums such as Twitter to assess the number of followers of Tweets.

The future of travel retailing

In Chapter 1, the theme of disintermediation was examined, which is the ability of tourism suppliers to use ICT to communicate directly with consumers in their homes. The travel agent once had a virtual monopoly on the distribution of travel services, especially inclusive tours, but the future is still unclear. To completely eliminate the travel agent would require new ICTs to provide all of the social, economic and psychological benefits that agencies offer the travelling public. Nevertheless, they will still remain the public face of the tourism industry in a retail setting, as the range of ICT makes travel a more complex process since more options and products are available. Far from disintermediation leading to the demise of travel agencies (see Figure 7.13), it may lead to a resurgence in the holiday market as technology proves to offer too much choice, is time consuming for travellers and does not provide the psychological benefit of a brochure as a purchase.

In 2013, Thomas Cook launched Dreamcapture, an initiative to use technology to engage with customers, unifying its retail activity with technological advances. Dreamcapture is designed to be a single approach to offer customers a personalized service, wherever they are and however they choose to interact. It is implemented through a one-to-one meeting between a travel consultant and the customer, identifying personalized holiday experiences to meet the needs specified by the customer. This leads to the creation of a wishlist which is e-mailed to the consumer with link-throughs to Thomas Cook webpages. The option of booking online, via the call centre or instore is available to link e-tail and retail, again offering the customer flexibility in how they interact with the company.

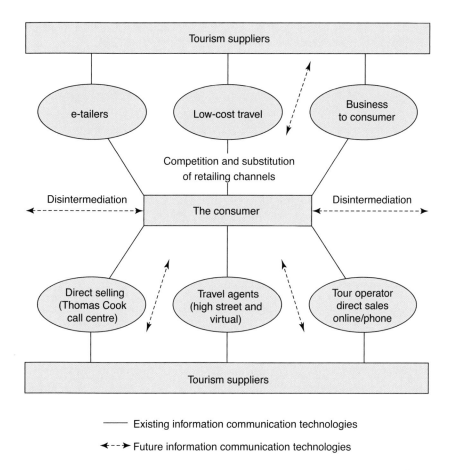

Figure 7.13
The future of travel retailing

Source: author

Figure 7.13 shows the existing and future forms of travel retailing, spurred on by the evolution of ICT in the reselling of travel products.

There is a significant decline in the share of the travel market enjoyed by the traditional high street travel agent: the majority of non-chain affiliated agents in the UK have a turnover of less than £5 million a year. Concentration and integration by the major holiday companies have provided a more competitive market environment to compete with large virtual e-tailers such as Lastminute.com. The company was established in 1998 and its turnover has grown from £188 million in 2003 to £590 million in 2006 (although it made pre-tax losses of £114 million in 2006) to £1–2 billion in turnover in 2009. The scale of its activities illustrates the challenge it has posed for the travel agency sector:

- it has 1.6 million online visitors a week in the UK
- it sold 750 000 airline tickets and has 62 000 hotels available online

- it is making around four bookings an hour and in the UK, the top destinations booked in 2009 were: Barcelona, Amsterdam, Prague and Paris.

Its unique position in travel retailing is that it can sell its own packages as a merchant and also as an agent for a third party.

Even so, new technology such as mobile phones (there are over 4.6 billion mobile phones worldwide) and other devices such as tablets are making internet access much easier and convenient. This will impose further pressures for shop-based agents. However, as the example of Australia shows (see Web Case 7.3) some travel agent chains have managed to go against the trend and embrace other technologies and markets to expand their travel agency business in recent years. The Flight Centre is a good example of a business which has transformed itself into a global operator, shifting from being a travel agency to a travel retailer. Even so, new technology such as mobile phones (there are over 4.6 billion mobile phones worldwide) and other devices such as tablets and iphones and ipads with their apps are making internet access much easier and convenient. This will impose further pressures for shop-based agents.

Conclusion

Travel agents will have to evaluate constantly how to protect commission levels and how to reach a highly fragmented travel market, as ICT establishes more niches. The pressure on independent travel agents in a highly competitive environment is set to continue, but new promotional tools and modes of distribution will see agents use marketing and advertising to maintain a presence. For example, rebranding holidays under agency names, such as Thomas Cook's initiative, or offering no deposit bookings; offering clients home-based sales visits; and using technology to retain face-to-face contact whilst improving ease of sales will certainly be a trend for the future. However, technology has certainly redefined the role of the agent and the tour operator with even the more traditional tour operator role in question, as dynamic packaging and low-cost airline and accommodation sales challenging the traditional notion of a package holiday. Whilst there is evidence during tough economic times that dynamic packaging may leave travellers vulnerable to the collapse of operators, the growing importance of technology has provided the potential tourist with many more travel opportunities.

CHAPTER REVIEW

 ## References

Holloway, J. C. (2001) *The Business of Tourism*, 6th edn. Harlow: Pearson.
Laws, E. (1997) *Managing Package Holidays*. London: Thomson Learning.

Further reading

There are few up-to-date sources on the tour operator and travel agent sector. The best sources of up-to-date information can be found in the following places:

Annual Reports of major tour operators and travel agents.
Business publications (e.g. *Financial Times*).
Consultancy reports/Market intelligence reports (e.g. Key Note).
Holloway, J., Davidson, R. and Humphrey, C. (2009) *The Business of Tourism*, 8th edn. Harlow: Pearson.
Laws, E. (1997) *Managing Package Holidays*. London: Thomson Learning.
Page, S. J. and Connell, J. (2009) *Tourism: A Modern Synthesis*, 3rd edn. London: Cengage Learning.

 # Questions

1 Why are tour operators important in the tourism industry? How is their role changing with the introduction of e commerce?

2 What is a package holiday? How is it assembled and sold? What other services and support do tour operators offer their clients?

3 How do travel agents operate? What are their main roles and responsibilities? What types of services and products do they sell?

4 What is the future of the travel agent as a retailer? Will their traditional high street location be maintained?

 # Access additional resources

- For students: Multiple choice questions for each chapter, video links and further reading.
- For instructors: PowerPoint slides with tables and diagrams, additional case studies, video links and further reading.

8 Visitor attractions and events

Joanne Connell and Stephen J. Page

Learning outcomes

This chapter examines visitor attractions as a key element of both the tourist's activities and as a business activity which has specific management requirements. After reading this chapter you will understand:

- how to define and classify visitor attractions
- the marketing and management issues associated with visitor attraction development
- the growing importance of events and meetings in the visitor economy and as an attractor of visitors to destinations
- the importance of managing the visitor experience at attractions and future issues for tourism managers.

Introduction

Along with the transport and accommodation sector, attractions and events form one of the central components of tourism, providing a vital element in the visitor's enjoyment and experience. Attractions are a central element in terms of what tourists visit at destinations as well as being something they may visit en route to a destination. In contrast, events may animate a destination and serve as a basis for a visit. UNEP (2009) indicated that over 80 million people attend a meeting or conference each year. The numbers attending trade fairs and exhibitions are much greater globally. As Swarbrooke (2000: 262) suggested 'visitor attractions are at the heart of the tourism industry, they are motivators that make people want to take a trip in the first place'. In many respects, they are the lifeblood of a destination, because they are part of the appeal, ambience and overall experience that visitors seek to consume in areas they visit. This argument can also be extended to events which have developed as shown in Case Study 8.1.

CASE STUDY 8.1
EVENTS AS ATTRACTIONS

In the research literature on the post-modern society, there has been a growing focus on how cities and places can become internationally competitive to attract further investment and mobile forms of capital to develop the economic base of localities. One consequence of this is that investment in tourism and leisure facilities is now seen as an important aspect of the quality of life for residents and workers in these cities, which is why it has become a higher priority for governments and decision-makers who seek to use marketing techniques to promote the attributes of individual cities as places to live, work and invest in. There has been a blurring of exactly what constitutes attractions to attract tourism, leisure and residents, with a growing interest in the arts and the expanding cultural industries of which visitor attractions and events feature prominently. This pursuit of competitiveness is most marked between world cities such as London, New York, Paris and Tokyo as reflected in recent attempts to stage international events to raise the profile of these localities and to enhance their cultural infrastructure. Events can take different forms as Table 8.1 shows.

Stevenson (2006) suggests that the shift towards the cultural industries reflects two important trends:

- the highly individualized nature of the leisure experiences being provided by the cultural and creative sectors
- the dominance of the commercial sector over and above publicly funded culture.

Stevenson (2006) also highlights a growing focus on the visitor experience and what Pine and Gilmore termed the experience economy. Recent studies (e.g. Haahti and Komppula, 2006) point to the importance of experience design in tourism, especially events to add value to the visitor experience which involves a detailed understanding of what the visitor is looking for from the attraction or event. Events perform a major role in helping to create an experience that can bring a place to life and create an emotional response in relation to fun, pleasure and satisfaction. Yet the development of events in any location is not without its impacts, some of which are positive and others are negative. Organizers and planners of events tend to focus on the economic benefits over and above some of the lesser-known social and environmental impacts. Events are often used to address issues of seasonality, and their

Table 8.1 Typology of events

Type of event	Explanation
Hallmark events	May be referred to, or encompass, 'special' or 'mega' events. A hallmark event is described by Ritchie (1984: 2) as being: 'major one-time or recurring events of limited duration, developed primarily to enhance the awareness, appeal and profitability of a tourism destination in the short and/or long term. Such events rely for their success on their uniqueness, status, or timely significance to create interest and attract attention'.
Festivals	Defined by Getz (1997: 8) as a 'public, themed celebration', they may help to maintain community values through increasing a sense of social identity, with historical continuity in the staging of the event (such as the Scottish Highland Games) as well as celebrating the survival of the local culture.
Fairs, exhibitions, expos and shows	May include commercial shows or exhibitions (e.g. the Ideal Home Exhibition) or a localized event such as an Agricultural Show. It is estimated that there are around 12 000 expos a year, which generate around 70 million visits a year.
Meetings and conferences	These range in scale and scope from conclaves (those meetings held in private/secret) to seminars and workshops which may have an educational and training function.

Source: Page, S. J. and Connell, J. (2010) *Leisure: An Introduction.* Harlow: Pearson Education

success as attractors of visitors by bringing a place to life and portraying its uniqueness and individual qualities will, as Getz (1997) suggests, depend upon:

- *a multiplicity of goals*, where the idea of *diversity* is implicit in the creation of the event
- *a festive spirit*, so that an ambience, joyfulness, revelry and freedom from constraint are built into the appeal such as through music
- *satisfying basic needs*, so that it appeals to a range of leisure motivations
- *uniqueness*, to create a must-see or a once-in-a-lifetime opportunity to experience something as well as featuring as a critical element in the experience of the place
- *quality*, so visitor expectations are exceeded
- *authenticity*, so that the local community feels that it is engaged and the event is embedded in their local history and traditions and it encourages them to participate alongside
- *flexibility*, so that events which require minimal infrastructure and investment are developed
- *tangibility*, where the event is the conduit and vehicle to encourage the visitor to experience the destination attributes and resources through a range of activities
- *theming*, to maximize the value of authenticity and increase interaction with visitors
- *symbolism*, where the use of rituals and symbols may give extra significance to the experience
- *affordability*, to encourage as wide a range of visitors as possible.

Further reading

Connell, J. and Page, S. J. (eds) (2011) *Event Tourism*, Vols 1–4. Routledge: London.

Getz, D. (1986) Event tourism: Definition, evolution, and research. *Tourism Management*, 29(3): 403–428.

Getz, D. (2007) *Event Studies: Theory, Research and Policy for Planned Events.* Oxford: Elsevier.

One of the major problems in identifying attractions is that they are patronized by tourists, but in terms of the scale and volume of visits, they are dominated by leisure and day trippers as well as local residents. In this respect the market for attractions is large and forms a vital part of the infrastructure of the destination area. For example, in Kyoto, Japan (the country's ancient capital), the cultural infrastructure provided by 1600 ancient Buddhist temples help attract 40 million visits a year to the city. Some 17 ancient temples are UNESCO World Heritage sites, with Toji Temple receiving 4 million visits a year. Kyoto City Council also seeks to grow tourist arrivals to over 50 million visits a year, illustrating the cultural and historical significance of the built heritage, dating to the eighth century. Attractions provide a vital nucleus for visitor spending in destinations, and when they are linked to regeneration strategies such as that of European City of Culture, they can be harnessed to create a new image and help reposition the city as a place to visit. Thus, a successful attraction industry is vital for a healthy tourism sector so that visitors have sufficient opportunity to undertake visits and to spend during their stay (see Table 8.2 for the key studies on attractions).

Plate 8.1
Universal Studios

Source: author

Not surprisingly, attractions and a programme of events are also a major draw for many visitors, and urban regeneration strategies by public- and private-sector agencies have pinned future tourism development around such hubs of visitor attraction activity. The process by which attractions may be integrated into urban regeneration strategies is shown in Figure 8.1. This shows that when an area or destination has declined, intervention by the private sector and public sector agencies can create a new focus, by pump-priming (i.e. stimulating redevelopment through incentives and through the

Table 8.2 Key studies on visitor attractions

Fyall, A., Garrod, B., Leask, A. and Wanhill, S. (eds) (2008) *Managing Visitor Attractions: New Directions*, 2nd edn. Oxford: Elsevier.

Newsome, D. and Dowling, R. (eds) (2010) *Geotourism*. Oxford: Goodfellow Publishing.

Page, S. J. and Connell, J. (2009) *Tourism: A Modern Synthesis*, 4th edn. London: Cengage.

Scottish Enterprise/Highlands and Islands Enterprise (2001) *New Horizons: International Benchmarking and Best Practice for Visitor Attractions*. Glasgow: Scottish Enterprise/Highlands and Islands Enterprise.

Swarbrooke, J. (2002) *The Development and Management of Visitor Attractions*, 2nd edn. Oxford: Elsevier.

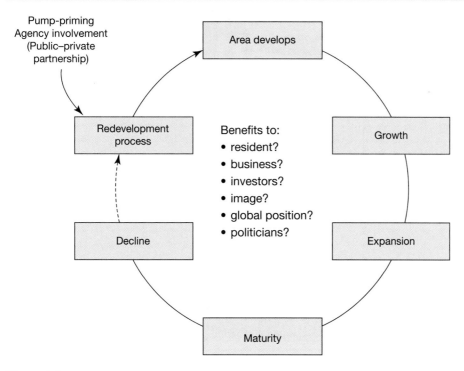

Figure 8.1
Tourism and regeneration

Source: author

development of infrastructure) to attract new investment. In principle this is not dissimilar to the resort life cycle, discussed in Further Web Reading 1, which is based on the marketing concept of the product life cycle. In many successful urban regeneration schemes where tourism has been a key component (e.g. Cardiff Bay in Wales, which was Europe's largest urban regeneration scheme), visitor attractions and the creation of a visitor environment around these attractions has contributed to the success of the regeneration scheme. In the case of Cardiff, locating a number of major anchor projects (i.e. flagship projects of national and international significance) together with supporting tourist infrastructure (i.e. accommodation, transport, retailing and restaurants) has enabled a new visitor destination to emerge around the attractions. Similar arguments cannot be made for the hosting of major events such as the Olympic and Paralympic Games. Recent evaluations of the London 2012 Games have criticized the tourism benefit of the Games (which generated an additional 1 per cent of international visitors in 2012), while the long-term regeneration benefits for East London residents, in employment generation and tourism development, remain unclear as a legacy of the investment in the Games. Yet one of the main problems in examining visitor attractions is in defining what comprises an attraction.

Plate 8.2
The Eden Project, Cornwall, has diversified by entering the summer music festival market, making use of its facilities after its normal closing

Source: author

Classifying visitor attractions

Within tourism studies, the issue of defining visitor attractions has proved difficult due to the diversity of users (tourists, residents, day trippers) who provide a marker broader than just tourists. As a result many researchers acknowledge that this diverse client base makes the most appropriate term to use 'visitor attractions'. One of the challenges for seeking to bring some order and logic to the scale and scope of visitor attractions is to find a framework that assists in the categorization process. Figure 8.2 provides one such overview. What Figure 8.2 highlights is the main attractor of visits – the core product – and structured around that are different factors and perspectives that assist in any attempt to categorize attractions (e.g. the nature of the environment it is located in, the charge to enter, structure of ownership, nature of the markets it attracts from residents through to international visitors). One useful definition used by the National Tourism Organizations in the UK outlines the scope of an attraction as:

> Where the main purpose is sightseeing. The attraction must be a permanent established excursion destination, a primary purpose of which is to allow access for entertainment, interest or education; rather than being primarily a retail outlet or

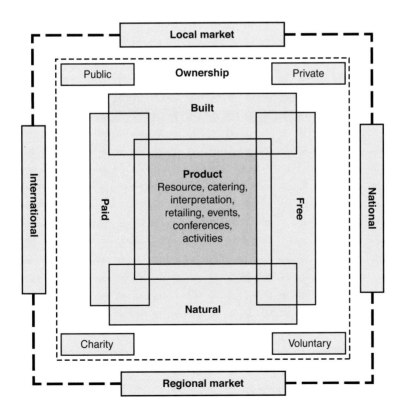

Figure 8.2
Framework for the categorization of visitor attractions
Source: Fyall *et al.* (2008) © Elsevier

a venue for sporting, theatrical or film performances. It must be open to the public, without prior booking, for published periods each year, and should be capable of attracting day visitors or tourists as well as local residents. In addition, the attraction must be a single business, under a single management, so that it is capable of answering the economic questions on revenue, employment.

(VisitScotland 2004: 8)

The scope helps to show how the sector incorporates a diverse range of attractions that combine to cater for visitors. However, it is also a somewhat restrictive and narrow definition because it does not acknowledge the significance of other elements of attractions including:

- the role of shopping as a key activity and drawcard for tourists, especially the diverse elements of the retail experience (i.e. shopping malls, markets, farmers' markets) which are an attraction in their own right. As Table 8.3 shows, London has 42 markets, promoted by Transport for London and London Underground as a Real London Markets brand. This is reflected in the way the Real London Markets' brochure conveys the atmosphere, image and character of the locality:

  there are so many reasons to visit, whether it's to savour the sights and smells of the Caribbean, the lure of finding that bargain antique or second-hand book

Table 8.3 Street markets as visitor attractions: London

Name of market	Speciality
Central London	
Covent Garden	Converted market with antiques and crafts and a piazza with performers and buskers
The Courtyard, St Martin in the Fields	Ceramics and arts
Gray's Antique Market	Antiques
Berwick Street, Soho	Food
Charing Cross Collectors' Fair	Flea market
London Silver Vaults	Silverware
North London	
Camden Market, Camden Lock	Clothing and all types of items
Camden Passage	Antiques
Chapel Market, Islington	Various
Nags Head, Seven Sisters	Various
Wembley	Clothing and various
Hampstead Community Market	Various

Table 8.3 *continued*

Name of market	Speciality
East London	
Petticoat Lane, Aldgate	Clothing
Spitalfields	Books, fabrics, clothing and food
Billingsgate Fish Market, Isle of Dogs	Fish
Columbia Road Flower Market	Flowers
Brick Lane (The Lane)	Various
Leadenhall Market	Food
Smithfield Market	Wholesale meat
Ridley Road Market (Dalston Market)	Various
Leather Lane	Various
Roman Road Market	Various
Whitechapel Market	Various
Hackney Stadium	Second-hand goods
Walthamstow Market	Various
Kingsland Waste (The Waste)	Second-hand goods
South London	
Borough Market	Food
Bermondsey Market	Antiques
East Street Market	Caribbean foods
Brixton Market	Handicrafts
Greenwich Market	Clothing and jewellery
Gabriel's Wharf	Clothing
New Covent Garden Flower Market	Flowers
Merton Abbey Mills Market	Weekend market
Riverside Market	Second-hand books
West London	
Bayswater Road Market	Art laid out on pavement
Chelsea Antiques Market	Antiques
Portobello Market	Antiques, clothing and jewellery
Shepherd's Bush Market	Local ethnic market (Afro-Caribbean dimension)
London Farmers' Markets, Notting Hill Gate	Fresh food from farms within 100 miles of London
North End Road, Fulham	Food
Church Street and Bell Street	Various

Various – a variety of food, clothing and mixed retailing

Note: There are also other famous London markets, some smaller and not easily accessible by London Underground, and some that are a major draw for leisure shopping, such as Romford Market in Essex. The above table is illustrative rather than all-inclusive

Source: developed from Transport for London and London Underground (2002) *Real London Markets*. London: Transport for London

or hearing the wit of a Cockney trader. When you've worked up a hunger from browsing and haggling, stop for a while to eat at an authentic pie and mash shop or snack on a falafel or crepe, before continuing your journey from stall to stall.

(Transport for London and London Underground 2002: 2)

In fact, the Gretna Green Outlet Village on the main tourist route between England and Scotland attracts over a million visitors a year, illustrating the scale of demand for a visitor retail experience

- events and festivals held on a periodic, non-permanent or one-off basis have an enormous potential to build the tourism capacity of a destination. They may also stimulate investment in tourism infrastructure to accommodate the short- or long-term impact of growth in demand. The most notable example is the Olympic Games, discussed in Further Web Reading 1
- the imagery created by using destinations as film or television locations can not only stimulate regional, national and global tourist interest, but also lead to a sudden influx of visitors. Some recent examples include filming the *Lord of the Rings* trilogy in New Zealand and *Harry Potter* in the UK, with some tourism organizations harnessing these media images to create tourism associations with the area, its attractions and the film tourism potential. For example, in northern Scotland, the BBC series *Monarch of the Glen* led to the branding of an area as Monarch of the Glen Country
- the geographical elements of a destination (termed 'GeoTourism') take the geological features of a region as the attraction and rationale for visiting. A unique landscape, such as lava flow (the Giant's Causeway in Ireland), effects of sand-based weathering of sandstone in western Australia (Bungle Bungle) or the white cliffs of Dover have powerful associations that create the attraction of the destination. Man-made elements in the region, such as local food and wine, crafts and vernacular (in the regional architectural style) buildings along with human elements such as the cultures of indigenous peoples also feature in defining the attraction of an area or destination.

Consequently, a broader definition of the term 'attraction' incorporates a wider range of locations as Pearce (1991: 46) suggests: 'A tourist attraction is a named site with a specific human or natural feature which is the focus of visitor and management attention'.

It is important to differentiate an attraction from a destination, since attractions are normally single units with a specific geographical focus. A destination may be based on a series of attractions, as the example of Cardiff Bay's regeneration illustrated earlier. However, there are exceptions to this, such as Walt Disney World, Orlando or EuroDisney (which attracts over 15 million visitors a year), which can be classified as a destination with an attraction and cluster of serviced accommodation. One of the perennial problems in studying visitor attractions is the global paucity of research data that measures visitor volumes at attractions. Even where data exist, they are rarely collected on a similar basis, making international comparisons problematic. One starting point in seeking to establish the basis of the scale and volume of visitor attractions in any destination or area is to seek to classify attractions.

There are three ways to consider the scope of attractions:

1   *natural or man-made attractions*, such as a National Park (natural) or the Tower of London (man-made). Natural attractions may be further divided into whether they are managed or left in a natural state

2   Holloway (2001) identifies attractions that can be *nodal or linear in character*. A nodal attraction may be a capital city, such as London, Rome or Paris, that is the focus of the visit and an attraction in its own right – a feature which many tourism organizations utilize in place-marketing strategies by using icons that reflect the place's image (e.g. the Eiffel Tower as representing Paris which attracts over 6 million visits a year). The linear resource most widely used by visitors is the coastal resort. Linear resorts act as attractions in their own right (e.g. Blackpool's Illuminations, which attract visitors to the town in the shoulder season; £2 million is spent on promoting this attraction, which can be dated back to 1912). A number of other UK seaside resorts have also used similar schemes very successfully, such as Southend in the 1950s and 1960s

3   the differentiation between *sites as locations, permanent attractions and special events*. Special events are temporary and short-term, and may be constructed or natural (see www.festivals.com for a global listing of festivals and events by category and a listing of the most unusual sporting events).

Many classifications and categorizations of attractions exist. One of the most interesting classifications is that developed by the English Tourism Council (now VisitEngland) which identifies the following attraction types and is a commonly used system of classification:

•   cathedral and churches
•   country parks
•   farms
•   gardens
•   historic houses and castles
•   other historic properties
•   leisure and theme parks
•   museums and galleries
•   steam railways
•   visitor centres
•   wildlife attractions and zoos.

The physical environment is also important, since attractions can be located in the:

•   natural environment, such as forests, mountains and other natural settings
•   built environment that has been adapted for visitor use (e.g. workplaces and historic houses)
•   built environment that has been designed for visitors.

In addition, one way of understanding how important the notion of an attraction is within a tourist's visit is to examine the main activities undertaken by tourists visiting a location. As Figure 8.3 shows, within a city context (Amsterdam), the city's built environment and its seventeenth- and eighteenth-century architecture from the Golden Age is a popular attractor. Similarly, shopping and hospitality are important activities, but other attractions (paid and unpaid) are also important as Figure 8.3 shows.

Walsh-Heron and Stevens (1990: 2) build upon and expand the function of a visitor attraction, defined as a place, venue or focus of activity. The elements of a visitor attraction are that it:

- sets out to attract visitors (day visitors from resident and tourist populations) and is managed accordingly
- provides a pleasurable experience and an enjoyable way for customers to spend their leisure time
- is developed to achieve this goal
- is managed as an attraction, providing satisfaction to customers
- provides an appropriate level of facilities and services to meet and cater to the demands, needs and interests of its visitors
- may or may not charge an admission fee.

Points of particular interest from Walsh-Heron and Stevens's list are that attractions have a psychological element – they provide a pleasurable experience and give satisfaction to visitors – as well as an appropriate level of services. Walsh-Heron and Stevens (1990: 3) define further criteria relating to management that assist in defining whether an enterprise is an attraction. The criteria are that management must: perceive and recognize

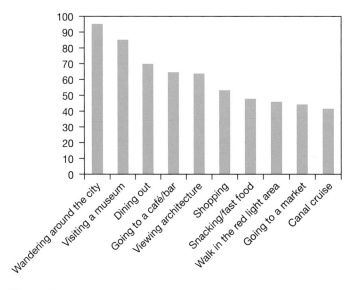

Percentage of activities undertaken by tourists in Amsterdam and surrounding area, 2011

Figure 8.3
Main activities undertaken by tourists visiting Amsterdam in 2011

Source: developed from data from Amsterdam Visitor Profile (2012)

itself to be a tourist attraction; promote and market the attraction publicly; provide on-site management and staffing; and be recognized as a 'tourist attraction' by the visitor.

The events industry classified

In contrast to visitor attractions, the scope and nature of the events industry can be classified into a number of discrete sectors as the following UK report found:

- the conference and meetings industry
- exhibitions and trade shows
- incentive travel
- corporate hospitality
- outdoor events
- festivals and cultural events
- music events.

Source: UK All Party Parliamentary Group Inquiry (2013)

The UK events industry was estimated to be worth £36 billion in 2012, supporting 25 000 businesses and 530 000 jobs. This categorization of the events industry extends the broad classification presented in Case Study 8.1 and highlights an additional phenomenon – the international meetings market (Case Study 8.2).

CASE STUDY 8.2
THE INTERNATIONAL MEETINGS MARKET AND WORK OF THE INTERNATIONAL CONGRESS AND CONVENTION ASSOCIATION (ICCA)

A recent study by ICCA (2013) outlines the historical growth of the international meetings industry, which is based on the main markets for these events: the corporate and non-corporate markets (Figure 8.4). Figure 8.4 shows that there are likely to be variety of event types (medical meetings, academic and trade-related meetings), scientific meetings and professional bodies. Choosing the venue and location for these events is a very competitive undertaking, as locations compete to attract the events, with ICCA estimating that there are 23 000 association meetings a year, 80 per cent of which ICCA record. The historic growth of the meetings market since 1963 is shown in Figure 8.5, which shows the exponential growth in the 1970s and 1980s, although ICCA show that the number of participants at meetings has also grown from 2 million in 1963–1968 to 22 million in 2008–2012. The popularity among delegates from Europe is shown in Figure 8.6 followed by Asia/Middle East, which has pushed North America into third place since the 1960s. The types of venue which these meetings use have changed since the late 1970s, as meetings in hotels have grown in popularity, whilst a drop in conference/exhibition centres has been recorded, although they still remain the

Figure 8.4
The international meetings market

Source: ICCA (2013: 9) *A Modern History of International Association Meetings 1963–2012*, ICCA, reproduced with permission

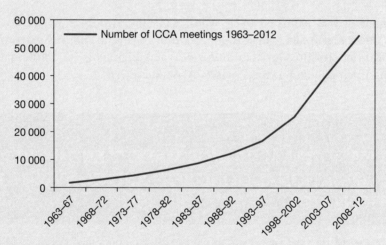

Figure 8.5
Number of ICCA meetings (based on 5 year aggregated data)

Source: simplified data extracted from ICCA (2013: 32), reproduced with permission

second most popular venue. Universities have also seen growth in popularity, whilst there has been a decline in size of meeting and shortening in duration of meeting (i.e. from 6.3 days in 1963–1967 to 3.8 days in 2008–2012). This has impacted upon the market for meetings as short duration events occur. In contrast, the average fee per delegate has risen from US$97 (1993–1997) to US$149 (2008–2012) and the average expenditure per delegate per day has risen from US$440 (1993–1997) to US$678 (2008–2012). The most popular countries for ICCA meetings are illustrated in Table 8.4 which highlights the importance of North America and Europe, as well as rising destinations reflecting their growing venue status in Latin America and China.

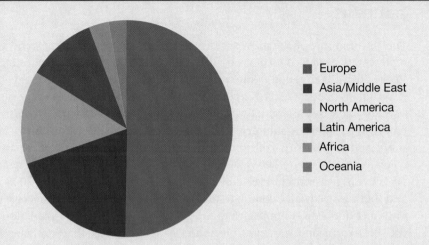

- Europe
- Asia/Middle East
- North America
- Latin America
- Africa
- Oceania

Figure 8.6
The regional distribution of participants in international meetings 2008–2012

Source: simplified data extracted from ICCA (2013: 32), reproduced with permission

Table 8.4 Top 10 countries for ICCA meetings in 2012

Rank	Country	Number of meetings in 2012	Rank	Country	Number of meetings in 2012
1	USA	833	6	Italy	390
2	Germany	649	7	Brazil	360
3	Spain	550	8	Japan	341
4	United Kingdom	477	9	Netherlands	315
5	France	469	10	China-P.R.	311

Source: simplified data extracted from ICCA (2013: 32), reproduced with permission

Further reading

ICCA (2013) A Modern History of International Association Meetings 1963–2012, iccaworld.com: 9.

Other data can also be obtained from the Union of International Associations.

Visitor attractions in the UK: Recent trends and patterns

The UK has some of the most accessible data on visitor attractions, and whilst it is not representative of all countries, we can use it to examine trends and patterns. Looking back to the 2001–2006 period is interesting as it highlights a number of key changes which government policy impacted upon. For 2001 and 2006, in almost every case, the volume of visits increased marginally or declined. As *Visitor Attraction Trends: England 2006* reported, in 2006 the summer, traditionally the peak season for visitor attractions, was warm and sunny. This contributed to a growth of visits in the paid attraction sector compared to 2004 and 2005. Overall, the larger attractions (i.e. those with over 20 000 visits a year) received a modest growth of 4 per cent in visitor numbers 2005–2006. London and south-east England dominate the list of top attractions which receive over a million visits a year; the most notable change 2001–2006 was in the free admission category after the UK Department for Media, Culture and Sport announced that admission to the national museums and galleries would be free (December 2001). Whilst admissions to Blackpool Pleasure Beach dropped by 11 per cent 2001–2006, other free-admission attractions in the top ten rankings expanded their visitor volumes, in the third to tenth rankings. These volumes typically doubled in some cases although one has to add a note of caution as the 2006 figures now have a caveat: they only include those admissions where the attractions agree to their publication.

The philosophy underpinning this government policy shift was informed by a desire to make these attractions more socially inclusive, to attract more visits from social groups D and E. In the period December 2001–June 2002, these attractions saw a 62 per cent increase in visitor numbers to 7 million, a 2.7 million increase. Yet, as Martin (2003) argued, these additional visits have not materialized from the social classes D and E. The profile of museum and gallery visitors has remained fairly static, being dominated by social groups ABC, although in numerical terms more social groups D and E have visited such attractions. Social exclusion among groups D and E has not been addressed, the reasons for which are cost of travel to cultural attractions, traditional leisure habits, lack of awareness of free admission, and geographical proximity to the attractions, since visits are dominated by those living in London and the South-East.

Visits to free attractions since 2001 have attracted a greater volume of visitors than paid attractions which in itself brings problems of management and planning for these sites. For example, in 2001–2002, the Victoria and Albert Museum experienced a 157 per cent increase in visitors after free admission was introduced although, as Martin (2003) observed, visitors gaining free admission were more likely to give a donation, buy a guide book and spend money visiting a special exhibition. Even so, the Natural History Museum had noted that a large proportion of visitors were spending no more than when admission charges were in place. This may call into question the viability of such a scheme if central government funding penalizes those large attractions which successfully attract high visitor numbers yet this does not convert to a major increase in visitor spending.

The visitor attraction market 2001–2006 did not see massive growth in the attractions charging for admission, whilst the flagship free attractions that stopped charging (e.g. the Victoria and Albert Museum, Science Museum and Natural History Museum) have seen visitor numbers almost double in most cases, posing major visitor management dilemmas. In 2004, the top five visitor attractions in the UK in terms of visitor volumes all had free admission. By 2006, this had risen to the top ten attractions. Since 2006, paid attractions' visitor numbers have been relatively stable with some fluctuation at the top ten attractions (Figure 8.7).

In contrast, the free attractions (Figure 8.8) have seen a greater degree of variation in visitation. For example, the British Museum numbers rose from 4.8 million in 2001 and 2006 to 5.9 million in 2009, stabilizing at that level in 2012. Similarly, the Tate

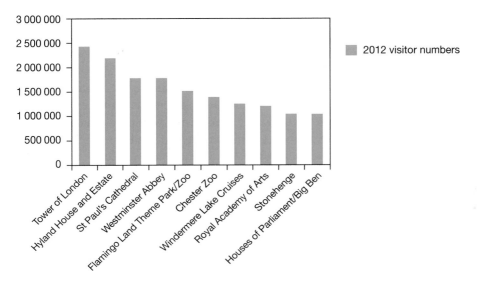

Figure 8.7
Visitor numbers to top ten paid attractions in England in 2012

Source: data from VisitEngland

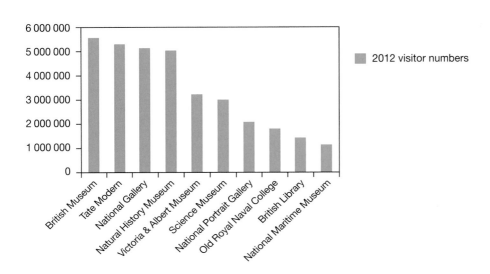

Figure 8.8
Visitor numbers to top ten free attractions in England in 2012

Source: data from VisitEngland

Modern saw its volume of visitors rise prior to 2009 and stabilized at 2.9 million visits in 2009, rising to over 5 million in 2012. In addition, the Natural History Museum saw its visitor volumes fluctuate from 3.7 million in 2006 to 3.2 million in 2008 and then to 4.1 million in 2009 and 5 million in 2012.

Visitor attractions: Product considerations

Visitor attractions offer both products and experiences. One of the main management issues for visitor attraction operators is matching the product to the benefits sought by the consumer. Kotler's (1994) view is that products consist of three levels (core product; tangible product; and augmented product), and Swarbrooke (2002) argued that this may be adapted to a visitor attraction setting. The core product is the central component and comprises the main benefits that will be identified by the visitor as a motivation for visiting. The second layer of a product is the tangible aspect, which visitors can purchase. The third aspect of a product is the augmented product, which includes the additional services a visitor receives and makes up the total product.

Gunn (1988) also conceptualized a tourist attraction in a way where the product basis can be considered. Gunn identified three zones in relation to the spatial layout of an attraction, the nuclei contains the core attraction and the zone of closure contains the ancillary services associated with the attraction, such as shops, car park and tea room. The inviolate belt is an area that protects the core product from the commercialized areas of the zone of closure (Figure 8.9). A more detailed model of attractions as products can be applied, as Figure 8.10 shows in the case of a historic garden such as Kew Gardens in London, where three levels of a garden visitor attraction product exist.

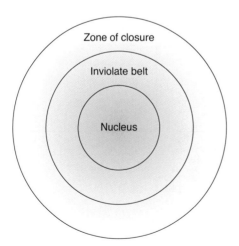

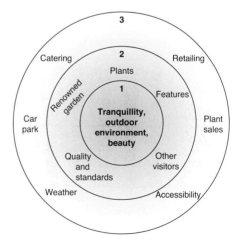

Figure 8.9
Gunn's model of a tourist attraction

Source: based on Gunn (1972) © 1972, *Tourism Planning*, C. Gunn, reproduced by permission of Taylor and Francis, Inc., www.routledge-ny.com

Figure 8.10
A garden as a visitor attraction product

Source: © Joanne Connell, reproduced with permission from the author

Attractions as a leisure product

Jansen-Verbeke (1986) developed a framework with which to analyse tourism visits to places and these ideas can be applied to attractions. Still focusing on the idea of a garden as a visitor attraction, the application of the leisure product idea is useful in helping to understand how the structure and presentation of visitor attractions can be analysed from a product perspective. As Table 8.5 shows, the facilities which gardens offer can be divided into primary elements, secondary elements and additional elements. While the range of elements available in gardens will vary, the framework identifies the scope of characteristics and facilities. This can also be applied to areas of cities such as London's West End where the leisure product can be constructed. However, such products will also have a life cycle.

Table 8.5 The categorization of the garden as a leisure product

Primary elements	Secondary elements	
Activity place	Leisure setting	
Leisure interest facilities:	**Physical characteristics:**	**Tea room:**
• Guided walks	• Design	• Shop
• Exhibitions	• Planting	• Nursery
• Routes	• Garden features	• Seats
• Self-guided trails	• Garden buildings	
• Events and festivals	• Water feature	
Physical features:	**Social features:**	**Additional elements:**
• Children's play area	• Welcome	• Accessibility
	• Friendliness	• Car parking
	• Helpfulness	• Signposting
	• Ability to answer questions	• Foreign language leaflets
	• Ambience	• Information
	• Health and safety considerations	• Plant labels

Source: © Joanne Connell, reproduced with permission from the author

Visitor attractions and the product life cycle

Within marketing, there is a widely accepted notion that products will evolve through time and follow a specific product life cycle (see Figure 8.11). This was adapted from marketing and applied to tourism, as the discussion of the resort life cycle in Chapter 1 suggested. For purpose-designed visitor attractions, the life-cycle concept is quite relevant. However, for those attractions that were not originally designed for visitation, Swarbrooke (2002) believes that the model is of less relevance because it is difficult to identify the start of the introduction phase. Motivations for opening may be based on the need to derive extra revenue for maintenance or conservation work and the attraction market is not viewed as the core business. For example, the 'core business' of the National Trust in England and Wales is conservation and education, not running visitor attractions, but it needs visitors to fund its work. However, it is still pertinent for operators of such attractions to be aware of market changes as it becomes more difficult to attract visitors in a market characterized by oversupply of attractions.

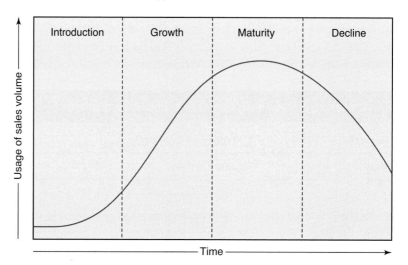

Figure 8.11
The product life cycle

Source: reprinted from Swarbrooke (2002: 51)

In a Scottish context, research by Lennon (2001) noted that those attractions that had invested and diversified their product base through retail areas (e.g. merchandizing), were receiving additional benefits in relation to visitor spending at attractions. In Scotland the average dwell time at an attraction was two hours and forty-two minutes, although this comprised eighty minutes at the attraction; twenty minutes' retailing; twenty-eight minutes at a catering outlet and thirty-four minutes at other elements of the operation. Therefore, by developing a broader product base attractions were seeking to expand the dwell time at their site. The significance of attractions is illustrated in that almost 6000 full-time employees work in Scottish visitor attractions, with almost 3000 unpaid volunteers helping at trusts and other sites. This illustrates the economic potential of broadening the product base in expanding employment opportunities.

A crucial fact to acknowledge in the management of visitor attractions is that the long-term quality of the product and the visitor experience can be adversely affected by external and internal threats. Consequently, a strategy to focus efforts in managing potential impacts from the internal environment (i.e. within the attraction itself) can assist a visitor attraction in striving towards a viable future. As research by Lennon (2001) found, the competition for leisure spending across the attraction, retail and entertainment sectors has led to a distinct visitor attraction life cycle. Lennon found that the following pattern emerged among paid and free attractions in Scotland with over 10 000 visitors a year:

- in Years 1–2 growth is apparent
- in Year 3 a decline in visitation occurs
- paid attractions maintain a greater stability in visitor numbers up to Year 4
- non-paid admission attractions see decline in Years 3 and 4 then stabilization.

Yet a range of attraction operators and their operational activities and business strategy explains this pattern. For example, there were those who saw an attraction decline cycle, where a decline set in after two years of growth following initial opening. The decline was a reflection of the failure to innovate and expand their visitor offering, and was typical of many public sector operations in Scotland. In contrast, a series of Year 4 revivalists also existed, which underwent a major refurbishment or reinvestment to nurture visitor interest again. A further attraction type was also discerned in terms of the constant innovators, where attractions constantly re-invest, seek to diversify their product offering, upgrade their facilities and pump-prime the attraction life-cycle model by intervening through ongoing reinvestment.

Stevens (1991: 110) notes that attractions provide a 'consumer product which is based upon the unique experience and immediate point of sale consumption', the implication of which is the need to emphasize visitor care. A clear understanding of the nature of the visitor experience and how it can be enhanced to achieve high levels of visitor satisfaction, according to the type of attraction and types of visitor, are variables over which owners/managers can have a greater degree of control in relation to the management of the attraction. One innovation by attractions in seeking to engage more fully with their actual and potential visitors is through the growing use of social media, as illustrated by Figure 8.12. Additional tools such as TripAdvisor and eWord of Mouth also help with visitor engagement.

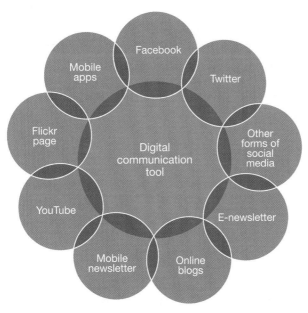

Figure 8.12
Use of digital communication channels by English visitor attractions in 2012

Source: data from VisitEngland

Visitor attractions and the visitor experience

Swarbrooke (2002) comments that the visitor attraction product is now usually viewed as an experience. The visitor experience is a somewhat nebulous concept because it is a complex amalgam of factors that shape the tourist's feelings and attitude towards his or her visit. The visitor experience is likely to be different for each individual visitor as it forms through a series of value judgements based on emotional and physical responses to a site, and resulting in satisfaction/dissatisfaction with one or more components of the site.

The visitor experience at attractions: Key influences

Yale (1997) states that the success of a tourist attraction lies in four critical areas:

1   accessibility
2   opening hours
3   on-site amenities, such as parking, visitor centre, signs and labels, shops, guides, refreshments, toilets, litter bins, seating and disabled provision
4   off-site amenities, such as signposting, local accommodation and local services.

Swarbrooke (2002) identified four key factors that influence the success of attractions:

1   the organization and its resources
2   the product
3   the market
4   the management of the attraction (see Table 8.6).

Table 8.6 Factors influencing the success of tourist attractions

The organization and its resources	Experience of developing and managing attractions	Financial resources	Marketing – see 'The management of the attraction'				
The product	Novel approach or new idea	Location	On-site attraction	High quality environment	Good customer service	Visitor facilities	Value for money
The market	Growth markets – targeting markets which are likely to expand						
The management of the attraction	Experienced professional managers	Adequate attention to market research	Realizing that marketing is not just about brochures and adverts	Long-term strategic view	Accepting importance of word-of-mouth	Planned marketing strategy with proper financing	Staff training

Source: after Swarbrooke (2002)

An intangible quality or '*magic*' is necessary, as well as highly professional management and innovative concepts.

Swarbrooke (2002) asserts that a range of elements affect the visitor experience on site beyond the core focus of the attraction. These elements include: the tangible elements of the product (such as retail outlets, cafes, toilet facilities and site cleanliness), the service delivery elements (including the appearance, attitudes, behaviour and competence of staff), the expectation, behaviour and attitude of the visitor and a number of factors that are largely outside the control of either the attraction or visitor, such as climatic conditions and the mix of people using the attraction at one time. The visitor experience is the combination and interrelationship of these factors and will be different for each individual visitor. Design issues, such as signposting and seating provision, present an image of the attraction to the visitor that may or may not be favourable. Thus the contemporary management of an attraction can influence the visitor experience through design and resource issues. As important as the physical management of the site are customer care and the acknowledgement of the crucial relationship between the staff, the service and the needs of the visitor. Each element is important and a lack of care – whether it is in the signage, car parking, quality of catering or cleanliness of the toilets – can destroy the overall visitor experience.

Visitor responses to perceived levels of crowding and impacts on the resource base materialize in terms of dissatisfaction with the site or, indeed, displacement of the visitor. In reality, the tourist experience at an attraction is likely to be affected by a wide range of factors, some of which are inevitably not linked with the destination *per se* but hinge on the mood and personal circumstance of the visitor. The experience is also likely to be affected by the expectations and preconceived ideas that the visitor may possess prior to a visit, as well as the cultural origin of the visitor and prior socialization. The recognition of these individual factors reflects previous consumer product experience or expectations, which influence the satisfaction/dissatisfaction process. It is impossible to control all the factors relating to the visit experience and it should be recognized that, while a visitor may be completely satisfied with the core product and the tangible service elements, an external factor, such as the weather or transport infrastructure, might spoil the experience. In addition, it is also worth noting that success in attraction development, particularly within a defined tourism region, can be dependent upon how the various sites are linked together through marketing and information to visitors. Providing brochures and advertising that create an awareness of visit opportunities can help to spread visitors across a region, especially when there is major investment at an attraction to stimulate tourism development.

Creating clusters of attractions can be successful, as with the regeneration of Stirling's old town through the public and private sector Stirling Initiative over the last 20 years. This used the drawcard of Stirling Castle, and a number of other attractions were created to fit a heritage theme to add to the range of heritage experiences (e.g. the Old Town Jail, Argyll's Lodgings and newly opened Tolbooth Art Centre). Other large-scale projects such as the Falkirk Wheel certainly assist in spreading the visitor impact and spending away from the 80 per cent currently focused on the Stirling region as well as creating a new destination, in this case in the Forth Valley area.

Attractions, when integrated into the product, can provide tangible economic impacts for the locality and tourism economy. Visitor spending at these attractions is often viewed as the basis of their contribution to the economy; for the visitor they may be the reason for visiting a destination. Bilbao's Guggenheim Museum has provided the catalyst for a growth in visitor activity and spending in a locality which did not historically have a highly developed tourism sector. Such iconic attractions can also create a 'must-visit' trend amongst certain segments of the tourism market (cultural tourists in the case of the Guggenheim). In Edinburgh, the location of the Royal Yacht Britannia at Leith combined with the development of Ocean Point retail complex has created a new nucleus for visitor activity and visitor spending in an area that has hitherto not been associated with tourism. Similarly, the economic impact of hosting events is often cited by developing organizations as a prime motive for progressing an attraction project. This is particularly apparent in one of the world's most ambitious attempts to develop an economy based on tourism: in Dubai, with unusual attractions requiring one of the largest injections of capital into attraction projects globally. For this reason, Web Case 8.1 outlines how Dubai has harnessed tourism and attractions to create a world-class tourism destination in a desert environment.

Managing the visitor experience: Potential and prospects

Two main factors underpin the need to ensure customers are satisfied with their visit experience. First, visitor satisfaction can encourage regular and repeat visits, and this is more cost effective than seeking new visitors. Second, positive word-of-mouth recommendations work in the favour of attraction operators since minimal marketing input is required to attract new visitors. Word of mouth can work inversely too and the communication of bad experiences to friends and family is likely to influence visit decision-making negatively. Managing the visitor experience is a vital, although complex, requirement in the operation of a visitor attraction and it is essential for attraction owners/managers to recognize the significance of the visit/visitor experience in sustaining visitor satisfaction and, inevitably, visitor numbers (see Table 8.6). Understanding the visitor experience is a key factor in determining the success of a visitor attraction, and has wider implications for the public perception of specific attractions as day-trip destinations.

A number of models have been developed to evaluate quality and customer satisfaction in business operations, the most notable of which is SERVQUAL (Parasuraman *et al.* 1985). Considered a seminal study in consumer behaviour, the basis of this evaluative framework is the difference between consumer expectation and perception of service, based on five generic service-quality dimensions necessary for customer satisfaction (see Table 8.7).

Table 8.7 Dimensions of service quality based on the SERVQUAL principle

Reliability	Ability to perform services dependably
Responsiveness	Willingness to assist customers and provide prompt service
Assurance	Courtesy, trustworthiness and knowledge of staff
Empathy	Display caring attitude to customers
Tangibles	Presentation of physical facilities

Parasuraman *et al.* (1985) identified five gaps between service providers and consumers, but later work suggested that another gap existed – that between the customer's and the provider's perception of the experience. These issues form the basis for managing the visitor at attractions and have to be viewed alongside future trends and issues affecting visitor attractions (also see Chapter 9 for more detail on service provision and the management of tourism experiences).

One of the key challenges for visitor attraction managers is to ensure the continued viability of an attraction, since the sector is littered with examples of business failure that can be attributed to poor financial management, a lack of understanding of the markets (including over-optimistic forecasts of visitor use and spending) that would be interested in the attraction and an inability to move with the times. For the attraction manager, the range of issues they will often have to grapple with is varied and diverse ranging from simple issues such as customer dissatisfaction or a complaint through to more protracted strategic and planning problems such as accommodating the car as a form of transport that connects the visitor with the attraction site. The management issues associated with the impact of visitors require a multi-talented team of staff able to grapple with these challenges including the day to day operational issues associated with human resources and finance and general management. For example, common issues reported in studies of attractions include: overcrowding, wear and tear (especially at natural and historic sites), vandalism, traffic related problems often associated with the car and accommodating peak numbers at popular times. In addition, the location of the attraction may indirectly lead to community impacts that occur between visitors and local residents who may feel 'under siege' at peak times. Other impacts which may arise for the attraction which can compromise the authenticity of the product and its portrayal to visitors are the need to alter or adapt the structure of the site or venue to accommodate the flow of visitors, make provision for disabled visitors and legal requirements such as complying with health and safety legislation that can affect the experience. For this reason, attraction managers have an arsenal of methods to manage the impacts including supply-led measures:

- queue management
- making the capacity at the attraction more flexible (extending the opening hours and providing additional staff at locations to cope with additional demand)
- increasing the capacity by hardening the site such as the Tower of London's Jewel House that has a travellator that is switched on during busy periods to limit the amount of time visitors can dwell at the point of interest

and demand-led measures including:

- price incentives to encourage visitation as many visitors to attractions are price sensitive
- marketing to encourage off-peak use

- education and interpretation to promote responsible behaviour and the provision of alternative routes to reduce pressure on sensitive sites.

Source: Fyall *et al*. (2008)

However, one of the key challenges for many attractions is the highly skewed nature of visitation in the peak season and for this reason, attraction managers need to be aware of measures which can assist in reducing the impact of seasonality such as extended opening hours or year round opening to promotions and incentives to attract visitor numbers. Conversely, some attractions accept the reality of coping with seasonality and reduce their opening hours or the areas available to visitors to cut costs as well as explaining to visitors that the full offer is not available to manage expectations. More proactive attractions may seek to create new markets in the low season through encouraging residents and leisure trips through the staging of events.

Other notable developments in the wider attraction and events sector is the greater concern with sustainability issues as illustrated in Innovation in Sustainability 8.1.

INNOVATION IN SUSTAINABILITY 8.1
THE GREENING OF MEETINGS AND EVENTS

The growth in global travel and concerns over the expanding role of business travel associated with meetings and events (i.e. trade shows and conventions) has seen a focus on the unsustainable nature of these activities. The principal problem associated with events and meetings lies in the short-term, concentrated impact of a large gathering of people in one place. Whilst these events may help to boost off-peak tourism, events and meetings are also all-year-round activities and some destinations have built their visitor economy around this lucrative market, nurturing high-spending visitors where the costs and spending are set against visitors' business or employers' costs.

To address sustainability concerns, UNEP (2009) launched its Green Meeting Guide. The underlying principles of how a green event or meeting should be constructed are shown in Figure 8.13.

Figure 8.13 illustrates the growing philosophy of sustainable events embodied in events such as the 2000 Sydney Olympic Games, 2006 FIFA World Cup and subsequent global events. The necessity of such a sustainability focus was illustrated by UNEP (2009), when it identified the impact of hosting the 2002 World Summit on Sustainable Development in Johannesburg, South Africa where:

- 322.59 tonnes of waste arose
- 136 000 tonnes of carbon emissions resulted
- 25 tonnes of paper were used
- 11 800 kl of water was used
- 2485 mwh of energy was used.

Consequently the UNEP (2009) report provides a guide to implementing a sustainable approach to event development as illustrated in Figure 8.14.

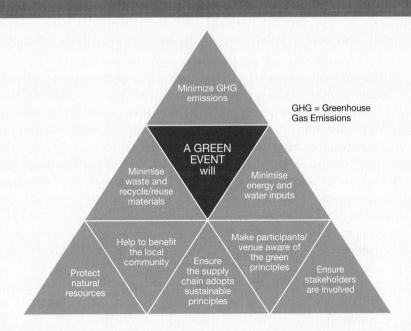

Figure 8.13
Underlying characteristics of a green event or meeting

Source: developed from UNEP (2009)

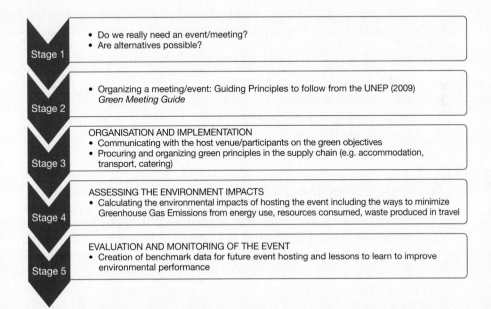

Figure 8.14
Greening meetings and events: Implementation process

Source: developed from UNEP (2009) *Green Meeting Guide*

The future for visitor attraction management

It is widely recognized that a range of factors impact upon the success or failure of visitor attractions to operate as tourism enterprises. This must be viewed against the visitor's growing expectations during their visit and the need for attractions to improve standards in many countries worldwide. It also involves the need for attractions to refresh their products in order to retain their market share. Even though some operate as trusts and are based in the not-for-profit sector, their future survival depends upon managing their assets and enterprise in an efficient and robust manner so that visitors are attracted and they remain viable in an increasingly competitive environment globally. Some of the key factors that will shape visitor attractions in the future have been identified by Swarbrooke (2001) as:

- coping with the scale and diversity of competition, especially in the leisure market
- recruiting, rewarding and retaining staff
- staying ahead of developments in marketing
- recognizing the role of marketing consortia in achieving economies of cost in advertising
- satisfying consumers
- meeting the needs of special groups of visitors such as the disabled
- offering unique selling propositions and the 'wow' factor at attractions to appeal to visitors.

Many of these factors can be grouped into a number of categories of challenges for the future:

1   product development and innovation
2   marketing and promotion
3   revenue generation and funding
4   education and training
5   community and public sector intervention.

Product development and innovation

This is vital if an attraction is to remain ahead of the competition and to take account of trends in the global and national marketplace. Chapter 11 examines innovation in more detail; here it is worth noting that most successful attractions seek to identify new concepts, business processes or techniques such as interpretation or technology to appeal to a sophisticated audience. One of the greatest developments for many attractions is in the use of film in interpretation and interactive technology to appeal to children, such as the Newseum in Washington DC: this cost US$50 million to develop and is a free admission museum of news and journalism. In its first nine months of operation it attracted 325 000 visitors – which is very interactive and mediaworthy! In a similar vein the Futurescope in Poitiers, France, which opened in 1987, incorporates film as the basis of the theme park's operation with IMAX and OMNIMAX, and also features roof projection and seat oscillation. Acting in much the same way as Lomond Shores in Scotland as a regeneration project led by the public sector, Futurescope has generated 1200 direct and 15 000 indirect jobs and received 2.8 million visitors in 2007 (largely domestic visitors). In the technology field, virtual reality attractions such as the New York Skyride and the Madame Tussaud Scenerama in Amsterdam offer simulated trips that also orientate the visitor to the destination.

Marketing and promotion

Whilst innovation is a key to success, ensuring that this is communicated to the potential customer through marketing and promotion is essential. Most attractions use limited budgets for public relations (PR) rather than media advertising, with many profile attractions having media kits, websites and virtual reality tours as well as targeting groups through promotional campaigns that are price driven. As discussed earlier, greater use of social media is also a new trend. These seek to make the public aware of the role of attractions in leisure spending and that they are venues for fun and enjoyment, as well as being safe and interesting. In the USA, the Smithsonian Museum in Washington DC and the Museum of Modern Art in New York both have very sophisticated websites and these have also provided a conduit for electronic trading such as retailing, ticket purchases and corporate hospitality bookings. In some cases, attractions have entered into strategic alliances and partnerships to develop synergies across the attraction and tourism sector to develop their business interests. For example, the Singapore Tourist Board screens all copy produced by attractions and places it in guide books and at strategic points of interest for visitors, ensuring the style and image of the tourist board is consistent. In New York, the Convention and Visitor Bureau links attractions and other tourist services with discount schemes and includes all attractions on an activities map. Other examples of partnership innovation include museums cooperating in Boston to undertake joint marketing initiatives and ultimately to raise public awareness. Other museums share best practice. Some attractions have introduced initiatives to extend their life cycle such as adding new visitor features or in-built regeneration strategies. One of the most interesting examples is Singapore Zoo's development of a nocturnal tour. Others have sought to extend the season through packaging the attraction with other products or services to create all-year-round opening opportunities as well as differential pricing mechanisms. Santa Claus Land in Finland has developed products to appeal to overseas markets at different times of the year and has created eight peak seasons. Joint marketing with rail operators such as ScotRail in Scotland can also yield significant results with free travel for children and entry concessions.

Revenue generation and funding

By presenting attractions as a series of products, managers can expand the scope for increasing the total spend per person while also appealing to the buoyant demand for retailing that has produced opportunities for themed development and linkage to the products and experiences offered by the attraction. Most successful attractions are heavily involved in hospitality, and have a prestigious cafe or restaurant that creates a nice ambience as well as good spending opportunities. In fact the Singapore Tourist Board has identified and themed food and hospitality into its tourism strategy for the twenty-first century – Tourism 21. It uses the Singapore Food Festival to add promotional opportunities and as a means to promote the ethnic diversity and 'Asia-ness' of the destination. Other attractions also have well-developed corporate hospitality functions, offering various places to host events and meetings as well as product launches. Many of the London museums have embraced this important source of funding, and also corporate membership. One of the principal tasks of revenue generation from existing visitors is to find ways to extend the dwell time on site, as discussed earlier in the case of Scotland. Greater division of attractions into sections/segments and experiences encourage a greater on-site time as well as increasing the range of retailing opportunities.

Education and training

The growth of awareness that many attractions now operate in what is called 'the cultural industries sector', and the growing need for education, training and management development activities, has led to recognition of the changing nature of attractions as businesses. It is evident that a series of cultural industries exist within a tourism context, and Myerscough (1988) identified the cultural events, artefacts and resources that are of vital significance to the tourism industry. Attractions provide the key element of this system. In an urban context, the cultural industries comprised a diverse group of attractions including nightclubs, libraries, museums and art galleries. In the UK these activities employed over 68 500 people in the 1990s, which is reflected in the fact that many countries (e.g. Scotland), towns and cities now have cultural industry strategies to promote these activities. This is shown in the European bids each year for cities to become European City of Culture with the perceived focus on attractions as a key element of tourism development and the associated controversy on how this will assist the attraction sector in developing its education and training needs to improve service delivery (see Richards and Palmer 2010).

The use of volunteers in many contexts provides many useful lessons for employed staff. Some countries (such as France) are exemplars of training in the visitor attraction sector since this is seen as gaining a competitive advantage. As Chapter 9 will show, certain tourism operators in the attraction sector such as Disney also lead the world in staff training and motivation to enhance guest care, the visitor experience and product development.

Community and public sector intervention

Visitor attractions are a vital element of any community and its tourism infrastructure and so local funding support for the low season is often seen as an essential element for success in cultural industry strategies. Off-season visits by local residents, who are also ambassadors for the local area, are important to the market for attractions. There are many good examples of country-level support for attractions in France and indirectly in the UK through Millennium funds. In contrast, the USA does not directly fund attractions through public funds, since donations, bequests or community efforts are more notable than public sector subsidies. Where the public sector intervenes directly, employment protection or development is usually justified as the basis for such intervention. In some cases states may seek to help develop an attraction in a destination and so funding for events and festivals can feature as a major element of public sector intervention in the attraction sector.

Conclusion

The post-modern age has witnessed a large increase in the range of visitor attractions in Britain and globally and the visiting public has to make certain decisions about visiting particular venues based on a complex mix of factors including location, appeal, cost and perceived benefit or a combination of these. Incentives such as free admission may have an impact, as the example of the UK's national museums and galleries illustrated. It is evident that professional approaches to researching visitor satisfaction are necessary as visitors' expectations increase and there is a greater urgency to ensure competitive advantage in the visitor attraction market. One of the major challenges for visitor attractions lies in harnessing new technology. Visitors are seeking greater interaction at attractions, which involves the integration of technology and 'high-touch' exhibits, whilst fulfilling a range of motivations for visiting. Yet, as the Web Case 6.1 of Dubai illustrates, attractions not only need to excite and surprise visitors, but they also need to have the 'wow' factor if they are to impress visitors and be world class.

CHAPTER REVIEW

 References

Fyall, Alan, Garrod, Brian, Leask, Anna and Wanhill, Stephen (eds) (2008) *Managing Visitor Attractions*. Oxford: Elsevier.

Getz, D. (1997) *Event Management and Event Tourism*. New York: Cognizant.

Gunn, C. A. (1988) *Tourism Planning*, 2nd edn. New York: Taylor and Francis.

Haahti, A. and Komppula, R. (2006) Experience design in tourism. In D. Buhalis and C. Costa (eds) *Tourism Business Frontiers: Consumers, Products and Industry*. Oxford: Elsevier, 101–111.

Holloway, J. C. (2001) *Business of Tourism*, 6th edn. Harlow: Pearson.

Jansen-Verbeke, M. (1986) Inner-city tourism: Resources, tourists and promoters. *Annals of Tourism Research*, 13(1): 79–100.

Kotler, P. (1994) *Marketing Management: Analysis, Planning, Implementation and Control*, 8th edn. London: Prentice Hall.

Lennon, J. (ed.) (2001) *Tourism Statistics: International Perspectives and Current Issues*. London: Continuum.

Martin, A. (2003) *The Impact of Free Entry to Museums*. London: MORI. www.mori.com

Myerscough, J. (1988) *The Economic Importance of the Arts in Britain*. London: Policy Studies Institute.

Parasuraman, A., Zeithaml, V. and Berry, L. (1985) A conceptual model of service quality and its implications for future research. *Journal of Marketing*, 49(4): 41–50.

Pearce, P. (1991) Analysing tourist attractions. *Journal of Tourism Studies*, 2(1): 46–55.

Richards, G. and Palmer, R. (2010) *Eventful Cities*, 2nd edn. Oxford: Elsevier.

Ritchie, J. R. B. (1984) Assessing the impacts of hallmark events: Conceptual and research issues. *Journal of Travel Research*, 23(1): 2–11.

Stevens, T. (1991) Visitor attractions. In C. P. Cooper (ed.) *Progress in Tourism, Recreation and Hospitality Management*, Volume Three. London: Belhaven Press.

Stevenson, D. (2006) The arts and entertainment: Situating leisure in the creative economy. In C. Rojek, S. Shaw and A. Veal (eds) *A Handbook of Leisure Studies*. Basingstoke: Palgrave, 354–362.

Swarbrooke, J. (2000) *Sustainable Tourism Management*. Wallingford: CABI.

Swarbrooke, J. (2001) Visitor attraction management in a competitive market. *Insights*, A41–52. London: English Tourism Council.

Swarbrooke, J. (2002) *The Development and Management of Visitor Attractions*, 2nd edn. Oxford: Butterworth-Heinemann.

Transport for London and London Underground (2002) *Real London Markets*. London: Transport for London.

UK All Party Parliamentary Group Inquiry (2013) *International Competitiveness of the UK Events Industry*. London: House of Commons.

UNEP (2009) *Green Meeting Guide*. Paris: UNEP. www.unep.org

VisitScotland (2004) *Scottish Visitor Attraction Monitor*. Edinburgh: VisitScotland.

Walsh-Heron, J. and Stevens, T. (1990) *The Management of Visitor Attractions and Events*. London: Prentice Hall.

Yale, P. (1997) *From Tourist Attractions to Heritage Tourism*. Huntingdon: ELM Publications.

 # Further reading

The most accessible source is:

Swarbrooke, J. (2002) *The Development and Management of Visitor Attractions*, 2nd edn. Oxford: Butterworth-Heinemann.

And on events, a seminal collection of papers can be found in:

Page S. J. and Connell, J. (eds) (2012) *A Handbook of Events*. London: Routledge.

Connell, J. and Page, S. J. (eds) (2011) *Event Tourism*, Vols 1–4. London: Routledge.

 Questions

1   Why are visitor attractions so crucial to the tourism sector?
2   What are the main factors associated with the successful management of visitor attractions?
3   Why are visitor attractions complex to categorize and classify?
4   What is the future for the visitor attraction with the growth of technology?

 Access additional resources

- For students: Multiple choice questions for each chapter, video links and further reading.
- For instructors: PowerPoint slides with tables and diagrams, additional case studies, video links and further reading.

9 The management of tourism

Learning outcomes

This chapter builds on the previous discussion of the tourism industry, reviewing the need to manage tourism businesses. On completion of this chapter, you should be able to understand:

- the principles of management and their application to tourism businesses
- the role of marketing as a management function
- the role of management in establishing standards and systems of service provision
- the significance of small tourism businesses in the tourism sector
- the role of innovation and tourism development as a management function.

Introduction

The previous chapters have highlighted the very fragmented nature of the business which many refer to as 'tourism', being a complex amalgam of businesses that cooperate and work together to supply services and products to tourists as consumers. Each of these businesses and bodies are known as 'organizations', which are formal entities such as businesses or corporations that exist to interact, trade and exchange goods, services and knowledge to create wealth or other outputs through the use of their staff, capabilities and know-how within a tourism context. Profit is the main driver of many businesses operating in the private sector. But there are also organizations within the public sector (see Chapter 10) and voluntary sector which interact in tourism in a regulatory or voluntary sense or as interest groups (i.e. a professional organization such as ABTA, the Association of British Travel Agents – now the Travel Association), and seek to influence and affect change and represent specific interests or viewpoints. All of these organizations impact upon tourism and its direction, nature and operation (this will be discussed more fully in Chapter 10). For businesses to exist and operate effectively some form of management and organization is needed. This chapter will examine and develop the theme of management already raised throughout the book in each chapter, with a focus on the manager as the conduit for such action.

Managing tourism businesses: Key principles

The vast array of business interests that are interlinked together in the production and delivery of tourism products largely operate for profit. For them to achieve this profit objective, they need management to get things done. In other words, management occurs in a formal sense in organizations, and in most cases, management is about harnessing the organization's resources (especially people, as its most valuable asset) to create services, outcomes or products in line with what the tourist requires as a consumer. In practical terms tourism management involves harnessing the power over resources (i.e. people, finance, technology and the organization) to bring some degree of order to the tasks that must be undertaken for the organization to function and achieve its objectives. This will require a manager (or teams of managers) to link with employees to undertake managerial tasks, which comprise managerial work.

Most tourism businesses work towards a set of common objectives. Tourism businesses are often organized internally into specialized functions (e.g. sales, human resource management, accounts and finance). This horizontal form of organization provides a structure for employees. Companies are also organized vertically into a hierarchy, and are characterized by different levels of power, authority and status. Within tourism organizations, managers are grouped by level (see Figure 9.1).

Managers can also be classified according to functional roles and include:

- *functional managers*, who manage specialized functions such as accounting, research, sales and personnel in large organizations

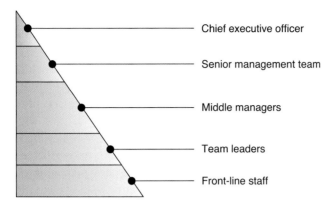

Figure 9.1
Levels of management

Source: author

- *business unit, divisional or area managers*, who exercise management responsibilities at a general level lower down in an organization; their responsibilities may cover a group of products or diverse geographical area and combine a range of management responsibilities
- *project managers*, who manage specific projects (a project is typically a short-term undertaking) and may require a team of staff to complete it.

The purpose of management in tourism organizations

The goals of managers within organizations are usually seen as profit-driven, but are often more diverse including:

- *profitability*, which can be achieved through higher output, better service, attracting new customers and cost minimization (for example, in 2005–2006, British Airways reduced its middle and senior management by 351 posts to save £50 million in order to reduce costs to try to remain profitable)
- in the public sector, *other goals* (e.g. coordination, liaison, raising public awareness and undertaking activities for the wider public good) that dominate the agenda in organizations
- *efficiency*, to reduce expenditure and inputs to a minimum to achieve more cost-effective outputs; in 2010, United Airlines merged with Continental Airlines to achieve greater efficiencies and to reduce competition
- *effectiveness* (achieving the desired outcome); this is not necessarily a profit-driven motive.

Yet in practical terms, the main tasks of managers are based on the management process, which is how to achieve these goals. Whilst management theorists differ in the emphasis they place on different aspects of the management process, there are four commonly agreed sets of tasks: organizing, planning, leading and controlling (see Chapter 1).

The process of management is an ongoing, ever-changing one in which the wide range of managers make decisions which affect the organization and nature of the business. Chief executive officers make decisions which have major impacts on the organization (e.g. the decision to downsize due to a drop in demand or to expand and grow the business) while more junior managers deal with more routine day-to-day decision-making. In managerial decision-making, two prevailing elements have to be balanced: technical skills and human skills. These are vital when interacting and managing people *within* the organization as well as those *outside* it such as clients and suppliers. This balancing of skills is often underpinned by an ability to communicate effectively and confidently with others, as well as an ability to lead and motivate people; it also highlights one other skill set that managers need to possess: cognitive and conceptual skills. Cognitive skills are those which enable managers to formulate solutions to problems and conceptual skills are those which allow them to take a broader view and consider the links with other areas of the business. These skills are apparent from studies of managers and their work.

A study by Carroll (1988) identified clusters of management tasks, which characterized managers as:

1   *representatives* of the organization
2   *investigators*, who research issues and problems
3   *negotiators*, who communicate with one or more people over a transaction to reach a desired outcome, such as a contract
4   *coordinators*, who ensure that the organization's resources are deployed to good effect to ensure flow in work tasks
5   *evaluators*, who observe, examine and control aspects of the organization's activities
6   *staffers*, who control human resource functions
7   *supervisors*, who direct the everyday work of junior staff.

These clusters inherently cause competing roles for managers, requiring them to have a wide range of competencies to be successful.

According to Inkson and Kolb (1995: 32) a competency is

> an underlying trait of an individual – for example a motive pattern, a skill, a characteristic behaviour, a value, or a set of knowledge – which enables that person to perform successfully in his or her job.

The main motivation for organizational interest in competencies is their desire to improve management through education and training, and competencies can be divided into three groups:

1   understanding what needs to be done
2   getting the job done
3   taking people with you.

Quinn *et al.* (1990) examined the skills, competencies and role of managers and concluded that the skill set of a manager often revolved around the following activities: mentoring, innovation, brokerage, as a provider, as a director, coordination, monitoring and facilitation.

The concern with competencies questions the simple notion of management as planning, organizing, leading and control; it emphasizes skills as the basis for management. However, relying upon only competencies may overlook the need for cognitive skills, which are related to personality and individual style, while conceptual skills are based on the natural abilities of individuals.

Above all, managers need to be adaptable and flexible to accommodate and lead change, particularly in fast-moving areas such as tourism. Among the common skills which a range of ecotourism businesses in Australia identified as critical to business performance were:

- business planning, financial planning, business plan skills, research
- general marketing skills, strategic marketing skills, an understanding of price, product, place and promotion
- operational skills, especially in terms of customers and business operations
- personal attributes, especially in dealing with people.

Source: McKercher and Robbins (1998)

This list highlights the diversity of skills and knowledge that business managers need.

Most significantly, change is a key feature for tourism businesses, and they need to be cognizant of a wide range of factors – sociocultural and economic issues (especially the nature of the economy), demographic changes, the role of legal and political changes, technological change (especially information technology), what the competition is doing, the global environment and role of change and uncertainty in markets. Internal resistance to change may be a problem for managers when seeking to move the business in new directions, and various techniques can be used to adapt to change including:

- education and communication
- participation and involvement
- facilitation and support
- negotiation and agreement
- manipulation and cooperation
- explicit and implicit coercion.

The ability to learn to manage in new situations where there are no guidelines or models to follow is, according to Handy (1989), how people grow, especially in a managerial role. The influential work of management writers such as Charles Handy offers many insights about the management challenges which organizations face in an ever changing world, such as the importance of employee knowledge, the growing use of more flexible labour and the changing shape of organizations. This reflects a concentration by organizations on their core business or their main purpose – to organize, as new trends such as outsourcing, the flexible organization structure and the impact of technology in the information society redefine the purpose and functions of traditional organizational structures. Some businesses such as Southwest Airlines (see Chapter 5) have embraced the need for more innovative forms of management, developing a teamwork-based approach to leadership and management structured around the idea of empowering employees to deal with organizational issues in a customer-facing organization. This is in contrast to the hierarchical model of management illustrated in Figure 9.1.

In fact managerial behaviour has been studied through the twentieth century, from the early work of Fayol, Mintzberg and others who observed and studied what managers did and why. In terms of how managers react to new challenges and tasks, research has illustrated that much managerial work is mundane, based on establishing ongoing reciprocal working relationships within and between businesses (i.e. networking). A number of stages in managerial responses to work are:

- taking hold of the job, normally three to six months in duration
- immersion, lasting four to eleven months
- reshaping, after a period of intense change, normally three to six months
- consolidation, running for three to nine months
- refinement.

Mintzberg argued that managers often work on a stimulus–response pattern, responding to problems, challenges and issues, and the nature of much of their work is fragmented and discontinuous, often being interrupted.

What do tourism managers manage?

Tourism is widely attributed as a service sector activity that has a high level of customer contact. Despite the wide range of tasks managers undertake, there are three principal management functions which tourism businesses need to be involved in when dealing with people as customers: marketing, operational issues and human resource management. Although other functions are important, these three are crucial where the service output is intangible. In a tourism context, marketing differs from other products because tourism is a service industry, the intangible elements, quality of delivery and evaluation of experiences being difficult to visualize. But with the growing importance of the experience economy, these issues of quality and the visitor experience are important: the crux of the issue is how businesses can add value to the visitor experience. The *heterogeneity* (i.e. diversity), *perishability* (i.e. a tour cannot be stored and sold at a different time) and *intangibility* of tourism services make marketing a challenge when combined with two other key problems:

1   the customer must travel to the product/resource base to consume it
2   the operator has little influence over the tourism activity (holiday).

The marketing focus belies the fact that tourism consumption is based upon the provision of a service and so marketing as a process acts to link the customer with the supplier (see the example of the holiday brochure illustrated in Chapter 9). Marketing is also vital to establishing the market research, market needs, specification and nature of service provision in consumer industries (see the example of establishing a tour programme in Chapter 7).

Marketing tourism as a management function

Marketing is widely acknowledged as a vital prerequisite to communicating the product or service offering of businesses or suppliers to the market. According to Kotler and Armstrong (1991), marketing is a process whereby individuals and groups obtain the type of products or goods they value. These goods are created and exchanged through a process, which requires a detailed understanding of consumers and their wants and desires so that the product or service is effectively and efficiently delivered to the client or purchaser (see Table 9.1 for key studies on tourism marketing).

Table 9.1 Key studies on tourism marketing
Fyall, A. and Garrod, B. (2004) *Tourism Marketing: A Collaborative Approach*. Bristol: Channel View.
Hall, C. M. (2011) *Tourism and Social Marketing*. London: Routledge.
Holloway, J. (2004) *Marketing for Tourism*. Harlow: Pearson.
Hudson, S. (2008) *Tourism and Hospitality Marketing: A Global Perspective*. London: Sage.
Kotler, P., Bowen, J. and Mackens, J. (2009) *Marketing for Hospitality and Tourism*. New York: Pearson.
Middleton, V., Fyall, A., Morgan, M. and Ranchhod, A. (2009) *Marketing in Travel and Tourism*, 4th edn. Oxford: Elsevier.

In particular, businesses need to understand, using market research, what markets they wish to serve and the service attributes they wish to offer; to establish the prices to be charged and to tailor the service to meet the clients' needs as closely as possible. They must then develop a communication programme to inform them about the service (e.g. create a brochure, advertisement or other method of communication, such as the internet).

To meet customer needs, a company analyses its own products or services in terms of its own business expertise and how competitors' products and services may affect them. This is frequently undertaken as a SWOT analysis, which considers the Strengths and Weaknesses of, Opportunities for and Threats to its products and services in the business environment.

For those tourism operators who may wish to grow and expand, a number of options exist. Horner and Swarbrooke (1996: 325) indicate these can involve:

- *marketing consortia*, where a group of operators cooperate to create and develop a product
- *strategic alliances*, where different businesses agree to cooperate in various ways (this varies by sector in the tourism industry, and includes such things as marketing agreements or technical cooperation)
- *acquisition*, which is the purchase of equity in other operations
- *joint ventures*, where operators seek to create new businesses
- *franchising*, where major operators use their market presence and brand image to further extend their influence by licensing franchisees to operate businesses using their corporate logo and codes.

However, the actual implementation of marketing for tourism ultimately depends on the 'marketing mix' a company chooses.

The marketing mix

The marketing mix is 'the mixture of controllable marketing variables that the firm [or company] uses to pursue the sought level of sales in the target market' (Kotler, cited in Holloway and Plant 1988: 48). This means that in any tourism organization there are four main marketing variables that need to be harnessed:

1   *product formulation*, which is the ability of a company to adapt to the needs of its customers in terms of the services it provides. Products are constantly being adapted to changes in consumer markets
2   *price*, which is the economic concept used to adjust the supply of a service to meet the demand, taking account of sales targets and turnover
3   *promotion*, which is the manner in which a company seeks to improve customers' knowledge of the services it sells so that those people who are made aware may be turned into actual purchasers. To achieve promotional aims, advertising, public relations, sales and brochure production functions are undertaken within the remit as promotion
4   *place*, which is the location at which prospective customers may be induced to purchase a service – the point of sale (e.g. a travel agent or another point of distribution such as the worldwide web).

These 'four Ps' are incorporated into the marketing process in relation to the known competition and the impact of market conditions. Thus, the marketing process involves the continuous evaluation of how a business operates internally and externally to meet customer requirements.

Managing operational issues in tourism businesses

Operational issues have traditionally dominated the focus of most service organizations centred on tourism, particularly where labour-intensive operations exist (e.g. at an airport).

Business operations in tourism assume a major role: the highly seasonal nature of tourism requires seasonal staff at resorts, airports, in hotels and for transport operators. Demand is largely concentrated in six months of the year and this is a key management challenge for many businesses. Seasonality shapes tourism demand from consumers due to a wide range of factors including the climate and environment of the origin area and the attraction of the destination, as well as exchange rates.

Managing seasonality

Seasonality remains a protracted problem for the tourism sector, although recent studies have begun to try to understand what the patterns of seasonality that exist mean for individual businesses and where they are located (see Connell, Page and Meyer 2015). Figure 9.2 outlines some of the issues which individual managers face in trying to assess how the mismatch of demand and supply caused through seasonality may be addressed. The first step for businesses is to understand the demand in the markets they are working in. For example, as Figure 9.3 shows, in the case of international tourism demand in Scotland (measured using overseas nights spent in the regions of Scotland), there are distinct trends to understand, as Coshall *et al.* (in press) indicate:

- using quarterly tourism data (which means data collected for each three-month period such as January to March) for international arrivals, visitor numbers dropped from 1997 to 2003 with the impact of major crises such as foot and mouth disease and 9/11, followed by a pattern of growth from 2003 to 2007. Demand then dropped again in 2009
- for the businesses depending on international tourists on holiday, visiting friends and relatives or those taking a business trip, Coshall *et al.* (in press) found that 73 per cent of all trips occurred in the period June to September. The study also found distinct geographical variations in the way in which seasonality is concentrated in certain regions of Scotland, with the major cities experiencing lower levels than many other regions. Factors such as accessibility are often used as explanations for the decline in demand outside of these major regions which contain the main gateways to Scotland (i.e. the main ports or points of entry such as airports) outside of the peak periods of visiting amongst international visitors.

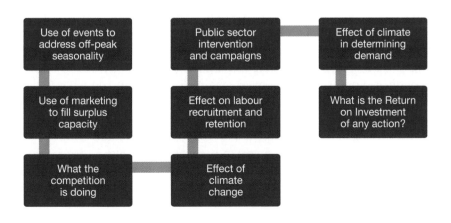

Figure 9.2
Tourism businesses and seasonality: Key issues for managers

Source: author

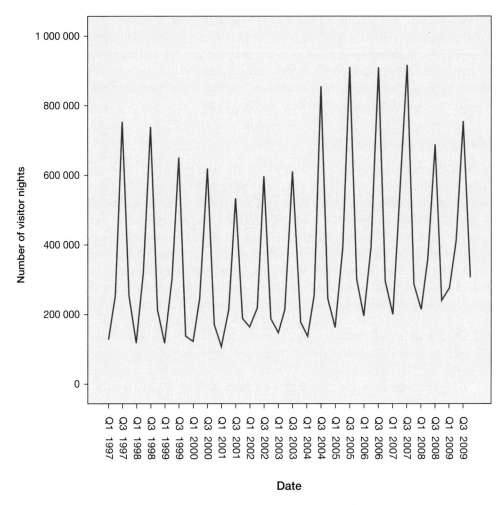

Figure 9.3

Total numbers of overseas visitor nights spent in the regions of Scotland 1997–2009

Source: Coshall *et al.* (in press)

Therefore, for individual businesses outside of the major cities, they need to decide how to respond to seasonality through: closing and operating seasonally if that is viable; responding to the market and diversifying into other markets (e.g. residents and domestic visitors); and thinking about what strategies to deploy to manage this issue.

Pricing is also used by tourism businesses to capitalize upon peak demand in popular summer months. In less popular seasons (e.g. autumn and winter), businesses may seek to leverage support from public sector bodies to host large-scale events (e.g. the Harbin ice festival in China) and attract visitors out of season. Events in the winter, such as Hogmanay in Scotland and new year celebrations in London (which attract around 250 000 people) are a way of providing a stimulus to reduce seasonality effects.

Some destinations experience *one-peak seasonality* (e.g. coastal resorts in the summer season) or *two-peak seasonality* (a summer and winter season) while many urban destinations experience non-peak seasonality, where the climate and environment do not cause peaks as different international markets' holiday taking habits shape the pattern of seasonal demand. Seasonality means that individual businesses have to be able to manage the peaks and troughs of demand and supply. The timing of travel by different markets is vividly illustrated by patterns of tourism to Iceland. Most of the visitor arrivals from continental Europe are concentrated in the months June to August, and occupancy rates for hotels in the capital exceed 75 per cent in these months. At the same time, the island has been able to accommodate a growth in seasonal visitor arrivals from 70 000 in 1982 to 300 000 in 2003 to 356 000 in 2005 and 500 000 in 2008 (and almost 60 000 cruise ship passengers). Iceland hopes to see growth rates of 8 per cent per annum to 2020, anticipating 1.2 million visitors in 2020 which required additional hotel capacity if demand was to be met.

Operational issues assume a dominant day-to-day role for many businesses, especially in places where large volumes of tourists are being managed, such as attractions or airports. To ensure the smooth flow and organization of these activities managers must delegate a great deal of responsibility in managing the interactions with visitors to front-line staff. The area is often termed 'operations management' and it focuses on five interrelated areas:

1   *capacity*, which is understanding the ability of the organization to produce something (such as service)
2   *standards*, which are those prevailing within the tourism sector (such as waiting times at an airport check-in or hotel reception)
3   *scheduling*, which is the planning of work and use of the organization's physical and human resources
4   *inventory*, which is understanding the organization's ability to meet supply and demand
5   *control*, which ensures the operations are managed in an efficient and systematic manner and brings the planning, preparation and readiness inherent in the four functions above into action.

Much of this is dependent upon having competent staff to undertake these tasks.

Managing service provision: Human resource issues and service delivery

According to Baum (1993: 4) tourism can be conceptualized as a client purchasing 'the skills, service and commitment of a range of human contributors to the experience that they are about to embark upon', highlighting the importance of human resource management (HRM) issues and the challenge this poses for tourism managers (see Table 9.2). Many of these issues are embedded in some specific problems which the tourism sector faces including:

- demographic issues related to the shrinking pool of potential employees and labour shortages
- the tourism industry's image as an employer
- cultural and traditional perceptions of the tourism industry
- rewards and compensation for working in the sector
- education and training
- skill shortages at the senior and technical levels
- linking human resource concerns with service and product quality
- poor manpower planning
- a remedial rather than proactive approach to human resource issues.

Source: Based on Baum (1993)

In line with management, HRM is concerned with planning, monitoring and control of the human resource as a management process (see Table 9.3 for a range of studies on tourism and HRM). More complex analyses of HRM identify the concern that the individual human resource system within any organization is able to realize the strategic objectives of the organization (i.e. the delivery of excellent customer service to tourism consumers) as will become evident later in the discussion of the Disney model.

For the medium- or large-sized tourism enterprise, human resource issues and the factors affecting their performance are usually linked to the staff and workforce;

Table 9.2 Managing human resource issues: Scope and extent for businesses

1	A critical awareness of the scope and nature of the labour market
2	The design of jobs
3	Recruitment, selection, appointment and retention of staff
4	Induction, equal opportunities, training and development
5	Evaluation of staff performance
6	Salaries and incentives
7	Employment termination, grievance and dispute procedures
8	Industrial relations and employment law
9	Motivation of staff

Source: modified from Baum (1993)

Table 9.3 Key studies on tourism and human resource management

Baum, T. (2006) *Human Resource Management for Tourism, Hospitality and Leisure: An International Perspective*. London: Cengage Learning.

Baum, T. (2008) Human resources in tourism: Still waiting for a change? *Tourism Management*, 28 (6): 1383–1399.

Baum, T. and Sziva, E. (2008) HRD in tourism: A role for government? *Tourism Management*, 29: 783–794.

World Tourism Organization (2001) *Tourism Challenges in the Twenty First Century – Human Resource Development in Asia-Pacific*. Madrid: UNWTO.

World Tourism Organization (2009) *The Tourism Labour Market in the Asia-Pacific Region*. Madrid: UNWTO.

World Travel and Tourism Council (2001) *Human Resource Task Force: Opportunities and Challenges*. London: WTTC.

---

therefore, recognizing the role of recruitment and ongoing development of the staff resource to achieve strategic goals becomes essential. The scale of the human resource function will often reflect the size of the organization and specific functions (e.g. training and development) may be allocated to specific individuals whereas in smaller organizations the commitment to core functions (recruitment and retention) may be all that is possible, due to work pressures and constraints on staff time.

The major challenges for the tourism industry in the new millennium are aptly summarized by Cooper *et al.* (1998: 458):

> the challenges facing the tourism industry will only be met successfully by a well-educated, well-trained, bright, energetic, multi-lingual and entrepreneurial workforce who understand the nature of tourism and have a professional training. A high quality of professional human resources in tourism will allow enterprises to gain a competitive edge and deliver added value with their service.

People do make a difference in what is undoubtedly a people business.

More sophisticated human resource policies need to be developed and implemented in the following areas for the tourism sector to be responsive to add value to its staff and change the sector's image as an employer:

- induction of staff
- appraisal and staff performance evaluation
- effective staff communication
- rewarding initiative and excellence

- empowering staff
- improved industry–education collaboration.

Source: Page and Connell (2014)

Therefore, the quality, commitment and effectiveness of human resources can be critical in businesses' competitiveness. Understanding how HRM issues interact and, more importantly, what types of service staff need to provide, are significant elements for managing tourism businesses.

Service provision in tourism: A perennial management challenge?

Service provision can be conceptualized as a system in which elements of the product are created and assembled and delivered to the customer. Whilst parts of the service are visible to the consumer, the manner of delivery is what will entail exposure to the tourist and will impact upon the company's reputation as a service provider. The tourist's satisfaction with the service delivered in tourism will focus upon two critical elements: the technical and the functional quality of the service. The technical quality relates to the measurable elements, such as whether an airline seat of a certain quality was provided and delivered. In contrast, the functional element relates to the impression one wants a client to receive: an overall impression that is more holistic and gauges satisfaction with what was consumed. Whilst the analysis of functional quality is more intangible, as Chapter 8 illustrated in terms of human behaviour in travel agencies, certain factors – such as posture, the use of a smile, voice, attitude, empathy and responsiveness – will have a major bearing. For tourism managers, seeking to achieve consistent levels of service in tourism will be measured by tourist satisfaction. This is a complex phenomenon since satisfaction is linked to a consumer's emotions and level of expectation of the service being consumed. This is partly dependent upon three interrelated factors: the level of equity in the service provided, whether expectations were met, and perception of the actual performance. This requires managers to understand in more detail the technical aspects of service provision in tourism, especially:

- what the final product is
- how it is produced
- the form and shape the service will take
- who ultimately delivers the service.

Therefore, recognizing that customer service is central to the satisfaction levels of tourism services is significant because consumers are often buying something they have high expectations of, based on the marketing mix (the price, product, place and promotion), which is shaped by people, physical attributes (i.e. was the weather good?)

and processes of delivery. In a customer contact business, managers need to be aware of the most commonly measured elements that determine service quality. These elements are known among researchers as SERVQUAL determinants:

- tangible elements
- reliability
- responsiveness
- communication
- credibility
- security
- competence
- courtesy
- understanding/knowing the consumer
- access/ease of approach and contact.

These are central in managing the service encounter with tourists and at an operational level will determine how customer expectations/needs are met.

Whilst SERVQUAL has been a long-serving concept associated with the quality of service delivery in business sectors such as tourism, a new way of thinking (a paradigm) has evolved in recent years to challenge this approach to managing service businesses such as tourism as shown in Case Study 9.1.

One area which is vital in meeting tourists' expectations is communication. This is important not only in marketing a company but also for the way in which individual companies locate and nurture their customer base. In some sectors of the tourism industry defined standards of service and provision may exist to meet visitor expectations. Despite the growth in new approaches to service-related research (Case Study 9.1), SERVQUAL has remained a dominant feature of many studies. Three key elements are associated with the staffing of tourism enterprises, based on the SERVQUAL model:

1 *the responsiveness of staff* – their willingness to help promptly (rather than ignore customers and leave them waiting, as many call centres now do with direct sales and the telephone waiting systems)
2 *the assurance of staff* – their ability to evoke images of trust and confidence associated with the company's offerings (as opposed to those staff who bemoan the problems of service delivery and weak elements in the system that have contributed to service failure)
3 *staff empathy* – their ability to provide tourists with individual attention and a commitment to the service they are providing (as opposed to more disaffected staff who do not have a stake in the business they are working for which may reflect poor levels of pay and motivation along with the use of casual staff).

When things go wrong, as they sometimes do when dealing with human behaviour that is not predictable and needs and attitudes to tourism services that are not

CASE STUDY 9.1
THE EVOLUTION OF RESEARCH ON SERVICES MARKETING

The evolution of research in marketing can be traced to the 1960s, and research on services (of which tourism is a component when it is classed as a service) developed comparatively later within marketing, as Baron *et al.* (2014) highlight in their review of the field. As research on services developed, this review highlighted key phases of growth (with three phases apparent prior to 2004). In phase one (pre-1988), ways of classifying services and tools to look at service quality (SERVQUAL) developed. In phase two (1988–97), a greater focus on the emergence of services research as a legitimate theme for research inquiry developed, including the further development of the service quality agenda, which had a major impact on tourism research with its consumer focus. In phase three (1998–2003), new research directions emerged which focused on themes such as the role of consumers and the relationship between consumers and their experiences of consumption, along with the global dimension in service provision and changes facilitated through e-services. Since 2004, three themes have dominated the research agenda as Figure 9.4 illustrates, where the three

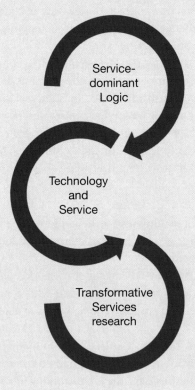

Figure 9.4
Current themes in services marketing research

Source: developed from Baron *et al.* (2014)

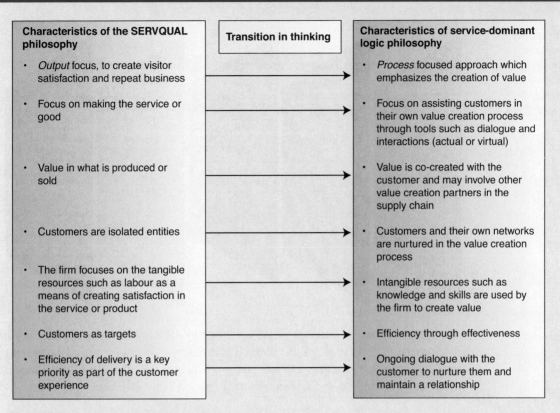

Figure 9.5
The paradigm shift from SERVQUAL to service-dominant logic

Source: based on Vargo and Lusch (2008: 254–259); Vargo, S. L. and Lusch, R. F. (2004) The four service marketing myths: Remnants of a goods-based, manufacturing model. *Journal of Service Research*, 6(4): 324–335

themes developed: service-dominant logic (associated with value and co-creation), technology and services (e.g. eservice), and transformative services research which can assist with the transformation of consumers' well-being.

Whilst SERVQUAL has focused on services and their output (i.e. service quality) in the 1980s and 1990s, new thinking from mainstream marketing has refocused attention to services as a process. This has been described as service-dominant logic where the new way of thinking has been described by Vargo and Lusch (2008: 258) as comprising a change as embodied in Figure 9.5. This approach to service delivery and the focus on value creation reflects a step change in thinking which fits with the theoretical research outlined in Chapter 1 on the experience economy where consumers are looking for value in the experiences they engage in.

Further reading

Baron, S., Warnaby, G. and Hunter-Jones, P. (2014) Service(s) marketing research: Developments and directions. *International Journal of Management Reviews*, 16(2): 150–171.

homogenous, staff and businesses can follow a number of simple principles in handling complaints as illustrated in Figure 9.6.

**Figure 9.6
How staff
should
respond to
complaints**

Source: author

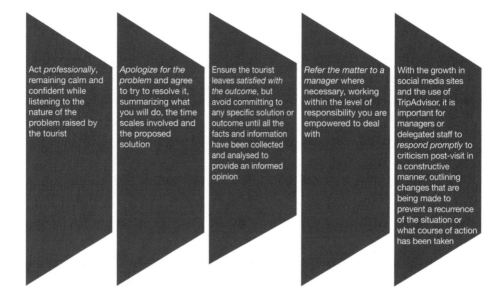

Act *professionally*, remaining calm and confident while listening to the nature of the problem raised by the tourist

Apologize for the problem and agree to try to resolve it, summarizing what you will do, the time scales involved and the proposed solution

Ensure the tourist leaves *satisfied with the outcome*, but avoid committing to any specific solution or outcome until all the facts and information have been collected and analysed to provide an informed opinion

Refer the matter to a manager where necessary, working within the level of responsibility you are empowered to deal with

With the growth in social media sites and the use of TripAdvisor, it is important for managers or delegated staff to *respond promptly* to criticism post-visit in a constructive manner, outlining changes that are being made to prevent a recurrence of the situation or what course of action has been taken

Yet there are some businesses such as the Disney Corporation which go far beyond that approach to service provision: their customer service is widely seen as an example of international best practice; a good example whose principles other businesses can emulate to be successful and to improve their performance (see Case Study 9.2).

Developing and managing tourism ventures in the small business sector

There is a tendency to assume that tourism has great potential to stimulate economic development if it is managed well. The basic argument is that the fledgling new business of today could develop and grow into the large international corporation of the future. This may occur in a few cases, such as the rise of the Virgin transport conglomerate which evolved from the Virgin Atlantic airline venture. Many governments have avidly supported small business development in tourism owing to its future employment-generating potential, although they were not overtly concerned until the 1980s with ensuring managers and owners had the skill set needed to manage such enterprises. The small business sector (also known as small- and medium-sized enterprises or SMEs; very small ventures are 'micro enterprises') does play a major role in most countries, not least for its employment role but also because it is a key element of the industry.

According to Morrison (1996: 400)

> a small tourism business is financed by one individual or small group and is directly managed by its owner(s), in a personalised manner and not through the medium of a formalised management structure . . . it is perceived as small, in terms of physical facilities, production/service capacity, market share and number of employees.

CASE STUDY 9.2
THE DISNEY MODEL OF CUSTOMER CARE

The Disney organization is acknowledged as one of the leaders in customer care, employing over 55 000 staff with revenue of US$23 billion in 1999 and profits of US$2 billion. In 2009, the company revenue had risen to US$36.1 billion, and by 2005 its workforce had expanded to 144 000. The company evolved from the Walt Disney business founded by its owner in 1923 and now encompasses four core businesses:

*   *studio entertainment* (including its purchase of Pixar)
*   *Disney consumer products* (including the highly successful merchandizing activities)
*   *Disney media networks*
*   *Disney parks and resorts*, launched in 1952 with the opening of Disneyland in Anaheim, California. Disney now has 11 parks and resorts it owns/operates on 3 continents, together with 35 resort hotels and luxury cruise ships. In 2005, Disney opened Hong Kong Disneyland, with a 43 per cent ownership of the venture. This is widely acknowledged as Disney's initial move towards a globalized strategy in the theme park sector, as it expands into the growing Asian market. This followed its successful opening of a theme park in Japan. An indication of the scale of Disney's business is illustrated by the 500 million guests who have stayed at the Disney World Resort in Florida since it opened. In 2011 the company opened a Disney resort – Aulani in Hawai'i – and the Chinese government has given approval for a theme park in Shanghai.

One notable feature of Disney is the level of repeat business in its theme parks, which has grown from 50 per cent to 70 per cent in recent years, despite major competition from other parks – a feature that many tourism businesses want to emulate to build a strong customer base. The concepts it uses are interesting in a customer service setting for the tourism industry because it uses a theatrical context – staff are referred to as *cast members*, and play their role *on stage*, which is at the point of customer contact. Staff are allowed to be themselves backstage, when they are not in front of customers, and there are a set of processes and procedures which are part of the Disney magic. The Disney formula for customer service is based on a set of values that come from integrating its commercialism with a quality experience for the visitor. It is based on three elements:

1   a quality staff experience, since each individual staff member impacts on the customer experience
2   a quality customer experience, based on the experience being customer driven; Disney seeks to exceed customer needs and expectations rather than simply meet them
3   a quality set of business practices, where knowledge, marketing, innovation and other elements are blended to ensure commercial success.

In particular, the Disney philosophy is to 'exceed customer expectations and pay attention to detail', with the visitor at the centre of all elements that drive business activities. Many of the failings in service sector provision in the new millennium are just that lack of attention to detail, unless you are purchasing a luxury product. In Disney jargon (which is a common feature of Disney internal communications), 'Guestology' is their approach to customer service, where staff need to know their customers and understand them in terms of psychographics (see Chapter 3 for more detail of psychographics). This requires an understanding of both the quantitative aspects of their visitors' experience and the more qualitative features (i.e. feelings, attitudes and reasoning), since the visitor experience is based upon these intangible elements. On the basis of this information, Disney develops its service theme – the type of service their guests want – which has four key service standards: safety, courtesy, show (to provide a seamless experience) and efficiency (to ensure smooth operations). To deliver these service standards, Disney uses a corporate brand.

A brand is a name, design or symbol (or combination of each) used to identify a service. This enables the customer to identify the product or service easily. For a company, a brand can help to build customer loyalty, since it implies less risk in a purchase – something that can help with further merchandizing opportunities, which the Disney brand has achieved through its international retail outlets. Disney recognizes the need for consistency in the way the organization conveys itself via its brand to the public. In one visit, a person may interact with 60 cast members in one day; to achieve consistency and a coherent brand image, Disney seeks to ensure staff are competent, attentive, trained, with managers providing service support for the cast and identifying how to 'reach out' to guests.

To achieve these goals, Disney has a number of processes and procedures to help the delivery of its service and recognizes that in the real world service breakdowns and interruptions may occur. Putting things right by empowering staff to alleviate the impact of such problems means that a negative event can be shaped into a positive response from staff (perhaps responding to problems with 'How can I help?'). 'Service debugging', as they refer to it, involves seeking solutions to problems so that good communication is achieved between visitor and staff member. One of Disney's major achievements, which is often held out as a model for the tourism industry, is its ability to deal with large flows of visitors at its theme parks: up to 30 000 a day in the case of Hong Kong Disneyland. It has introduced visitor management tools (see Chapter 11 for more discussion of this concept) including *Early Bird Programmes*, to allow early entry before the main visitors; *Fast Passes*, to avoid waiting; and *Tip Boards*, which advise people how long a wait is required at a specific attraction. The aim is to optimize the operation of the attraction, guest flow and queue experience so the visitor experience is enhanced.

In seeking to manage the visitor experience at Disney, sending the right message to the visitor is seen as vital, from the entry point until the point of departure. By paying careful attention to detail, Disney seeks to create a positive image (it calculated that the average duration of a visit to Hong Kong Disneyland was nine hours, which is a long time for the visitor attraction sector). It does this by ensuring it creates the right ambience and feeling among visitors by harnessing details such as design, landscaping, lighting (which can affect visitor mood), colour, signage, texture of surfaces, music and ambient noise as well as elements that appeal to the other senses: smell, touch and taste. Above all, tidiness and cleanliness in mass visitor attractions are seen as critical to the image created. This highlights how integrated the visitor experience is at an attraction and that customer service is not just about visitor contact and interaction, but about the entire environment and how service systems are designed and managed to enable satisfaction to be achieved. Above all, Disney is constantly reinventing itself, innovating and seeking to stay in front of the competition. Management research has termed this 'business re-engineering' – seeking to reintegrate processes (i.e. tasks, labour and knowledge) to make continuous improvements to its business performance. In fact some commentators see Disney as the market leader in attraction management.

Whilst many of these Disney principles may seem quite alien to some service organizations, this example highlights a range of experiences that tourism businesses can adapt and develop in understanding how to deliver services to visitors. The culture of the workforce is important in terms of its willingness to embrace such principles to deliver services. However, one of the problems that this poses for tourism operators in many countries is their scale of operation, especially when they are based in the small business sector that has specific managerial concerns, particularly in the early set-up stage.

Further reading

Capodagdi, B. (2001) *The Disney Way: Harness Secrets of Disney in Your Company*. New York: McGraw Hill.

Hannigan, J. (1998) *Fantasy City*. London: Routledge.

Miles, S. (2010) *Spaces for Consumption*. London: Sage.

Morrison goes on to argue that

> traditionally the tourism industry has been dominated by the small business and this still remains true in the 1990s. Currently in Ireland ... firms with less than fifteen employees account for around 79 per cent of all Irish tourism businesses.
>
> (1996: 401)

Indeed, it is notable that the success often attributed to Ireland as a booming tourism destination up until 2009 can be directly related to activity across the tourism sectors, in which SMEs play a role.

However, in terms of small tourism firms, entrepreneurship seems weakly developed because tourism is perceived as having low entry barriers (i.e. you do not need large amounts of capital and investment to start a venture like a bed-and-breakfast establishment). The main management issues affecting tourism SMEs is highlighted by Carter (1996: 4504) who suggested that

> irrespective of the relative size of each country's small business sector, the main management characteristics of small firms remain similar regardless of nationality. Researchers have consistently noted that small firms play an important role in new product and process innovation and are characterised by their product specialisation ... [and] ... that these firms are undercapitalised, product-led, family-owned concerns in which the management function is confined to one person or a few key individuals.

The short-term planning horizon of many tourism SMEs, their limited knowledge of the business environment and their owner-managed structure influences the way tasks are managed. SME managers rely upon attitudes, personal qualities (i.e. leadership skills) and experience. The differences between small and large firm management is that the preparation of ongoing business plans and the marketing function in SMEs is seen as peripheral to the management task of running the business. Many of these characteristics are borne out in the studies by Shaw and Williams (2002), where few businesses had formal marketing strategies, skills or knowledge of the tourism business, as is reiterated in the studies listed in Table 9.4.

Table 9.4 Key studies on tourism and SMEs
Ateljevic, J. and Page, S. J. (eds) (2009) *Tourism and Entrepreneurship*. Oxford: Elsevier.
Getz, D., Carlsen, J. and Morrison, A. (2004) *The Family Business in Tourism and Hospitality*. Wallingford: CABI.
Page, S., Forer, P. and Lawton, G.R. (1999) Small business development and tourism: Terra incognita? *Tourism Management*, 20: 435–459.
Shaw, G. and Williams, A. M. (2010) Tourism SMEs: Changing research agendas and missed opportunities. In D. Pearce and R. Butler (eds) *Tourism Research: A 20:20 Vision*. Oxford: Goodfellow Publishing.
Shaw, G. and Williams, A. M. (1987) Firm formation and operating characteristics in the Cornish tourism industry. *Tourism Management*, 8: 344–348.
Shaw, G. (2014) Entrepreneurial cultures and small business enterprises in tourism. In M. Hall, A. Lew and A. Williams (eds) *Companion of Tourism*, 2nd edition. Oxford: Wiley Blackwell.
Thomas, R. (ed.) (1998) *The Management of Small Tourism and Hospitality Firms*. London: Cassell.
Thomas, R. (2004) *Small Firms in Tourism: International Perspectives*. Oxford: Pergamon.
Thomas, R. and Augustyn, M. (eds) (2007) *Tourism in the New Europe: Perspectives on SME Policies and Practices*. Oxford: Pergamon.
Thomas, R., Shaw, G. and Page, S. J. (2011) Understanding small firms in tourism: Research, trends and challenges. *Tourism Management*, 32(5): 963–976.
Wanhill, S. (1999) Small and medium tourism enterprises. *Annals of Tourism Research*, 27(1): 132–147.
Williams, A. M., Shaw, G. and Greenwood, J. (1989) From tourist to tourism entrepreneur, from consumption to production: Evidence from Cornwall, England. *Environment and Planning A*, 21: 1639–1653.

Many localities promote tourism business development because it has the potential to form linkages with businesses that supply it ('backward linkages') and with those it supplies ('forward linkages') and so has the potential to generate economic development. An example of a backward linkage is a new hotel sourcing local food supplies. These types of supply chain, using local networks, have attracted a great of attention from public and private sector organizations seeking to promote local collaboration, where collaborations can also become the basis for expanding regional tourism products and events. This can help to create a distinctive local and regional product offering and when these networks evolve into producer groups they can also add value to the tourist experience.

Research focused on the accommodation sector has shown that many new entrants to this sector have little experience of the business and have a wide range of motives for entering the market. What is interesting in the tourism sector is that the sources of venture capital for new businesses are varied, with a proportion often coming from families and contacts in small business ventures. However, tourism entrepreneurs need to harness managerial skills if their business idea is to work. In Cornwall, research by Shaw and Williams (2002) found that more than 50 per cent of capital came from these sources, especially for older entrepreneurs. The grounds given by over 80 per cent of these entrepreneurs for establishing their businesses included lifestyle reasons (i.e. a better way of life), as they were new migrants to the region.

There is also evidence that where these businesses are operated by family members, there are social benefits that are additional to the lifestyle reasons for operation. Similar reasons are also evident in a new form of business venture now appearing in the UK – home-working travel agents.

Home-working travel agents have started to become established as a new form of business venture to offset the decline in the conventional high street travel agent in the face of massive competition from the online agencies discussed in Chapter 7. A number of travel agent companies have set up home-working as a self-employed model of a franchised travel agency where the employee is based at home and works the hours to suit their clients and their lifestyle. Travel Counsellors, Hays Travel and Instant Holidays are three examples of home-working business brands. They support the home-workers with state-of-the-art ICT, a head office function, advertising and the provision of leads to generate business. This provides many travel agents with the flexibility of working from home as well as the opportunity to operate when clients want to contact them (e.g. out of normal office hours), competing with the way consumers use the internet and plan/book travel. Clients are provided with a dedicated person for each booking and enquiry. In 2005, Travel Counsellors had recruited 560 travel consultants and has recently been licensed to offer dynamic packaging; the company expanded its £150 million turnover in 2006 to £255 million in 2009. In contrast, organizations such as the high street chain Going Places closed 110 locations which were no longer profitable. By 2008 it had 900 consultants supported by 200 staff at its Bolton head office and in 2010 the number of consultants had reached 1100.

In 2007 with two mergers of major holiday companies (TUI and First Choice; Thomas Cook and MyTravel) the travel agency ownership was reconfigured thus: TUI and First Choice had 650 shops, MyTravel 458 shops and Thomas Cook 548 shops (a combined 1006 shops for the Thomas Cook Group).

With many countries having a strong dependence upon small businesses in the tourism sector, it is not surprising that many government agencies are concerned with improving the performance and managerial skills of new businesses when they do not enter the market for profit-only motives. For example, in New Zealand, 99 per cent of the country's businesses are based in the SME sector, which employ 60 per cent of the working population. Over 85 per cent of these businesses employ fewer than five people and this is replicated through the tourism and hospitality sector, though the hospitality industry tends to employ more staff.

What is apparent is that new business start-ups and small business ventures in tourism have specific management requirements, with a common range of obstacles to improving business performance including:

* high rates of inflation
* high labour costs

- high interest rates
- high rents or rates
- debtors/poor cash flow
- lack of external guidance on business development
- competition from other businesses
- low labour productivity
- lack of skilled employees
- insufficient customer demand
- government regulations and bureaucracy
- limited access to finance
- competition from large firms.

This highlights the scope of management challenges faced by many small tourism and hospitality businesses. Addressing these through good management skills is critical, and in the initial set-up stage of the business venture particular attention should be paid to the obvious financial issues through a feasibility study or business plan. Among the common issues new tourism start-up businesses need to address are:

- how do I get started?
- marketing
- knowing your market: Who will be my customers?
- networking: Who will I need to do business with?
- staff-related issues: Who will I need to employ?
- what are the risks in setting up a business?
- what business ownership model will I choose to set up?

Underpinning these issues is the importance of developing a good business plan and the role of innovation.

Tourism and innovation

Challenges for tourism managers

Innovation is often seen as one way in which businesses may seek to gain competitive advantage, especially where innovation in the face of competition leads to growth, survival or enhanced profitability. Innovation implies change of some sort (Plate 9.1) and can be divided into a number of areas: diffusion of new ideas, products or processes; adoption by individual organizations and levels of innovativeness. Much of the existing research on innovation emerged after Schumpeter's study (1952) which identified five principal routes to innovation (demonstrated in Figure 9.7) with a number of tourism applications. What this highlights is that much of the focus of innovation centres on creative thinking and inventiveness. For tourism managers, the challenge is to understand the ways it is adopted, used by organizations and diffused to the business and commercial/non-commercial environment to provide solutions to problems or generate ideas that can make a difference to the way a business operates or functions.

Plate 9.1
The hovercraft was an important transport innovation in the late 1960s, overtaken in the 1990s by new technology – the high-speed catamarans

Source: author

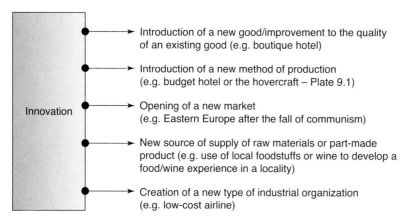

Figure 9.7
Schumpeter's types of innovation and their application to tourism

Source: author

How and why does innovation occur and what is its significance in tourism?

Human actors, environmental factors such as turmoil and crisis, idea champions and external factors such as government intervention and competition can induce innovation. What is not clear in existing research is whether management is necessary to encourage innovation, or whether it will occur without the influence of management. However, managers need to understand the role of innovation and its potential to improve business processes and the client–organization interface and to add value to the business (i.e. it may lead to cost savings). This is important in a people industry such as tourism, which is reliant upon new ideas, experiences and destinations for the generation of new product ideas. Business research highlights that there are pioneer adopters in some organizations who embrace innovation and the change that it may induce, and adapt the innovation to fit the company's needs. In contrast, innovation laggards hold out against innovation and change until the majority of the workforce accepts it. Innovation in organizations is seen to pass through a number of stages including:

- invention
- application
- adoption
- diffusion, where a number of sub-stages exist including: marketing the idea, interest arousal, trial implementation, continued use and full implementation.

Plate 9.2
One innovation which visitor attractions have developed to fill capacity in the low season is events such as this Halloween event aimed at children so they bring accompanying parents and so boost spending

Source: author

One of the key stages for a tourism business is the adoption stage, which may reflect the receptiveness of the organization – highlighting its degree of innovativeness and willingness to experiment with new ideas. This will often depend upon the level of innovation, which can range from mildly new to radically new (from the producer's perspective), and is also reflected in how the consumer might perceive the innovation. Two contrasting examples can be seen in the field of air travel: a mildly innovative idea is the reduction in the number of cabin crew to reduce costs and service levels; a very radical one is the removal of all in-flight service.

Innovation is critical in tourism, given the sector's fast-evolving nature. Being trend driven means that tourism has to adapt and innovate to meet consumers' needs for improved quality and new products and experiences. In Scotland, the Work of Scottish Enterprise (Scottishenterprise.com), which was highlighted in the Scottish Tourism Framework for Action 2002–2005, and its successor, which ran to 2010 (see Web Case 10.3), illustrated their key role in stimulating economic development and strategic change in Scottish tourism. Since 2012 other tourism industry stakeholders have taken ownership of the strategy process. This led to the creation of a new strategy in 2012 entitled Tourism Scotland 2020. In 2001, a Tourism Innovation Group was formed by the tourism industry to promote such processes to make Scottish tourism more competitive. One intended outcome of their actions and why they are engaged in such a process as a result of intervention by Scottish Enterprise, is to promote greater levels of innovation. Much of their work in this area is world leading, since few other public sector agencies have pursued and championed such an ambitious innovation programme. Scottish Enterprise, which covers 93 per cent of the Scottish population through its regional offices, has a fourfold approach to involvement in tourism to promote a competitive edge and improvement to the visitor experience. The areas are:

- improving market intelligence and knowledge (tourism-intelligence.co.uk)
- business leadership
- destination development
- product development
- innovation.

In previous years, its programmes have embraced the following areas of innovation activity:

- *the Tourism Innovation Group*, with its resulting Pride and Passion programme for encouraging new ideas, with passionate people able to promote it
- *learning journeys* to destinations deemed to be innovative and able to provide learning experiences for participants, generating ideas to introduce into their businesses
- *a Tourism Innovation Day*, where members of the tourism industry can gather to hear about and share new ideas and best practice in innovation
- *a Tourism Innovation Toolkit* and training programme to facilitate in-company innovation and training
- *an annual Innovation Development Award* to help fund promising new ideas by financially assisting the development of a feasibility study to implement the idea

- *a Destination Development programme* to help focus resources geographically into leading destinations to foster excellence in key areas
- *an Ambassadors Scheme* aimed at encouraging enhanced product development.

Each initiative was driven by a desire to see innovative businesses fostered to cater for tomorrow's tourists and their changing needs, while also acting as a high-profile model for other businesses to learn from; the successes are shown in Web Case 9.1.

This approach to tourism intervention was based on the perceived need for leadership in the tourism sector, which was dominated by many SMEs. SMEs are predominantly operationally focused and not renowned for their long-term vision and strategic assessment of how tourism markets are evolving and what new products are needed to cater for these markets. However, with reduced public funding and budget cuts, not all of these activities can be pursued, even though it was a world-leading programme.

For small businesses to be innovative, they must often overcome the barriers of size and resources, especially in terms of financial, technical and human resources. They may also be inhibited by a lack of marketing expertise. Yet where innovation occurs, it can be very significant and some researchers have focused on the concept of *niche tourism* (i.e. new forms of specialized tourism products and experiences) as one outcome of the innovation process. Being innovative as a manager also requires being aware of the wider business environment and how this may impact on one's business, especially given the growing interest in tourism and competitiveness. Pechlaner *et al.* (2005) point to where leadership needs to occur for innovation to flourish in a destination, also requiring cooperation among different actors and players to the extent that the innovation process can only be successfully implemented if the following are involved:

- *leaders*, such as political authorities and members of regional development agencies, such as Scottish Enterprise, with an understanding of the regional context and destination
- *managers* in tourism businesses, including entrepreneurs who understand the market and likely take-up of an innovation.

The recognition of these different players illustrates why networking and encouragement of cooperation and collaboration by agencies to facilitate this activity is vital.

Competitiveness among tourism destinations is often framed in terms of their ability to attract an increasingly demanding consumer, seeking new experiences and attractions that stimulate their senses and feelings. This is evident in major tourist capital cities such as London where large attractions like the London Dungeon (Plate 9.3) develop a growing interest in new trends such as dark tourism which focuses on past events that have a dark history.

Equally, destinations may focus upon iconic elements in their built envrionment which have a worldwide appeal and recognition as another way of attracting visitors. For example, Plate 9.4 shows a San Francisco cable car, which is a popular 'must do' attraction for visitors, given the city's role as a film tourism destination. The cable car is a familiar feature in many films and has a global role in promoting visits to the city. One of the key features of competitiveness is how destinations compare against each

Plate 9.3
London Dungeon on a busy day, illustrated by the long queue to buy a ticket to gain entry to the attraction

Source: author

other in terms of their performance, measured using indicators such as visitor arrivals and tourism growth. Such studies are often undertaken by analysts and this is part of a growing interest in benchmarking. Benchmarking is a research tool used to understand one's competitive position in relation to other destinations. This may involve compiling rankings of performance which are used by organizations to measure their relative position as a destination as well as for targeting areas to improve one's performance from a management perspective. Above all, competitiveness focuses destinations and managers on how to constantly strive to improve their tourism product and experience, so as to try to stay ahead of other competing destinations and businesses. Since tourism is very much a trend driven activity, so then an understanding of competitiveness is vital to any business operating in this sector.

One form of innovation that is constantly evaluated and examined by tourism managers is growth options and the need to pursue new business ideas such as establishing new developments, and the next section examines how managers need to approach such ideas.

Plate 9.4
A San Francisco cable car, a major tourist icon

Source: author

Tourism management in action: Designing and developing a visitor attraction

One of the key features inherent in tourism is the tourist's search for something new – a new experience, a new place to visit or new activity. Part of the innovation development process for businesses is how they evaluate the feasibility of new ideas and potential business ventures or developments. This is usually undertaken in two stages: the construction of a business plan that sets out the ideas and then a more detailed feasibility study if investment of external or large sums of money is involved. The formulation of a business plan will usually need to examine the fairly standard set of issues, many of which are listed in Table 9.5 in a simplified form. This is a fairly reflective exercise for a company, entrepreneur or planner and asks a range of questions. Many lending institutions also offer advice to new ventures regarding creating a business plan, and provide software to assist in the development of the final plan to a predetermined structure. The business plan is the stage where many of the issues are scoped out and identified, and the proposal will identify what might be expected to occur.

However, for a much larger venture, such as the building of a new tourist attraction, or modification and expansion involving the investment of large capital sums, a feasibility study will normally be undertaken, which is often contracted out to consultants who

Table 9.5 The possible structure for a simplified tourism business plan

Executive summary

- What type of business are you planning? What type of product or service will you provide?
- What do you believe are the critical success factors for this type of business?
- Why does it promise to be successful?
- What is the growth potential?

Market for the business

- Who are your potential customers and what is the market?
- How will you price your product or service?
- What market share can you expect?
- How will you promote your business?

Management

- Who will manage the business?
- What skills and characteristics will they need?
- How many employees will you need?
- What tasks will they be deployed in?
- What will their remuneration be?
- Are there potential threats to your business?

Financial elements

- What will the business cost to open?
- What will be your projected assets, liabilities and net worth?
- What is your total estimated business income for the first financial year?
- What sources of funding will you seek/use?

Many elements of a business plan can now be prepared with the aid of business planning software available from banks and their small business venture/start up units.

can offer specialist advice on certain aspects of the project. It requires detailed research or the compilation of existing research knowledge, and analysis of a range of issues, as the example in Case Study 9.3 will show.

This is a typical framework for many feasibility studies. The critical element which has proved so controversial in the UK relates to the availability of Millennium Fund grants to new visitor attraction developments. In many cases, consultants have overestimated the market for these developments and in some cases the developments have run into financial trouble within a year to 18 months of opening; some closed. This highlights the problems that employing consultants can pose for entrepreneurs and businesses: managers need to have a degree of understanding of the business process involved in a business plan and feasibility study. In each case, an impartial view or

CASE STUDY 9.3
A FEASIBILITY STUDY FOR A NEW TOURISM ATTRACTION: THE SCOPE AND RANGE OF ISSUES

The example which follows is a real-world example that has been modified for reasons of commercial confidentiality so that the identity and location are not revealed. The project, which was initially released to three consulting firms as an invitation to tender, consisted of a brief to evaluate the existing business plan for a new attraction on a greenfield site, with no local competition. The brief asked for a detailed project proposal that would outline the expertise of the consultants, time scale in which they could complete the tasks, their track record in previous projects and the costs for undertaking the task. Any area of feasibility work in tourism requires a multidisciplinary team to be assembled. In this case, quantity surveyors, a tourism planner, a tourism development expert with detailed knowledge of the region in which the attraction was to be sited and a managing partner were assembled to work on different aspects of the project. The brief identified certain misgivings with the existing business plan prepared previously, and questioned whether the financial assumptions and model used to base the development on were sufficiently robust. As a result, the project examined:

- the objectives of the visitor centre development
- the business requirements of the visitor centre (i.e. the requirement from the client that it had to be self-financing from visitor numbers and spending)
- planning regulations for new developments in the region
- existing and future tourism trends in the region, to understand if the domestic and international tourism markets would generate enough business for the new project on existing and future forecasts
- local tourism statistics and surveys that illustrated visitor behaviour within the region and their willingness to travel to a new attraction, based on existing travel patterns
- the impact of seasonality in visitor numbers and their impact on the business model
- visitor attraction trends in other countries and experiences of new developments
- infrastructure constraints and opportunities to make the new development less or more accessible, such as road improvements to cut journey times
- the market segments that were likely to use the new attraction, particularly the schools market, tour groups and independent travellers
- methods of revenue generation, including visitor spending among domestic and international visitors as well as day trippers
- financial assumptions and projections for the visitor centre, including ownership structures, assumptions about visitor spending, refined assumptions based on actual experiences at other attractions, and a model of the visitor mix and projected numbers
- construction budgets, space usage and fit-out within the new visitor centre and project programming to show the timelines for completion of each stage of the development and cost implications of different options
- the preferred model of development and likely management model that would work.

evaluation by a third party may help managers validate or reject the outcome of the study, rather than simply reiterate the findings which they are looking for simply to secure funding, which may lead to financial problems if the plan is implemented and it is not viable and realistic. In other words, the multi-skilled nature of managing a tourism business and new opportunities requires a balance of risk-taking counterweighted by financial prudence and a questioning mind to ensure that any investment is well used as well as the skills to understand business plans and feasibility studies when seeking to develop and expand (or start) a business.

Conclusion

Managing tourism is a dynamic activity: change, more change and upheaval is a function of managing a fast-changing business. Tourism businesses are subject to the vagaries of consumer tastes and market conditions, and can easily be sent into crisis by catastrophic events such as swine flu or other disease outbreak; civil disturbances (i.e. riots); and environmental disasters such as hurricanes or floods. There is a growing recognition among large tourism organizations that they need to have contingency plans to plan for such events and to engage in an understanding of crisis management (see Chapter 12). However, this is probably less challenging than day-to-day operational issues and responding effectively in a competitive market where cost, service quality and delivery at a suitable price are now dominant. Nevertheless, there is a growing need for businesses to understand the anatomy of a crisis and its different phases (i.e. pre-crisis; crisis; and post-crisis) so they can begin to understand the management challenges it poses at each stage.

Even normal operating conditions can prove challenging as market trends, unforeseen events, structural problems in a business and corporate philosophy can have a substantial bearing on business performance. The following example illustrates the significance of these respective factors in relation to the airline industry.

Southwest Airlines is one of the world's most profitable airlines in the USA. The full-cost service airlines like Delta and United had massive cost and management structures that were out of line with current models of profitable airline production, making it difficult for them to compete with the likes of Southwest on an equal basis. Therefore, these full-service carriers have sought to restructure to reduce their cost base. At the same time, these airlines have been seeking to reposition, restructure and redesign their major company offerings reflected in the United merger in 2010. The low-cost carriers in the USA have provided many examples of innovative provision, tailoring their products to the changing market. Some analysts have argued that the low-cost carriers have evolved the market so that demand now follows the low-cost supply model, causing full-service provision to be completely overhauled in the USA.

These examples show that the business model airlines use, marketing, operations management and human resource management functions are critical to delivering their service to the tourist. Even in the face of adverse conditions such as 9/11, businesses responded to the market conditions and adapted, innovated and responded to new situations. In the case of the US airline industry, the scope for innovation was limited by negative publicity and a reduction in air travel. But in other sectors of the tourism industry, innovative advertising, moving capacity such as cruise ships to new destinations and routes, promoting domestic travel and allowing managers to re-orient their business activities to fit supply with demand, occured. Ultimately, management of tourism in the private sector is about marrying supply with demand, and in managing capacity so that peaked demand through seasonality is accommodated and profitability is achieved. Yet there are various agencies and organizations that work alongside the private sector businesses and act as facilitators of tourism, to ensure it is planned, managed and developed in a manner that befits each locality. For this reason, Chapter 10 turns to the role of tourism agencies and the public sector in managing tourism.

CHAPTER REVIEW

 References

Baum, T. (ed.) (1993) *Human Resource Issues in International Tourism*. London: Butterworth-Heinemann.

Carroll, S. (1988) Managerial work in the future. In G. Hage (ed.) *Futures of Organisations*. Lexington: Lexington Books.

Carter, S. (1996) Small business marketing. In M. Warner (ed.) *International Enyclopedia of Business and Management*. London: Thomson Learning.

Connell, J., Page, S. J. and Meyer, D. (2015) Visitor attractions and events: Responding to seasonality. *Tourism Management*, 46: 283–298.

Cooper, C., Fletcher, J., Gilbert, D. and Wanhill, S. (1998) *Tourism, Principles and Practice*. London: Pitman.

Coshall, J., Charlesworth, R. and Page, S. J. (in press) Seasonality of overseas tourism demand in Scotland: A regional analysis. *Regional Studies*.

Handy, C. (1989) *The Age of Unreason*. London: Business Books Ltd.

Holloway, J. C. and Plant, R. V. (1988) *Marketing for Tourism*. London: Pitman.

Horner, S. and Swarbrooke, J. (1996) *Marketing Tourism, Hospitality and Leisure in Europe*. London: International Thomson Business Press.

Inkson, K. and Kolb, D. (1995) *Management: A New Zealand Perspective*. Auckland: Longman Paul.

Kotler, P. and Armstrong, G. (1991) *Principles of Marketing*, 5th edn. New Jersey: Prentice Hall.

McKercher, B. and Robbins, B. (1998) Business development issues affecting nature-based tourism operators in Australia. *Journal of Sustainable Tourism*, 6(2): 173–188.

Morrison, A. (1996) Marketing the small tourism business. In A. Seaton and M. Bennett (eds) *Marketing Tourism Products: Concepts, Issues, Cases*. London: International Thomson Publishing.

Page, S. J. and Connell, J. (2014) *Tourism: A Modern Synthesis*, 4th edn. London: Cengage Learning.

Pechlaner, H., Fischer, E. and Hammann, E. (2005) Leadership and innovation processes – Development of products and services based on core competencies. In M. Peters and B. Pikkmaat (eds) *Innovation in Hospitality and Tourism*. Binghampton, NJ: The Haworth Hospitality Press.

Quinn, R., Faerman, S., Thompson, M. and McGrath, M. (1990) *Becoming a Master Manager: A Competency Framework*. New York: Wiley.

Schumpeter, J. (1952) *Can Capitalism Survive?* New York: Harper and Row.

Shaw, G. and Williams, A. (2002) *Critical Issues in Tourism: A Geographical Perspective*, 2nd edn. Oxford: Blackwell.

Vargo, S. L. and Lusch, R. F. (2004) The four service marketing myths: Remnants of a goods-based, manufacturing model. *Journal of Service Research*, 6(4): 324–335.

Vargo, S. L. and Lusch, R. F. (2008) From goods to service(s): Divergences and convergences of logics. *Industrial Marketing Management*, 37: 254–259.

Further reading

One of the most digestible sources is:

Leiper, N. (1995) *Tourism Management*. Victoria: TAFE.

On tourism, SMES and entrepreneurship see:

Page, S. J. and Ateljevic, J. (eds) (2009) *Tourism and Entrepreneurship*. Oxford: Elsevier.

On innovation see:

Hall, C. M. and Williams, A. (2008) *Tourism and Innovation*. London: Routledge.

Questions

1 Why is innovation important to tourism? How do businesses embrace and harness the potential of innovation?

2 Why do tourism managers need to understand the role of management in tourism? How far are good managers 'people persons'?

3 Why do small businesses dominate the tourism sector? What particular management challenges does this pose?

4 Can the Disney model of customer care be widely rolled out to be adopted in tourism firms? Outline the reasons why or why not this may be the case.

Access additional resources

- For students: Multiple choice questions for each chapter, video links and further reading.
- For instructors: PowerPoint slides with tables and diagrams, additional case studies, video links and further reading.

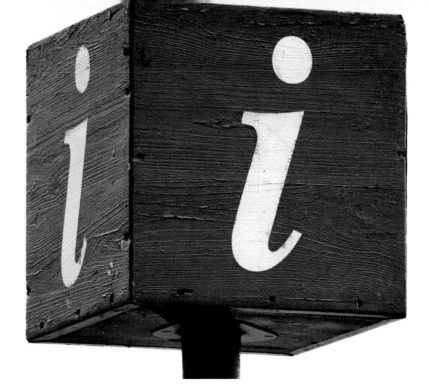

The public sector and tourism

Learning outcomes

This chapter examines the role of the public sector and the ways it facilitates and constrains the development, operation and management of tourism. On completion of this chapter, you should be able to:

- identify the roles and responsibilities of the public sector in tourism
- explain what is meant by tourism policy and why it is developed to guide tourism planning and development in different contexts and destinations
- present a coherent argument as to why the public sector needs to intervene in the tourism sector
- present examples of best practice in developing public sector models of intervention that balance the needs of stakeholders
- recognize why tourism planning is used as a tool and what are its problems in implementation.

Introduction

Chapter 9 introduced the concept of tourism management in relation to the way private sector businesses interact, operate and perform in market economies. It highlighted the importance of management to ensure that for private sector companies profitability is ensured. Yet tourism operates in a wider macro-economic environment beyond the level of the firm and that environment can be indirectly and directly managed, influenced and directed by government. According to Elliot (1997), there are four main questions that need to be asked in relation to the involvement of government in tourism:

1   why are governments important to tourism, and why do governments get involved in tourism management?
2   who are the main participants in the tourism policy system?
3   how is management of tourism policy carried out, and how do such managers manage?
4   what are the effects on tourism – has it led to success or failure?

This chapter will explore these questions and explain how the public sector manages tourism, emphasizing the role of policy-making, the implementation through planning and the impact on the management of tourism.

Governments and tourism

Governments become involved in tourism either through direct action to develop facilities and areas or indirectly by nurturing organizations that foster tourism (see Table 10.1 for key studies on governments and tourism). To the political scientist, tourism is an interesting phenomenon because for it to thrive, the ideal conditions are political stability, security, a well-defined legal framework and the essential services and infrastructure (roads, water supplies and a suitable environment) that the state is able to provide at both the national level and also at a regional and local level, through local councils (see Table 10.2). In addition, national governments are the main organizations which negotiate on immigration, visa requirements and landing rights for airlines. These statutory responsibilities are often delegated to different government departments and do not take account of more active involvement in tourism. The main factor at work here is *power* – the ability to use influence and authority to effect decisions and change. Whilst governments are expected to perform statutory tasks such as immigration and negotiating aviation rights for the wider public good, it is their degree of involvement and commitment to tourism over and above these statutory functions that is important. In other words, if power is about 'who gets what, when and how in the political system' (Elliot 1997: 10), then the political system is worthy of consideration. This is because it can explain why some countries, regions and localities are characterized by high levels of public sector management (PSM) and involvement and others are not. PSM is how the government influences tourism through actions and policies to either constrain or develop tourism. To governments, PSM is expected to effect change due to interventions

Table 10.1 Key studies on tourism policy and the public sector

Canadian Tourism Commission, World Tourism Organization and World Tourism Organization Business Council (2003) *Co-operation and Partnerships in Tourism: A Global Perspective.* Madrid: UNWTO.

Dredge, D. and Jenkins, J. (2007) *Tourism Planning and Policy.* Milton, Qld: John Wiley and Sons Australia Ltd.

Elliot, J. (1997) *Tourism, Politics and Public Sector Management.* London: Routledge.

Hall, C. M. (2007) *Tourism Planning: Policies, Processes and Relationships,* 2nd edn. Harlow: Prentice Hall.

Hall, C. M. and Jenkins, J. (1995) *Tourism and Public Policy.* London: Routledge.

Jeffries, D. (2001) *Governments and Tourism.* Oxford: Butterworth-Heinemann.

OECD (2012) *Tourism Trends and Policies 2012.* Paris: OECD.

UNWTO (2010) *Handbook on Tourism and Poverty Alleviation – Practical Steps for Destinations.* Madrid: UNWTO.

UNWTO (2010) *Joining Forces: Collaboration Processes for Sustainable and Competitive Tourism.* Madrid: UNWTO.

Table 10.2 The scope of local authority involvement in tourism in Scotland

There are 32 local authorities in Scotland, called councils, and their main area of involvement is in:

- infrastructure provision (e.g. roads, water, refuse collection, food safety and hygiene licensing)
- ensuring visitor facilities are accessible
- provision of information to visitors.

This is largely a tourism-support role.

A lesser-known role for local authorities is in tourism operations. They:

- fund local tourism activity, via partnership agreements with the main tourism organization – VisitScotland
- promote tourism initiatives at the local level
- own and manage visitor attractions (around 900 free admission attractions in Scotland), approximately 21 per cent of the total of Scottish visitor attractions
- engage in tourism development through the planning process as well as in promoting specific initiatives (e.g. city centre renewal strategies)
- promote tourism marketing via promotional campaigns, sponsoring and facilitating events.

Source: adapted from Scottish Local Authority Economic Development (SLAED) Group (2002) *The Role of Scottish Councils in Tourism.* Edinburgh: SLAED; COSLA and Economic Development and Planning Executive Group (2002) *Review of the Area Tourist Boards.* Edinburgh: COSLA

in the 'public interest' and based on principles of accountability, which are determined by the political and legal system and PSM culture. In other words, PSM is the way in which governments manage tourism although few tourism commentators would adopt that perspective, preferring to deny that government has an active role in management directly, since it is often delegated to purpose-designed tourism bodies such as National Tourism Organizations. The level of government involvement in society and the notion of PSM have been significantly challenged in many developed countries since the global credit crunch and state intervention in the financial sector to safeguard the financial stability of the banking system. This has generated increased levels of state debt, and attempts to reduce state spending so it is a lower proportion of GDP has seen a sudden sea change in the levels of expenditure now being directed to different areas of state activity at a time of relatively low levels of economic growth. There has been a greater questioning of the social and economic benefits which can arise from state spending, particularly in the wider area of the cultural industries of which tourism is one component. In this respect, tourism is not seen as a high priority for state spending when other pressing issues arise at a time of public sector cuts and a downward spiral of debt and economic growth. This signals a new era of frugality among many countries and the way they allocate public sector resources and tourism is one area of potential cuts.

Why governments intervene in the tourism sector

At the country level, governments traditionally had an interest in tourism because it is an environmentally damaging activity if left uncontrolled, and may affect the people and economies of areas in positive and negative ways (see Chapter 11). In other words, governments have a strong interest in tourism in terms of its benefits to the economy and society. It is usually argued that the government's utilization of the concept of leverage, namely investment in facilities and infrastructure to promote and stimulate tourism, brings wider benefits of tourism for the well-being of the population (i.e. it can create jobs and raise tax income). This is illustrated by the World Tourism Organization (now UNWTO) (1998: 29) *Guide for Local Authorities on Developing Sustainable Tourism*, which highlighted the preconditions, benefits and effects of government intervention:

> Tourism requires that adequate infrastructure such as roads, water supply, electric power, waste management and telecommunications be developed. This infrastructure can also be designed to serve local communities so that they receive the benefits of infrastructure improvements. Tourism development can help pay for the cost of improved infrastructure. Tourism can provide new markets for local products . . . and thereby stimulate other local economic sectors. Tourism stimulates development of new and improved retail, recreation and cultural facilities . . . which locals as well as tourists can use.

The report also acknowledged that tourism can contribute to environmental improvements as tourists seek out unpolluted places, also promoting cultural and heritage protection. In fact Middleton and Hawkins (1998: 6) identified the attraction of state-encouraged tourism in the developing world because of its potential to expand rapidly as an economic sector. It is widely acknowledged that only the state has the resources to create the necessary infrastructure to promote economic development. A good example is the South African World Cup in 2010 where the state provided the infrastructure and stadia with a view to the development of private sector business activity associated with the event and beyond the event. This illustrates the argument that the state is vital in pump-priming tourism development and investment by providing the environment where the private sector is encouraged to become an active partner in business development. This shows that tourism is a global phenomenon which can have major economic (e.g. foreign currency) benefits, can promote employment growth and create value in natural, cultural and heritage resources for visitors. According to OECD (2008: 7), 'The state can stimulate this process [of helping tourism-related industries improve their competitiveness] by offering macro-economic stability, a tourism-friendly business environment, attractive public goods and an innovation-oriented tourism policy' as highlighted in Chapter 9. In contrast to other sectors of the economy it has been described as a smokeless industry (i.e. it is perceived as low polluting compared to developing heavy industry) and can contribute to the quality of life of residents and visitors. But there are sceptics who question the positive reasons behind state intervention, since it can induce social and cultural change amongst the resident population, and alter the character and ambience of places as tourism development is followed by the resort life cycle and mass tourism. Furthermore, the economic benefits of tourism are not necessarily oriented to generating local wealth and employment, as in less developed countries (LDCs) and non-urban areas, the benefits leak out and low-paid, seasonal employment is the norm rather than full employment for all. The economic drawbacks become more serious when external control by multinational companies results in the environmental costs being borne by the locality while the profits are expropriated back to the company, often located overseas. This has been reinforced by concerns over policies designed to liberalize barriers to trade, such as the World Trade Organization General Agreement on Trade in Services (GATS). Critics pointed to the potential removal of entry barriers in LDCs which may intensify the impact of foreign direct investment on the tourism sector.

Jeffries (2001) also pointed to wider political objectives by governments that affect tourism development:

- in Spain, the Franco regime in the 1960s sought to use tourism to legitimize its political acceptability, as well as recognizing its economic potential
- since the 1930s, France has used the concept of social tourism (similar to the former Soviet Union's idea of recreational tourism, to improve the quality of life of workers at resorts, spas and holiday camps), especially among low-income groups, to enhance the welfare role of the state. A similar approach has also been adopted in Belgium
- the UK government in the 1980s emphasized the employment potential of tourism to create new jobs and wealth in an era of high unemployment
- some countries and transnational bodies such as the EU actively promote grants and aid to the peripheral regions to help develop the tourism infrastructure (e.g. road improvements in the Republic of Ireland and the Highlands and Islands of

Scotland) to encourage the expansion of the tourism potential. Since the expansion of the EU to include 27 member countries, its tourism policies have particularly focused on new member states in Eastern Europe and Southern Europe to improve the competitiveness and capacity of their tourism sectors

- in LDCs, tourism expansion is often politically justified as a means of poverty eradication and a number of developed countries' governments (e.g. the UK, Australia, New Zealand and the EU) provide aid to assist with this objective, as evident in the case of the Pacific islands. This has been more recently focused on pro-poor tourism initiatives, where notable successes have occurred in countries such as the Gambia and South Africa.

Government intervention and tourism performance

Governments also intervene in the tourism arena because it is perceived to be a complex industry, being an amalgam of different businesses and sectors, where benefits accrue if these businesses are coordinated better to achieve common goals – the development and improvement of the quality of tourism. A more controversial argument for intervention is that it can prevent market failure. Indeed, some commentators argue that when the public sector gets too involved in tourism, such as through major investment in business activities like visitor attractions, failure is never far away. There are many examples in the UK of Millennium Grants used to fund visitor attractions which subsequently failed. This is because the imbalance with public sector intervention may deter private sector investment if tourism becomes overly bureaucratized with a multiplicity of agencies involved in its management and regulation. In extreme cases, too much public sector investment may lead to a dependency culture where tourism is protected from market forces, becomes uneconomic due to the subsidies, is unattractive to investors and fails to reach its full potential.

But intervention is often politically justified since the highly seasonal nature of tourism activity in some regions and countries means that there is often insufficient business to support all-year-round operation. In extreme cases, there may not be adequate flows of tourists to support a tourist attraction. State subsidies, grants and assistance to the tourism sector in this context is justified, supporters argue, because without support the attraction may not be able to survive, and therefore would not provide a vital element of the region's attractiveness. This is highly controversial in countries where the performance of the tourism sector (in terms of visitor arrivals, productivity per business and high levels of seasonality) has been supported by public subsidies to operators and the tourism sector. Critics of such policies point to the obvious advantage of allowing the tourism sector to operate in a market economy with no subsidies or state intervention: it improves competitiveness. They argue that a market forces culture is important to stimulate innovation and new ideas, exciting developments and a dynamic tourism industry. For example, one concept which has informed such intervention by the public sector concerns the use of the triple helix model (Figure 10.1). The triple helix model in simple terms suggests that where mutual benefits exist in the intersection of the three stakeholders (public sector, private sector and universities/research institutes) it may be possible to foster innovation. To lead the nurturing of mutual benefits, it is

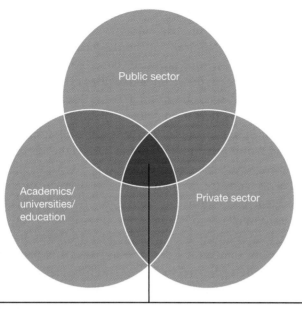

By intervening in the system at this point, the intersection of the triple helix, to foster interaction, the public sector as a lead partner should be able to encourage cooperation and collaboration, and it should be feasible to encourage innovation by pooling expertise and resources so that the opportunities for business development are shared

Figure 10.1
The triple helix concept

Source: author

vital that one of the stakeholders (e.g. the public sector) leads and champions the process, initially through networking and then through the creation of a smaller community of like-minded individuals committed to promoting innovation. This particular focus in Norway on the triple helix has informed its thinking on collaboration and cooperation in many of the networks which Innovation Norway (which has absorbed the roles of the National Tourism Organization) has supported and funded. Enterprise, development and innovation may need support and assistance at a fledgling stage, but first ideas on innovation need to be generated.

If there is no incentive for such activity due to dependency, and the tourism sector operates in a protective environment and does not have to compete globally, then public sector support may actually dampen vital activity. The result of increased competition may well be the loss of businesses without a viable market to support them in the short-term if subsidies were removed. Yet a decline in the number and range of tourism operators may actually be desirable if it removes marginal and poor-quality operators with low service standards, who may depress the market for other businesses seeking to promote a quality product.

The perceived impact of such changes on marginal tourism regions, which have a heavy dependence on seasonal tourism for local employment, is viewed as politically unacceptable. Removal of subsidies are only implemented where public sector funding for tourism is reduced owing to financial stringencies in central, regional or local government budgets. Yet critics of state subsidies for tourism argue that few other sectors of the economy with significant private and public sector involvement enjoy such levels of state-related support to facilitate economic activity.

Advocates of continued state support, often described as 'lobbying' or 'interest groups' (e.g. the British Hospitality Association in the UK and Tourism Industry Association in the USA, which represents its tourism members) highlight the wider benefits of state involvement in tourism. Even in the USA, where Congress suspended funding of the US Travel and Tourism Administration in 1996 and pushed the marketing and promotion of the US to an industry body (the Tourism Industry Association), it re-intervened in 2005 to provide federal funds for marketing the USA overseas since a combination of problems had damaged the country's attractiveness as a destination. Industry lobby groups argue that improvements to the range of infrastructure (e.g. roads), attractions and business activity may also have benefits for residents of areas. In many local council areas, especially in towns, tourism is seen by residents as a problem in that cleansing, rubbish collection, policing and marketing/promotion that arises from tourism adds to the tax burden. Yet the beneficial effects of tourist spending on the local economy (see Chapter 11) arguably can reduce rating levels, as tourism supports local businesses, which pay business rates, create employment and generate greater revenue for councils, thereby reducing the potential rates burden for local residents.

The following statement in the Parliament of New South Wales in relation to Byron Bay, a popular coastal tourist destination and community on the east coast of Australia, highlights many of the reasons why the public sector is involved in tourism, particularly planning, because of the problems which may arise from uncontrolled development and the negative consequences of tourism development. It also shows how small communities may be forced to take the pressure of seasonal tourist development and be forced to pay for it through the rates charged by local authorities to meet tourist and resident needs.

> I want to raise the general issue of the pressure that is placed on people and the facilities in the popular tourist destination of Byron Bay . . . Everyone knows that the beaches and landscape around Byron Bay are simply magnificent. During the past 10 years in particular Byron Bay has become a significant international destination, especially for backpackers . . . Whilst tourism is the economic lifeblood of Byron, and tourists generally are most welcome, if the amenity of Byron for locals and the atmosphere of Byron which attracts tourists in such large numbers are not preserved it will end up being neither attractive for locals or tourists. I believe the Coalition's policy is an enlightened one because it recognizes that a community with a small population, and therefore a small rate base – in the case of Byron some $7.3 million a year only for the whole of shire – which hosts 1 million tourists a year is deserving of some special assistance ahead of a community of similar size which hosts no tourists.
>
> Another problem is that the sewerage system at Byron cannot cope with the demand on it. Some progress at last is being made on this front, but overloads are not uncommon. Water consumption is up, sewerage loads are up and it is doubtful

that the upgraded sewerage plant at West Byron, which is due to come on line in 2004, will provide more than temporary respite ... On the positive side, council has commissioned a tourism plan to be developed for Byron Bay specifically, and the voice of the local community is being heard more than in the past. The locals are fighting back. A recent public meeting of residents looked at ways of bringing under control the worse excesses of backpacker and other visitor behaviour – namely public drunkenness, using the streets as toilets, loud all night parties and overcrowded houses ... The Byron tourism plan needs to be developed to address all the key issues. It must include strategies for protecting the amenity and the beauty of Byron Bay for locals and tourists alike.

(Page 2002)

Such arguments are highly controversial and different facets of each argument are invariably highlighted by interest groups, depending upon the evidence used and points raised to advocate or reject public sector support. There is often a great deal of conjecture, supposition and value-laden arguments used by interest groups and stakeholders when debating tourism. This may explain why some local councils, which periodically change their political complexion, can be described as 'blowing hot and cold' towards tourism, exemplified in the policies and planning approaches they adopt towards tourism. This is one reason why governments have endorsed better research methods to understand, analyse and explain how local economies are impacted by tourism. As Chapter 11 will show, the use of Tourism Satellite Accounts has begun to provide some objective data to support the wider economic arguments on the importance of tourism to national economies. This has started to address the ongoing tension associated with situations where objective tourism data do not exist.

Inevitably, government involvement in tourism at any level is about the resolution of conflict, seeking to achieve a balance between actively promoting tourism and acting as guardians of the public interest in the manner, form, direction, impact and effect of tourism from a national to local level. For example, state intervention in Spain, Greece and Cyprus in 2008 was critical due to drought and water shortages, requiring Barcelona and Cyprus to import water to address a strategic crisis facing their tourism sector upon which their economies depend. Thus the state has a crucial role as a strategic planner and crisis manager. This conflict resolution process will often mean balancing the protagonists (i.e. the tourism industry) and antagonists (often residents) who are both valid stakeholders in the tourism economy, in seeking to meet the needs of the visitor in a sustainable and locally appropriate manner (see Web Case 10.1).

A more active role for governments, and a potential reason for intervention in the tourism economy or markets, is related to strategic objectives aside from the development process. Here one dimension of public sector management has been divided into two perspectives by Jeffries (2001):

1   strategic seasonal redistribution of tourists
2   strategic geographical redistribution of tourists.

In the first instance, seasonal redistribution is a major global issue, given the problems of seasonality in tourism discussed in Chapters 7 and 8. Seasonality can lead to a highly skewed pattern of business for tourism operators outside major urban areas but tourism organizations responsible for tourism promotion, development and management may intervene in the market, as the case of Destination Northland (north of New Zealand, www.destinationnorthland.co.nz) suggests. It was able to:

- provide a new series of innovative new products for visitors in the low season that are less weather dependent, by emphasizing the appeal to the domestic market (e.g. through hosting sporting events and promoting sightseeing on the twin-coast highway route, and wine and food tourism based on local products)
- operate marketing campaigns via printed media and the worldwide web to highlight the region's indigenous culture (i.e. the Maori of Tai Tokerau iwi) and the built heritage, at Russell, the country's first capital, as the birthplace of New Zealand. It also recognized the appeal of the marine environment of the Bay of Islands, with the attraction for yacht-based tourists to winter over in the region.

Even so, the tourism industry in many localities remains highly fragmented, lacks cohesion and the ability to have political clout and influence change, since the individual operators are focused on their own activities rather than the strategic development of the region or destination. By seeking to extend the tourist season, and expand the range of opportunities for low season visitation, public sector agencies argue that they will encourage increased business activity and turnover that will lead to greater profitability, as well as possibly increasing employment and gaining a higher profile as a tourism region. The problem is that research studies are sometimes dubiously used to inflate the potential economic benefits to justify or to continue funding an event.

The public sector directly intervenes in tourism planning and development by seeking directly to achieve a geographical redistribution of tourists and the volume of visits. For example, in the 1960s the French government produced a plan to develop a coastal region to the south of Montpellier, known as Languedoc-Roussillon. The initial plan was to develop a resort area with 150 000 bed-spaces; this was subsequently revised and expanded in the 1970s and 1980s. This is a widely cited example of state-led tourism development in a peripheral area, and reveals the state's motives: seeking to direct tourism to an undeveloped region to assist with regional development. In contrast, tourism in London, which is the gateway for UK tourism, saw residents' views, congestion, overcrowding and high occupancy rates in hotel accommodation result in the London Tourist Board commissioning the *Tourism Accommodation in London in the 1990s* report (Touche Ross 1988). This formed the basis for policies to limit further hotel growth in London's West End, while encouraging out-of-town accommodation development. The result was the development of tourism accommodation after 1988 in districts adjacent to the West End of London and the expansion of accommodation in London's urban fringe adjacent to Heathrow and Gatwick airports – especially budget accommodation next to the M25 motorway junctions. This policy of constraint and directed development has taken a number of years to evolve, but despite the lead-time for new accommodation and over a 20-year period, changes are notable.

London is a crucial gateway, with 48 per cent of all overseas visitors to the UK entering via London. Other leading cities also handle a high proportion of their country's international arrivals (e.g. Sydney 50 per cent; Dublin 54 per cent; Amsterdam 52 per cent) although this does not apply to all capital cities (Paris only accounts for 12 per cent of all arrivals in France and Rome for 10 per cent of arrivals in Italy). What many public sector analysts recognize is that London is competing globally as a world city and tourism is a necessary component of that globalization. Therefore, policies constraining tourism have had to be replaced with those seeking to facilitate growth.

In the wider scheme of tourism, key elements identified in this dispersal strategy are:

*   improving the supply of London's accommodation with a further 26 000 rooms as well as improved value for money and quality control
*   developing new attractions and accommodation to achieve the dispersal strategy in outer London boroughs
*   improving transport and infrastructure to facilitate this dispersal in areas identified for economic growth (as well as safeguarding the West End of London as a key element of London's international appeal as an entertainment district).

One area that has seen considerable growth is the night-time economy in London both for tourist and leisure use, with a rise in restaurant and bars opening since the 1990s. This in itself has been stimulated by a greater provision of all-night buses by Transport for London. However, a number of problems also exist and these can impact upon the tourist image of London. They include crime and antisocial behaviour, and street-cleanliness, all of which are aggravated by the expansion of the night-time city. In 2005 controversial legislation in the UK allowed pubs to open for 24 hours in approved instances, in a bid to address the problems of binge drinking and a yob culture among 18- to 30-year-olds in city centres. Thus, whilst policies to decentralize tourism in London have seen a degree of success, the expansion in central and suburban London's nightlife, where residents and visitors co-exist, may prove a major social and environmental nuisance for residents and affect the image of London as a destination for tourists.

More explicit state intervention is evident in many of Europe's small historic towns, where local planning authorities have adopted radical measures to constrain the saturation effects of mass tourism in cities such as Canterbury, York, Stratford-upon-Avon and Cambridge. But how do organizations in the public sector affect such change, and what processes and procedures are used to manage tourism? This begins through the development of tourism policy.

Tourism policy

According to Hall and Jenkins (1995: 2), tourism public policy can help the causes and consequences of policy decisions, since it indicates the way in which policy influences tourism through:

*   the political nature of the policy-making process
*   the degree of public participation in the tourism policy and planning process

- the sources of power in the tourism policy-making environment, and the choices and decisions made by civil servants towards complex policy issues
- the perceptions of stakeholders as to the effectiveness of tourism policies.

This illustrates that tourism policy-making is inherently a political activity, affected by the formal structures of government. A wide range of forces affects policy-making. According to Hall and Jenkins (1995: 5) public policy in tourism is 'whatever governments choose to do or not to do', and it is a function of three interrelated issues according to Turner (1997):

- the intentions of political and other key factors
- the way in which decisions and non-decisions are made
- the implications of these decisions.

Figure 10.2 illustrates the continuous nature of policy-making, which requires one to understand the nature of the institutions and organizations involved in shaping policy, since policy-making is filtered through a range of different institutions that may seem complex to the uninitiated observer. These institutions help shape policy outcomes because they are involved in negotiation and bargaining to achieve their own organization's objectives. At the same time, interest groups (producer groups such as national tourism associations), non-producer groups (e.g. environmental organizations) and single issue groups (e.g. opponents of an airport project) seek to influence the decision-making element of policy-making.

Tourism policy does not exist in a vacuum because various agencies exist to implement policy. The implementation is, again, a resolution of conflict and an attempt to meet the needs of stakeholders whilst meeting national or local tourism development needs. Policy cannot be viewed in isolation from political decision-making, which determines the direction of policy, which is constantly evolving. For example, in the case of China, a series of policy changes post-1978, when the country first opened its doors to tourists, required major policy changes. After 1978, policy success has often been measured through one simple barometer of tourism – international visitor arrivals. In 1978, international visitor arrivals in China were a modest 1.8 million; these subsequently increased to 17.8 million in 1985 and 33.3 million in 1991. Five years later, visitor arrivals exceeded 51 million, and in 1997 some 57.5 million arrivals were recorded. This incredible rate of growth in inbound tourism required a shift in policy from the pre-1978 socialist idea that tourism was a vehicle to educate visitors about the virtues of communism to one that was accommodating a large influx of visitors who were only allowed to visit certain areas. A similar rationale characterized inbound tourism policy in the former Soviet Union and pre-1990s Albania (see Web Case 10.2 for more discussion of China).

Yet it is not just governments which influence tourism policy, but also a range of international non-governmental agencies (NGOs) such as the World Tourism Organization. The UNWTO, based in Madrid, seeks to assist its member countries to work in a cooperative and collaborative manner to provide statistical information on tourism, and to advise on policies and practices to improve tourism planning and

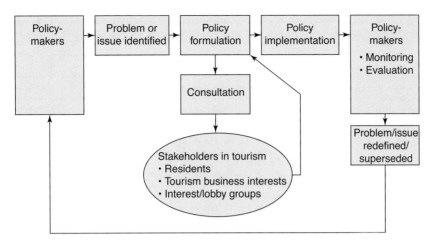

Figure 10.2
The policy-making process in tourism

Source: author

education and training. Other international lobby groups seek to influence the air transport and its industry groups (i.e. the IATA, ICAO, ATAG and ACI – see Chapter 5). These bodies promote the interests of their members, who have vested interests in tourism.

One additional agency that is influential in government tourism policy is the EU. The 27 member countries of the EU represent an important trading bloc, which is mirrored by similar blocs in other parts of the world. The EU seeks to promote tourism as a free-trade activity in and between member states by trying to simplify and harmonize policies and procedures to facilitate the free movement of travellers. The EU also seeks to develop measures to improve the quality of tourism in member states although tourism policy remains the remit of individual governments. The scale and extent of the EU's impact on the wide range of issues which affect tourism are shown in Table 10.3 which highlights the diversity of EU measures affecting tourism (see www.europa.eu.int for more up-to-date information as EU policy and developments in tourism are constantly evolving).

Among the most influential agencies that develop policy for tourism in individual countries are:

• ministries of tourism, which fund or part-fund National Tourism Organizations (NTOs) such as VisitBritain (which replaced the former British Tourist Authority)
• NTOs
• Regional Tourism Organizations, which manage the implantation of national and regional policy in their respective areas
• local authorities and other agencies, which set policies at the local area level.

This vast array of public sector agencies is complemented by *ad hoc* agencies set up within specific areas such as inner city regeneration projects (e.g. the London Docklands

---

Table 10.3 The range of European Community measures affecting tourism

- Economic policies
- Enterprise policy towards tourism businesses
- Competition issues and mergers
- State aid for tourism (e.g. subsidies)
- The internal market and tourism
- Fiscal policies and tourism (e.g. taxation)
- Employment and social policy (e.g. the minimum wage)
- Enhancing Europe's potential for tourism
- Tourism and employment
- Exchange and dissemination of information
- Training, skills and the workforce
- Education and vocational training
- Qualifications, employability and lifelong learning
- Social rights, social protection, social integration and inequality
- Social dialogue
- Quality issues in tourism destinations
- Improving the quality of tourism products
- Safety in tourism installations, food safety and health
- The environment and sustainable development
- Environmental protection
- Natural and cultural heritage
- Transport
- Energy

The European Commission has produced guidelines or reports for each of these areas, all of which can be accessed at: www.europa.eu.int

---

Development Corporation in the 1980s and 1990s). These specific area-based initiatives by local economic development agencies have been reintroduced in England and Wales; they highlight how policy changes can affect the actual structure of provision. In Scotland, Scottish Enterprise's regional enterprise companies set out policies for the tourism sector and intervene, using public funds, to meet specific tourism objectives as is explained in considerable detail in Page and Connell (2009).

It is apparent that in many countries, while tourism policy may rest with the Ministry of Tourism or department responsible for tourism, a host of agencies interact to produce a multilayered system of public sector support. Figure 10.3 illustrates this model of support in the UK, a model that has been described as chaotic and extremely bureaucratic. At the time of writing, this framework in England was under review, as public sectors may eradicate the Regional Development Agencies, removing the funding base of tourist boards. Whilst there is a growing debate over whether governments are still about direct control of tourism, or whether they should be encouraging other agencies to manage tourism, in the UK the model is in abeyance as austerity cuts are proposing to remove the middle tiers of administration and public sector management of tourism, although the future model remains unclear. At present the UK model is characterized by:

- one national organization, VisitBritain, to market the UK overseas
- our country-based NTOs – VisitEngland, VisitScotland (formerly the Scottish Tourist Board), the National Ireland Tourist Board and VisitWales (the former Wales Tourist Board now incorporated into the Welsh Assembly). In some cases, these NTOs market each country to domestic and international tourists, which may seem as a duplication of the efforts of VisitBritain, which markets the UK as a united destination overseas
- an amalgam of destination-marketing organizations and local economic partnerships (LEPS) in England, regional tourism partnerships in Wales, and the former network of area tourist boards in Scotland which are now part of the VisitScotland networks. These agencies are funded by grants from the devolved governments in Wales and Scotland
- in the UK, the development of Local Economic Partnerships (LEPs) has been the new focus for the regional organization of tourism and, from the LEPs currently operating, 7 have placed tourism as a priority, a further 26 have a tourism interest and 2 are not interested in this activity. This has to be understood against the background of 90 local tourism destination organizations also operating in England at a local level. For example, in the County of Dorset in south-west England, the LEP has membership and a working relationship with the following public sector organizations that are working at the local level and involved in tourism: Bournemouth Tourism, Poole Tourism Services, Dorset and New Forest Partnership, West Dorset District Council, Dorset County Council, East Dorset District Council, Purbeck District Council, Weymouth and Portland Borough Council
- local authorities in England of which there are 387 – 34 are non-metropolitan county councils, 238 are non-metropolitan district councils, 36 are metropolitan councils, 46 are unitary councils, 32 are London boroughs, plus the City of London Corporation
- according to OECD (2008), the funding arrangement in 2006 for UK tourism comprised the Department for Culture, Media and Sport (DCMS) (see Figure 10.3) providing £50 million to VisitBritain, £38 million to VisitScotland (£44 million in 2012) and £22 million to the Welsh Assembly; £50 million was provided by the former Regional Development Agencies in England. In addition, English local authorities spent around £120 million on tourism. This provides a conservative estimate (excluding special cross-government initiatives) of £280 million of public sector expenditure on supporting UK tourism, which must rate amongst the highest amount of any developed country.

Through their role in managing services for visitors, such as tourist information centres (TICs) (some local authorities undertake this role in other countries), regional and area

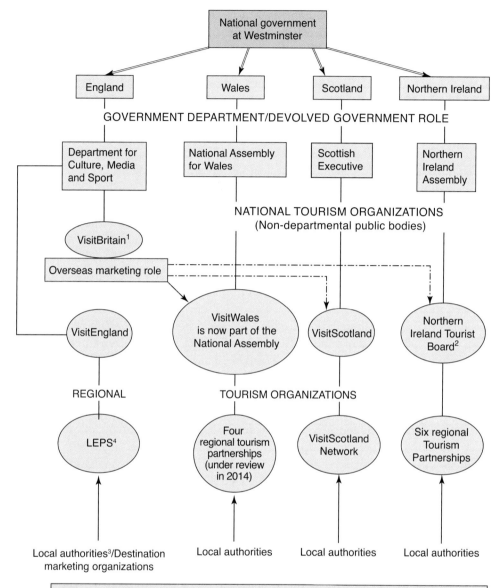

Figure 10.3

The statutory framework for the administration of tourism in the UK

Source: author

tourist boards provide a network of contact points for visitors. This function is discussed more fully in Further Web Reading 1 where their significance and role in tourism is explained. Given the scope and nature of the public sector agencies in tourism, attention now turns to how these organizations plan for tourism.

How government organizations influence tourism

In the UK, the DCMS is the government department responsible for tourism. Like its counterpart in many countries, it is not seen as a high-profile ministry, since tourism is not accorded a portfolio that reflects its economic role in most countries. As a result, other government departments make a significant contribution directly and indirectly to infrastructure development (e.g. the Department of Transport in terms of roads, ports and aviation). The DCMS has a broad responsibility for leisure, tourism and the cultural industries in the UK, including tourism, the arts, broadcasting, cultural artefacts, film, art, heritage, libraries, museums, galleries, the press, the royal estate, sport and recreation. Whilst such an integrated approach to the leisure industries is intended to achieve the ministry's objectives to improve the quality of life through cultural industries and sporting activities, and by contributing to job creation, there is a danger that tourism is subsumed and lost among so many functions.

Having outlined which organizations and bodies are involved in policy-making for tourism at different levels, attention now turns to how these policies are implemented – through the planning process.

Planning and tourism

So far this chapter has highlighted the tensions that exist in the formulation of policies to guide the development of the tourism sector, as a process of negotiation between stakeholder groups brokered by public sector agencies. At a practical level, the implementation of public sector policies requires an understanding of how agencies plan, manage and use tools in tourism destinations. The context in which agencies involved in tourism planning operate is also important, because underlying principles and ideas shape planning. For example, although the concept of sustainability is not the focus of this chapter, it is an important theme to explain, given its widespread use in tourism planning. In simple terms, sustainability is a common-sense approach to the use, consumption and management of the resources upon which tourism relies (see Chapter 11). In essence, the arguments developed on sustainability, and embodied in the Brundtland Report (World Commission on the Environment and Development, 1987), are that we need to use resources in such a manner that they can be enjoyed today but also conserved and managed for future generations. They question the historical pursuit of resource depletion in the name of progress and development, with no concern for the future use. This concept, which was guided by environmentalism in the 1960s and 1970s, recognizes that there are limits to the growth of the planet, with many resources being finite and non-renewable (e.g. oil).

In a tourism context, the question of sustainability has emerged as a major debate for planners because of the global growth of tourism. Tourism equates to the consumption of environmental resources and this poses problems for destination areas. In practical terms, planners face the challenge of balancing tourism demand and supply, and of recognizing the future effects of tourism if the concept of sustainability is not considered. The public sector therefore intervenes in tourism and planning terms, to implement tourism policy objectives and to avoid over-development from tourism, as the tourism sector pursues short-term profits. This means that without public sector intervention, the environment and resource base for tourism in destination areas could be irreversibly damaged and the potentially beneficial effects of tourism may easily be lost.

In terms of the implementation of sustainability as a theme to manage the future development of tourism activity in destinations, a champion of the idea or organization tasked with developing an idea is often needed from a management perspective to lead an innovative idea. This is illustrated in more detail with the example of the Global Sustainable Tourism Council as a global organization set up to champion the principles of sustainability in tourism business activities and in destination management.

If we return to the basic premise of tourism management, then tourism planning in its practical form is about the public sector leading to organize, plan and control tourism development in relation to policies in each destination area. This requires the complex coordination of stakeholder interests (private sector businesses, public sector agencies, residents and visitors). These tasks also have a time horizon, known as 'the strategic dimension', where tourism planning has a five- to ten-year time frame during which the impact and implications of policies and plans can be monitored and evaluated. This was illustrated above in the case of London's tourism accommodation 1988–2000, where policies directly shaped the nature, form and location of accommodation development. But does tourism planning actually exist and, if it does, how does it operate and how is it organized?

Does tourism planning exist?

There is an ongoing debate amongst tourism professionals as to whether tourism planning exists as a phenomenon, since much of the planning activity for tourism is based upon public sector planning as opposed to planning led by tourism agencies. In many cases, planning exists within regional (i.e. county councils) and local (i.e. district councils) agencies in the UK and their equivalents in other parts of the world. These bodies typically subsume tourism within economic development departments, which seek to accommodate future demands and change. As Hall (2007) argues, much of the planning for tourism is based on an *ad hoc* approach, lacking continuity, cohesion and strategic vision.

Even so, Getz (1987) has described four traditions that have evolved towards planning tourism:

1 boosterism
2 an economic-industry approach
3 a physical-spatial approach
4 a community-oriented approach.

The GSTC (www.gstcouncil.org), established in 2010, is a global lead organization with public and private sector support and members which has a number of specific objectives within its broad remit of seeking to create universal principles upon which sustainable tourism can be developed into reality:

- to establish a common language on sustainable tourism given the varying terms and interpretations of sustainability and its application to tourism
- to make tourism destinations more sustainable
- to promote market access for sustainable tourism, so it is seen less as a niche activity and more as a mainstream form of tourism
- to increase knowledge on the subject
- to help with the verification of the standards of sustainable tourism through harmonization of the different criteria and measures used by accreditation schemes as discussed in Chapter 6, such as the Green Tourism Business Scheme.

Its work spans the promotion of sustainable practices, the adoption of sustainable tourism principles and the promotion of sustainable tourism demand. It has taken a lead role in establishing and launching its sustainable destination programme in 2013, where destinations need to demonstrate, through various indicators and evidence, how they are sustainably managing their destination using a very detailed set of criteria. Among the early adopters of this new programme that fulfil the criteria are: the Okavango Delta in Botswana, the Cosco region in Peru in which Macchu Picu is located, the Norwegian fjords, Yellowstone National Park, Lanzarote in the Canary Islands and a number of other destinations. These represent early examples of where the sustainability ethos is at the forefront of their work in seeking to manage and develop tourism around the criteria of what constitutes a sustainable destination and are examples of best practice and leaders in the field.

Further reading

www.gstcouncil.org

This can also be extended to give a fifth approach – sustainable tourism planning, which is 'a concern for the long-term future of resources, the effects of economic development on the environment, and its ability to meet present and future needs' (Page and Thorn 1997: 60) although the implementation and management of sustainable tourism indicators remain problematic for many destinations despite the guidance recently issued by the UNWTO in a report. The UNWTO argued that sustainable tourism should:

- make optimal use of environmental resources (while maintaining the essential ecological processes while helping to conserve the natural heritage and bio- diversity)

- respect the sociocultural authenticity of host communities (helping to conserve the cultural heritage and traditional values as well as seeking to engender intercultural understanding and tolerance)
- ensure viable, long-term economic operations, providing socio-economic benefits to all stakeholders.

This illustrates both the environmental focus and the sociocultural and economic dimensions in relation to the nature of tourism and its impact. It is these elements that the UNWTO argue should be the focus of any planning activity.

Inskeep (1994) has indicated that the effective management of tourism requires certain 'organizational elements'. The most important of these in a planning context are organizational structures, which include government agencies and private sector interest groups as well as local and regional government bodies, which are all involved in planning for tourism activity as well as tourism-related legislation and regulations. These bodies utilize the statutory planning frameworks such as planning acts, government ordinances and directives from central government, which in turn condition the parameters for planning. Where the planning process focuses on tourism, a process akin to the way policy-making is developed is followed.

The planning process for tourism

There is normally a set of pre-defined steps that characterize the planning process for tourism including:

1   *study preparation*, which is where the planning authority within the local or regional government (although on small island states that do not have a complex planning structure it may be the NTO) decide to proceed with the development of a tourism plan. Normally a statutory body undertakes to prepare the plan but in more complex urban environments, where a local and regional agency both develop a tourism plan, it is important that they are integrated to ensure a unified approach to tourism. This was a problem in London in the 1990s, when the 33 London boroughs each had unified development plans but pursued different approaches to tourism. This meant that some councils promoted tourism development while others positively discouraged it despite the efforts of the London Tourist Board, which sought to coordinate their activities in tourism. The result was a pattern of uneven development across the city

2   *determination of objectives*, where the objectives of the plan are identified (e.g. is the agency seeking to promote an explanation of tourism to pump-prime economic development or trying to manage the problems of mass tourism and the associated effects?)

3   *survey of all elements*, where an inventory of existing tourism resources and facilities are reviewed, requiring the collection of data on the supply and demand for tourism and the structure of the local tourist economy. It will need to recognize which other private and public sector interests are stakeholders in tourism within the destination

4   *analysis and synthesis of findings*, where the information and data collected from the previous stage are used to begin formulating the plan. This typically involves four techniques: asset evaluation, market analysis, development planning and impact analysis (see Chapter 11) to establish the future for tourism

5   *policy and plan formulation*, where the data are used and synthesized (i.e. sifted, sorted and organized) to establish development scenarios for tourism. This will invariably lead to the preparation of a draft development plan with tourism policy options. These policies must have three elements to be able to meet the varying needs of the tourism stakeholders – visitor satisfaction, environmental protection and ensuring a pay-back for investors

6   *consideration of recommendations*, where the full tourism plan is sent to the organization's planning committee. A public consultation would normally follow after the planning committee's acceptance of the plan. The general public and interested parties are then able to read and comment on the plan. A number of public hearings may also be provided to gauge the strength of local feeling towards the plan. Once this procedure is completed, the plan will then be sent back to the planning authority in a revised form for approval with any changes incorporated, so the final plan can be prepared

7   *the implementation and monitoring of the tourism plan* then follows, which includes various actions. Legislation may be required in some cases to control certain aspects of development (e.g. the density of development) that need to be implemented as part of the plan. However, the political complexity of implementing such a plan is substantial since the political balance of elected representatives on the statutory planning authority may change and cause the priorities to change. Where an action plan is produced that causes intense political debate over each issue, it may allow for some degree of choice in what is implemented and actioned in a set period of time. At the same time as the plan is implemented, it will also need to be monitored and evaluated, and frequently criticized by commentators. The planning agency will need to assess if the objectives of the plan are being met. The operational time frame for a tourism plan is normally five years after which time it is reviewed

8   *the periodic review*, is the process of reporting back on progress after the plan has run its course. When analysing the reasons for the success or, more commonly, failure of the plan to achieve all its objectives a range of reasons may be suggested. These may include a lack of resources to achieve the goals, political infighting by elected members of the planning authority, inadequate transport and infrastructure provision, public opposition to tourism among residents, and a lack of investment by public sector businesses.

Government tourism strategies

To guide the multitude of public sector agencies and stakeholders involved in tourism, government departments will often embody many of the policy objectives in a strategy document. This strategy document will identify what the government wishes to achieve in broad terms in tourism, and identifies objectives and action points for other agencies, as Web Case 10.3 shows.

Plate 10.1
Management of queues

Source: author

As Web Case 10.3 suggests, concerns with the industry's competitiveness, value for money, travel costs, unfavourable exchange rates and the problems of seasonality are not necessarily issues that a strategy can easily address. Above all, lateral thinking, industry–public sector cooperation and more visionary central government legislation aimed at tackling obstacles to improve business performance are needed to find ways to reposition Scottish tourism. With 50 per cent of overseas and 30 per cent of British visitors to Scotland visiting July–September each year, seasonality adds pressures on businesses and raises costs of production (see Plate 10.1 for an example of seasonal pressure in tourism evident in queues). This illustrates the need to reposition Scotland with new products and experiences to encourage a more even spread of visitation.

The public sector marketing of tourism

The majority of National Tourism Organizations (NTOs) are not producers or operators in a tourism context, but seek to influence the images which visitors and potential visitors may hold of the country or region. However, prior to NTOs marketing destinations, private transport companies worked in collaboration with destinations to promote their attraction as Plates 10.2 and 10.3 show from the 1920s and 1930s. Plate 10.2 is an

Plate 10.2
Seaside Excursions, Kate Burrell, 1927

Source: TFL

Plate 10.3
Southend-on-Sea, Surfing, by Charles Pears, 1932

Source: TFL

example of one of the posters produced by London's Underground Electric Railway Ltd (now the London Underground) to encourage travel to the seaside ('*Seaside Excursions*' by Kate Burrell). Plate 10.3, produced in 1932 and based on the painting commissioned from the artist, Charles Pears, promoting a nearby resort patronized by Londoners, Southend-on-Sea, was also published as a poster by the Underground Electric Railways Company to encourage holiday travel and excursions from London by train. These posters are very good illustrations of the urban demand for coastal tourism and leisure. For example, research by the National Railway Museum in York, UK has found that Southend was a popular summer destination. On one Bank Holiday in the 1930s, 100 special trains conveyed 70 000 people from London to the resort.

Today, the London Underground is still a conduit for place promotion with many NTOs using large-scale posters to promote holidays and travel to a captive audience whilst travelling to work or for leisure. Such posters may cost a couple of thousand pounds for a single campaign but they have the potential to reach millions of travellers in a short space of time.

Imagery and place promotion then is not a new task, but in recent years this has been largely undertaken by destination organizations like NTOs. As a result of the evolution of place promotion, there are four models widely used to undertake this task:

1   full state intervention, where the state promotes the brand image; this is not a common occurrence outside the former Eastern Europe, Africa (excluding South Africa) and South America

2   a public–private sector partnership, where the private sector contributes to the marketing, an approach that is widely used in Australia and Europe (excluding Germany, Italy and Greece)

3   a minimalist public sector role, as in the Netherlands, Japan and the USA, where private sector promotion is dominant

4   other models that are entirely funded from taxation of tourists and tourism rather than state support for destination marketing as a concept.

Most NTOs are engaged in destination promotion, usually aimed at the international market (though in large countries they may also target the domestic market). NTOs are also involved in the maintenance of a network of tourism offices in key international source markets, though this is more restricted in less developed countries whose budgets are very restricted. The most up-to-date figures on NTO budgets are shown in Table 10.4, updating Pike's (2003) excellent review of this area.

Expenditure on marketing is only one of the influences that affect tourism volumes to a country. There is no easy way to link marketing spend to performance in attracting visitors even though many NTOs use visitor numbers and their spending as a Return on Investment (ROI) for their expenditure on advertising. Marketing of a destination is more about the subliminal changes to visitor perceptions to encourage and shape their interest in a place rather than a direct influencer of demand, in the same way that advertising affects fast-moving consumer goods.

There is new research evidence in tourism that the cultural and psychological association which people develop with a place, known as 'place bonding', may be important in developing the desire to visit a destination. This is still a relatively new idea in tourism research but has a long history of research in other areas such as recreation, and could begin to help us understand how NTOs and marketing strategies can target the very qualities to which visitors have an emotional attachment in a destination. In this respect, destination marketing is only the first stage in trying to raise the visitor's awareness of the place, and provoking the notion of what bonding associations they have and whether these can be fostered to create an image of a highly desirable and must-see place. There is also a more substantial marketing effort by the tourism industry, much of which has often been led by airlines and tour operators. Indeed, given the low levels of industry membership of tourist boards, NTOs only have a limited influence in developing an industry-led campaign that seeks to send a specific message to potential visitors. Even so, in some countries (e.g. Scotland and Singapore), the efforts are very successful in harmonizing marketing messages where they are directed towards target

Table 10.4	Examples of National Tourism Organizations and destination-specific marketing organization spending on tourism/tourism initiatives
Country/organization	**Budget (year)**
Tourism Ireland	€60 million (2013)
Hawaii Tourist Authority, USA	US$82 million (2014)
Choose Chicago, USA	US$32.6 million (2013)
Orlando, Florida, USA	US$49.8 million (2013)
Los Angeles, USA	US$24.5 million (2009–2010)
New York City, USA	US$40 million (2013)
San Francisco, USA	US$27.4 million (2012)
Montreal, Canada	C$24.5 million (2009)
VisitLondon, UK, reformed as London and Partners, London, UK	£17 million (2009/10) £20.2 million (2012)
Miami, USA	US$23 million (2009)
Las Vegas Convention and Visitor Authority, USA	US$113 million (2013)
Atout France (formerly Maison de la France)	€87.9 million (2012)
Tourism Australia (formerly Australian Tourist Commission)	AUS$160 million (2012–13)

Source: compiled from National Tourism Organization and City Tourism websites

markets and specific segments with growth potential. This approach recognizes that the NTO has an influence far beyond that of individual businesses and industry-sector groups such as tour operators as shown in Innovation in Sustainability 10.2.

There are many other marketing initiatives that seek to promote a destination using conventional print and new forms of media such as the worldwide web. They do this by creating promotional messages and symbols/messages, and using promotional media to provide merchandizing opportunities as well as providing incentives to buy. In each case the work of NTOs in place and product marketing is to develop a product substitute role (i.e. come to our destination as opposed to a competitor's), by using advertising opportunities to access the destination's products and thereby provide a purchasing mechanism in some cases. The launch of an e-commerce site is now seen as a vital element of any NTO strategy for destination marketing, since it offers a mechanism for generating a sale and a convenient method of communicating with the customer. It has been evident throughout this book that e-commerce is now a vital element for all sectors of the tourism industry in a rapidly changing business environment. It can be beneficial for NTOs to engage in e-commerce for the wider tourism sector, since tourists select particular place products (i.e. destinations) in their holiday decision-making process. Tourists normally consider a limited set of place products, often on the basis of limited knowledge of the destination and available options. Yet the holiday may be as much

INNOVATION IN SUSTAINABILITY 10.2
DEVELOPING A COUNTRY-BASED APPROACH TO
SUSTAINABLE TOURISM MANAGEMENT

The case of Scotland, Dr Joanne Connell, Exeter University Business School

Sustainability is a concept that transcends borders, and its evolution from a global way of thinking to a local application through national, regional and local policy and strategy is crucial to its success. Sustainability as a concept means only using resources at a rate which allows replenishment and does not exceed environmental capacity and implies that:

- sustainable development does not enrich one group of people over another
- we need to replace the current philosophy of economic growth/development with sustainable growth/development
- under current market conditions we need to work towards this as a goal.

This innovation insight looks at how policy and strategy are formulated and implemented in relation to sustainable tourism at a country level in the case of Scotland. However, prior to focusing on Scotland and the rationale for examining this case, it is useful to highlight that there are a myriad of organizations and bodies responsible for progressing the implementation of sustainable tourism, as Chapter 9 indicated. This is represented in the case of the UK in Figure 10.4 which looks at examples of policy and the organizations progressing this at different geographical scales from the global to the local level, with a focus on the UK. As was illustrated earlier in this chapter, Local Economic Partnerships (LEPs) have been the new focus for the regional organization of tourism in England but a different structure exists in Scotland under devolved government structures.

In Scotland, Scottish Government Economic Strategy (2011) identifies the six strategic priorities which will accelerate recovery, drive sustainable economic growth and develop a more resilient and adaptable economy, which provides a context in which tourism can be located at a policy level. Its six priorities are:

C1 Supportive Business Environment
C2 Transition to a Low Carbon Economy
C3 Learning, Skills and Well-being
C4 Infrastructure Development and Place
C5 Effective Government
C6 Equity.

All of these embrace the principles of sustainability, and sustainable tourism is one of the priorities for development. This is a logical step for Scotland given that 55 per cent of visitors come for landscape and scenery, and the natural environment is a key attribute in its brand proposition. Sustainable tourism is a primary issue for Scotland's National Tourism Organization, VisitScotland, which has been viewed very positively internationally for its innovative approach to embracing sustainable principles through its quality assurance scheme to drive up performance (the Green Tourism Business Scheme – see Chapter 6). It has clearly aligned its activities and actions on tourism directly to the

Scottish Government strategy so it dovetails with it and complements the overall ambitions of a more sustainable Scotland.

For VisitScotland, sustainable tourism means:

- greener transport, encouraging visitors to use public transport and innovations in cleaner forms of transport (such as the greater use of electric vehicles as piloted in National Parks such as the New Forest in England)
- addressing seasonal and geographical pressures to try to achieve a greater spread of visitors to avoid adverse impacts on the natural environment at peak times and spreading the load across the year with campaigns such as *Surprise Yourself*
- understanding the impacts of tourism through a better measurement of the impacts on the environment and communities
- greener accommodation through expanding further the membership of the Green Tourism Business Scheme which is the largest in Europe with over 800 members.

One strand of promoting the natural environment and sustainability by VisitScotland was its 2013 Year of Natural Scotland, which was a chance to enhance Scotland's reputation as a place of outstanding natural beauty. Its underlying rationale was *to promote Scotland's stunning natural beauty and*

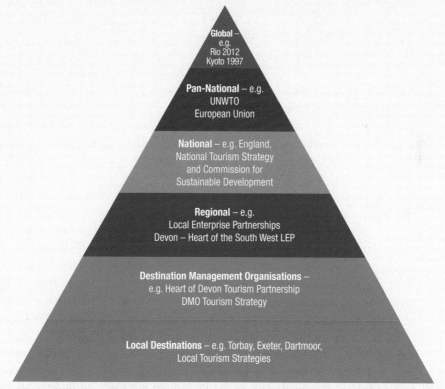

Figure 10.4
The sustainable tourism policy pyramid

Source: © Joanne Connell, reproduced with permission from the author

biodiversity, and promote ways in which visitors can enjoy our beautiful landscapes, wildlife and heritage responsibly.

The VisitScotland Natural Scotland Growth Fund has supported marketing projects aimed at increasing tourism spend throughout Scotland while showcasing its natural heritage.

Eight key themes were developed to cover Scotland's vast wealth of natural product (Natural landscapes, Built heritage, Natural larder, Sustainable tourism, Natural playground, Flora and fauna, Art in nature and Nature in cities). The Year of Natural Scotland was a chance to enhance Scotland's reputation as a place of outstanding natural beauty, underpinned by a clear link with the sustainability objectives that VisitScotland wished to achieve within a strategic context (Table 10.5).

Table 10.5 The strategic aims of Year of Natural Scotland

Sustain and build upon the momentum generated by major events

Enhance Scotland's reputation as a place of oustanding natural beauty with a landscape and biodiversity to enjoy responsibly

Increase awareness of the activities available in Scotland's natural and built tourism attractions

Promote Scotland as a beautiful and accessible destination for active pursuits

Promote Scotland as the perfect stage for sporting and outdoor events and festivals, and reinforce Scotland's natural heritage at existing events

Bring together the work of relevant industry bodies and public sector organizations across Scotland under one themed campaign

Source: J. Connell, developed from VisitScotland

the place as the place is the holiday for the tourist. In contrast, the various businesses and organizations associated with tourism focus on specific aspects of the place product (e.g. an attraction or facility). For this reason, NTOs may often seek to address any shortcomings in the destination through the application of more sophisticated marketing techniques that change the visitor's perception of the destination. For example, enjoyEngland.com seeks to portray 'England as real, fun, and indulgent, incorporating these into the brand essence that everyone can share' (VisitEngland 2005) to address negative images of England that have arisen because of the cost of being a tourist, the unreliability of the weather and quality issues in tourism provision. The e-commerce strategy of the NTO and the ready provision of visual information and images may help to broker the tourist as purchaser with the business as a seller. It can help to promote an initial interest registered by a potential tourist after they became aware of the destination, and encourage a follow-up visit to a website. This linking the purchaser and seller electronically often requires NTOs and the tourism industry to work collaboratively through a partnership approach.

The growing collaboration between public and private sectors in countries such as Canada and Australia has indicated how powerful these new NTO partnerships can be in marketing a dynamic industry. In 2012, tourism revenue in Canada was C$82 billion (C$67 billion from domestic tourism), with 608 000 employed in tourism. The Canadian Tourism Commission (CTC), which has a remit to seek private sector partnerships,

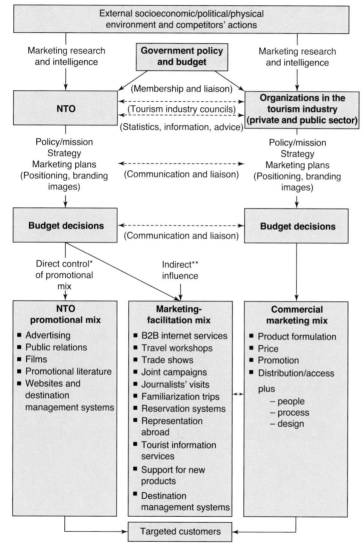

Figure 10.5

The destination marketing process for National Tourist Organizations

Source: reprinted from V. Middleton and J. Clarke (2001) *Marketing for Travel and Tourism.* Oxford: Butterworth-Heinemann with permission from Elsevier

raised its funding for marketing from C$15 million in 1995 to C$100 million in 1998/99, with the private sector contributing 50 per cent of the funds. By 2004, this core funding from the public sector had risen to C$79 million, with matched funding from the tourism sector, and by 2007 core funding was almost C$100 million and C$132.9 million in 2009. In 2012 this reached C$138 million. The ratio of partner contributions to CTC annual funding was 1.26:1 in 2009 and 1:0.80 in 2012 (ahead of a target of 1:0.60). The CTC calculated that for every C$1 it invested in marketing, it generated C$56 for the visitor economy in 2012. The marketing activities of NTOs are outlined in Figure 10.5 which highlights the different options available such as developing a visionary promotional strategy. They may involve branding as a process, though the range and nature of activities will be dependent upon the nature of the budget, and may also be controlled by the NTO's remit, established by legislation (such as the 1969 Development of Tourism Act in the UK). Figure 10.5 also reiterates the coordination and liaison roles the NTOs perform and how tourism businesses interact with the public sector.

Below the level of the NTO, regional or area tourist boards perform a similar function. These bodies emphasize the attributes of their local area and many local authorities seek to promote their city or locality, in a lesser way, to establish a destination as a distinctive and unique place to visit, emphasizing the unique selling proposition (USP). In Northern Ireland, there are six regional tourism partnerships (RTPs). These are themed to reflect the destination they represent and unique attributes of the area and comprise: Derry Visitor and Convention Bureau, Causeway Coast and Glens Tourism Partnership, Visit Belfast, Western Regional Tourism Partnership, Flavour of Tyrone, and Fermanagh Lakeland Tourism. Each RTP has funding from the public and private sectors in line with other parts of the UK. They are largely membership organizations, so businesses have to pay a fee to join and in return they are able to draw upon the RTP's services, which include marketing, advertising, training and research and development. The RTPs' income streams are supported by the Northern Ireland Tourist Board (NITB) and local authority contributions as well as through commercial income (e.g. sales of goods to visitors and commissions on sales).

The future of the public sector in the management of tourism

At a global scale, there has been a growing consensus among governments that private sector tourism interests (i.e. stakeholders) need to work more closely with the public sector to manage the marketing, planning, control and development of tourism. Part of the marketing logic here is to gain industry ownership of what is being marketed in terms of sales and promotion. The term 'tourism collateral' is now in vogue to describe how the tourism sector gets buy-in to the collateral of the destination from the private sector (e.g. the brochures, websites, posters and visual material to promote the destination) so as to feel an integral part of the messages, images and focus of how the area is being sold to tourists. This is part of a withdrawal of central government from direct management of many areas of public activity, reflecting a desire to see a greater use of public–private partnerships to govern the tourism sector, where the private sector are seen as joint owners of the tourism collateral. In many countries, national or devolved government still plays a role in funding NTOs and other tourism-related functions. There is a recognition of the need for the tourism sector to be in charge and responsible for its own destiny. Whilst public sector-led marketing remains the norm in most countries, there is a greater awareness of the need for tourism to be a self-financing activity and debates over the possible value of tourist taxes (e.g. bed taxes) to fund public sector planning and management of tourism. For example, the Las Vegas Convention and Visitor Authority levies a 12 per cent room tax that generates U$213 million, around 80 per cent of the organization's budget. Around half of its budget is allocated to marketing the destination.

In some cases, the withdrawal of central government involvement in tourism and the replacement with quangos (quasi-autonomous government organizations) reflects a changing philosophy that industry-led bodies are more appropriate entities to deliver tourism policy and its implementation as the case study in Web Case 10.3 highlighted. However, this is not being accompanied by the rationalization of tourism organizations that input into policy and planning. To the contrary, with the growth of tourism associations and interest groups, there is a greater need than ever for the public sector to coordinate, liaise and interact with such bodies to monitor and evaluate the needs and issues that impact upon the performance and management of tourism. However, since policy-making is an inherently political process, the historical role of the public sector as the main agency formulating tourism policy seems set to continue. But tourism policy monitoring and evaluation still remain a neglected area for many public sector agencies, and there is a need for more critical evaluation of the assumptions behind policy (i.e. if we do A will it lead to B and if so, with what effect?).

If the public sector is to play a greater role in tourism, understanding the consequences of specific tourism policies, requires a more explicit recognition of whether policy is successful or a failure. Indeed, there is a degree of introverted, inward-looking thinking that fails to question the need for government intervention in tourism. Policy analysis and evaluation in the public sector has remained generalized in many tourism contexts, since poorly specified objectives and goals may contribute to perceived failures in policy. There is also a widespread recognition that performance measures to evaluate policy impacts on tourism are poorly developed. The result is that many crude measures associated with visitor arrivals, spending and impacts are used which may not necessarily be directly affected by tourism-related policies. If the policy is flawed, its implementation and integration into planning mechanisms will not deal with the issues it originally was intended to address. The growth in the number of agencies involved in tourism inevitably delays the speed at which change in policy and planning can be affected. It is no surprise, therefore, that urban development corporations in the UK in the 1980s, despite criticisms about their lack of accountability, did remove planning obstacles, allowing areas to be regenerated quickly. In many cases the tourism development process was thereby streamlined to remove endless tiers of consultation, strategy development and disagreement over development goals. In 2001, for example, South Africa Tourism (SAT) took a policy decision to shift from a more traditional approach to marketing the destination as a place to visit, to one which was consumer-oriented and aligned to destination marketing objectives (VisitScotland also did this). By adopting a focused and targeted segmentation strategy, SAT has evaluated 'who its tourists are, where they come from and why'. This served as a basis for identifying the range of actions necessary to invest in and develop these markets. As part of a wider global competitiveness study, SAT was able to recognize what marketing it needed to undertake to remain a competitive destination.

Whilst such a radical approach is not advocated for the public sector in tourism, there are compelling arguments for nationally determined tourism policy, strategy and planning to remove some of the layers of administration and bureaucracy. A more centralized approach that avoids a multitude of agencies, each having to review policy and planning at each level, would provide the context for area-based tourism planning and strategies, requiring cooperation at the local level to implement policy and planning. At the national level, the NTO would simply market the destination, with research and market intelligence managed by an agency led and funded by the industry, with regional or area-based tourism organizations driving policy and planning at the local level. This structure for tourism may be radical but is unlikely to be implemented due to politics, as lobby groups and vested interests in the existing system resist change if they perceive it as leading to a loss of power and input in decision-making in relation to policy.

CHAPTER REVIEW

 ## References

COSLA and Economic Development and Planning Executive Group (2002) *Review of the Area Tourist Boards*. Edinburgh: COSLA.

Elliot, J. (1997) *Tourism, Politics and Public Sector Management*. London: Routledge.

Getz, D. (1987) Tourism planning and research: Traditions, models and futures. Paper presented at the Australian Travel Research Workshop, Bunbury, Western Australia, 5–6 November.

Hall, C. M. (2007) *Tourism Planning: Policies, Processes and Relationships*, 2nd edn. Harlow: Prentice Hall.

Hall, C. M. and Jenkins, J. (1995) *Tourism and Public Policy*. London: Routledge.

Inskeep, E. (1994) *National and Regional Planning*. London: Routledge/World Tourism Organization.

Jeffries, D. (2001) *Governments and Tourism*. Oxford: Butterworth-Heinemann.

Middleton, V. and Hawkins, R. (1998) *Sustainable Tourism*. Oxford: Butterworth-Heinemann.

OECD (2008) *Tourism in OECD countries 2008: Trends and Policies*. Paris: OECD.

Page, D. (2002) Byron Bay tourism. Private Member's Statement to the House. Parliament of New South Wales, 7 May. *Hansard*: 1623.

Page, S. J. and Connell, J. (2009) *Tourism: A Modern Synthesis*, 3rd edn. London: Cengage Learning.

Page, S. J. and Thorn, K. (1997) Towards sustainable tourism planning in New Zealand: Public sector planning responses. *Journal of Sustainable Tourism*, 5(1): 59–78.

Pike, S. (2003) *Destination Marketing Organisations*. Oxford: Pergamon.

Touche Ross (1988) *London Tourism Accommodation in the 1990s*. London: Touche Ross.

Turner, J. (1997) The policy process. In B. Axford, G. Browning, R. Huggins, B. Rosamond and J. Turner (eds) *Politics: An Introduction*. London: Routledge.

VisitEngland (2005) *Enjoy England Strategy*. London: VisitEngland.

World Commission on the Environment and Development (1987) *Our Common Future*, Bründtland Commission's Report. Oxford: Oxford University Press.

World Tourism Organization (1998) *Guide for Local Authorities on Developing Sustainable Tourism*. Madrid: WTO.

Further reading

The most digestible overview of tourism policy is:

Hall, C. M. and Jenkins, J. (1995) *Tourism and Public Policy*. London: Routledge.

For the most interesting overview of tourism planning with many good examples and case studies see also:

Dredge, D. and Jenkins, J. (2007) *Tourism Planning and Policy*. Milton, Qld: John Wiley and Sons Australia Ltd.

Hall, C. M. (2007) *Tourism Planning: Policies, Processes and Relationships*, 2nd edn. Harlow: Prentice Hall.

www.visitscotland.com

Questions

1   Why does the public sector need to intervene in the tourism market? Are its reasons driven by political concerns or the pressure exerted on it by lobby groups?

2   How is tourism policy formulated? Who are the main actors and stakeholders in policy formulation in tourism?

3   How does tourism planning occur in practice?

4   Should public support for tourism be driven by arguments surrounding the wider social benefits which accrues to destinations? Or should the public sector support mechanisms for tourism be equally financed by the public and private sector?

Access additional resources

*   For students: Multiple choice questions for each chapter, video links and further reading.

*   For instructors: PowerPoint slides with tables and diagrams, additional case studies, video links and further reading.

11 Managing the visitor and their impacts

Learning outcomes

This chapter examines the practical ways in which visitors and visitor sites are managed by agencies and the tourism sector. It discusses the typical range of economic, social, cultural and environmental pressures that tourism exerts on the resource base on which it depends and the ways management tools may be used to develop a more sustainable resource base. On completion of this chapter, you should be able to understand:

- what the problems induced by visitor activity are
- how researchers approach the study of the economic, social, cultural and environmental impacts of tourism
- what visitor management is and the tools available to address visitor impacts in soft and hard ways
- the role of tourism planning, development and management in the case of Venice, which highlights the economic, social, cultural and environmental problems induced by tourism.

Introduction

Many of the previous chapters have examined how the members of the tourism industry manage and develop their businesses to produce a product or experience for a tourist. In this chapter the consequences of these actions in terms of tourist consumption are considered in relation to destination areas. This requires an understanding of the visitor as an agent of change in destinations due to the impacts induced directly or indirectly by their actions. Quite simply, it discusses where, why and how such impacts occur and with what effects. Promotion and advertising by the tourism sector (i.e. tour operators, NTOs and other promotional organizations) assist in generating tourism demand as a consumptive activity, which culminates in both positive and negative effects for the places it affects. These effects often co-exist, making policy-making, planning and management problematic owing to the tendency to create beneficial and undesirable impacts simultaneously. For this reason, this chapter will focus on some of the tools and approaches used in tourism studies to understand how tourism generates impacts, how these can be managed and the lessons that can be learned.

In any discussion of tourism's impacts, three principal areas of concern exist: the economic effects of tourism; its social and cultural effects and, of course, the environmental dimension upon which the consumption of tourism experiences is often based. Since many of these impacts are site- or place-specific, it is useful to have some understanding of the geography of tourism to identify who goes where, when and why, and what impacts occur where.

The geography of tourism: Its application to impact analysis

Geography is about the study of the environment, people and the co-existence of man with the environment at different scales, ranging from the international through the national and regional to the local level. More advanced studies of tourism have shown that the contribution of geography can be significant, with its interest in place and space (i.e. how activities are organized in different locations) because tourism is an inherently dynamic activity that requires movement from an origin to destination area. Many studies of geography and tourism are highly academic and based on theory and concepts to understand the complexity of tourism in time and space (i.e. how it operates at different times and in different places). But there are certain research skills that geographers use, the application of which to tourism can help in understanding why tourists go on holiday to certain locations, when they go, what they do when there, where the impacts of such visitor activity occur and what can be done to minimize the effects. As data in Chapter 5 on airport arrivals suggest, the scale of tourist travel is substantial and so understanding the dynamics and elements of tourist mobility are vital to managing tourism activity. As geographers look at the scale of travel, it is then possible for them to begin to understand more about the dynamics of tourist travel within a specific region, such as Europe, and the trends in the market, and then to consider these issues as a basis for understanding how tourism operates in the region.

European tourism: Trends and patterns

According to the European Travel Commission (ETC) (2007), France and Spain are the leading tourist destinations in the EU. In Spain, an interesting trend is the tendency for up to half of tourists to make their own travel arrangements using the internet, which reflects the impact of the low-cost airlines in creating demand for seat-only sales. The ETC noted that the low-cost airlines' impact was less pronounced on capital cities than it was on many smaller secondary destinations which have seen major growth.

The geography of European tourism based on air transport: Key trends and impacts

There are two techniques that can be used to address some of these issues surrounding visitor behaviour to understand the geographical patterns of tourism, particularly the nature of tourist flows, so that the scale and extent of tourism can be understood at different scales. The first technique is a simple analysis and mapping of tourism flows between origin and destination countries, to highlight the main flows. At the EU level, the largest tourist flows occur from the UK to Spain whilst the next most important flow is Germany to Spain. The top city-to-city flows of travellers are dominated by holiday and business travel. The top ten city–city pairs account for around 50 per cent of all intra-regional travel in the EU. Here the above-mentioned large numbers of flights from the UK and Germany to Spain and the Mediterranean, including business travel, are clearly shown. In addition markets that are near to a land border and a popular destination (e.g. flows from France to Spain) have a strong propensity to use car-based travel, which results in seasonal effects upon the roads and airports in each respective destination area. Even at such a rudimentary level, such patterns begin to explain the seasonal rhythms of tourism, the effect of mass travel on destination areas and the pressure this causes on infrastructure, the environment and people in the resort areas. Research by Eurostat (the European Statistical Agency) on the stability of tourism flows in the EU based on hotel occupancy data shows that tourism is largely concentrated in the June–September months although this does vary by country. These variations therefore highlight the importance of understanding the timing of tourist trips and where they are destined if one is to begin to identify where impacts will occur. This historic pattern for 1999 has changed significantly with the introduction of low-cost airlines which now have almost 20 per cent of the market for air travel in Europe. In 2007, ten of the top 25 low-cost country-pair flows involved the UK. The UK had almost 570 daily low-cost flights serving domestic destinations. This was followed by 366 on the Spain–UK route, 281 on German domestic services and 196 on UK–Ireland flights and 173 on France–UK flights. A more up-to-date assessment of the low-cost airlines (LCAs) is provided by Dobruszkes (2013) who analysed LCAs in Europe, highlighting their contribution to 70 per cent of the growth in intra-European flights (i.e. within Europe) and 64 per cent of seat kilometres travelled in 1995–2012. This reflects the dominance of the LCA model, which accounted for 31 per cent of the intra-European flight market. Figure 11.1 shows that the main focus of LCAs in Europe is on major urban centres, as discussed earlier, and coastal tourist destinations, using a combination of main and secondary airports. Dobruszkes (2013) illustrates that LCAs also serve island destinations not accessible by land transport. The expansion of the EU to 27 member states since 2004 explained the rise of LCAs in eastern and southern Europe, as new open sky agreements such as between the EU and Morocco contributed to growth in North Africa. At a country level, the effects of LCA traffic growth can be seen in the case of Spain. Figure 11.2 illustrates the impact of such LCA growth within Spain, illustrating how coastal areas and secondary airports have contributed to local tourism development compared to the major urban centres for the period 2002–2010. What this discussion illustrates is that the market for LCAs is extremely fluid, where growth in some markets had seen contraction in others; as markets are no longer deemed viable, carriers withdraw services. However, Dobruszkes (2013) noted that in 2004 the median distance flown by an LCA was 634 km. By 2012 this had risen to 896 km, as LCAs seek new unserved routes/destinations, although 1500 km seemed to be the furthest distance for optimum route operation. The outcome is a greater geographical diversification of routes leading to destinations served by LCAs, which are often the sole operator to some secondary destinations, although these are

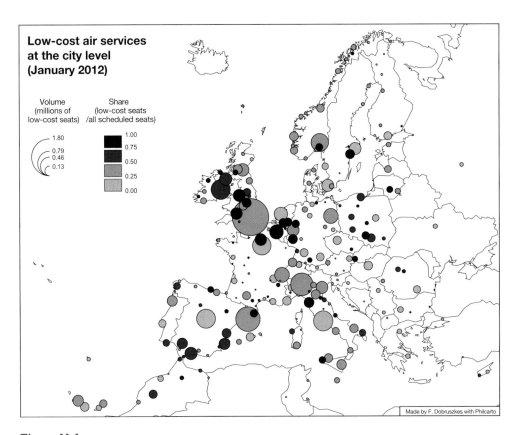

Figure 11.1
Low-cost services at the city level: Take-offs within, from and to Europe (EU 27), Iceland, Norway and Switzerland

Source: Dobruszkes (2013: 79)

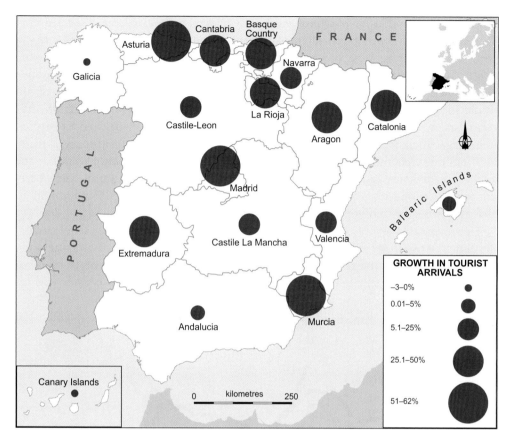

Figure 11.2
The geography of low-cost airline development in Spain 2002–2010

Source: based on UNWTO data

only a smaller component of the overall European route network. This has also developed a dependency by some more regional airports on single LCAs as the main service upon which their tourism sector is dependent for arrivals.

The second more sophisticated method of analysis used to understand how visitors can impact upon destinations through their activities is to study their activity patterns (what they do when, where, for how long and the variations according to market segment). This can utilize the recent advances in information technology made by geographers in terms of the new Geographical Information Systems (GIS). GIS uses sophisticated computer programs, typically the industry standard ArcInfo and variants, to collect data on tourism with a geographical dimension. The geographical elements of the data (i.e. a tourist's travel pattern and specific activities undertaken at each point on an itinerary) can then be recorded, mapped and modelled to understand how overall patterns of tourist activity exist in a location or region. This was recently undertaken for Loch Lomond and Trossachs National Park by Connell (2005) as a basis for establishing the nature and hierarchy of visitor destinations that existed in the Park for the new National Park plan. These destinations could then be used to establish how to manage visitor impacts and what planning mechanisms were needed to cope with seasonal demands. On the basis of such an exercise, we can then begin to identify where particular impacts are occurring as shown in Figure 11.3 based on car-based stopping points. We would also be able to identify the geographical patterns of tourism business development, to establish where the main development opportunities exist. The exercise would be useful in identifying what planning measures are needed where and when to constrain or facilitate tourism development and the tools that might need to be used to manage different patterns of visitor behaviour (see Plate 11.1). Not surprisingly, many local authority planning departments use such techniques in their daily work but the application to tourism has been quite limited to date. GIS is a powerful, yet greatly under-utilized research tool in tourism. It has an enormous potential application to assist in managing, developing and understanding the dynamics of tourism.

The integration of different data sources in GIS has a major potential to visually illustrate the dynamics of tourism, and the different impacts that exist, by linking other sources of data together (e.g. records of land degradation, environmental pollution, economic data). This helps us to identify and understand some of the impacts of tourism and where management measures will need to be developed. Therefore, with these issues in mind, attention now turns to the different impacts to understand what

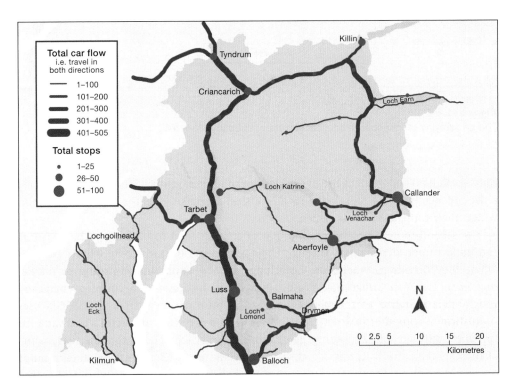

Figure 11.3
Visitor destination management and infrastructure survey

Souce: Connell, J. and Page, S. J. (2008) Exploring the spatial patterns of car-based tourism in Loch Lomond and Trossachs National Park. *Tourism Management*, 29(3): 561–580

Plate 11.1
Clovely, Devon: A former fishing village and historic attraction. Visitors pay for entry to the steep cobbled village

Source: author

relationships exist with tourism, how to measure them and what management tools may be used.

Analysing the impact of tourism

One of the major problems facing planners in assessing tourism impacts is the establishment of an appropriate baseline against which to measure the existing and future changes induced by tourism. This is a problem mentioned in scientific studies of Environmental Assessment (EA) which seek to combine different data sources to understand how tourism development affects the environment. EA acknowledges the practical problems of establishing baseline studies and in disaggregating the impact of tourism from other economic activities since it is hard to isolate tourism from other forms of economic development. Mathieson and Wall (1982) highlight the precise nature of the problem since in many tourist destinations it is almost impossible to reconstruct the environment minus the effects induced by tourism (see Table 11.1 for key studies on tourism impacts).

Table 11.1 Key studies on tourism impacts

Forsyth, P. *et al.* (2008) *The Carbon Footprint of Australian Tourism*. Sydney: Cooperative Research Centre for Tourism.

Gössling, S. and Hall, C. M. (eds) (2006) *Global Environmental Problems*. London: Routledge.

Gössling, S., Peeters, P., Ceron, J., Dubois, G., Patterson, T. and Richardson, R. (2005) The eco-efficiency of tourism. *Ecological Economics*, 54: 417–434.

Hall, C. M and Lew, A. (2009) *Understanding and Managing Tourism Impacts*. London: Routledge.

Holden, A. (2008) *Tourism and the Environment*, 2nd edn. London: Routledge.

Mathieson, A. and Wall, G. (1982) *Tourism: Economic, Physical and Social Impacts*. Harlow: Longman.

Murphy, P. (1983) *Tourism: A Community Approach*. London: Metheun.

Wall, G. and Mathieson, A. (2006) *Tourism: Change, Impacts and Opportunities*. Harlow: Pearson.

A range of key studies on tourism impacts are also reproduced in:

Connell, J. and Page, S. J. (eds) (2008) *Sustainable Tourism*, Vols 1–4. London: Routledge.

While it is widely acknowledged that tourism is a major agent affecting the natural and built environments, isolating the precise causes or processes leading to specific impacts is difficult: is tourism the principle agent of change or is it part of a wider process of development in a particular destination? As Mathieson and Wall (1982: 5) argue

> tourism may also be a highly visible scapegoat for problems which existed prior to the advent of modern tourism. It certainly is easier to blame tourism than it is to address the conditions of society and the environment.

The complex interactions of tourism with the built and physical environments make it virtually impossible to measure impacts with any degree of precision. Even so, impacts may be large scale and tangible (e.g. where a destination is saturated by visitors) or small scale and intangible.

Further factors complicating the analysis of tourism's impact are the extent to which the effect of tourism is necessarily continuous in time (i.e. how seasonal is it?) and the geography of tourism (as tourism activity tends to concentrate in certain locations such as destinations where the supply of services and facilities occurs). At this point, one needs to begin to identify specific indicators of tourism impacts chosen to represent the complex interaction of tourism and the destination to guide the impact assessment. Whilst this involves complex methods of analysis which may be aided by GIS and computer modelling, it is clear that impacts are more than just costs and benefits for specific destinations.

One useful starting point in analysing the impact of tourism in a practical context is to establish how to measure visitation levels as a basis for calculating visitor numbers

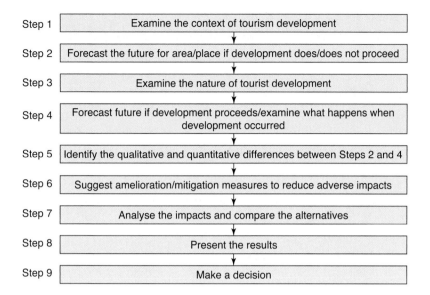

Figure 11.4
Potter's tourism impact framework
Source: after Potter (1978); Pearce (1989); Page (1995)

for a destination. Yet one of the ongoing problems with visitor surveys is their value, as they are often undertaken at visitor attractions or based on accommodation occupancy rates as a means to establish the scale of visitors. Their ability to yield a representative sample of visitation at the destination, and thus their reliability, is debatable. Therefore, where visitor information is collected, it needs to be related to other forms of statistical information to establish the volume of tourism.

An early work by Potter (1978) provided a general framework for impact assessment. This is shown in Figure 11.4 where the impacts incorporate environmental, social and economic issues. Potter's approach has a number of steps, starting with the context of the development and proceeding through making a decision on a particular development that is useful in a planning and management context.

The economic impact of tourism

The economic measurement of tourism has a long history in many countries. The study by Ogilvie (1933), *The Tourist Movement*, is one of the early attempts to illustrate the significance of outbound tourism's impact on the national economy. Ogilvie (1933: 135) compiled tourist expenditure by British residents in Europe and outside Europe in the 1920s and early 1930s (Table 11.2) using Ministry of Labour and other official statistics. Ogilvie estimated average expenditure by visitors to show that UK residents spent over £24 million in 1921 using an adjusted Cost of Living Index which rose to over £33 million in 1928 but then dropped due to the stock market crash and subsequent recession. What is interesting from Ogilvie's study is that he observed a £10–£11 million

Table 11.2 Expenditure of United Kingdom tourists abroad, 1921–1931

Year	British residents		Foreign residents (average £20)	Unadjusted total	Final total, adjusted to Cost of Living Index (Ministry of Labour: 1929 = 100)
	On tour to countries outside Europe and the Mediterranean area (average £100)	On tour to Europe and the Mediterranean area (average £30)			
	£	£	£	£	£
1921	1 948 800	14 405 000	1 205 000	17 558 800	24 231 000
1922	2 009 500	16 679 200	1 222 300	19 911 000	22 300 000
1923	2 233 400	20 284 700	1 190 400	23 708 500	25 131 000
1924	2 192 800	20 946 500	1 068 100	24 207 400	25 902 000
1925	2 645 300	24 118 600	1 065 400	27 829 300	29 777 000
1926	2 717 000	25 044 500	1 072 000	28 833 500	30 275 000
1927	2 926 100	25 486 500	1 020 100	29 432 700	30 021 000
1928	3 193 500	28 546 000	1 029 700	32 769 200	33 097 000
1929	3 271 700	28 548 100	974 000	32 793 800	32 794 000
1930	3 245 100	29 365 800	952 500	33 563 400	32 221 000
1931	2 797 000	26 882 800	848 800	30 528 600	27 476 000

Source: Ogilvie (1933)

deficit in the 1920s and early 1930s in the balance of UK outbound tourist spending and inbound tourism from other countries. This is one of the most notable studies to make the vital point that tourism is important to the economy of many countries.

Ogilvie's innovative and landmark study also compiled a number of European sources to develop this point for many of the world's leading countries in the late 1920s/early 1930s. This not only illustrates the scale of their inbound tourists but also the scale of their outbound markets and the scale of spending, to calculate the impact on national travel accounts as they would later be called. Table 11.3 outlines these features for 24 countries and offers further detail for each country. Even in the late 1920s, France was established as the leading inbound destination whilst the USA and UK had a travel deficit, features which still exist today.

On the basis of this early economic analysis, one can see why tourism is used by many national and local governments as a mechanism to aid the development and regeneration of economies. Politicians and decision-makers see that it offers renewed opportunities for work, income and revenue for the local economy as places are affected by global, national and local economic restructuring. There is a prevailing perception among national and local governments that economic benefits accrue to tourism destinations, which then create employment opportunities and stimulate the development process in resorts and localities. The economic development process is often cited by public and private sector developers to pump-prime regeneration initiatives in declining areas (e.g. the inner city) to stimulate tourism-led economic growth as shown in Figure 8.1. For the local population, it is often argued by proponents of tourism development that investment in tourist and recreational facilities provides a positive contribution to the local economy. One very controversial illustration of this can be seen in the debate on the impact of casino development on localities: this is very topical, given the reform of legislation governing the development of casinos in the UK. Taxes levied from gambling generate positive economic benefits for localities in terms of visitor spending and employment, and this is being emphasized by proponents of plans for casino development in Blackpool. In Auckland, New Zealand, a casino constructed in the 1990s acts as the city's main drawcard. The scale of the impact on the local economy can be gauged from the 12 000 visitors a day it receives, but around 80 per cent of visitors are residents or New Zealanders. Gaming revenue averages NZ$595 000 a day (including goods and service tax at 12.5 per cent) and the operating company employs 2400 people.

Tourism is not necessarily a stable source of income for destinations because tourists are not noted for their high levels of customer loyalty to tourism destinations. Page and Hall (2003) identify a number of features to support this argument based on urban tourism destinations:

- tourism is a fickle industry, being highly seasonal, and this has implications for investment and the type of employment created. Tourism employment is often characterized as being low skill, poorly paid and low status, and lacking long-term stability. One of the very serious problems that has been raised in developed countries is the rise of zero hours contracts in the tourism and hospitality sector. Zero hours contracts imply that employers are not under any obligation to provide a minimum number of hours of work, but can keep a workforce supply available. The use of such contracts may offer the employer a flexible workforce to accommodate seasonal and weekly peaks in demand, but offers no stability for employees. In the UK, it was estimated that around half of the 7 million employees in the hospitality sector were part-time employees and a proportion were on zero hours contracts, a phenomenon that is expanding in the UK
- the demand for tourism can easily be influenced by external factors (e.g. political unrest, unusual climatic and environmental conditions) which are beyond the control of destination areas
- the motivation for tourist travel to urban destinations is complex and variable and constantly changing in the competitive marketplace
- in economic terms, tourism is price and income elastic, which means that it is easily influenced by small changes to the price of the product and the disposable income of consumers
- many cities are becoming alike, a feature described as 'serial reproduction'. This means that once an idea for urban economic development is successful in one location, the concept diffuses to other places. The example of waterfront

Table 11.3 International tourist balances, 1928–1930

Country and year		£ thousands			
		Receipts from foreign tourists	Expenditure of national tourists abroad	Balance Credit	Debt
Albania	1928	159	12	147	—
	1929	198	12	186	—
	1930	198	32	166	—
Argentine (now Argentina)	1928–29	2379	5947	—	3568
	1929–30	2379	4956	—	2577
	1930–31	1982	3965	—	1983
Austria	1928	9078	1879	7199	—
	1929	7517	1879	5638	—
Bulgaria	1928	74	89	—	15
	1929	74	185	—	111
	1930	74	133	—	59
Canada	1928	54 802	20 671	34 131	—
	1929	61 480	22 870	38 610	—
	1930	57 370	23 281	34 089	—
Czechoslovakia	1928	4689	4263	426	—
	1929	4933	4324	609	—
	1930	4842	4263	579	—
Denmark	1928	551	826	—	275
	1929	826	1377	—	551
	1930	826	1377	—	551
Dutch East Indies (now Indonesia)	1928	578	8508	—	7930
	1929	496	7104	—	6608
	1930	413	5039	—	4626
Finland	1928	881	932	—	51
	1929	984	1140	—	156
	1930	984	1140	—	156
France	1928	72 450	12 075	60 375	—
	1929	80 500	12 075	68 425	—
	1930	—	—	68 425	—
Germany	1928	8811	14 685	—	5874
	1929	8811	14 685	—	5874
	1930	13 706 (a)	13 706	—	—

Table 11.3 *continued*

Country and year		£ thousands			
		Receipts from foreign tourists	Expenditure of national tourists abroad	Balance Credit	Debt
Hungary	1928	740	1369	—	629
	1929	787	1880	—	1093
	1930	960	2049	—	1089
Italy	1928	28 100	3600	24 500	—
	1929	26 100	3400	22 700	—
Japan	1928	3851	3831	20	—
	1929	4568	4312	256	—
Jugoslavia	1928	1307	1245	62	—
	1929	1481	1242	239	—
Lithuania	1928	240	286	—	46
	1929	277	312	—	35
	1930	279	436	—	156
New Zealand	1927–28	683	1657	—	974
	1928–29	720	1650	—	930
	1929–30	719	1671	—	952
Poland	1928	2266	3895	—	1629
	1929	3852	3801	51	—
Roumania	1929	615	430	185	—
	1930	492	344	148	—
Sweden	1928	—	—	—	1542
	1929	—	—	—	1652
	1930	—	—	—	1377
Switzerland	1928	15 700	3200	12 500	—
	1929	—	—	11 100	—
	1930	—	—	9700	—
Union of South Africa	1928	1076	4291	—	3215
	1929	1125	4461	—	3336
United Kingdom	1928	22 108	33 097	—	10 989
	1929	22 445	32 794	—	10 349
	1930	21 622	32 221	—	10 599
United States	1928	33 500	169 000	—	135 500
	1929	37 500	178 000	—	140 500
	1930	32 200	167 000	—	134 800

revitalization is a case in point; many projects are similar in structure and character across the world.

Source: modified from Page and Hall (2003)

Pearce (1989: 192) argued that 'the objective and detailed evaluation of the economic impact of tourism can be a long and complicated task'. This is because there is little agreement on what constitutes the tourism industry although it is normally classified in relation to:

- accommodation
- transport
- attractions
- the travel organizers' sector (e.g. travel agents)
- the destination organization sector.

Hospitality and ancillary services are also important. Understanding the economic impact of these disparate sectors of the economy requires a method of analysis that allows us to isolate the flow of income in the local tourism economy. This is notoriously difficult because of attributing the proportion of tourist expenditure on goods and services in relation to the total pattern of expenditure by all users of the destination (e.g. residents, workers and visitors). What we usually need to do is identify the different forms of tourist expenditure and how they affect the local economy. Typically these include:

- the nature of the destination area and its products, facilities and physical characteristics
- the volume and scale of tourist expenditure
- the state of the economic development and economy in the destination
- the size and nature of the local economy (i.e. is it dependent on services or manufacturing or is it a mixed economy?)
- the extent to which tourist expenditure circulates around the local economy and is not spent on 'imported' goods and services
- the degree to which the local economy has addressed the problem of seasonality and extends the destination appeal to all year round.

Source: modified from Page (1995)

On the basis of these factors, it is possible to assess whether the economic impact will be beneficial or have a detrimental effect on the economy. In this respect, it is possible to identify some of the commonly cited economic benefits of tourism:

- the generation of income for the local economy
- the creation of new employment opportunities
- improvements to the structure and balance of economic activities within the locality
- the encouragement of entrepreneurial activity.

In contrast, there is also a range of costs commonly associated with tourism and these include:

- the potential for economic over-dependence on one particular form of activity
- inflationary costs in the local economy as new consumers enter the area, and potential increases in real estate prices as the tourism development cycle commences and tourism competes with other land uses
- depending on the size and nature of the local economy, a growing dependence on imported rather than locally produced goods, services and labour as the development of facilities and infrastructure proceeds
- seasonality in the consumption and production of tourism infrastructure and services leading to limited returns on investment
- leakages of tourism expenditure from the local economy
- additional costs for city authorities.

Source: modified from Page (1995)

Constructing the economic impact of tourism

In seeking to understand the extent, scale and consequences of tourism on the economies of countries and destinations, a range of analytical methods have been developed by economists. These usually involve collecting data to model the expenditure from tourism and its impact, as information gathered in visitor surveys can be used to identify:

- *direct expenditure* by tourists on goods and services consumed (e.g. hotels, restaurants and tourist transport services), although this is not a definitive account of expenditure due to leakage of tourist spending to areas and corporations outside the local economy
- *indirect expenditure* by visitors is often estimated by identifying how many tourism enterprises use the income derived from tourists' spending. This money is then used by enterprises to pay for services, taxes and employees, which then recirculates in the urban economy. In other words, tourist expenditure stimulates an economic process which passes through a series of stages (or rounds)
- *the induced impact*, by calculating the impact of expenditure from those employed in tourism and its effect on the local economy.

Source: modified from Page (1995)

These three impacts are then used to estimate the nature of tourist spending, as illustrated in Figure 11.5, which highlights the interrelationships that exist between tourism, tourist spending and other sectors of the economy. Figure 11.5 also introduces the concept of leakage, in which expenditure is lost from the local system to other areas. For planners and managers, maximizing local economic linkages (e.g. buying local produce and employing local people) can enhance the benefits of tourism to a locality. Where the local economy is very vulnerable, and dependent upon a large number of imports (e.g. labour, goods and services), leakage will be high and so reducing the openness of the tourism economy will help to improve the impact locally. Many rural

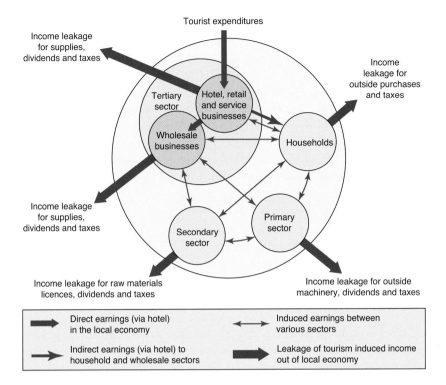

Figure 11.5
The economic impact of tourism

Source: after Murphy (1985); Page (1995)

areas are characteristically open economies and high levels of leakage in tourism occur there, whereas in urban areas leakage is reduced as the economy is more closed. In many less developed countries and island nations that depend upon tourism, the leakage is also high due to external control by multinational companies and a reluctance of tourism businesses to use local products. Instead, high-volume imports reduce the beneficial local effects of tourism. Economists use various tools to measure tourism demand in local economies; one is Multiplier Analysis, where a formula expresses changes that tourism spending can generate.

More recently, governments have tried to understand how tourism affects the national economy. In conjunction with the UNWTO and Organization for Economic Co-operation and Development, some countries have developed tourism satellite accounts (TSA) to measure more precisely the economic impact of tourism. In 1999 the New Zealand government launched the results of its TSA, updating it in 2006 and 2009 and then every year after, which used a wide range of economic data to identify six main themes regarding the impact of tourism:

1   the direct impact of tourism on GDP
2   tourism expenditure expressed as a percentage of GDP
3   the level of tourism employment in the economy

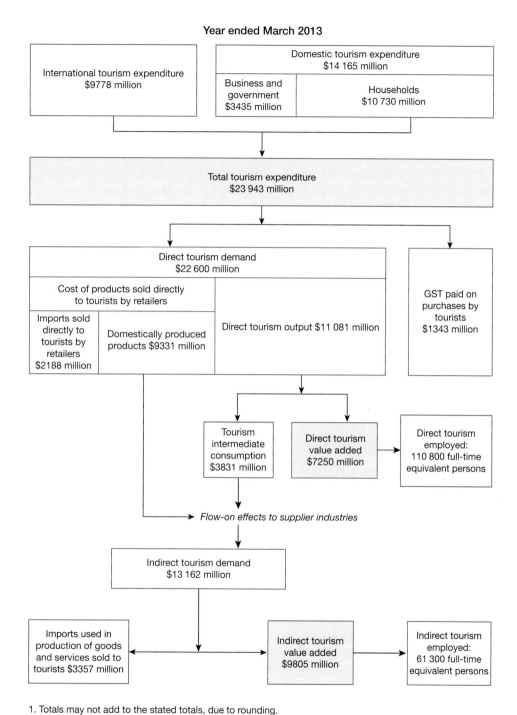

Year ended March 2013

1. Totals may not add to the stated totals, due to rounding.
2. Tourism expenditure is measured in purchaser prices. Other monetary aggregates are measured in producer price.

Figure 11.6
Flows of expenditure through the New Zealand economy year ended March 2013

Source: Statistics New Zealand

4   the proportion of international travel-related expenditure as a percentage of total travel-related expenditure

5   domestic personal expenditure as a percentage of total travel expenditure

6   domestic business and government expenditure as a percentage of total travel expenditure.

The example of the New Zealand TSA is shown in Figure 11.6.

This modelling of the tourism economy is increasingly gaining credence in many governments, since reliable information on the economic impact of tourism is useful:

- for policy-making
- for planning and macro-management of the economy
- for allocating public sector resources towards tourism projects
- for internal government processes to secure additional resources for the Ministry of Tourism and the NTO.

In the New Zealand example, the TSA also helped to raise the profile of the tourism sector, since the magnitude of the economic impacts were far in excess of existing estimates of tourism's effects on the national economy. Yet while it is now becoming easier to gauge the economic effect of tourism, as researchers use more refined methods of analysing its impact, it is much less visible and tangible than the social and cultural impacts which tourism induces.

Social and cultural impacts of tourism

Tourism can emerge as a source of conflict between hosts and visitors in destinations where its development leads to perceived and actual impacts. There has been a wealth of studies of the social and cultural impacts by anthropologists and sociologists, embodied in the influential studies by Valene Smith (1977, 1992). The attitudes of residents towards tourism represent an important way in which this stakeholder group contributes to policy and public support for or dissent towards tourism. At a simplistic level, resident attitudes may be one barometer of an area's ability to absorb tourists. However, the analysis of tourism's social and cultural impacts is related to the way in which it affects or induces change in a number of elements, as Figure 11.7 implies.

The focus of any analysis of host–guest impacts is a function of the interaction between these two groups and will be dependent upon:

- the nature and extent of social, economic and cultural differences between tourists and hosts
- the ratio of visitors to residents
- the distribution and visibility of tourist developments
- the speed and intensity of development
- the extent of foreign investment and employment.

Source: Douglas and Douglas (1996: 51)

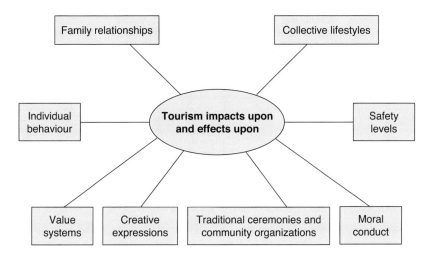

Figure 11.7
The social and cultural impact of tourism

Source: author

In the context of the Pacific islands, Douglas and Douglas (1996) highlighted the differing ethnic origins of residents, and the history of colonialization and tourism development, which provide a backcloth to any analysis of tourism's sociocultural impacts. The scale of development varies enormously across the region, with over 6 million visitors in Hawaii (1.2 million population) through to less than 1000 per annum on Tuvalu (resident population 9000). In each case, the physical presence of tourism is huge and dominates the island. Similarly, high levels of foreign ownership have provoked the indigenous population's antagonism towards tourism in some islands, with some multinational corporations expecting employees to adopt certain behaviour towards visitors. In many of these fragile and ancient cultures, indigenous people's art and culture have been over-commodified, resulting in the derided 'airport art'. Similar criticisms have been levelled at the demand for cultural performances, which create income, but result in indigenous cultures being portrayed as a 'human zoo'. Indeed, in many of these island contexts, tourism has led to host–guest relationships that are:

- limited in duration, and so require distinct behaviour from residents where a service or performance is sold
- transitory in nature, especially where a packaged experience or performance is provided
- geographically isolated, since visitors stay in resort enclaves, where hotel companies meet all their needs and only encourage temporary staged visits to engage with locals. This creates relationships that lack spontaneity, and an unequal and unbalanced experience. As Figure 11.8 shows, Sharpley (2014) indicates that a continuum of host encounters exist which are conditioned by the level and type of contact between hosts and guests.

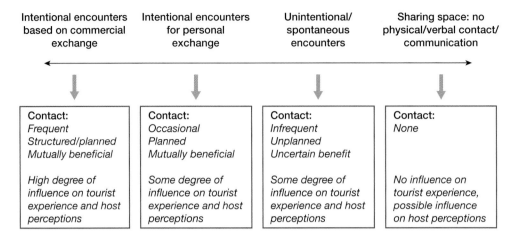

Figure 11.8
A continuum of tourist–host encounters
Source: Sharpley (2014) Host perceptions of tourism: A review of the research. *Tourism Management*, 42(June): 37–49

Pearce (1989) also cited a range of other social and cultural impacts resulting from tourism including:

- the impact of migration from rural areas to urbanized tourism resort areas to secure employment in service industries due to the higher income levels. This can often modify the population structure in destinations, putting pressure on services
- changes in occupational structure, as the demand for low-skill, female and seasonal labour expands
- changes in social values, with greater levels of community turnover
- the impact of gentrification in inner city districts where urban regeneration with a strong tourism element transforms the local housing market, and leads to residents having to move to accommodate development
- increased levels of crime when special events and hallmark events, such as the Olympics, are held
- potentially negative effects related to the increase in prostitution and gambling to meet visitor needs. In some destinations such as Sydney, Bangkok and Amsterdam a distinct sex zone has emerged, changing the social structure of the area
- a decline in the use of native language because the universal method of conversation in tourism is in European languages (English and French).

But how do we understand the way these changes affect resident attitudes?

Probably the most widely cited study that sought to explain how residents react, respond and interact with tourism is Doxey's Index of Tourist Irritation. This is based on Doxey's (1975) study, in which resident responses in the Caribbean and Canada were observed to identify a series of stages through which they passed. These were:

- *euphoria*, following the initial development of tourism
- *apathy*, as tourism developed further and becomes part of the local way of life

- *annoyance*, as tourism began to interfere with everyday life and cause a level of disturbance
- *antagonism*, where residents became tourist averse and tensions, conflict and anti-tourism feeling became widespread.

More detailed research by Ap and Crompton (1993) questioned the validity of such an approach, arguing that it was too simplistic. Instead, they pointed to the diversity of views in any community at any point in time, especially the significance of difference stakeholders (i.e. businesses and residents) – which make the Doxey model problematic as minority and majority views will exist. Indeed, a community will not necessarily progress through a simple set of phases, but may well react according to the seasonal impact of tourism and reflect the overall analysis of tourism's general impact on residents' quality of life. A wide range of studies have been published that seek to encapsulate residents' attitudes to tourism, but comparatively few studies have been longitudinal, to try to understand attitude change through time. One notable exception was Getz's (1993) longitudinal study of resident attitudes in Scotland. Without such a framework, it is not feasible to assess how attitudes have changed as tourism development progresses. Many *ad hoc* resident attitude studies are not sufficiently detailed or methodologically sophisticated and are unable to adopt a longitudinal approach to help understand how social values, community feelings and everyday life are affected by tourism.

Attention now turns to the last major impact associated with tourism – the environmental effects of tourism.

Tourism and the environment

Throughout this book, the link between tourism and the environment has been emphasized as one that has been assuming greater significance, particularly with the rise of the sustainability debate. Yet this relationship between tourism and the environment has evolved over a much longer time period, namely the last 50 years. For example:

> In the 1950s it was viewed as being one of coexistence . . . However, with the advent of mass tourism in the 1960s, increasing pressure was put on natural areas for tourism developments. Together with the growing environmental awareness and concerns of the early 1970s the relationship was perceived to be in conflict. During the next decade this view was endorsed by many others . . . at the same time a new suggestion was emerging that the relationship could be beneficial to both tourism and the environment.
>
> (Dowling 1992: 33)

To foster a beneficial relationship between tourism and the environment requires public sector intervention to plan and manage each element, whilst highlighting the benefits for the tourism industry. For example, the UK government-led study on *Tourism and the Environment* (English Tourist Board/Employment Department 1991) examined and established the scale and nature of environmental problems induced by mass tourism at major tourist sites, and produced guidelines on how such problems were to be addressed. The study pointed to the need to maintain the resource base for tourism activities. As part of their study, they identified common problems resulting from tourism, including wear and tear on the urban fabric, overcrowding and social and cultural impacts between the visitors and local communities.

Indeed, other authors have portrayed tourism–environment impacts as running along a continuum where the effects may be positive in inner city environments (that benefit from tourism-led regeneration), but more negative as one passes into other tourism environments (e.g. coastal areas, rural areas, upland and mountain environments). Depicting this dependent relationship between tourism and the environment, Mathieson and Wall (1982: 97) argued that:

> In the absence of an attractive environment, there would be little tourism. Ranging from the basic attractions of sun, sea and sand to the undoubted appeal of historic sites and structures, the environment is the foundation of tourism.

This is nowhere more evident than in the South Pacific, where stereotypical images of palm trees, beaches, lagoons and sun create an impression of an idyllic tourist landscape. Yet many of the Pacific islands encapsulate the environmental problems which tourism creates.

Many Pacific islands are fragile ecosystems, where the impacts of tourism are highly visible, particularly given the tendency for tourism development to concentrate on coastal areas. As Hall (1996: 68) observed

> because of the highly dynamic nature of the coastal environment and the significance of mangroves and the limited coral sand supply for island beaches in particular, any development which interferes with the natural system may have severe consequences for the long-term stability of the environment.

As a result, inappropriate tourism development in coastal areas creates:

- erosion, where vegetation clearance exposes the beach to sea storms, and building activity on beaches makes sand deposits loose and more vulnerable to erosion
- the salination of fresh ground water sources, which are usually in limited supply
- sewage outfall into shallow waters, which cause nutrients to build up and algal growth that adversely affects coral reefs.

Furthermore, the modification of mangrove swamps on lowland areas to create harbours and marinas, or for land reclamation, leads to loss of ecological diversity and a rich environment for wildlife. It also removes a barrier to sediment build-up. As a result tourism's environmental impacts on Pacific islands create:

- environmental degradation and pollution
- the destruction of habitats and ecosystems

- the loss of coastal and marine resources
- coastal pollution
- impacts on ground water.

As island ecosystems are characterized by limited space and species, the impacts are very obvious, especially where the geographical isolation of an island state is suddenly affected by the rapid development of tourism. Some attempts to address these concerns have been seen with the development of ecotourism. In the South Pacific, Hall (1996) indicated that ecotourism could be construed in two ways:

1   as green or nature-based tourism, with a niche market as part of special interest tourism (e.g. scuba diving)
2   as any form of tourism development that is considered to be environmentally responsible.

Both of these should pay attention to the sustainable use of very fragile resources. In many island microstates (IMS) in the Pacific, the significance of environmental issues in tourism are apparent as a number of common themes characterize tourism's development and the pressures on the resource base:

- scale, where impacts can easily be damaging to fragile resources
- the high levels of dependency on external international tourism interests that do not have a long-term stake in the local environment
- an absence of indigenous sources of capital to develop tourism, removing many opportunities for sustainable tourism development that is community owned and locally managed
- the predominance of colonial patterns of control in the tourism sector limiting the permeation of new ideas such as environmentalism
- an economic system characterized by outward migration, a dependence upon remittances back to families, aid to assist economic survival, and bureaucracy (known as the MIRAB model)
- increasing competition among IMS for tourists in the Pacific and resulting compromises in tourism planning and development to attract visitors.

There is also a growing dependence upon tourism, which is politically promoted as a solution to problems of under-development. The main problem is the consumption of a finite resource – the environment to meet tourism aspirations in IMS in the Pacific.

In many ways the environmental impacts in the Pacific islands can be combined with the more general problems that Mathieson and Wall (1982) identify in resort areas, which include:

- architectural pollution owing to the effect of inappropriate hotel development on the traditional landscape
- the effect of ribbon development and urban sprawl in the absence of planning and development restrictions (as is the case on many Spanish resorts in the Mediterranean)

- the resort infrastructure becomes overloaded and breaks down in periods of peak usage
- tourists become segregated from local residents
- good quality agricultural land may be lost to tourist development
- traffic congestion may result in resort areas
- the local ecosystem may be polluted from sewage
- litter and too many visitors in the peak season.

So how has the tourism industry responded to criticisms over its impact on the environment?

The tourism industry response

A substantial lobby has emerged amongst environmental groups to question the seemingly unstoppable march of tourism as a consumer of environmental resources. The hotel industry has responded with environmental initiatives in the 1990s such as the International Hotels Environment Initiative, which promotes recycling, codes of conduct, best practice among members, accreditation schemes and improved standards of energy efficiency (features of this were discussed in Chapter 8). These elements of environmental management are non mainstream. In some hotels, waste minimization strategies have resulted from environmental audits of the tourism and hospitality operations to reduce costs. They may include purchasing more eco-friendly products, waste reduction (e.g. not laundering guests' towels every day), reusing resources and packaging and adopting a green policy towards operational issues. In the Balearic islands, the development of an ecotax in 2002 has been used to fund environmental improvements to address decades of tourist development. Yet this has had a negative impact on one market – the Germany package holiday market. In Germany the ecotax was called 'Limonadensteuer', a lemonade tax, because hotel owners have been giving guests drink vouchers in lieu of the tax. It was also dubbed a 'Kurtax' (a cure tax) that has raised ecological issues among visitors. This approach to attempting to remedy the impacts of mass tourism development is at least beginning to move the sector towards a greater understanding of its effect on the environment. So how does the tourism industry manage the impacts of visitors?

Visitor management

The tourism sector, even if it seeks to be socially inclusive and permit access to different resources, has to address an ongoing problem: it needs to permit access to sites and yet needs to protect the resource base upon which tourism is based. This requires a wide range of management tools to balance the needs of the visitor, the place (i.e. the resource base), the host community and other tourism stakeholders (e.g. the industry) in providing a quality tourism experience. As a result the area known as 'visitor management' has emerged in a tourism context. Visitor management develops and adapts many of the principles and practices used in the outdoor recreation and leisure areas. There are two types of measures which are usually used – 'hard measures', which are place extensive and place permanent restrictions on visitor activity, and 'soft measures', which involve improving marketing, interpretation, planning and visitor coordination. These are summarized in Table 11.4 (p. 401).

In terms of managing the impact of visitors, the car and its management remains a key element of any strategy to reduce tourism's carbon footprint, since the mobility of visitors is what contributes to the geographical concentration or dispersion of impacts on the environment and communities. With the car being such a culturally ingrained element of many developed economies, and seen as a means of flexible transport associated with personal freedom to travel, introducing any measures that will add restraint or limit individual freedom is a huge challenge. This highlights the need for all of us to think about our own carbon footprint in terms of our leisure time. Consequently, managing the impact of the car is a challenge that is central to introducing a sustainability ethos into tourist behaviour and the way we live. For this reason, it is helpful to look at successful examples of where car use has been reduced in sensitive environments such as the New Forest National Park in the UK. By examining what has been done to make changes to visitor behaviour, we may begin to understand what innovations we need to introduce in other settings to replicate such success, as the Innovation in Sustainability 11.1 shows.

An example of a country taking hard measures is the kingdom of Bhutan in the eastern Himalayas, which places major restrictions on tourism. It only allows a limited number of visitors to enter on organized packages as independent travellers and backpackers are discouraged. Visitors have to spend US$200 a day during their visit to Bhutan. The majority of the population (Drukpa) follow an ancient Bhuddist culture which has been conserved by the king, and a policy of limited modernization has been followed since the 1970s (radio broadcasting was introduced in 1973 and internet provision was permitted in 1999). Tourism has been developed as a means of deriving foreign revenue for the country. Bhutan's ecological diversity has made it a major nature tourism destination and it also has a rich heritage and culture among the population combined with a traditional lifestyle (including the wearing of traditional dress). Bhutan has a population of 870 000 and visitor numbers have grown from 287 in 1974 to 2850 in 1992, 7000 in 1999 and 6261 in 2003, rising by 30 per cent to 9249 in 2004. The government's ninth Five-Year Plan set a target of around 15 000 tourist arrivals in 2007, which were forecast to rise to 20 000 arrivals in 2012. This actually reached 44 000 in 2012, generating US$63 million from international tourism. In 2004 the market was largely dominated by high-spending tourists from the USA (35 per cent), Japan (11.8 per cent), the UK (10.3 per cent) and Germany (7.3 per cent). This model of the strict control of tourism has been accompanied by examples of community-based tourism development, where those who benefit from tourism are local people. One good example is the Jigme Singye Wangchuck National Park which has a trekking trail and opportunities for local people to benefit from provision of services (e.g. portering, providing refreshments and cultural activities, and guiding). However, current concerns about managing tourism are associated with the effect of external influences upon Bhutanese culture and the possible change to cultural values that increased numbers of visitors and increased modernization measures may have on the population. Similar

INNOVATION IN SUSTAINABILITY 11.1
GETTING TOURISTS OUT OF THEIR CARS ONTO PUBLIC TRANSPORT – THE EXPERIENCE OF NEW FOREST NATIONAL PARK, UK

The New Forest National Park, located in southern England, was designated in 2005 as one of the most recent National Parks to be created in the UK. As a destination for visitors, around 90 per cent arrive by car, illustrating the scale of the challenge facing the Park Authority to manage as this leads to congestion and reduced air quality in many Park honey pots. The Park has set itself an ambitious target for 2015 to get 370 000 people out of their cars and to do this it has secured a share of a £3.8 million grant (shared with the South Downs National Park, also in southern England). Progress has been impressive to date, with 40 653 passengers using the seasonal hop-on-hop-off open top bus services that offer a tour and an opportunity to stop off at various locations in the Park. This figure increased by 40 per cent on 2012 figures and resulted in 223 000 journeys being switched from the car to the bus. Marketing and promotion of the public transport alternatives alongside the introduction of electric care hire (Twizzies) and cycle hire at key locations provide a novel alternative alongside some horse drawn options and rail transport. In 2012 the Park won the Virgin Holidays Highly Commended category of award at the Responsible Tourism Awards, reflecting the innovative work of the Park Authority in championing sustainability.

Similar successes in innovative sustainable transport action by Northumberland National Park in northern England have seen its patronage of tourist bus services rise from 600 passengers a year in the 1980s to 36 000 in 2012. Other notable achievements are the trialling of electric car use in the Park and the roll out of electric charging points. Electric vehicles are acknowledged as emitting half of the CO_2 of conventional combustion engines, which has helped the National Park Authority to reduce its carbon footprint by 39 per cent.

Further reading

New Forest National Park, www.newforestnpa.gov.uk
Northumberland National Park, www.northumberlandnationalpark.org.uk

concerns may also be raised in relation to other destinations experiencing rapid tourism growth (see Case Study 11.1 on Vietnam).

In a heritage tourism context, Hall and McArthur (1998: 123) review the value of these management tools to achieve the twin goals of conserving the resource and contributing to improving the quality of the visitor experience. Table 11.5 (p. 411) is a qualitative assessment of each approach they identified, and suggests that hard measures to regulate visitor activity are the dominant mode of control. The table also illustrates the need for managers and planners to consider ways of integrating these approaches to manage tourism. One approach is to develop visitor management models that seek to assess the capacity of a site or location and the types of management needed to

Table 11.4 Examples of visitor management techniques in tourism

Technique	Examples
Regulating access by area	Excluding visitors from sacred sites such as aboriginal lands
Regulating access by transport	Park and ride schemes to prevent in-town use of cars, or car-free environments and pedestrianization schemes as part of town centre management programmes
Regulating visitor numbers and group size	The use of group size restrictions in Antarctica
Regulating types of visitors permitted	Discouraging certain groups through marketing and products on offer
Regulating visitor behaviour	Zoning of visitor activities in marine parks in Western Australia to allocate certain activities to certain areas
Regulating equipment	Prohibiting off-road driving except in permitted areas (e.g. in Forest Enterprise's four-wheel drive track in the new Loch Lomond National Park)
The use of entry or user fees	Charging visitors to Kenya's National Parks and Reserves so that some of the fee is used for conservation
Modifications to sites	Constructing hardened paths to direct visitors
Market research	To identify reasons for visiting, to understand how to develop tools to modify visitor behaviour
Promotional marketing campaigns	The provision of alternative destinations in the Lake District, UK to relieve pressure on congested sites
Provision of interpretation programmes	Provision of guided tours or guides to avoid congestion at key sites

Source: modified and developed from Hall and McArthur (1998)

CASE STUDY 11.1
THE CHALLENGE OF MANAGING TOURISM GROWTH: THE CASE OF VIETNAM

Vietnam is one of Asia's rapidly expanding tourism destinations, with a dynamic tourism economy worth over US$12 billion a year. The country has seen over US$100 billion in foreign direct investment attracted to the country since the late 1980s. It remains one of Asia's rising stars of economic development, with a population of 89 million (2011) and its growth trajectory in tourism has been impressive. This has to be set against the country's chequered history of conflict with its colonial rulers (France) and the subsequent war with the USA (the Vietnam War) that ended in 1975 at a huge human cost (estimates of 2 million military personnel and 5 million civilians killed). The communist control of the country resulted in continued internal conflict, with the country a most unlikely candidate for development as a tourism destination prior to the 1980s.

Forecasts of Vietnam's tourism sector suggest it will grow by over 7.5 per cent per annum through to 2015, making it one of Asia's fastest-growing destinations, and one of the world's top ten areas for tourism growth. The country's international arrivals have grown from 92 500 in 1988 to just over 1 million in 1995, to almost 4.2 million in 2008 and 6.8 million in 2012, dominated by Chinese inbound visitors, followed by visitors from South Korea, Japan and the USA as shown in Figure 11.9.

In 2011/2012, growth in tourism arrivals had slowed to just under 14 per cent but for 2009/2010 it had reached almost 35 per cent and 19 per cent for 2010/11. International tourism accounts for US$6.6 billion. Vietnam has remained one of the fastest growing regions globally, while it was a major driver of tourism in Asia (i.e. Asia achieved 7 per cent growth per annum in 2011–12 and South-East Asia 9 per cent growth, compared to almost 14 per cent in Vietnam). Therefore Vietnam is one of the key drivers of international tourism growth in the region. The government has forecast that, by 2015, international arrivals will be around 7 million and domestic tourism will rise from around 17 million in 2009 to 36–37 million arrivals, creating a US$10 billion tourism industry for the country. By 2020, the government expect international arrivals will reach 10 million and by 2030, 20 million. By any standards this is a rapid growth rate and poses many challenges for developing a sustainable tourism product.

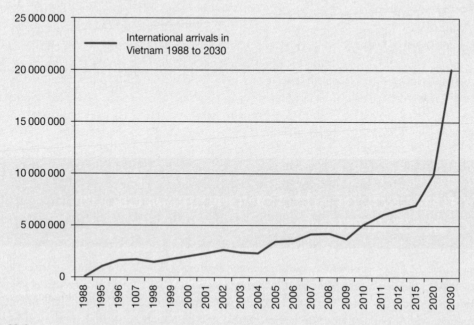

Figure 11.9
International arrivals in Vietnam, 1988–2030

Source: based on data from UNWTO

Much of the country's rapid growth can be attributed to the free-market reforms (Doi Moi) which created a climate of economic liberalization. These were created in advance of the wider commitment to creating a free trade area in Asia among the member countries of the ASEAN trading bloc, which announced the phased introduction of liberalization measures in 2008 for a single aviation market for all passenger services by 2015. The rapid expansion of the country's tourism economy has been accompanied by massive growth in its tourism capacity and infrastructure. In 2008, for example, 130 companies were investing in 68 major tourism-related projects ranging from hotels, to casinos and resort developments, and golf course development. Much of the investment has been focused on the economic hubs of Hanoi and Ho Chi Minh City, where around US$21 billion in capital investment is occurring. Ho Chi Minh City, for example, has an ambitious tourism development strategy, receiving over 3 million visitors a year. Such ambitious growth plans have meant that airports such as Da Nang, which currently handles over 80 000 arrivals a year, will need to expand to 4 million by 2010 and 6 million by 2015 to achieve growth forecasts. The result is that over US$312.5 million of investment is needed for the airport to grow its capabilities to handle increased capacity. Investment in tourism has also been leveraged from overseas aid budgets which were running at US$2.2 billion per annum in 2007; in 2008 one project alone was receiving US$11.1 million in aid for the Greater Mekong sub-region Sustainable Tourism Development programme to assist five of Vietnam's poorest areas to benefit from tourism-led economic development.

The history of conflict in the country in the period 1954 to 1975 created an unusual attraction which fits the definition of dark tourism (see Chapter 1) on the largest island in Vietnam – Phu Quoc, where its military prison was renovated in 2009 and now attracts over 75 000 visitors a year. The island is one of Vietnam's popular beach holiday destinations in the Gulf of Thailand. The prison was initially used by the French and then the US army as a camp for Viet Cong fighters where it housed over 40 000 detainees at its peak, and around 4000 are estimated to have died when interned there. In 1975 after the communist government took control of the south of the country, the prison was turned into a re-education camp for people deemed in need of rehabilitation for their political views or attitudes, with average stays of three to five years depending on the severity of the misdemeanour. In 1996 the prison was opened as a tourist attraction and, like many other sites of torture and death, it has developed a fascination among visitors such as the 350 000 who visit Robben Island, off the coast of Cape Town where the former South African President Nelson Mandela was imprisoned for 18 years. Similarly, the number of visitors to the former Second World War concentration camp, Auschwitz-Birkenau, reached a peak in 2012 of 1.43 million visitors, the largest number in the site's 65-year history. These three examples of dark tourism illustrate the fascination visitors have with the macabre as well as the important role that visitation plays in the healing process for people in post-conflict environments.

Further reading

Truong, V. and Hall, C. M. (2013) Social marketing and tourism: What is the evidence? *Social Marketing Quarterly*, 19(2): 110–135.

ensure a maximum visitor experience without affecting the sustainable use of the resource and its long-term appeal. A number of technical models have been developed and applied in visitor management contexts across the world, as Table 11.6 (p. 412) shows. Each approach is reviewed in terms of its key characteristics and its ability to meet the varying needs of different stakeholders and be applied in practical contexts. As Table 11.8 (p. 415) suggests, these models (widely used and understood in the recreation and tourism management literature – see Pigram and Jenkins, 1999, for more detail) adopt different management approaches which are useful in illustrating the diversity of tools available to managers. The case study of Venice is examined in Case Study 11.2 and illustrates the practical problems that visitor management poses and the conflicting challenges of economic, environmental and socio-cultural impacts.

With the global spread of tourism, the growth in the demand for domestic and international travel is creating an insatiable demand for leisure spending in the new millennium. As new outbound markets such as China and India develop, there will be a huge increase in the rate of tourism growth in certain regions such as Asia-Pacific. The consequences of such growth if it is allowed to develop in an unplanned, unconstrained and unmanaged manner is clear: the continued impact on the environment, people and ecosystems that will be irreversibly damaged by tourism consumption.

Since tourism is a powerful force in many economies, some degree of planned intervention by the public sector, as well as the increasing number of public–private sector partnerships, will be essential in terms of implementing visitor management plans and tools. If the example of Venice tells us one thing, it is that the excesses of tourism can quickly destroy the visitor experience, the resource base and the potential for sustainable tourism if it goes unchecked (see Case Study 11.2).

CASE STUDY 11.2
MANAGING THE TOURIST IMPACT IN VENICE

Stephen J. Page and C. Michael Hall

Venice is acknowledged as one of the world's leading cultural and art cities with its acclaimed fifteenth-century Renaissance art. It is a magical place for many visitors, with its elegant architecture, ambience and artistic qualities (Plates 11.2 and 11.3). Many of its buildings have iconic qualities, not least due to their association with poetry, writing and the work of different artists (e.g. Canaletto). Indeed Canaletto popularized many images of Venice as a place to visit in his picturesque, almost idealized, cityscapes that have contributed to the pursuit of cultural and heritage consumption by visitors. Venice is located on a series of islands in a lagoon with 117 islets, and is the capital of the Veneto region of Italy. The impact of tourism has resulted in continued population loss from the historic city of Venice. The resident population dropped from 175 000 in 1951 to 78 000 in 1992 and 65 000 in 2001 and is now around 60 000 (a decline of 60 per cent since 1952); the city receives 47 000 commuters daily. The age and condition of many of Venice's buildings are under constant threat. The environment in Venice is suffering from:

Plate 11.2
1908 tour of Italy and Venice to fulfil the renewed interest in the Grand Tour

Source: Thomas Cook

Plate 11.3
1953 brochure advertising tours to Venice by Thomas Cook

Source: Thomas Cook

- a sinking ground level
- a rising sea level
- pollution of the lagoon in which it is located
- atmospheric pollution
- congestion on the main canals from motorized traffic
- over-saturation at key locations for tourists
- increased flooding: in the 1970s and 1980s there were 50 high tides a year; in 1996 there were 101, and in 2000 some 80. This illustrates the range and extent of environmental concerns amidst a booming visitor industry.

Visitor arrivals have developed greatly. In 1952 500 000 tourists spent 1.2 million bednights in the historic city of Venice. By 1987 these figures had risen to 1.13 million tourist arrivals and 2.49 million bednights; by 1992, to 1.21 million arrivals and 2.68 million bednights. The average length of stay was 2.21 nights in 1992. These visitor numbers are swelled by a large day visitor market from other parts of Italy, especially the Adriatic beach resorts and Alpine areas. In 1992, the day tripper market was estimated to be 6 million visitors, providing a total market in excess of 7 million visitors a year. In 2007, 5.4 million Italian visitors stayed 25 million nights in the Venice region and 8.72 million international visitors spent 36 million nights in the region. Estimates new put visitor numbers at 16 million or as high as 22 million. To accommodate tourists, 41 new hotels were opened 2000–2007. As tourists have expanded and property has been turned to accommodation, residents have left. In 2007, a peak of 20 million was exceeded. Only 20 per cent of visitors are domestic Italian visitors. The majority of international visitors were from Germany, USA, Austria, the UK and other mainland European countries. Whilst these statistics are not actual arrivals in Venice *per se*, they are a good proxy for the scale and volume of visitation which the city experiences.

Russo's (2002) study of tourism in Venice highlighted tourists' motivations for visiting cultural attractions and described Venice as being in the latter stage of the resort life cycle – nearing stagnation and decline. Montanari and Muscara (1995) recognized that Venice was saturated at key times in the year (e.g. Easter) and that the police have had to close the Ponte del Libertà when the optimum flow of 21 000 tourists a day has been exceeded (60 000 at Easter and 100 000 in the summer). There is increased competition between residents and visitors in the use of space within the historic city. Up to 34 per cent of the public space in the historic square is used by visitors and 49 per cent by residents. During special events, the use by visitors increases to 56 per cent and this adds to congestion in the city, competition for facilities and a declining visitor and resident experience.

Since 1987, on selected spring weekends, the land route from the mainland to Venice has been closed to visitors as an extreme form of crisis management. Montanari and Muscara (1995) developed a ninefold classification of tourists based on differences in their spatial behaviour (i.e. where and what they visit in the city), perception and spending power, which can be summarized thus:

- the first-time visitor on an organized tour
- the rich tourist
- the lover of Venice
- the backpacker camper

- the worldly wise tourist
- the return tourist
- the resident artist
- the beach tourist
- the visitor with a purpose.

This large number of different categories reflects Venice's unique tourism environment and the diversity of motivations for visiting the city.

Yet Russo (2002) argues that the city does not manage visits prudently. The time tourists spend on queuing at well-known attractions leads to lost opportunities to see lesser-known cultural attractions, heightened by poor marketing and communication with the visitor. This is complicated by the existence of ten agencies responsible for museums in the city. Venice is dominated by excursionists (83.1 per cent) in comparison to tourists (16.9 per cent), with a very even pattern of distribution throughout the year: January–March 14 per cent of visitors arrive; 30 per cent come in April–June; 32 per cent in July–September and 24 per cent October–December. Russo (2002) noted that the average duration of a visit was eight hours, with many tour operators promoting day trips rather than overnight stays. The destination's accessibility has also been increased with the recent advent of low-cost airlines in Europe. Venice's tourist market is comprised of 26.3 per cent of arrivals from within Italy, 36 per cent from the rest of Europe, 17.7 per cent from the USA, 11.1 per cent from Japan and 8.8 per cent from other countries/regions.

The social impact of the existing patterns of demand led van der Borg *et al.* (1996) to calculate the visitor to resident (host) ratios for Venice and a number of other European heritage cities. In Venice's historical centre, a ratio of 89.4:1 existed while for the wider Venice municipality this dropped to 27.6:1. This level of visitor pressure reflects the scale of the problem facing Venice. Incoming visitors have also purchased holiday properties which have driven up prices and excluded the local population at a time when this has dropped to around 60 000 Venetians.

Venice's capacity for tourism

To assess the capacity of the historic centre of Venice, Canestrelli and Costa (1991) undertook a complex mathematical modelling exercise to examine the parameters to consider in any future visitor management plan. This established what is called the 'carrying capacity' (i.e. how many visitors can the historic city accommodate). The optimal carrying capacity for the historic city of Venice would be to admit 9780 tourists who use hotel accommodation, 1460 tourists staying in non-hotel accommodation and 10 857 day trippers on a daily basis. Even if the day trippers who currently visit Venice were evenly spread this would still amount to 11 233 trippers a day. In fact it is estimated that an average of 37 500 day trippers a day visit Venice in August. Canestrelli and Costa (1991) argued that a ceiling of 25 000 visitors a day is the maximum tourist capacity for Venice. Some estimates suggested that around 50 000 visits occur on peak days.

There are important implications for the environment and its long-term preservation if the tourist capacity is being exceeded. Once the capacity is exceeded, the quality of the visitor experience is eroded and the physical fabric may be damaged; extra strain is placed on the infrastructure. Yet the large volume of visitors which descend on Venice each year not only exceeds the desirable limits

Plate 11.4
The Grand Canal, Venice

Source: Istock

of tourism for the city, but also poses a range of social and economic problems for planners. For example, over 1.5 million visitors go to the Doge's Palace each year while small numbers visit lesser-known attractions, illustrating the massive congestion at flagship and iconic attractions and areas such as St Mark's Square. As van der Borg *et al*. (1996: 52) observed:

> the negative external effects connected with the overloading of the carrying capacity are rapidly increasing, frustrating the centre's economy and society . . . excursionism [day tripping] is becoming increasingly important, while residential tourism is losing relevance for the local tourism market . . . [and] . . . the local benefits are diminishing. Tourism is becoming increasingly ineffective for Venice.

Thus, the negative impact of tourism on the historic centre of Venice is now resulting in a self-enforcing decline. Excursionists, who contribute less to a local tourism economy than staying visitors, supplant the staying market as it becomes less attractive to stay in the city. Up until 2000, changing the attitude of the city's tourism policy-makers was difficult: the pro-tourism lobby heavily influenced it. Since 2000 a number of positive measures have been enacted to address the saturation of the historic city by day visitors including denying access to the city by unauthorized tour coaches via the main coach terminal.

In 2001 a new mayor was elected and introduced a number of emergency measures to safeguard the future of tourism by:

- the introduction of a tourist tax to recover some of the external costs of tourism
- imposing a strict control on motorized traffic in the canals to reduce the wash effects on gondolas and buildings
- the introduction of a multi-million pound mobile flood barrier, despite protests from ecologists, to reduce the regular flooding, to be in place by 2012.

Another serious issue that impacts upon the quality of the tourist experience is the effluent problem in the city: the absence of sewers results in algal growth and a notable stench in the summer season.

Environmental processes that affect both the local and tourist population must also be recognized – such as flooding. Flooding in Venice now means that St Mark's Square, an icon for visitors, floods forty to sixty times a year compared to four to six times a year at the beginning of the twentieth century. As a result, tourism must be balanced with measures of environmental protection and management. Positive steps are needed to provide a more rational basis for the future development and promotion of tourism in the new millennium. Glasson *et al.* (1995: 116) summarized the problem of seeking to manage visitors and their environmental impact in Venice:

> every city must be kept as accessible as possible for some specific categories of users, such as inhabitants, visitors to offices and firms located in the city, and commuters studying or working in the city. At the same time, the art city needs to be kept as inaccessible as possible to some other user categories (the excursionist/day-trippers in particular).

The behaviour of visitors combined with the volume of visits has led the Mayor's office to introduce a Tourist Code of Conduct based on a range of principles including some of the following:

- visitors should obtain a map and look beyond the iconic attractions (although visitors visit to see these very features); this is to try to geographically disperse visitors around the city. It is widely argued that overcrowding due to tourists has affected the residential ambience of the city, which is why many residents have left. If this trend continues Venice could become a living museum with a minimal resident population – at worst a cultural Disneyland
- tourists should keep to the right in the streets to help reduce congestion and to improve the flow of people.

In addition, new laws have been passed to regulate tourist behaviour in St Mark's Square (Articles 12, 23 and 28 of the Regulations of the Metropolitan Police of the City of Venice) which prohibit visitors from:

- lying down in public places
- sitting or lingering on the street, or eating picnic lunches
- throwing litter on the floor
- swimming in the canals or in the St Mark's Bay area
- riding bicycles or other vehicles in the city
- performing unsafe or bothersome activities

- undressing in public places
- walking about the city shirtless or in bathing costumes.

Any breach of these rules will be receive a 50 euros fine.

Source: www.commune.venezia.it

The example of Venice shows that, while tangible economic benefits accrue to the city, social and environmental costs are substantial. Montanari and Muscara (1995) argued that Venetian water transport plays a major role in tourism (including as a spectacle for the 128 regattas it hosts each year) within the city and could be used to manage visitors, while the city needs to plan to separate the access, circulation and exit of the resident/commuting population and tourists. Russo (2002) expanded this debate, and argued that the better matching of tourism demand (i.e. visitors) with the available supply of attractions through improved marketing and information would bring some economic benefits to the city. It would also assist in geographically spreading the impact of visitors. But a much more visitor-focused management strategy is also needed, with policies and actions to:

- increase the attraction potential in some areas
- place access restrictions in some areas.

This could be achieved through a range of visitor management measures listed in Table 11.7 (p. 414). These combine soft and hard controls, listing the problem (causation), reviewing the context of addressing it and suggesting potential interventions. In some respects, the recent growth in cruise-ship traffic (short-term high-volume day trippers) has also placed additional strains on the city's tourist infrastructure. The introduction of the Venice Card (now the Venice Connected pass) in 2004 to give pre-booked visitors priority entry to attractions has been a move in the right direction, as it allows the city to limit the number of visitors to 25 000 on peak days when up to 50 000 people can descend on the city. Russo's (2002) advocacy of greater taxation/tariffs to 'disincentivize' excursions is likely to be implemented. Russo rightly advocates tourism management as a starting point to plan the future for tourism in the city, to raise the industry from saturation and stagnation. The continued growth in the numbers of day trippers has led to a deterioration in the quality of the tourist experience. This case study is significant in that it highlights the prevailing problems affecting many historic cities and both the political and policy issues that must be addressed to manage the impacts so that tourism does not destroy its vital resource – the environment.

Venice may be an extreme example of a city under siege. The management of visitor numbers and flows of these visitors is central to the long-term management of the destination. Venice has long passed any level of what might naively be called 'sustainable' tourism, meaning that tourism management must adopt a model of crisis management and deploy a radical solution, although the city authorities are now promoting the Venice Sustainability Project for businesses to adopt sustainability principles. It is also promoting 'the golden rules for the sustainable tourist in Venice' (veniceconnected.com): to book a trip in advance, to visit during the off-peak period and to book tickets from Veniceconnected.com, to travel by train or bus and to choose accommodation adopting environmental practices.

Table 11.5 Qualitative assessment of visitor management techniques

Visitor management technique	Ability to address heritage management paradox		Other aspects of performance		
	Conservation of heritage	Improve quality of visitor experience	Create support for heritage management	Proactiveness	Reliance by management
Regulating access	•••	•	•	•	•
Regulating visitation	••	••	•	•	••
Regulating behaviour	••	•	•	•	•
Regulating equipment	••	••	•	••	••
Entry or user fees	••	•	•	••	•••
Modifying the site	••	••	••	•	•••
Market research	••	••	•	•••	•
Visitor monitoring and research	••	•••	•	•••	•
Promotional marketing	•••	••	•••	•••	•
Strategic information marketing	•••	•••	•••	••	••
Interpretation	•••	•••	•••	•••	••
Education	•••	••	••	•••	•
Profile of heritage management	•••	••	•••	••	•
Alternative providers – tourism industry	••	•••	••	•••	•
Alternative providers – volunteers	•••	•••	•••	•••	••
Favoured treatment for accredited bodies bringing visitors to a site	•••	•••	•••	•••	•

Performance in relation to heritage management paradox: •, Limited; ••, Reasonable; •••, Good

Performance in relation to other criteria: •, Limited; ••, Reasonable; •••, Good

Source: Hall and McArthur (1998: 123), reproduced with permission from the authors

Future issues for visitor management

In the future, the impacts of tourism will continue to pose ethical dilemmas for planners and managers. On the one hand, governments are seeking to develop more socially inclusive societies, where principles such as 'Tourism for All' are pursued to facilitate a greater inclusion of special needs by tourism businesses and agencies. This argues against management measures to limit access to those with the purchasing power. Running counter to such ideological arguments on tourism is the recognition that visitor management needs to limit rather than expand the access to many tourist sites and resources. The introduction of charging to enter religious sites such as Canterbury Cathedral in the face of problems caused by unlimited access is one example that raised

Table 11.6 Applications of visitor management models

Visitor management model	Applications across the world
The Recreation Opportunity Spectrum (ROS)	• In Australia ROS has been developed for Knarben Gorge, Fraser Island National Park • In an innovative study ROS was applied to the urban parklands around Newcastle, Australia • ROS has been an underlying principle behind the development of management strategies for National Parks in New Zealand and the USA
Carrying Capacity Model	• Yosemite Valley, Yosemite National Park, USA – implemented by the United States Parks Service • Boundary Waters Canoe Area, USA – investigated but not fully implemented by the United States Parks Service • Angkor World Heritage Site, Siem Reap Province, Cambodia – the Angkor Conservation Office implemented an annual and daily capacity, as well as a capacity for any one moment in time • Green Island, Queensland, and the Queensland Department of Environment and Natural Heritage, Australia – implemented an annual and daily capacity, as well as a capacity for any one moment in time • In the early 1990s, the New Zealand sub-Antarctic islands had a limit of 500 visits per year • Waitomo Caves in New Zealand has a carrying capacity set at 200 persons at any one moment in time • Bermuda in the USA has set a capacity of 120 000 cruise-ship passengers during the peak visitation period • Lord Howe Island in the Tasman Sea has a limit of 800 visitors at any time
Visitor Activity Management Programme (VAMP)	• Cross-country (Nordic) skiing in Ottawa, Canada – partially implemented by the Canadian National Parks Service. • Mingan Archipelago National Park Reserve, Canada – implemented by the Canadian National Parks Service to help establish the new park

Table 11.6 *continued*

Visitor management model	Applications across the world
	• Point Pelee National Park, Canada – implemented by the Canadian National Parks Service with an interpretation focus • Kejimkijik National Park, Canada – partially implemented by the Canadian National Parks Service
Visitor Impact Management Model (VIMM)	• Florida Keys National Marine Sanctuary, Florida, USA – pilot implemented by the US Travel and Tourism Administration and the US Environmental Protection Agency • Netherlands – pilot explored for expansion by the World Tourism Organization • Buck Island Reef National Monument, Virgin Islands, USA – implemented but discontinued by United States National Park Service • Youghiogheny River, Western Maryland, USA – implemented but discontinued by Maryland Department of Natural Resources • Price Edward Island, Canada – pilot implemented by Parks Canada and the World Tourism Organization • Los Tuxtlas, Veracruz, Mexico – pilot implemented by the World Tourism Organization • Jenolan Caves, New South Wales, Australia – fully implemented and monitored by the Jenolan Caves Management Trust • Villa Gesell, Buenos Aires Province, Argentina – pilot implemented by the Buenos Aires Province Tourism Authority and the World Tourism Organization • Peninsula Valdes, Northern Patagonia, Argentina – pilot implemented by the World Tourism Organization
The Limits of Acceptable Change (LAC)	• Bob Marshall Wilderness Complex, Montana, USA – tested and implemented by the United States Forest Service • Selway-Bitteroot Wilderness, Idaho, USA – tested by the United States Forest Service • Cranberry Wilderness Area, West Virginia, USA – tested by the USDA Forest Service and West Virginia University • The Wet Tropics World Heritage Area, Queensland, Australia – prepared for but never fully implemented by the Wet Tropics Management Authority • The Nymboida River, New South Wales, Australia – prepared for but never fully implemented by the New South Wales Department of Water Resources • Wallace Island Crown Reserve, New South Wales, Australia – developed but never implemented by the Wallis Island Reserve Trust and New South Wales Department of Water and Land Conservation
Tourism Optimization Management Model (TOMM)	• Kangaroo Island, South Australia, Australia – implementation in progress by the South Australian Tourism Commission, Department of Environment and Natural Resources and Tourism Kangaroo Island

Source: Hall and McArthur (1998: 123), reproduced with permission from the authors

Table 11.7 The problems, causes, measures and future actions needed to manage tourists in Venice

Causation	Context	'Hard' interventions	'Soft' interventions
1 Increase of tourist demand → enlargement of tourism region, shorter visits	Difficult expansion of tourism supply, irreproducible heritage (*small centres, islands*)	Zoning, regional planning, enlargement of accommodation capacity in the city centre	Entrance ticket, incentives based on advance booking, discrimination policies, tariffs, creation of a supra-local 'tourism authority'
2 Shorter visits → increasing congestion costs, asymmetric information	Many cultural resources, difficult mobility (*medium-sized art cities*)	Zoning, access regulation, closing of portions of city centre, infra-structure policy, decentralization of cultural supply	Information and discrimination policies, promotion, creation of 'alternative routes'
3 Asymmetric information → decline in the quality of tourism supply (primary and complementary)	Limited competition, low controls, scarce homo-geneity of cultural institutions (*mature destinations, transition countries*)	Licensing regulations, law enforcement, police controls in central areas, interpretation and welcome centres	Integral management of the cultural system, incentive to start ups, quality labels, virtual access to cultural products, tourism e-commerce
4 Decline in quality → incentive to commuting and disincentive to cultural visits	Sensitiveness to reputation, international attention, prevalence of tour-operated holidays, presence of alternatives in the hinterland (*mature metropolitan destinations, high accessibility*)	Regional–national planning	Reputation policies, promotion, diversification of tourism supply, fidelization, marketing, rejuvenation of products

Source: reprinted from A. Russo (2002) The 'vicious circle' of tourism development in heritage cities. *Annals of Tourism Research*, 29: 165–82, with permission of Elsevier

many moral issues. The dilemma pricing as a management tool introduces is that political arguments on allowing all members of society to engage in tourism and leisure trips became redundant. Instead a caveat has to be added – participation for all in a defined range of activities and events. Tourism only becomes accessible if one has the disposable income.

Globally, the application of sophisticated management tools used in niche markets such as ecotourism is beginning to permeate other destinations and sites. As Page and Dowling (2002) noted, soft measures in ecotourism management designed to influence visitor behaviour, in order to mitigate impacts, seek to change users' attitudes and behaviour, and even out the distribution of visits between heavily and lightly used sites. An intermediate category of visitor management seeks to lower usage levels by balancing

Table 11.8 Qualitative assessment of visitor management models

Visitor management model	Key characteristics of visitor management model	Level of sophisti-cation	Range of contributing stakeholders	Actual application by heritage managers
The Recreation Opportunity Spectrum (ROS)	• Determines the threshold level of activity beyond which will result in the deterioration of the resource base • Its main dimensions are biophysical, socio-cultural, psychological and managerial • Used for planning, site design and development, and administration	**	**	***
Carrying Capacity Model	• Creates a diversity of experiences by identifying a spectrum of settings, activities and opportunities that a region may contain • Helps to review and reposition the type of visitor experiences most appropriate to a heritage site	*	**	**
Visitor Activity Management Programme (VAMP)	• Is a planning system that integrates visitor needs with resources to produce specific visitor opportunities • Is designed to resolve conflicts and tensions between visitors, heritage and heritage managers • Requires heritage manager to identify, provide for, and market to designated visitor groups	***	***	*
Visitor Impact Management Model (VIMM)	• Focuses on reducing or controlling the impacts that threaten the quality of heritage and visitor experience • Uses explicit statements of management objectives and research and monitoring to determine heritage and social conditions, then generates a range of management strategies to deal with the impacts	**	**	**
The Limits of Acceptable Change (LAC)	• Focuses on the management of visitor impacts by identifying, first, desirable conditions for visitor activity to occur, then how much change is acceptable • A monitoring programme determines whether desirable conditions are within acceptable standards • A decision-making system determines manage-ment actions required to achieve the desired conditions	****	***	**

continued

Table 11.8 *continued*

Visitor management model	Key characteristics of visitor management model	Level of sophisti- cation	Range of contributing stakeholders	Actual application by heritage managers
Tourism Optimization Management Model (TOMM)	• Instead of limiting activity, it focuses on achieving optimum performance by addressing the sustainability of the heritage, viability of the tourism industry and empowerment of stakeholders • Covers environmental and experiential elements, as well as characteristics of the tourist market, economic conditions of the tourism industry and sociocultural conditions of the local community • Contains three main parts; context analysis, a monitoring programme and management response system	****	****	*

* Low; ** Moderate; *** High, **** Very high

Source: Hall and McArthur (1998: 123), reproduced with permission from the authors

decisions on whether to concentrate or disperse visitors. Last, hard measures seek to ration use by controlling tourist numbers; this often requires advance reservations, different pricing strategies and queuing.

These tools and techniques will begin to gather momentum at many tourist sites and destinations, with taxing tourists as the most radical measure being seriously considered by destinations under extreme pressure. This tool is really a manager's last resort to control tourism. The World Travel and Tourism Council (WTTC) does not want to see its industry members saddled with massive tourist taxation, since it is seen that this may stifle growth. It objected to unfair measures like tourism taxation, fees and levies in its 2002 report *Taxing Intelligently*. Yet the WTTC is not faced with managing tourism in Venice. Venice illustrates what happens in a free-market economy, where pricing and taxation may be the only tools left to radically manage the destination. In locations such as Venice debates on issues such as 'Tourism for All' may be arcane, given the fact that tourism is not a basic human need, but a consumer good purchased in a free market. Reducing costs of access such as the low-cost airlines have done has actually placed additional stresses on locations such as Venice. Making them potentially more accessible to a larger range of people due to price will conversely add problems for visitor management.

In an ideal world, Page and Dowling (2002) identify the value of environmental planning for ecotourism that destinations can extend and apply in other locations. Here the principles of identifying discrete planning zones (see Plate 11.5), with well-defined conservation values that also accommodate tourist activities and development, require

Plate 11.5
A very controversial development in the Cairngorms National Park was the construction of a
funicular railway up the side of the mountain to create a visitor attraction and convey skiers
(replacing former ski lifts). The environmental impact of this development raised considerable
controversy

Source: author

a detailed classification of visitor activity in relation to the need for protection and
compatibility with the resource base (see Plate 11.6). This involves identifying types of
zones for tourism where ecotourism or environmental issues are critical, such as:

- sanctuary zones, with special preservation provisions
- nature conservation zones, where protection and conservation are balanced
- outdoor recreation zones – natural areas where a wide range of outdoor activities
  are accommodated
- tourism development zones, with clusters of tourist activities and attractions/
  infrastructure
- other land uses to accommodate social and economic activity.

This approach allows tourism management to combine the reduction of environmental
impacts with enhancing the visitor experience.

These principles can be modified and refined for application in resorts and urban
tourism destinations to achieve a more coordinated and rational approach to tourism.

Plate 11.6
Rotorua, New Zealand, and its internationally acclaimed geysers and thermal area require careful visitor management; board walks and prepared paths are used to avoid visitor pressure on this natural attraction

Source: author

In sum, the activities and freedom of tourists will have to be curtailed in the future as resorts, destinations and sites realize the imperative of visitor management tools to implement a more rational and managed use of resources. This is to maintain a viable and dynamic tourism industry. To do this will require more innovative thinking and planning, partnerships between stakeholders and good communication to explain to visitors the rationale and need for such measures. The resolution of conflict, balancing tourism, non-tourism and other interests, will require planners and tourism managers to cooperate in the best interests of the locality in an increasingly competitive marketplace. With these issues in mind, attention now turns to the discussion of future management challenges for tourism in Chapter 12.

CHAPTER REVIEW

 # References

Ap, J. and Crompton, J. (1993) Residents' strategies for responding to tourism impacts. *Journal of Travel Research*, 32(1): 47–50.

Canestrelli, E. and Costa, P. (1991) Tourist carrying capacity: A fuzzy approach. *Annals of Tourism Research*, 18(2): 295–311.

Connell, J. (2005) Analysing coach tourism in Scotland: Trends and patterns. In S. J. Page, *Transport and Tourism: Global Perspectives*, 2nd edn. Harlow: Pearson Education.

Dobruszkes, F. (2013) The geography of European low-cost airline networks: A contemporary analysis. *Journal of Transport Geography*, 28(1): 75–88.

Douglas, N. and Douglas, N. (1996) The social and cultural impact of tourism in the Pacific. In C. M. Hall and S. J. Page (eds) *Tourism in the Pacific: Issues and Cases*. London: International Thomson Business Press.

Dowling, R. (1992) Tourism and environmental integration: The journey from idealism to realism. In C. Cooper and A. Lockwood (eds) *Progress in Tourism, Recreation and Hospitality Management*, Vol. 4. Chichester: John Wiley and Sons.

Doxey, G. V. (1975) A causation theory of visitor–resident irritants: Methodology and research inferences. In *Proceedings of the Travel Research Association 6th Annual Conference*. San Diego, CA: Travel Research Association.

English Tourist Board/Employment Department (1991) *Tourism and the Environment: Maintaining the Balance*. London: English Tourist Board.

European Travel Commission (2007) *European Tourism Insights 2007 – and Outlook for 2008*. Brussels: ETC.

Getz, D. (1993) Impacts of tourism on residents' leisure: Concepts, and a longitudinal case study of Spey Valley, Scotland. *Journal of Tourism Studies*, 4(2): 33–44.

Glasson, J., Godfrey, K. and Goodey, B. with Absalom, H. and Van der Borg, J. (1995) *Towards Visitor Impact Management: Visitor Impacts, Carrying Capacity and Management Responses in Europe's Historic Towns and Cities*. Aldershot: Avebury.

Hall, C. M. (1996) Environmental impact of tourism in the Pacific. In C.M. Hall and S. J. Page (eds) *Tourism in the Pacific: Issues and Cases*. London: International Thomson Business Press.

Hall, C. M. and McArthur, S. (1998) *Integrated Heritage Management*. London: The Stationery Office.

Mathieson, A. and Wall, G. (1982) *Tourism: Economic, Physical and Social Impacts*. Harlow: Longman.

Montanari, A. and Muscara, C. (1995) Evaluating tourist flows in historic cities: The case of Venice. *Tijdschrift voor Economische en Sociale Geografie*, 86(1): 80–87.

Murphy, P. (1985) *Tourism: A Community Approach*. London: Routledge.

Ogilvie, I. (1933) *The Tourist Movement*. London: Staples Press.

Page, S. J. (1995) *Urban Tourism*. London: Routledge.

Page, S. J. and Dowling, R. (2002) *Ecotourism*. Harlow: Prentice Hall.

Page, S. J. and Hall, C. M. (2003) *Managing Urban Tourism*. Harlow: Prentice Hall.

Pearce, D. G. (1989) *Tourism Development*. Harlow: Longman.

Pigram, J. and Jenkins, J. (1999) *Outdoor Recreation Management*. London: Routledge.

Potter, A. (1978) The methodology of impact analysis. *Town and Country Planning*, 46(9): 400–404.

Russo, A. (2002) The 'vicious circle' of tourism development in heritage cities. *Annals of Tourism Research*, 29(1): 165–182.

Sharpley, R. (2014) Host perceptions of tourism: A review of the research. *Tourism Management*, 42: 37–49.

Smith, V. (ed.) (1977) *Hosts and Guests: The Anthropology of Tourism*. Philadelphia: University of Pennsylvania Press.

Smith, V. L. (ed.) (1992) *Hosts and Guests: An Anthropology of Tourism*, 2nd edn. Philadelphia: University of Pennsylvannia Press.

Van der Borg, J., Costa, P. and Gotti, G. (1996) Tourism in European heritage cities. *Annals of Tourism Research*, 23(2): 306–321.

World Travel and Tourism Council (2002) *Taxing Intelligently*. London: WTTC.

 Further reading

This is probably one of the most comprehensively documented subject areas in tourism. A number of good books exist on the impacts of tourism, notably:

Wall, G. and Mathieson, A. (2006) *Tourism: Change, Impacts and Opportunities*. Harlow: Pearson Education.

And with reference to the less developed world:

Schyvens, R. (2002) *Tourism for Development: Empowering Communities*. Harlow: Prentice Hall.

And with an urban bias:

Page, S. J. and Hall, C. M. (2002) *Managing Urban Tourism*. Harlow: Prentice Hall.

 Questions

1   Why does tourism create impacts?
2   How can tourism impacts be managed?
3   In what situations does a tourism manager decide to use 'hard' and 'soft' visitor manager approaches?
4   What would you do, as Mayor of Venice, to address the problems and potential of tourism?

 Access additional resources

- For students: Multiple choice questions for each chapter, video links and further reading.
- For instructors: PowerPoint slides with tables and diagrams, additional case studies, video links and further reading.

2 The future of tourism

Post tourism?

Learning outcomes

This chapter discusses the future range of management problems that the tourism industry will have to address in the new millennium. On completion of the chapter, you should be able to understand:

* why the tourism industry needs to be proactive in managing its impacts
* how tourism has developed to a point where it may be uncontrollable in relation to the snowball concept
* what the main drivers of change will be in the tourism sector in the next decade
* the significance of crises for tourism managers.

Introduction

Throughout the book, there has been only a limited discussion of the way in which the global growth of tourism will change, develop and require new forms of planning and management to control its effects. One of the most pressing concerns for planners, decision-makers and businesses is: *will tourism stop growing and will it stop spreading across the globe?* Major challenges, such as the pressing demand among environmentalists to address the issue of climate change in relation to tourism is now apparent and this chapter will assess some of the issues shaping the future of tourism. For example, one key question which policy-makers and the tourism industry continues to ponder is: will climate change and other factors dampen the demand and volume of tourism in the future? In other words, will the spread of tourism stop? Or is it unstoppable?

The spread of tourism

One of the enduring themes in the history of travel is the pursuit by individuals, ruling elites and, latterly, the increasing numbers of leisure travellers, of unique, special and unspoilt locations to visit. This is part of the increasing geographical spread of tourism across the world to many countries that now embrace it as a method of stimulating economic activity, particularly where global trade barriers have frozen many developing countries out of engaging with lucrative trading blocs as a means of generating foreign currency. This has been one reason behind the GATS proposals to reduce such barriers to the trade in tourism services, although doing so is not without potential problems. The main issue is that some of these new tourist destinations have not been able to control tourism to retain their vital unique elements. The result is what was described in Chapter 1 in terms of the resort life cycle concept, where the growing popularity (demand) and supply by the tourism sector create a vibrant and dynamic business activity that begins to expand and develop. At that point, planning and policy issues need to be explicitly stated so that sustainable development is implicit in the future rationale for the destination. In 2003 the World Travel and Tourism Council (WTTC) launched a *Blueprint for New Tourism* which recognized that all stakeholders involved in tourism (including tourists, the tourism industry and destination communities) need to adopt a longer-term planning horizon as opposed to taking the short-termist commercial perspective that dominates the tourism sector approach globally (with some exceptions). Implicit in the WTTC's approach to tourism was a concern for sustainable tourism so that everything associated with tourism and the environment in which it is developed remains in balance.

This seemingly logical and phased approach to tourism destination management by WTTC assumes that tourism will continue to grow, and that the destinations can manage and accommodate the effects. It does not support a halt to tourism growth as it is an industry-funded body with its own agenda to continue to grow global tourism. This approach is very much based on the notion of growth management. *Growth management* as a concept is based on the idea that simple notions of tourism success (e.g. a growth in visitor arrivals and expenditure and value added to GDP by tourism) do not portray the real costs and benefits to communities and destinations. Some visionary locations embraced concerns about the problems which economic growth posed for the environment during the 1970s (e.g. California, Florida and Hawaii) while Whistler in British Columbia, Canada, has developed a tourism plan based on the notion of growth management which does not negate future growth: it states it needs to be managed. The evidence from Whistler is that the resident community endorsed such an approach where the environmental challenges which tourism poses are writ large in the landscape. Yet the evidence from the post-war period in terms of tourism development in many countries is that the growth in visitor arrivals has been far from orderly, phased, consistent and based on principles of managed growth. As the case of Spain in the 1960s illustrates, mass tourism rapidly established itself with few mechanisms in place to control development and growth. Indeed, public sector backing for tourism in Spain utilized the foreign exchange and political benefits of international tourism with little concern for long-term sustainability or environmental protection. Ironically, though not surprisingly, the introduction of a tourist tax to address environmental degradation in Spanish resorts in the new millennium, has had negative impacts in some mass markets (e.g. Germany), where it has contributed to a decline in visitor arrivals. It was removed as an ecotax in 2003 after a short period of implementation. This illustrates the power of the tourism lobby and its reluctance to see measures which may inhibit growth in either the volume or value of tourism in given locations. Newly discovered destinations, marketed and promoted by tour operators, have witnessed phenomenal growth (as illustrated in the case of Vietnam in Chapter 11), over and above the annual growth rates of global tourism. This has been compounded in some cases by the opening of new outbound markets, such as South Korea in the 1990s and China in the new millennium. Growth is expected in other Asian middle-class markets and the BRIC market, which have new-found wealth: travel (more specifically tourism) is the new must-have consumer product not only in the developed world but increasingly among those with the means to buy it in the developing world. It is for this reason that notions of growth management are crucial and different tools can be used (some of which were introduced in Chapter 11). Such tools include those based on controlling the quality of the environment for tourism (e.g. controls on architecture and building styles, landscaping and the density of development) as well as those which focus on the quantity of tourism (i.e. those associated with volume controls and impacts) such as permits to limit numbers at key sites, visitor management strategies for entire destinations, zoning of tourism land uses to control the spread of tourism and imposing limits on the size of tourism, as well as more wide-ranging strategies that can either disperse or concentrate tourism at specific sites or locations.

So will tourism stop growing? Some mature destinations that have passed through all the stages of the resort life cycle have probably reached the end of their growth period unless the public sector intervenes. The Sociologist John Urry (2004) pointed to places that die, which are exhausted in terms of capacity and the experience they offer (this may also result from a natural disaster like a volcanic eruption). The UK coastal resorts in east Kent provide an example of the worst-case scenario. Margate, Ramsgate and Broadstairs in Kent, UK reached their heyday in the 1950s and 1960s before low-cost overseas package holidays became more appealing to domestic tourists. There have been substantial interventions from the public sector (e.g. the local authorities and county council), funding from the EU and new attractions such as the Turner Gallery at a cost of £17.5 million, receiving 156 000 visits in three months. Whether this will be the catalyst for the area to rejuvenate the resorts successfully and address the post-tourism social and economic deprivation is unclear. Yet a number of other UK seaside resorts have been able to reinvent themselves successfully by repositioning and reimaging themselves (to use the current in-vogue marketing jargon): in simple terms, these destinations have found new products and ways to intervene in the resort life cycle to create a new demand for the destination. An example of this is Brighton, through business tourism and the pink market (gay and lesbian tourism products).

In many urban areas, new destinations have been created and the towns reimaged and remodelled to generate a new economic sector based on tourism and the cultural industries (e.g. Glasgow after hosting European City of Culture in 1990, Bradford and East London's Docklands area, and Liverpool with its hosting of the 2008 European City of Culture). In each case of urban regeneration, visitor growth has been significant although the public sector cost of stimulating these regeneration schemes has been massive, as the case of London's Olympic bid illustrated in Further Web Reading 1 and earlier in the book. At a time of scarce public resources, with endemic poverty in some areas of major cities seeking to regenerate their future based on pleasure and leisure, there have been few attempts to stop and question whether this is the most appropriate economic strategy. Tourism has been seen almost unquestioningly within the public sector, in a naive and simplistic manner, as a good development option: it can always be justified if visitors are generated. What consultants and analysts prefer not to say to these public sector bodies is that tourists will visit many major cities irrespective of their massive infrastructure development, although exceptions to this exist such as the case of Bilbao in Spain where the construction of a flagship project – the Guggenheim Museum – put the city on the international culture map. This reflects the poor understanding by some organizations in the public sector of tourism as a development tool. One major criticism is their reliance upon consultants and external advice rather than employing staff with an intuitive knowledge and understanding of what tourism is and the success factors needed in creating new developments. Equally they can be a useful scapegoat when public or private sector managers make the wrong decision on a project or development or they misjudge the market potential of a project.

Coastal resorts created in the 1980s and 1990s across the Mediterranean and Asia-Pacific (e.g. Pattaya in Thailand) have experienced growth in excess of 10 per cent per annum when many other destinations and countries have been content to receive growth of around 3–4 per cent per annum. Given the time lag involved in new tourism supply coming on stream, this has often had major impacts on local infrastructure, the environment and residents. Likewise, developing countries facing problems of a lack of clean water, scarce water supplies for agriculture and their population (see Chapter 1) in a fragile environment have seen inappropriate forms of tourism developed following public policy decisions. One example, is the development of golf tourism in South-East Asia and Goa, southern India: the maintenance of golfing greens requires large quantities of water and fertilizers, resulting in pesticides leaking into the water table, which pollutes the ground water and compromises its drinking quality. One of the most large-scale proposed expansions of tourism is described in Case Study 12.1 in relation to Turkey.

The snowball and amoeba concepts in tourism

The resort life cycle was used above to explain the linear growth of tourism through a series of stages of development ending in either stagnation or rejuvenation to stimulate the development process once again. This linear growth is best described as a snowball which begins to gather momentum as it rolls down a hill (see Figure 12.1). The agents of change that have the idea of stimulating tourism development as a small snowball (i.e. the public and private sector) do not envisage the rapid transition to mass tourism. Initial visions of tourism are rapidly compromised, despite the best intentions of the public sector to control it. The pressure exerted by entrepreneurs, tour operators and other stakeholders takes precedence in early stages of development. Through time, these interest groups impact upon policy and the growing economic dependence upon tourism in the resort adds further pressure. The snowball grows and gathers momentum, almost unstoppable and out of control; public sector interventions become less effective, only able to work around the edge of the problem to try to control an uncontrollable phenomenon that takes on a prominent role in the resort or locality.

Although local antagonism grows, tourism cannot be restricted due to the inevitable political fallout because of employment dependency issues. Yet if the development process continues, it may saturate and destroy the destination and its resource base. This means that the destination will be unable to sustain tourism any longer in that form. The destination becomes unattractive, overdeveloped and an environmentally compromised location (i.e. visual and physical pollution prevail). Images of saturation lead tour operators to use it as a low-cost, mass resort while high-spending visitors seek more attractive locations.

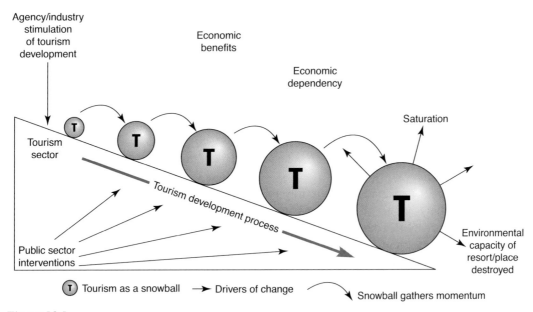

Figure 12.1
Tourism growth and development – the snowball concept

Source: author

CASE STUDY 12.1
THE TOURISM STRATEGY OF TURKEY TO 2023

In 2007, the Ministry of Culture and Tourism launched the new tourism strategy for Turkey to 2023. It fits with the country's Ninth Development Scheme, an economic development strategy to 2013. The strategy recognizes that a focus on the development of mass tourism has led to:

- the geographical concentration of tourism on the Mediterranean and Aegean coast
- distorted urban development patterns
- environmental and infrastructure problems.

The new strategy seeks to address these problems by creating a master plan for tourism in Turkey. This will establish nine tourism development areas, seven thematic tourism corridors, ten tourism cities and five ecotourism zones by focusing investment and public sector interventions on areas of priority. It will be supported by improving transport infrastructure – building motorways, and establishing cruise ship and yacht marinas and fast links. The plan seeks to grow tourism to 63 million arrivals by 2023 to expand the tourism economy to US$86 million. The ambition is to establish Turkey as world brand in tourism and to be in the top five receiving countries for overseas visitors.

This seems to be a massive expansionist programme for a destination that has already faced many problems linked to tourism. It is also somewhat surprising to find such an expansionist strategy when many other countries are recognizing the problems of climate change associated with travel and tourism and the difficulty in balancing the sustainability of tourism with environmental concerns. Like Dubai, Turkey is seeking to substantially reposition its economy and future prosperity on the market for tourism. This raises many issues for the way in which tourism is embraced as a development option, the consequences for the way it spreads and the problems of controlling growth. This will be discussed in the next section.

Although this is a gross simplification of the public and private sector role in tourism development, the basic principles have been replicated across the world. Locations have embraced tourism without really appreciating how complex and powerful it can be – or become – once vested interests begin to drive it forward so that they can reap short-term profits.

Another explanation of the way tourism grows and expands might be described as the 'amoeba effect'. The amoeba, as a single-cell, simple form of life has the ability to reproduce itself. Tourism is not dissimilar because once the initial amoeba is introduced to a locality, and finds a welcoming home that embraces it as a mechanism to help stimulate economic activity, the process has begun (see Figure 12.2). The ability of tourism to replicate itself, but then adapt and change to meet customer needs in certain cases, means that the amoeba keeps dividing and producing new entrepreneurs, as innovation and change lead to more development.

Taking the example of London's tourism accommodation stock: constraints in central London led to development elsewhere as the amoeba looked for a new niche where it

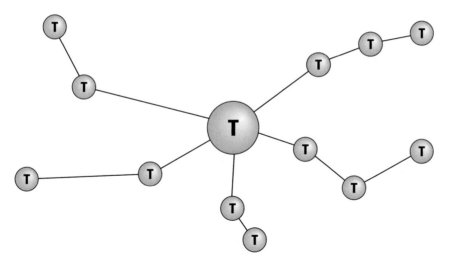

Figure 12.2
The amoeba concept

Source: author

could survive and prosper. This simplistic explanation of tourism as a development process makes control, planning and management extremely difficult because the ground rules keep changing as tourism assumes a new form and nurtures new visitors. It is only at the point where the resort or destination reaches total saturation and is destroyed as an attractive location that the amoeba moves to a new home and the process begins again. However, there are good examples of public sector interventions managing tourism and seeking to encase the amoeba and prevent it growing any more, especially at sensitive environmental sites. The amoeba's ability to thrive beyond a controlled level is shifted. Unfortunately, these are the exceptions rather than the rule.

So, to re-examine the question: *will tourism continue to grow?* If one considers the snowball and amoeba analogies, then there will almost certainly be tourism growth at a global scale. At a national and regional/local level, growth will largely be dependent upon the attractiveness of the locality in providing a conducive location for tourism to root itself and begin developing. The example of tourism and regeneration in Chapter 10 explained how this might occur. The challenge for the public and private sector stakeholders is to try to control and direct tourism – constrain it if necessary – to meet local social, environmental, economic and political objectives while ensuring it does not escalate too quickly and get out of control. Yet with governments positively encouraging the boom in low-cost air travel (which is artificially subsidized due to an absence of fuel tax on aviation fuel), questioning the efficacy (i.e. the rationale) of continued tourism growth is problematic: too many vested interests wish to see it grow due to the economic benefits they receive. This is increasingly difficult: organizations intent on promoting global tourism growth do not want to see limits imposed on tourism growth. Given this assessment of tourism, it is interesting to review briefly the ways in which researchers, analysts and policy-makers consider the future of tourism in different contexts.

Understanding the future of tourism

The highly variable nature of tourism, particularly its vulnerability to change due to fashion, trends and shock events such as 9/11, requires that public and private sector interests try to understand these fluctuations (see Table 12.1 for a range of studies of different aspects of the future of tourism).

Table 12.1 Key studies on the future of tourism

Climate change, transport and energy

Becken, S. (2008) Indicators for managing tourism in the face of peak oil. *Tourism Management*, 29(4): 695–705.

Becken, S. (2009) Global challenges for tourism and transport: How will climate change and energy affect the future of tourist travel? In S. J. Page, *Transport and Tourism: Global Perspectives*, 3rd edn. Harlow: Pearson.

Bristow, A., Tight, M., Pridmore, A. and May, A. (2008) Developing pathways to low carbon-based transport in Great Britain by 2050. *Energy Policy*, 38: 3427–3455.

Dubois, G., Peeters, P., Ceron, J., Gössling, S. *et al.* (2011) The future tourism mobility of the world population: Emission growth versus climate policy. In *Transportation Research Part A: Policy and Practice*, 45(10): 1031–1042.

Forsyth, P. *et al.* (2008) *The Carbon Footprint of Australian Tourism*. Sydney: Cooperative Research Centre for Tourism.

Gössling, S., Peeters, P., Ceron, J., Dubois, G., Patterson, T. and Richardson, R. (2005) The eco-efficiency of tourism. *Ecological Economics*, 54: 417–434.

Forecasting and scenario planning

Duinker, P. and Greig, L. (2007) Scenario analysis in environmental impact assessment: Improving explorations of the future. *Environmental Impact Assessment Review*, 27(3), 206–219.

Page. S. J., Yeoman, I., Greenwood, C. and Connell, J. (2010) Scenario planning as a tool to understand uncertainty in tourism: The example of transport and tourism in Scotland to 2025. *Current Issues in Tourism*, 13(2): 99–137.

Page, S. J., Yeoman, I., Munro, C., Connell, J. and Walker, L. (2006) A case study of best practice – VisitScotland's prepared response to an influenza pandemic. *Tourism Management*, 27(3): 361–393.

UNWTO (2010) *Demographic Change and Tourism*. Madrid: UNWTO.

Tourism and growth management

Gill, A. (2004) Tourism communities and growth management. In A. Lew, C. M. Hall and A. Williams (eds) *A Companion of Tourism*. Oxford: Blackwell, 569–597.

BRIC markets

World Tourism Organization (2008) *The Chinese Outbound Travel Market*. Madrid: UNWTO.

World Tourism Organization (2009a) *The Russian Outbound Travel Market*. Madrid: UNWTO.

World Tourism Organization (2009b) *The Indian Outbound Travel Market*. Madrid: UNWTO.

Table 12.2 The ten key issues affecting global tourism in 2014

1. Continued impact on the travel and tourism industry resulting from the global economic slowdown

2. Concerns for safety and security remains an important issue for the travel and tourism industry

3. Necessity for increased local/regional/national leadership in tourism policy and strategic planning

4. Importance of maintaining a destination's sustainability of social, cultural, natural and built resources

5. Educating users about optimization of technologies and online applications in the tourism industry

6. Understanding the transformative effect travel and tourism has on global socio-economic progress

7. Responding to increased interest in potential long-term consequences of climate change on tourism

8. Negative impact on the travel and tourism industry of increases in fuel prices and airline fees

9. Effect on travel and tourism from natural and manmade disasters and world political disruptions

10. Changes in tourism demand resulting from increased travel by emerging nations

Source: © David Edgell (2014), reproduced with kind permission of D. Edgell

Understanding the changes and trends likely to affect tourism in 2014 and the next year or so (see Table 12.2) is much less problematic than trying to anticipate the nature and shape of tourism in 2020. This is because we can never be certain about the future because we do not know what will happen and the processes which will shape the future. In particular, one needs to understand how tourism activity, especially trends, are likely to affect countries, localities and places in the short term (up to five years) and long term (up to ten years).

To try to envisage how tourism will perform, analysts attempt to forecast the future of tourism, but they must be aware of underlying trends that may pose problems as well as crises and disasters. Glaeßer (2006) observed that natural disasters and shock events are becoming more common in tourism and thus there is a greater demand for crisis management tools to manage their effects. It is not surprising to find tourism analysts utilizing research techniques such as forecasting and scenario planning, which seek to construct a number of scenarios of how future trends might play out. This involves:

*   framing the issues involved such as the drivers (i.e. the key trends and factors affecting these trends) of demand and supply for tourism (see Case Study 12.2)
*   identifying people who may be involved in providing input and critical reviews of the scenarios

CASE STUDY 12.2
UNDERSTANDING THE FUTURE DRIVERS OF CHANGE FOR GLOBAL TOURISM

Stephen J. Page, Ian Yeoman and Chris Greenwood

According to the World Tourism Organization the principal determinants and influences that will impinge on the development and growth of tourism activity into the future include:

- prosperity and affordability: according to research by the Future Foundation, holidays are perceived by consumers as the number one luxury product. They desire holidays over houses, fast cars, perfumes and designer clothes. The desire for holidays has been driven by affordability and prosperity. Prosperity is about rising incomes, which over the last 20 years have doubled in real terms, whereas affordability is about falling prices. This is exemplified by consumers who will stay in luxury hotels but travel by low-cost airlines. Over the next two decades we will see the rise of the middle classes of China, India and Eastern Europe, who will be the travellers of tomorrow

- accessibility: the tourists' world is shrinking due to technological advances. The advent of the internet to inform and break boundaries allows consumers to choose a tourist destination anywhere in the world and beyond. With the restructuring of the economies of scale brought on by the online economy, travel and tourism is becoming a buyer's market. In recent years the low-cost airline has come to represent the pinnacle in the adoption of technology. Travel is so much more easier today, with more direct flights between destinations and the cost in real terms, that is yield per passenger per airline kilometre, is the lowest since statistics begun. The world is opening up to travel

- events: with the worldwide expansion of tourism destinations, the individual is increasingly exposed or influenced by events, whether sporting or environmental disasters. With arbitrary acts of terrorism from nation-less organizations and the increasing occurrences of extreme weather events in popular tourist destinations, the role of government policies in all areas of society determines the individual's feeling of safety in a particular situation

- globalization and competition: the globalization/localization divide is formed of two concurrent but apparently conflicting developments in which the world is increasingly polarized between the macro and the micro. All countries are integrally locked into the global economy and no market can succeed without operating in all major established and emerging markets. Populations are responding to this globalization of economies and cultures by looking to their own identities. The openness of the world economy means the tourist has more choice and increased competition means better value.

More individual drivers which will shape the tourism proposition and the motivation to travel for consumers include:

- the 'anxiety society', health and safety: in the short term, fear will lead to risk minimization and tourists will avoid perceived dangers. However, over time a sense of complacency occurs where travellers start to believe that 'whatever will happen, will happen', at which point a wider choice of experiences opens up to them. Associated with this is the events mega driver: specific events in a location will affect tourism in the short term but the resilience of the consumer invariably returns quickly

- longevity: there is a continuing trend towards ageing populations in the established economies. This means contracting workforces with fewer younger people and therefore pension payment constraint. Society is changing demographically; there are higher divorce rates, people are marrying and starting families later in life, remarriages and second families are becoming more common. All these alter the perceptions of households. Predictions are that in the short term, highly mobile mature consumers with high disposable incomes will seek an experience-based economy, with the long term showing changes to tourism demands to take into account protracted family associations and varying financial levels

- image and brand: destinations will become a fashion accessory with the traveller increasingly adopting this as fundamental in the choice of destinations. Tourism products that have something that the consumer can associate with (such as heritage or celebrity endorsement) and new tourist destinations that are seen as 'untouched' will develop an associated cachet. Brand will become increasingly used to distinguish between destinations where the market is saturated with lots of messages. Further, brands and images will become more important in the future as destination choice will be shaped by the values that the consumer holds. Destination brand values of the future will have to be trustworthy, ethical and sustainable

- technology: the tourist of tomorrow will be better informed, have wider choice and be able to purchase holidays in an instant, all driven by technology – whether it is the internet, video on demand or online bookings

- environment: travellers are increasingly aware of the social and environmental issues around tourism. This is leading to conflict between their conscience and their desire to travel. Sustainable travel products are intended to bridge the gap between the two states of mind. However, the consumer will untimely decide which factor is of greater importance

- individualism: a main challenge to marketing tourism destinations will be the increasing diversification of interests, tastes and demands among travellers. The availability of products to supply and the range of demand will see a split in provision, with mainstream products being provided to the majority. Through the use of technology, smaller-scale micro marketing will target individuals and provide highly tailored products to meet their requirements

- time pressures: with changing work practices and a blurring of the traditional boundaries of work and leisure time, the trend is increasingly towards escapism and indulgence. Several shorter breaks are replacing the established long break as greater pressure is put on people's time and there are greater levels of stress at the workplace. There is a change in people's perception of a holiday, moving towards something which captures an experience through relaxation or through a sensory overload of excessive adrenalin and is concentrated to enable a physical and mental recharging before the return to normality

- the movement from an experience economy to authenticity: the industrialized world is in transition from the service to the experience economy. As the experience economy matures, the desire for authenticity emerges, a trend based on a desire for the real rather than something that is false

- perceptions of luxury: luxury is becoming less about materialism and increasingly about enrichment and time. The consumer is increasingly aware of the importance of luxury as a concept of fulfilment. Destinations are adapting to this demand by diversifying into niche areas where the traditional perceptions of luxury and opulence are sharing the market with providers of wellness and remoteness
- quality: there is little doubt that quality is the hallmark of consumer expectations today and in the future. Consumers look for a degree of individual treatment. More sophisticated technology tracks and records consumer preferences and desires, and using this allows the operator to engage with a more individualized relationship with the customer. The consumer is certainly becoming more sophisticated: there is no clear cause–effect relationship between consumer spending and social class. The waters have become muddied by trends such as less affluent consumers who 'trade up', seeking to pay for that little extra luxury on a package holiday by paying for business class or extra legroom. Conversely, the purchaser of a low-priced airline ticket may be using the flight to travel to enjoy a luxury experience and the mode of transport becomes less significant to consumption, given their cultural acceptance of low-cost travel to reach the destination where few options may exist and their awareness that the entire flight will be non-segmented in terms of class of travel – the only distinguishing feature is how much you pay for the right to travel.

Source: Developed from Page *et al.* (2007)

- drawing a picture or pictures of the future using trends, themes, critical relationships and issues associated with the problem that is being considered (i.e. how would we respond as a destination to three different severities of earthquake?)
- providing known uncertainties that could impact upon the scenarios and upset the status quo, and factors that are critical in moving a scenario from a pre-crisis, to crisis and post-crisis stage (i.e. tipping points)
- identifying possible paths for different scenarios
- testing the plausibility of the scenarios
- anticipating how people and organizations associated with tourism might respond during the different scenarios
- identifying strategies to manage the future scenarios.

Whilst critics of such approaches argue that such 'crystal gazing' exercises may never result in accurate predictions of how the future may evolve, there is a growing acceptance in public and private sector organizations of the need for such exercises. The July 2005 terrorist bombings in London are a case in point: the rapid responses and the mobilization of a disaster plan had already been tested after a scenario planning exercise and dry run of the crisis some months previously. Concerns over tourist safety, terrorism, sustainability, climate change and the impact on future configurations of tourist travel have made such exercises all the more valuable. An example of such an exercise was the joint project between the author and VisitScotland to assess the possible impact of avian flu and a flu pandemic on Scottish tourism, with one outcome being a contingency plan for the management of Scottish tourism and its implementation in 2008–2009 during the outbreak of swine flu (see Chapter 1 for more detail).

One other tool which is far more commonly used by managers in tourism is forecasting. Forecasting uses quantitative research methods (especially mathematical models – see UNWTO 2008 for a review). Forecasting in tourism is far from an exact science. This is because of the effects of so many unknown factors (e.g. exchange rates, fuel prices, cost of travel, political stability in the origin and destination area and impact of inflation). Yet forecasting still helps planners to measure the order of magnitude of potential change that may occur in tourism. It will be important in a commercial context in trying to match future supply with likely demand (i.e. will an airline need to invest in additional capacity to meet demand?), and in maximizing revenue and profits through the optimum efficiency in resource or asset use. This has been summarized by Archer (1987: 77) in a management context as

> no manager can avoid the need for some form of forecasting: a manager must plan for the future in order to minimise the risk of failure or, more optimistically, to maximise the possibilities of success. In order to plan, he must use forecasts. Forecasts will always be made, whether by guesswork, teamwork or the use of complex models, and the accuracy of the forecasts will affect the quality of the management decision.

In essence, forecasting is about the assessment of future change in the demand for tourism, estimating future traffic and a range of possible scenarios to gauge likely changes in the scale of demand. This invariably involves looking at past tourism trends to statistically model future demand, using a variety of models, formulae and developments in the sub-field of economics known as 'econometrics'. In constructing these models, the analyst will normally build in key tourism variables such as number of tourist trips, tourist expenditure, market shares of tourism and tourism's share of gross domestic product. The resulting models will look at the factors that are likely to have a bearing on demand, to develop the forecasts. For example, the UN World Tourism Organization has produced forecasts for global tourism to 2030 called Tourism Towards 2030, which anticipates 1.8 billion international visitor arrivals. The types of changes which the study identified that will impact upon global tourism include:

- tourism growth of 3.3. per cent per annum for the period 2010–2030, slowing to 2.9 per cent by 2030, with arrivals increasingly globally at 43 million a year
- arrivals will grow the fastest in Asia, Latin America, Central and Eastern Europe, at 4.4 per cent, which is twice the rate of growth forecast for advanced economies
- by 2015, arrivals in emerging economies will reach 57 per cent of the total, an increase from 30 per cent of the total in 1980
- Asia Pacific will see the greatest increases in tourism, reaching 535 million arrivals by 2030.

Source: UNWTO

However, when examining any tourism forecast, one needs to look at the assumptions used by the analyst, what data sources are being used and what the analyst is intending to produce. Regardless of forecasts there will always be pressures for tourism to change.

The pressures for tourism to change

At a global scale, and particularly in the industrialized Western countries, there is evidence from consumer attitudes towards tourism that the self-destructive nature of tourism causes some visitors to question the impact of where they travel. A greater consciousness of the effects of tourism is now permeating both the consumer and the more environmentally responsible tour operators. This is a slow and gradual process of change, and there is always likely to be a role for the mass packaged, low-cost, high-volume, sun, sea and sand holidays. However, at the upper end of the market, a greater demand for environmentally sensitive and conservation-oriented niche products may begin to permeate the activities of the tourism sector, as airlines, tour operators and accommodation providers introduce environmental products to recognize these consumer tastes as illustrated in Chapter 2 and 3 (e.g. the rise of slow travel as a new trend). The factors involved in pressurizing tourism to change can be divided into those that are external to tourism and beyond its control (e.g. exchange rates) and those that are within its grasp.

An ageing travelling public

In many of the Western industrialized countries, tourism markets are becoming characterized by an ageing population. This has been termed the 'senior market' (also called the silver market in Japan, or mature traveller), which, internationally, exceeds 100 million arrivals, or one in six of all international trips. The senior market is particularly notable in the USA, Europe and Japan, which are major contributors to outbound travel globally. In many European countries, the over-55s now comprises 25 per cent of the total population – although, statistically, the likelihood of travel decreases with increasing age. Senior markets are less seasonal, able to utilize high disposable incomes in those cases where mortgage payments are negligible, and require more attention to their needs. This is reflected in the growth of specialist tour operators (e.g. Saga in the UK and Elderhost in the USA). What is evident is the continued growth in this market and the potential for tourism businesses to adapt to meet these consumers' needs. For example, the revival of coach tourism for long holidays in many parts of Europe reflects one niche product that is particularly favoured by the grey market, since it is perceived as safe and convenient and meets the travellers' needs.

New social trends

New social trends have emerged over the last decade in developed outbound markets. For example, women are playing a more dominant role in the labour market than they were 20 years ago. People in the 20- to 40-year age bracket are marrying later and deferring having children; as a result they have more disposable income, making them a lucrative expanding niche market. This niche market and much of the senior market places a renewed emphasis on the consumption of luxury tourism products. Whereas luxury products in the 1970s and 1980s were often associated with consumer goods and a house, now travel products have become far more fashionable among both the elite and the general population, who are willing to spend more money on a luxury experience.

New outbound markets

In the 1990s, much of the attention on the future growth of tourism was focused on the rise of the Chinese outbound market and the growth in outbound middle-class travellers in Asia. Since then, other markets have followed a similar growth path and now the attention for future outbound markets has shifted to the BRIC economies (i.e. Brazil, Russia, India and China). The significance of the BRIC economies is reflected in the rising economic power where they control 50 per cent of the world's exports and also have large foreign currency reserves alongside a growing middle class. Yet for these economies only around 5 per cent of the population has travelled overseas before and so their growing middle classes will have a substantial impact on future tourism demand as their wealth and affluence increase (see recent UNWTO reports on the BRIC markets in Table 12.1). One of the most obvious forms of tourism growth will be linked to global travel to visit family and kin in other parts of the world. What is certain is the scale of such markets is huge and has the potential to change dramatically the nature of international travel. This reflects the importance of economic and political changes, such as allowing outbound and inbound travel as well as the significance of growing affluence which are notable in shaping future tourism trends: governments can also constrain, facilitate and prevent tourism according to the policies they promote in terms of domestic and international tourism.

Crises and disasters in tourism

One of the principal external factors that can affect tourism and is highly unpredictable for organizations and countries is a crisis or disaster (man-made or natural). The challenge of coping with catastrophic events poses many issues for an organization's ability to adapt to change, as reflected in the foot and mouth crisis in the UK in 2001, 9/11, the 2004 tsunami and the hurricanes that affected the USA in 2005 as well as the 2010 earthquake in Christchurch, New Zealand and the 2011 floods in Queensland, Australia.

Crises in tourism and business response: A management challenge?

Although such crises may be short-term in nature, the exposure of the tourism sector is significant and apparently stable business activities can be transformed into chaos. However, such crises may also have the potential to stimulate innovation, as Chapter 9 highlighted. Ultimately, crises and chaos illustrate tourism's highly volatile nature and indicates how adaptable organizations need to be to change. In a management context, Faulkner and Russell (1999) identified the typical modes of operation for entrepreneurs in tourism, who instituted chaos and change, and for those who were planners and regulators of change. This has important implications for how tourism ventures are managed. Chaos makers were characterized by being:

- individualistic
- flexible
- innovative
- experimental
- intuitive
- risk takers.

Regulators were characterized by being:

- risk-averse
- rational
- controlled
- planners
- rigid in their outlook
- concerned with reaching consensus on decision-making.

Therefore, the profitability of tourism organizations is increasingly being linked to the ability to:

- innovate
- manage and adapt to change and crises
- manage, recruit and retain high-quality human resources
- develop competitive business ventures by understanding the economic, social, political and managerial challenges of operating tourism enterprises
- react to public policy, and influence its formulation and implementation, particularly the growing concerns over regulation and its cost to business (see Web Case 12.1)
- think creatively and globally, with an ability to apply international best practice in a local context
- understand how tourism trends affect one's day-to-day business operations.

In order to react and embrace change, many tourism organizations need to be able to understand and implement technology.

Technology and tourism

Technology is globally connecting tourism businesses and clients together. In tourism environments, the harnessing of technology to achieve entertainment and enhance fun has been widely embraced in the theme park sector. In the USA, the theme park industry generates over US$11 billion a year, while globally over 120 large theme parks exist, each attracting over a million visits a year. Indeed, from a management perspective, the creation of man-made tourism environments such as theme parks may fill a niche in the market for accommodating mass tourism without compromising the local environment. Theme parks allow large numbers to be accommodated, using technology, fantasy, escapism and a safe, monitored and highly managed experience (as with the Disney model illustrated in Chapter 9). This is certainly a trend which will continue, as continuous improvements and innovation help these tourism environments to adapt to new consumer tastes and trends.

At an individual business level, information communications technology or ICT is the main driver of change, requiring better management for tourism operations to harness their potential. ICT provides up-to-date, managed client data and the scope to search and select a wide range of products and experiences. ICT has enabled forward-looking businesses to respond to the demand for more up-to-date information and tailor-made products. The worldwide web also allows the customer to undertake this process themselves (dynamic packaging software makes this much easier), challenging the supply chain and its traditional role in selling tourism products, some industry analysts suggest. The rapid growth in online booking may have stabilized in terms of large corporations, but it continues to make inroads into traditional travel agent business. ICTs are now widely adopted in the tourism sector, and innovation is likely to push further developments that allow tourism products to reach a wider audience. Above all, ICTs are making society, and the consumer, more demanding and more conscious of getting value for money. Yet technology will not address all the future processes likely to shape tourism trends, especially environmental issues such as climate change.

Climate change, tourism and the environment: Its impact on future tourism trends

There is major concern among scientists that the world's climate is changing. Global warming resulting in climate change could affect the climate and weather in many of the world's major tourism destinations by 2050. Tourism related CO_2 emissions arise from tourist mobility (75 per cent of emissions) and from on-site consumption (26 per cent) and recent research by Peeters and Dubios (2010) indicates that tourism-related CO_2 emissions will continue to grow at a rapid rate up to 2050. Many of these longer-term changes associated with climate change are also likely to have some shorter-term effects on tourism including:

- temperature increases of up to 0.5°C per decade causing many destinations with Mediterranean and African climates to become too hot for normal tourist use in the peak summer season, thereby changing the likely use of many coastal resorts in the long term
- a drop in summer rainfall in many arid locations, such as small islands, making technological solutions to water supply (e.g. desalination) critical and ensuring that tourism growth is dependent upon the viability of technology

- global warming which will lead to sea level rises. Vulnerable islands located around sea level, many of which have thriving tourism industries, will be lost unless expensive flood protection schemes are put in place
- changes to weather patterns, such as an increased severity of storms, which may make access to many island destinations problematic, if sea access is the only viable option
- the possible removal of snow cover by global warming in locations dependent upon winter sports, reducing their appeal and attraction
- the need for destinations to think more strategically about the risk assessment associated with climate change in terms of their physical environment as a context and attractor of tourism activity, whilst changes to weather patterns may cause significant disruption to tourism and alter visitors' perception of resorts and areas.

According to UNWTO and UNEP's (2008) climate change report, there are four mitigation strategies for tackling greenhouse gas emissions in tourism as Figure 12.3 indicates.

Of the four strategies in Figure 12.3, the most effective is reducing energy use but it also highlights the need for more radical strategies whereby people may need to have

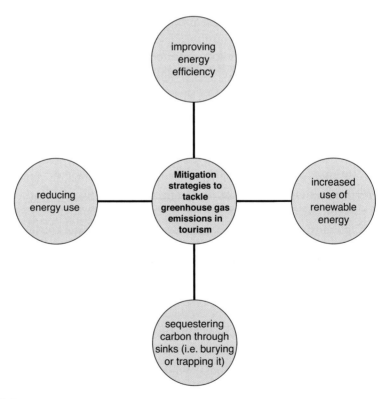

Figure 12.3
Mitigation strategies for tackling greenhouse emissions in tourism

Source: author

their holidays (or the carbon emissions they produce) limited in the future through carbon allowances. This may be critical if the reduction of CO_2 is to be achieved given the predictions of future growth in tourism and the corresponding need to reduce emissions to tackle climate change. In other words, despite the potential technological solutions which are heralded for transport to reduce CO_2 emissions in the future, the scale of demand for travel and tourism seems an insurmountable problem for future policy-makers without a radical shift in the desire and availability of cheap travel by air and car. Alternative strategies such as decarbonizing the entire tourism supply chain may be the only long-term option if the global climate change problems associated with tourism are to be addressed. These environmental concerns will certainly begin to feed into the changing nature of tourism as a business activity, once consumers start to more fully recognize how important climate change and environmental risks associated with global warming become.

New business trends

Change is rapid in the tourism sector: today's trends are redundant tomorrow. Tourism has gathered momentum since the 1980s as technology has increased the scale, extent and rate of communication across the tourism sector. ICT has forced many tourism businesse to scrutinize their operations, to assess whether they are operating in an efficient and profitable manner. Greater industry concentration through mergers and acquisitions will certainly continue, premised by perceived economies of scale and efficiency gains. This also reflects competition strategy in the tourism sector, with larger players seeking to dominate certain sectors (e.g. retailing, aviation and tour operation) or adopt integrated operations to raise profitability (e.g. TUI in Europe). This leads to a new operating environment in which evolving trends can create recognition of the need to participate in certain products if businesses are to compete.

In an ICT context, software launched by RWA – its 'sell it' software package – is also allowing more tour operators to compete for the online market by allowing clients to search by destination, departure point and holiday type. Canadian research on travel since 9/11 noted that these new trends have seen changes in travellers' behaviour, including demands for increased evidence of security, more road-based trips, shorter trips and cruises, a growth in the demand for safer destinations and a larger number of discounted travel offers to stimulate demand.

Furthermore, new business processes, called hypercompetition, now characterize the fast-growing tourism sector. D'Aveni (1988) cited in Page and Connell (2009), characterized hypercompetition in this sector of the tourism industry in terms of:

- rapid product innovation
- aggressive competition
- shorter product life cycles
- businesses experimenting with meeting customers' needs
- the rising importance of business alliances

- the destruction of norms and rules of national oligopolies such as state-owned airlines which still dominate South American and South-East Asian aviation.

D'Aveni (1988) identified four processes that are contributing to the hypercompetition. These are:

1 customers want better quality at lower prices
2 rapid technological change, enhanced through the use of ICT
3 the expansion of very aggressive companies who are willing to enter markets for a number of years with a loss leader product (e.g. low-cost airlines), with a view to destroying the competition so that they will harness the market in the long term
4 the progressive removal of government barriers towards competition throughout the world.

Hypercompetition changes how competitors enter the marketplace and how they disrupt the existing business:

- by redefining the product market by offering more at a lower price
- by modifying the industry's purpose and focus by bundling and splitting industries
- by disrupting the supply chain by redefining the knowledge and know-how needed to deliver the product to the customer
- by harnessing global resources from alliances and partners to compete with non-aligned business as competition becomes more global.

But given such changes, will tourism be limited by governments in the future – and if so, how?

Limiting tourism: The beginning of the end?

With global concerns for environmental impacts generated by the pollution tourism induces, environmental management has emerged as a new buzzword for the tourism sector. This has also been embodied in a much larger debate on the ethical issues involved in how and what form of tourism governments will allow to develop. For example, legal and moral issues surround the exploitation that sex tourism causes in many countries and this has produced a great deal of debate on how tourism fuels such activity. NGOs such as the UNWTO and End Child Prostitution and Trafficking have pursued a campaign since 1996 to eradicate this unacceptable element of tourism. Similarly the work of other organisations like Tourism Concern (see Chapter 1) acts as an important counter-weight to the impact of big business with its unwieldy effect on people and their communities and environment.

One notable development has been the introduction by the tourism industry of voluntary codes of conduct (see www.world-tourism.org for the UNWTO view on these codes and its own Ethical Code of Conduct). This is seen as one attempt by the industry to try to reform some of its bad practices and impacts.

Similar debates are also emerging concerning the impact of air travel and transport on global warming, initially illustrated by the 2002 World Summit in South Africa. Global warming highlights the interdependencies that exist between different ecosystems and man's damaging effects through tourism. If tourism continues to make a major contribution to such environmental problems, then it will be one more economic activity that is self-destroying. Tourism as a consumer activity is also accentuating the socio-economic extremes between the 'haves' and 'have-nots' in society at a local, national and international scale, especially in less developed countries. This has led to a greater interest in community-based tourism development which has been rebranded to widen the role for tourism in poverty reduction in less developed countries (called pro-poor tourism).

Proponents of peace have argued that tourism can aid understanding between cultures and societies. Yet the visits of Westernized travellers to less developed areas simply highlights the poverty and income gap, further fuelling discontent, envy and, in some cases, crime and political upheaval – failing to generate peace. Human nature is such that the real impact of tourism and the wealth and consumption of visitors on places with low levels of development can be psychologically and culturally damaging. At the same time, it may bring economic benefits. This highlights the conundrum – tourism's internal tension and tendency to be both positive and negative. In this context, more forceful policy and public sector management will be required to manage these relationships if potentially damaging effects are to be limited.

But should tourism be allowed to spread to all parts of the planet in an uncontrolled or even planned manner?

The evidence is that tourism's growing influence is set to impact on every corner of the globe. Even pristine wilderness areas and very fragile environments such as Antarctica are not immune from the visitor phenomenon. Attempts to license and manage visitors to such pristine environments and charge premium prices have not limited their impacts: they have simply accentuated the demand for visits. For example, the first recorded overflight (i.e. a scenic flight) of Antarctica was by the Chilean national airline (Linea Aerea Nacional) in 1957, the first commercial ship visited in 1958 and regular tourist voyages began in the 1960s with around 1000 visits a year up to 1993. By 1998, tourism had expanded to 15 000 ship-borne visits per annum, concentrated in the November–February period. Some forecasts suggest that this could grow to 20 000 by 2010 but by 2004/2005 it had already exceeded 30 000 visits a year. In 2010–2011, it had reached 26 000 visits and it exceeded 35 000 in visits in 2012–2013. Whilst Antarctica is a large continent, the geographical distribution of landings by tourists are confined to a limited number of locations. Various policies exist to limit the development of commercial tourism in Antarctica, such as the 1999 Madrid Protocol, the 1994 Antarctic Treaty Consultative Meeting in Kyoto and a voluntary Code of Practice among the International Association of Antarctic Tour Operators (formed in 1991). Yet it is patently obvious that tourism has developed: it exists as a business activity if only as scenic flights and ship-borne visits by Western visitors who are typically prosperous, well educated and professional. Antarctica highlights both the amoeba principle and the evolution of the snowball concept: attempts by vested interests (i.e. tour operators) and conservation agencies to limit visits are slowly being eroded – though arguably limitation is in their interest, as restricting supply keeps the prices high. Whilst many scientists do not accept that tourism is a detrimental activity to the continent at the current time, there is compelling physical evidence of actual and potential risks including:

- increased litter and rubbish disposal
- accelerated degradation of tourist landing sites including footpath erosion, soil erosion and the effect of souvenir hunting
- air pollution from sulphur emissions from ship engines
- growing marine pollution from fuel spillages, sewage dumping and contamination of the environment from engine emissions from different modes of transport used to access the region and extreme events like the sinking of the MS *Explorer* in 2007
- disturbance of wildlife through tourist viewing and damage to fragile ecosystems as well as the introduction of plant diseases from such visitation (Plate 12.1).

Some studies have highlighted the dichotomy that visitation to Antarctica causes. Interaction with the physical environment does not necessarily enhance a visitor's understanding of the fragility of the Antarctic ecosystem. What is clear is that the ecological effects of tourism on the region are substantial. In many respects tourism here is irresponsible if one adopts a logical review of the prevailing evidence and concerns over the effects of climate change. The region itself is receiving massive media coverage to document the effects of these changes on its ecosystems, which in itself is adding additional pressure through non-essential visits.

This is part of a trend described by Lemelin *et al.* (2012) as Last Chance Tourism (also called disappearing tourism), focused on visitors travelling to places or resources (natural and man-made) under threat of disappearing or extinction. Examples of destinations under threat include Antarctica, the Arctic, some alpine ski resorts (due to global warming) and the Great Barrier Reef (Plate 12.2) (for wildlife habitats under threat, see the World Wide Fund for Nature, wwf.org.uk for more details). These destinations have been highlighted by media coverage such as crews visiting Antarctica to report on the melting of the polar ice cap and tour operators who charge premium prices to visit such locations. There is something almost surreal about this trend: people understand the threat that visitation poses and yet they choose to add to the problem by visiting rather than exercising restraint. These instances have led some commentators to argue that tourism is becoming less rather than more sustainable. In fact Hall (2013) claims that this trend of tourism becoming less sustainable is evidenced through the following characteristics of global tourism: there is a growth in emissions from tourism (in absolute terms), greater resource use and biodiversity loss. It is clearly unfashionable to discuss such issues challenging the tourism sector as a powerful lobby group but, without a degree of rethinking the current and future implications of tourism growth to 2030, we will see more examples of what Urry (2004) described as the 'death' of destinations. At a theoretical level, some studies have pointed to the role of transition management as one way of getting greater stakeholder involvement in implementing policies to shift towards sustainable tourism.

The tourism industry's pursuit of the next business opportunity has led to even those countries that limit visitors, such as Bhutan, allowing in more visitors to gain additional foreign currency. It would appear that tourism knows no bounds. Planning and self-management by industry codes of conduct have only had a superficial effect on visitor damage in sensitive environments. Rather than being phrased in restrictive ways, they need to be phrased in positive ways (e.g. 'Do not dump your rubbish here' might be replaced with 'Please take your litter home to help minimize your impact on the environment'). To the critic, however, this is the industry policing itself – and this usually only kicks in when serious problems begin to emerge. Is it time that commentators and researchers began to make a stand and pose some of the following questions in order to engage in a greater debate about tourism, now that the impacts are so important to all of our lives?

- Is there a real need now to make certain parts of the world 'tourism-free'?
- Should not certain pristine areas be kept pristine and be free of the vagaries of tourism?

Plate 12.1
Last chance tourism: Antarctica – should the tourist really be visiting this location given its fragile nature?

Source: Istock

Plate 12.2
Last chance tourism: The Great Barrier Reef – should tourists really be visiting this location given its fragile nature?

Source: Istock

- Is there not an opportunity to retain Antarctica as a natural wilderness as opposed to a media playground reporting climate change and as an attraction for the rich traveller?
- Should nature have some respite from the continuous pressures of tourism?

The notions implied in these questions seem to be common sense, as well as taking a stance on environmental preservation, but they remain controversial. This is because the very implementation of such a position would limit the personal freedom of the affluent tourist and, more importantly, prevent business from exploiting the tourism potential of an area. Yet surely with the introduction of virtual reality, these environments can be experienced in more novel ways than in a manner that destroys the resource base? In visionary destinations, tourism revenue has been used to protect and conserve nature and heritage, but these examples are not the norm. One of the problems that tourism development has posed in China is in areas of environmental sensitivity where there is demand for economic revenue for development from large-scale tourism when the areas are better suited to small-scale, locally owned and operated ecotourism developments. Given the scale of demand for domestic and international travel, tourism can only really be described as an uncontrollable process once the basic elements of economic development become established which drives the ideological development of the sector: therefore, when tourism gets out of control it becomes a destructive force. There is just not enough public debate or academic discussion regarding the justifications for halting tourism or even making a stance and saying *no tourism here please*. This may have major political overtones, but in public policy contexts, alternative economic development options will be required if tourism is not the solution. It is not necessary to be anti-tourism, but it should be realistically understood what a future committed to tourism means for people, their locality and environment, and to consider the measures to control it.

One indication of a sea change in thinking has been the recent development of the idea that we need to move towards a green economy (see Figure 12.4). What this idea suggests is that as well as using investment and development to give better returns on human and natural assets, it needs to be accompanied by reducing greenhouse gas emissions. This was showcased at the 2008 conference on Tourism and Travel in the Green Economy. Specific areas for targeting greenhouse gases in tourism include the way tourism is produced and consumed and the critical role of transport as an emitter of such gases. This is seen as one way of accelerating the move towards more sustainable tourism. The shift in emphasis is to promote investment in tourism that can meet the new Global Sustainable Tourism Council Criteria so that the future development of the tourism economy is rooted in this approach whereby the benefits in employment, the environment and community (including poverty alleviation) are leveraged from new investment in tourism as opposed to continuing with the status quo. These may be ambitious targets and ideas but as major tourism developments illustrate, such projects often run in the face of all the environmental indicators of sustainable development. But as this example shows, political objectives override wider strategic environmental issues such as safeguarding an area of major scenic and wildlife value. Unless the ideals of the green economy are embraced by big business (and small business for that matter) then the negative impacts of tourism will continue and the notion of the green economy will seem a distant memory.

Although there is a growing sophistication among some travellers who are beginning to understand the link between travel, environmental damage, personal consumption and development, they are the few rather than the majority. Just as the education of consumers about the impact of domestic waste and environmental cost, there needs to be better education to raise awareness of the impact of consumer behaviour in relation to tourism. If tourism is not subjected to greater control in many destinations, self-destruction will lead to *post-tourism* and destinations suffering *tourism trauma*, where they are deluged by demand and stretched to a point where they cannot cope effectively with visitors or the demands placed on their resource base. Such a scenario exists in many destinations, which look forward to the shoulder season to allow the area to recover from 'tourist shock', so that psychologically and environmentally the local population once again feel they are not marginalized and pushed out by the influx of visitors. This is noticeable in many small historic cities in Europe that experience such pressures. Post-tourism and tourism trauma should be developed as a new element of the resort life cycle. Here, the loss of attractiveness and damage induced has led to overdevelopment, and the tourist seeks new pastures once the destination goes past its sell-by date. Tourism is a free-market activity, where price, affordability and appeal remain

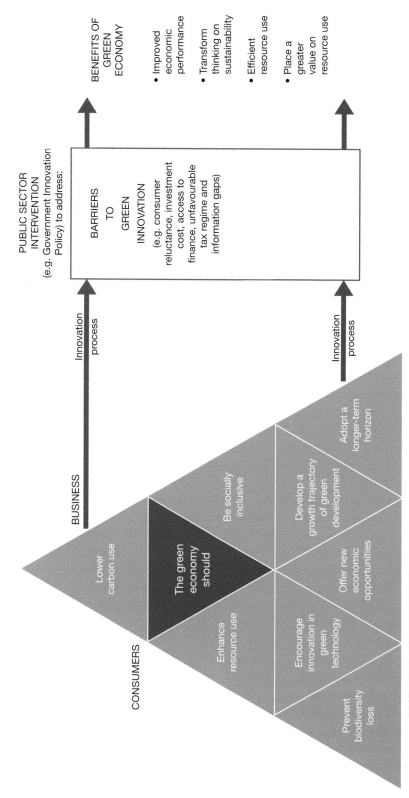

Figure 12.4

Principles of green economic growth for tourism

Source: developed from OECD (2013)

the determinants of consumer demand. If the destination loses its appeal, it may have an economic crisis to address. As examples in this book have shown, many destinations have never returned to their tourism heydays and the redundancy that is now apparent in many former coastal resorts is a permanent reminder of what happens when the resort cycle hits the decline stage. Therefore, striking the right balance between development, sustainable use and destination or tourist appeal is a dynamic element that needs constant review given the ability of tourism to change rapidly. This is why an understanding of tourism, how to manage it and how to take action quickly when things go wrong is fundamental to a healthy, prosperous and enriching tourism environment for all stakeholders. One suggestion may be to rethink how we manage tourism – and one possible and quite radical approach might be the development of a new concept of *managed tourism*.

Towards a new tourism management concept: Managed tourism

Given the increasing cynicism from tourism analysts about the green lobby and the unwillingness of almost every government globally (with the exception of Bhutan) to limit tourism growth, a more radical approach is needed. The 1990s have seen an excessive amount of research activity associated with the notion of sustainable tourism but few examples exist of where this has been developed with the degree of sophistication needed for it to work properly: one notable exception is Calvià in Mallorca that has embraced the principles to redevelop a mass resort into a more sustainable destination. The concept of sustainable tourism is quite simply too vague, imprecise and lacking in detailed measures for an assessment to be made of how it should be implemented and monitored in different contexts so that limits and thresholds of tourism activity can be established. The tourism industry does not want to see anything implemented that could damage its commercial viability (e.g. limits to growth), and without decrying the validity of much of the academic research activity on sustainable tourism, it has not led to wide-scale changes in the way tourism is developed or promoted. The theory of sustainable tourism has not been widely applied in practice, and so it is probably time for a more radical concept to be introduced that governments and policy-makers can understand in simple terms: it is *managed tourism* (MT).

There are global processes at work in terms of both tourism demand and tools by which tourists can begin to assess and understand their own impact on the environment. One of these, as Table 12.3 shows, is a new tool: *ecological footprinting* (EF), which now allows us to measure and assess how resource consumption occurs in terms of our pleasure and leisure time. It also highlights how unnecessary some forms of excessive consumption of the earth's finite resources are when compared with the effects this may have on the planet. For this reason, and given the prior discussion on the snowball concept in tourism, there is a real need for MT to develop a number of principles to manage such activity in the future. Figure 12.5 illustrates how these principles are starting to arouse interest from tourists in terms of growing numbers of people becoming aware of the effects of tourism on climate change and resource use.

Figure 12.5
The concept of managed tourism

Source: author

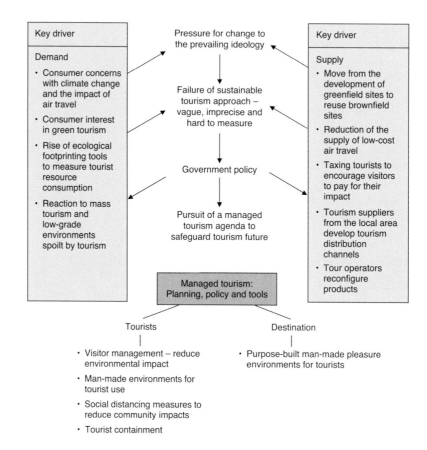

Yet the key element in Figure 12.5 is the willingness of governments to see an alternative path to tourism development through policies that may embrace MT and, for this reason, some of the following principles and ideas may need to shape how MT is implemented in different contexts:

- EF needs to be developed more extensively across the tourism sector to show consumers exactly what the environmental costs of their activity are for destinations and the environment. This may need to be introduced as a legislative requirement in the same way that foodstuffs now have to be labelled with their contents or cigarettes carry a warning on their impact on your health
- holidaymakers need to be taxed more fully to reflect their impact and use of resources: this may raise issues of equity and social inclusion/exclusion, but with growing environmental problems, there is a need once again to make international tourism more of a luxury than a mass product. It should also be emphasized that tourism is not a basic human need such as food, water and shelter. We do not need it to survive, but only to enrich our lives and as a consumer product
- governments need to reconsider the ill-advised and short-termist view that low-cost airlines are major contributors to tourism growth and development: in simple terms, these transport providers do not pay the full cost of their environmental impact on the environment, and ridiculously low-priced air fares not only stimulate

Table 12.3 Ecological footprinting

- There is a growing interest among environmental researchers on developing measures and indicators capable of accounting for the tourist's impacts on the environment. One technique now being developed and debated in tourism is the ecological footprint (EF). EF is a tool by which an estimate of resource consumption and waste generated by an economic activity, such as tourism, can be generated in a given area.

- The technique examines the consumption of energy, foodstuffs, raw materials, water, transport impacts, waste generated and loss of land from development. While criticisms do exist over the methods of analysis used to calculate the EF, it is now being used by public sector agencies to highlight issues of tourist resource use as one approach to assessing tourism and its sustainability in terms of resource use.

- Gössling (2002) used this technique to illustrate the EF for tourism in the Seychelles per tourist, using the common unit of measurement 'gha' (global hectares), which is the way demand of an activity on natural resources results in its consumption. In the Seychelles, values of 1.9 gha per year for the EF were 90 per cent the result of air travel.

- For a typical two-week holiday in the Mediterranean, a World Wide Fund for Nature study observed that a gha of 0.37 resulted in Majorca and 0.93 in Cyprus. In each case, air travel was the contributor to over 50 per cent of the EF. The value of the EF technique is that it allows comparison of the overall ecological impact of tourism products on global biological resources.

demand, but create a perception that international air travel and tourism are now a universal right with no associated impacts

- companies need to reassess the effect of business travel for long-haul activities (as well as short-haul trips using low-cost airlines). Governments could easily remove some of the tax incentives for companies to offset excessive business-class and first-class travel as part of the perks of being an employee, limiting the nature of this wasteful activity: many good alternatives exist such as video and phone conferencing. This would need a major culture shift but legislation on the tax breaks gained from business travel in company accounts may need to be looked at

- governments could treat this issue in the same way that they tax company car benefits if they wish to reduce the extent of excessive use of resources for travel that may net only marginal benefits to business. The same also applies to all public sector bodies (including universities) with their staff's appetite for travel which takes them away from the daily work routine. As appropriate technology now exists to reduce the need for conference travel, reducing the public and private sector carbon footprint must be a priority as opposed to the current situation where many people promote the ethic of sustainable tourism and in the next breath fly to far flung places to give a 20- or 60-minute presentation at a conference and to network

- destinations need to delimit precisely areas in resorts and man-made areas where tourism activity can be concentrated so that they are *tourist-resilient* and not in fragile natural environments: no new greenfield development should be permitted for tourism, given the loss of the earth's resources to this activity. Instead, tourism should be concentrated on brownfield sites (i.e. those with former tourism or industrial developments that are no longer in use), especially existing resort areas that can be environmentally improved. This would reduce the impacts on the natural environment as far as is possible given the available technology

- residents should be sheltered and socially distanced from resort areas to reduce unnecessary impacts and effects on their culture; they should not be swamped by tourist districts as many Mediterranean resorts have been since the 1960s
- local tourism suppliers should be developed from the existing business networks in areas to remove unfair and externally dominant commercial relationships that favour global companies which then take control of the tourism sector
- government policies need to reflect a commitment to strongly control MT and the way tourism develops. Without a very active involvement, MT will not be a reality. This commitment would require the use of planning tools that are able to protect destinations, contain tourism and prevent it spilling over to other areas. It is bizarre that aviation fuel is not taxed globally to provide a level playing field with other more sustainable forms of transport to remove the key impetus for low-cost air travel. Surely the time has come to acknowledge that cheap low-cost air travel is not in the environment's long-term interest and it needs to be curbed as efforts to tackle greenhouse gas emissions will be undermined by the insatiable growth for travel fuelled by low-cost carriers
- where governments choose a path based on mass tourism, the future development will need to utilize a wide range of visitor management tools so that the tourist experience is provided in a way that the resource base can easily maintain. This may involve demolishing and rebuilding brownfield tourism sites or upgrading infrastructure rather than allowing resorts to keep expanding whilst other parts become rundown and redundant. This points to a need for resort renewal and regeneration using the existing land area of the resort as opposed to new landtake. This would require a visionary masterplan.

Whilst many of these principles may seem draconian, they are based on many of the tools and principles of visitor management and efficient resource use. They question the logic of constantly expanding tourist resort areas and districts without really looking at an area's capacity to absorb visitors. Managers of destinations need realistically to assess what visitors they can accommodate, limit the numbers and develop a tourism industry based around more rational principles, rather than allowing it simply to grow and mutate along the lines of the amoeba concept. The aim of MT is to tightly control and manage tourism activity given its propensity for resource consumption, while controlling the places where it takes root. A more definite and practical approach to tourism management is needed that is not shrouded in the vagueness and mystery of 'sustainable tourism'. Many sectors of the tourism industry have harnessed this term for marketing purposes to make tourism look more attractive in certain destinations, yet have done little to implement it. Sustainable tourism is also seen as making the tourist feel more environmentally responsible when in fact the very pursuit of tourism to many sensitive environments is the least responsible and sustainable activity in which a consumer can engage. Whilst some examples of genuine sustainable activity exist in sensitive environments, they are not the norm in tourism and this is why it is time for a new approach, radically rethinking how governments perceive and manage tourism. Tourism may seem like a panacea to solve all our ills in economic terms, but the environmental and social costs may be too great in the long term without a stronger commitment to radical principles of MT that require substantial state intervention to direct and manage the tourism sector.

There is no doubt that the new millennium is a very testing time for tourism. The pressure to continually pursue tourism growth is unrelenting from business interests and government agencies who see tourism as a legitimate route to enhanced economic development. The challenge for the tourism sector, policy-makers and governments is to ask a number of very fundamental questions:

- Why do we want tourism?
- What does it mean for our locality or country?
- How will it impact upon our society?
- How will it be managed to make a win–win situation for all stakeholders?

A further dimension to the public policy-making process on the future of tourism in a locality or destination is posed in countries with a substantial indigenous population with ancient rights over tourism resources. In Australia, New Zealand, the Pacific Islands and many parts of Asia, the indigenous people are an integral part of the cultural tourism product. Being sensitive and able to accommodate their needs is assuming a higher priority for many governments that have belatedly recognized how integral these groups of people are to the tourism industry. If integrated and managed in a sensitive manner, such cultural diversity can actually provide destinations with a competitive edge by offering a unique and memorable element in the tourist experience. If managed badly, it can destroy any tourism development potential.

Ultimately many destinations and businesses will seek to develop a 'sustainable tourism industry' – it is good for the marketing of the destination, businesses and may appeal to the environmentally conscious traveller. As Page *et al.* (2007) have argued, one way this is increasingly being communicated to the consumer in a highly competitive market for tourists, is through destination branding. Destination branding is assuming a key role in tourism as Anholt (2004) suggests, and many of the key tourism destinations globally (especially cities) have iconic status due to their historic position in the destination hierarchy or have been highly successful in positioning themselves in specific markets. These brands help to communicate to an increasingly complex tourism marketplace, transforming the place into something tangible, trading on international tourism images of the nation state and its tourism attributes (as reflected in Innovation in Sustainabilty 10.2) (also see UNWTO 2009). The association with branding and quality means that countries developing national brands will need to ensure that quality assurance delivers the promise. The promise is made in the proposition to the customer: the destination should not over-promise and fail to deliver.

For very sensitive environments the best form of tourism may be *no tourism*, unless the benefits are reinvested back in protection and preservation, such as in some of Africa's game reserves. Arguably, the best way to manage mass tourism is to concentrate it in purpose-built man-made developments. Many of these developments have already degraded the environment and are now experiencing measures to improve their impact and image. At least, from a planning perspective, this keeps the destructive effects of tourism in one place – but it then limits the economic benefits to the wider population. Some countries are seeking to appeal to a specific type of market and not to drive ahead for large numbers. All too often, however, the efforts of industry supersede such plans, because ultimately tourism remains a free-market activity with few major constraints on incremental growth. Limits are the exception rather than the rule. There is no doubt that tourism is a dynamic industry. Yet the rhetoric of using the latest buzzwords and jargon to appeal to tourists can only be judged by actions. Can tourism really be developed in a way in which profits and demand are balanced by the long-term needs of the environment and the people it affects? That is the future challenge for tourism.

CHAPTER REVIEW

References

Anholt, S. (2004) Nation brands and value of provenance. In N. Morgan, A. Pritchard and R. Pride (eds) *Destination Branding*. Oxford: Butterworth-Heinemann.

Archer, B. (1987) Demand forecasting and estimation. In J. R. B. Ritchie and C. R. Goeldner (eds) *Travel, Tourism and Hospitality Research*. New York: Wiley.

D'Aveni, R. (1988) Hypercompetition closes in. *Financial Times*, 4 February (Global Business Section).

Faulkner, B. and Russell, R. (1999) Chaos and complexity in tourism: In search of a new perspective. *Pacific Tourism Review*, 1(2): 93–102.

Glaeßer, D. (2006) *Crisis Management in the Tourism Industry*, 2nd edn. Oxford: Butterworth-Heinemann.

Hall, C. M. (2013) Tourism, slow consumption and slow tourism. Presentation to The Business of Sustainable Tourism: Past, Present and Future Research Symposium. Curtin University, Western Australia, 18 February 2013. http://canterbury-nz.academia.edu/CMichaelHall

Lemelin, H., Dawson, J., and Stewart, E. (eds) (2012) *Last Chance Tourism*. London: Routledge.

Page, S. J. and Connell, J. (2009) *Tourism: A Modern Synthesis*, 3rd edn. London: Cengage Learning.

Page, S. J., Yeoman, I. and Greenwood, C. (2007) *Accommodation in Scotland to 2015*. Edinburgh: VisitScotland.

Peeters, P. and Dubois, G. (2010) Tourism travel under climate change constraints. *Journal of Transport Geography*, 18(4): 447–457.

UNWTO (2008) *Handbook of Tourism Forecasting Methodologies*. Madrid: UNWTO.

UNWTO (2009) *Handbook of Destination Branding*. Madrid: UNWTO.

UNWTO and UNEP (2008) *Climate Change and Tourism: Responding to Global Challenges*. Madrid: UNWTO.

Urry, J. (2004) Death in Venice. In M. Sheller and J. Urry (eds) *Tourism Mobilities, Places to Play, Places in Play*. London: Routledge, 205–215.

Further reading

The best starting point is the websites of the World Tourism Organization, World Tourism Council and National Tourism Organizations to assess market trends and future strategies for tourism growth and development.

A number of good sources exist to examine future tourism scenarios, including:

Future Foundation (2005) *The World of Travel in 2020*. London: Futures Foundation. www.futures-foundation.net

Page, S. J., Yeoman, I., Greenwood, C. and Connell, J. (2010) Scenario planning as a tool to understand uncertainty in tourism: The example of transport and tourism in Scotland to 2025. *Current Issues in Tourism*, 13(2).

UNWTO (2011) *The Best of UNWTO: Policy and Practice for Global Tourism*. Madrid: UNWTO.

Questions

1   What are the crises in tourism? And how should individual businesses respond to them?

2   What is the future growth potential of tourism in relation to the earth's resource base?

3   What are the principal management problems facing tourism managers in the new millennium?

4   How would you develop an action plan for managing tourism in a destination area you know or have recently visited? Will you need to take radical action to limit or prohibit tourists?

Access additional resources

* For students: Multiple choice questions for each chapter, video links and further reading.
* For instructors: PowerPoint slides with tables and diagrams, additional case studies, video links and further reading.

Index

Note: Page numbers in **bold** type refer to **figures**. Page numbers in *italic* type refer to *tables*